"A very important and successful book....Few people, if any, could write a book of this scope....A fine job."
—Jeffrey Mishlove, Ph.D., psychologist, author of several books and Director of the Intuition Network

"A valuable and intriguing book."
—Professor George Araki, Ph.D., Director of the Holistic Health Institute, San Francisco State University (retired)

"I believe this is the best single book available on intuition and its applications. While there are many books out on the subject, no one book other than William Kautz's provides as knowledgable and comprehensive a balance between a solid examination of the nature of the subject and a rich description of how it can be used....Kautz has had more experience than anyone I know in using expert intuitives to successfully bring their unusual information accessing abilities to problem solving tasks in the real world."
—Prof. Jon Klimo, Ph.D., author of *Channeling: Investigations on Receiving Information from Paranormal Sources* (Tarcher, 1987)]

Opening the Inner Eye

Opening the Inner Eye

Explorations on the Practical Application of **Intuition** in Daily Life and Work

William H. Kautz

iUniverse, Inc.
New York Lincoln Shanghai

Opening the Inner Eye
Explorations on the Practical Application of Intuition in Daily Life and Work

iUniverse, Inc.

For information address:
iUniverse
2021 Pine Lake Road, Suite 100
Lincoln, NE 68512
www.iuniverse.com

Cover: Boddhinath Stupa from "Nepal: The Himalayan Kingdom" (Lustre
Press, 1996); photo © Mani Lama, re-printed with permission.

ISBN: 0-595-27584-2

Printed in the United States of America

This book is dedicated to the late

Dr. Willis W. Harman
whose committed and devoted life of exploration of human consciousness, and his many rich contributions to the growing science of noetics, including intuition, have inspired so many persons—including this most appreciative student.

Thank you, Bill.

ACKNOWLEDGMENTS

The content of this book is based heavily upon the work of the **Center for Applied Intuition** (CAI) and all those who participated in it. Every one of CAI's several programs was a collaborative undertaking involving from two or three up to dozens of individuals. Some of the projects were carried out in conjunction with universities in the San Francisco Bay Area or organizations in the United States or abroad. I am greatly indebted to all these individuals and organizations for their encouragement and support over the fifteen-year period in which CAI functioned, and especially during its difficult times when plans had to be changed more than once, grand hopes were dashed and patience and finances were in short supply.

I want to acknowledge here especially my many wonderful personal associations with those who worked with CAI as participating employees, volunteers (many!) and consultants. Others lent their support as friends, members and clients. Many freely shared their time, labor, financial support and sometimes their private personal experiences—their "inner lives" of intuitive and spiritual development—at a time when intuition was still an unpopular and controversial notion. I want to thank especially the several expert intuitives who carried out the personal intuitive "life readings" for individuals, business consultations, and the many topical research readings that constitute the main basis of the presentations in Part III of this book. Contributors who participated as expert intuitives (on the CAI staff and a few others) are tagged here with their initials, which are used in the text to identify particular contributions.

I see no way to acknowledge fully and fairly these many contributions or to rank them from least to most supportive. Worse, the list which follows is incomplete, since a few names (but not the faces!) are forgotten. Several volunteers and the participants in my intuition development programs in the Czech Republic are not included here by name. To those not specifically acknowledged, please accept my apologies.

To all of you listed on the next page, please accept my sincere thanks for your willing part, large and small, in this extensive undertaking.

CAI was not alone, of course, in probing the mysteries of the inner mind and intuition in particular. I have used footnotes and text references to credit the sources of most quoted material and specific findings, whenever these could be readily traced. However, much of the growing body of knowledge on intuition emerged from the creative and cultural mileau at the time and cannot be individually credited. Included in this category are the authors of dozens of articles and books on which I have drawn for my own understanding and inspiration. They played their part as background material, in my long attempt to grow a credible picture of the workings of intuition. My appreciation extends to these contributors as well.

Aron Abrahamsen [AA]
Marsha Adams [MA]
Dan Hawkmoon Alford
Dean Anderson
George Araki
Anne Armstrong [AAA]
Angeles Arrien
Marta Aura
Betty Bailey
Tina Bell-Gumaer
Gabrielle Blackburn [GB]
Stanislav Bohadlo
Melanie Branon
Vonnie Brenno [VB]
Anne Breutsch
Alan Brickman
Janet Kiyo Brockmann
Ellen Brogren
Matthew Bronson
Judy Brooks
John Broomfield
Karen Wilhelm Buckley
Cindi Burklo
Robert Butts
Susan Campbell
Sally Carter
Mary Carouba
Debi Carvallo
Lorna Catford
Gladys Chase
Sárka Fellegi Christová
Jo Coffey
Thomas Condon
Diana Conti [DC]
Thomas Condon
Audrey Contente
Jay Cornell
Kate Costello
Kay Croissant
Mary Croxall
Michael Crumbacher
Henry Dakin
Christy Anne Davidson

Catherine Dees
Constance Demby
Lisa Dickson
Jonathan Driscoll
Christian Eddleman
Jane English
Earl Ettienne
Lisa Faithhorn
Georg Feuerstein
Barbara Findeisen
Donna Flegal
Rene Floyd
Deki Fox
Jon C. Fox [JF]
Yuko Franklin
Sharon Franquemont
Sandra Freeman [SF]
Yukio Funai
Phil Gang
Marylyn Genovese
Mary Gillis [MG]
Yvonne Ginsberg
Evelyn Glassmeyer
Bridgett Gleason
Philip Goldberg
Kathleen Hobbs Golden
Kathy Goss
Paul Grof
Stanislav Grof
Frances Hailman
Willis W. Harman
Alison Harolde
Stephanie Harolde
Shari Harter
Arthur Hastings
Katherine Hensley
Allen Hicks
Bruce Honig
Gudrun Hoy
Lenora Huett [LH]
Paul Hwoschinsky
Minoru Imabeppu
Shizue Inagaki
Kazue Iwamoto
Marta Johnson
C. Scott Jones
Jeannine Kagan
Nancy Kautz
Alain Kermarec

Robert Kimball
Sara Kittleson
Jon Klimo
Minoru Kodera
Ivana Kostková
Jarmila Koudelková
Pavel Krivka
Rowena Pattee Kryder
David Latimer
Richard Lavin [RL]
Monte Leach
Judy Linden
Patricia Livingston
Maria Teresa Lonsdale
Kathy Lund
Mori Machida
Anne Maiden
Michael Marsh
Annette Martin [AM]
Lin David Martin [LDM]
Colleen Mauro
Bill Mayben
Diane McCarney
John McKenzie
Sally McReynolds
Barry McWaters
Katherine Metz
Jean Millay
Elaine Miller
Jeffrey Mishlove
Joan Grigsby Moriah [JG]
Joan Morton
Nancy Nadaner
Zachery Nicholson [ZN]
Diana Nicoletti
Nel Noddings
Paul Nortia
Charles Nunn [CN]
Suzanne Owings [SO]
Richard Page
Helen Palmer
Julan Pekkain
Penney Pierce [PP]
Rosemary Quinn
Kay Ramsey
Wanda Ransdell

Debra Reynolds [DR]
Jane Roberts [JR]
Sherry Rochester
Helen Hoban Rogers
Shirley Rogers [SR]
William G. Roll
Barbara Rollinson [BBR]
Sanaya Roman [SSR]
Betty Rothenberger
Barbara Rowan [BR]
Richard Ryal [RR]
Kevin Ryerson [KR]
Lynn Ryerson
Susan Schneier
Rex Schudde
Jody Lang Santry
Nancy Sharpnack [NS]
Leslie Shelton
Donna Signorelli
Lezlie Skeetz
Standa Slanina
Diana Soash
Jerry Solfvin
Paula Underwood Spencer
Anita Stover
Kimiko Sugano
Mae Swanbeck
Gabrielle Thomson
Nel Thomson [NT]
Richard Toomey [RT]
Ruth Topham
Karen Turner
Yuko Uritani
Michael Vancura
Martha Turner Vargas
Frances Vaughan
Helen Wallace
Elaine Weissman
Pam Whidden
David Wick
Bryan Wittine
Richard Wolinsky [RW]
Mary Kaye Wright Malear
Verna Yater [VY]

CONTENTS

PREFACE

You have acquired this book out of tens of thousands of others from your local library, bookstore, Internet or a friend, and will soon be deciding if you really want to read it. In the few pages to follow I would like to help you make this decision.

Over the past fifty years we have watched the subject of intuition rise from an obscure and rarely mentioned notion, sometimes an embarrassing topic of conversation, to a concept at least worthy of qualified respect and a tolerated subject of curiosity. Intuition may not yet be well understood but it is now acknowledged to be largely responsible for human capacities such as creativity, problem solving and decision making. It has found an effective nitch within both psychological counseling and business management, and to a lesser extent in education and psychology. Dozens of books and other publications on intuition have appeared. The personal development of intuitive skills is taught in workshops and training programs in the U.S. and in Europe and is beginning to show up in a few college curricula and schools of business management.

But intuition is still "underground" stuff in America: it has not yet reached the mainstream. The voices of an informed and experienced minority are eloquent, informed and persuasive when they speak out about it, but the subject is still not popularly understood for what it actually is, nor is it regarded realistically. Professionals and business leaders often acknowledge intuition, but usually incorrectly. The media mention it from time to time, though rarely accurately and fairly. Even though an intuitive undercurrent is visible in many undertakings, both individual and societal, there is still much common misunderstanding about intuition: what it is, how it works, what it is good for and especially what it has to do with daily life and work.

Indeed, intuition is not what most people think it is. It is not synonymous with a good idea or a discovery, for these may arise by non-intuitive means as well, and often do. It is not the same as a "gut feeling" either, though it is certainly related. Intuition reveals itself largely through feelings, but most human feelings are not intuitive at all. Neither is its practice confined to so-called "women's intuition," for the faculty is not solely or even primarily a female quality. Nor is it limited to what has been dubbed its male counterpart, the occasional insights of executives and creative discoverers. It is not just an intellectual topic to be pondered over by philosophers and psychologists. Intuition is a deeper mental capacity or attribute. It is responsible for man's most valuable ideas, insights, decisions, visions, dreams, revelations and creativity. All of these originate internally, out of view of the conscious mind and its feeble attempts to control them.

The Value of Intuition. We will see below that intuition belongs to everyone, and is practiced naturally by everyone, albeit to a varying extent and not necessarily with awareness of the extent to which it is being used, or could be used, on a daily basis. Actually, *intuition is accessible to all who want to learn to use it better*—and to their great advantage. That is, everyone is free to develop his inherent intuitive ability into a refined and practical skill, even though relatively few persons choose to do so.

We will see in the text to follow that intuition has both a broad and a deep relevance within many of modern man's most worthy endeavors. At the least it has a huge potential for application within society at large—in fact, in almost every human activity in which the *acquisition of knowledge and understanding plays a significant part.* Societal enterprises expend immense resources in their attempts to acquire new knowledge through data collection, communication, analysis, experimentation and various kinds of research. It is difficult to name a field of study or practice that does not involve the acquisition of new knowledge to at least some extent. Intuition can aid all of these endeavors.

Of course, some of society's greatest problems, such as war, hunger and overpopulation, are limited more by a lack of individual or political will than a shortage of knowledge, since it is already well known what needs to be done. Even here, though, the right kind of new knowledge can often encourage effective collective action and soften the misery until better solutions can be worked out.

But intuition's greatest value by far lies in what it can do for the individual, simply because the personal experience of intuition is where its more conspicuous and practical societal facets have their origin and their basis. Intuition is becoming an ever more acceptable gateway through which motivated persons are able to discover the deeper and normally obscure (that is, unconscious) parts of themselves, those realms that govern the mental forces of attention and will, which underlie their daily thoughts and activities and are truly running the drama of their lives. Those who have found ways to cooperate with their intuition have a powerful and practical means for connecting with this hidden part of themselves—their best ally for self-understanding and their prime source of inspiration and guidance in both their personal lives and their work.

In simplest terms intuition may be thought of as the communication channel between one's outer, conscious mind and his inner, unknown, mysterious and (to many) frightening unconscious mind. The unconscious, which we all experience through our feelings more than our intellect, holds various aspects of the self but is mainly the locus of one's true essence or beingness. Intuition is everyman's main access to inner self-identity and his primary source for new knowledge, guidance, strength and inspiration.

In the chapters to follow we will be exploring, mainly through various examples, just *how* intuition impacts these various areas of human life, individual and societal. We will focus mainly on how to actually *use* intuition to help solve a range of specific human problems, individual and societal, broad and specialized, and how it may be used to solve an even wider range of such problems in the future.

You will find here descriptions of a dozen or so experiments on applied intuition, including how the experiments were actually carried out: how the topics were selected, how "expert" intuitives were chosen and worked with, how questions were derived and posed, what kind of information arose from the inquiries, how it was corroborated with other sources and how it was applied when this was possible. Also addressed are some broader questions: What are the inherent limitations on the kinds of information available through intuitive inquiry? What general conditions must be satisfied if inquiries are to be successful? What sort of results can be expected? How to ask good questions? How to check intuitive information and communicate it to those who wish to use it?

Verification. The observations and conclusions reported here are grounded in careful observation, critical examination and (at the time) much skepticism. This is a legacy from my own scientific background, I suppose, for I too had to be convinced that what I was discovering about intuition was real and valid. All findings have been screened through two filters—my background as a critical scientist and my personal experiences with intuition. Both had to "make sense." In the world of intuition, just as in several other fields, the validity of conclusions derives not so much from voluminous bodies of information and formal knowledge, which the researcher has acquired through his education, subsequent study and working experience, nor does it derive solely from his analytical abilities—though this hard-won background certainly plays its part. Rather, it comes from his direct experience with his own intuition. This experience, often intense and challenging, involves his own self-development, which changes and expands as his understanding of intuition changes and expands.

Therefore, much of the strength of these findings on intuition rests on the fact that I have had to undergo these experiential processes for myself. This self-development took place partly from interaction with highly skilled intuitives, partly from the research studies themselves and the rest from personal efforts to enhance my own intuitive skill. When teaching intuition development, describing the practices and reporting the experiences and findings of others, I felt the need to confirm experientially whatever I could. This confirmation underlies this text, unless specifically mentioned otherwise.

Justification. Perhaps thirty books and a magazine devoted to intuition have appeared during the twenty years since intuition began to recover its respectability. You have a right to know why yet another book is needed.

The main reason is the simplest and most obvious one: every decade since the 1950s has brought an improved understanding and appreciation of intuition. New evidence has come out to substantiate the applicability and importance of intuition and how anyone may develop it. Many of the earlier publications have partially and gradually fallen out of date and need to be updated. At the same time it is now easier to discuss and explain intuition. Both practitioners and researchers have been exploring how intuition relates to established knowledge domains such as psychology, philosophy and science, and to the broader realm of human experience with which we all can identify. In the following pages of description and explanation I have tried to take advantage of this new understanding of intuition's place in these other domains, though a full analysis of intuition's evolving history is not relevant here and is not included.

Finally, almost nothing has been published up to now on *applications* of intuition in human activities that rely upon specific information and collectively held knowledge for their significance and effectiveness. These activities include most professional fields such as the various sciences, health, politics and education. They also cover individually held knowledge, used for decision making, problem solving, creative activity, self-understanding and personal growth generally. This book describes for the first time several experiments in intuitive application in these and other areas.

The broad purpose of this book, then, is to explain and illustrate with examples how the direct-knowing faculty of the human mind called *intuition* can be used (1) to solve a wide variety of problems, both individual and societal, and (2) to enhance the quality of individual human life by acquiring practical knowledge not ordinarily accessible.

I am aware that many readers will view intuition as just a phenomenon, and this report as yet another enthusiastic report on "psychics at work." And isn't it amazing what they can do! Many of these readers will persist in believing that there must be some trickery in it, or in the reporting of it, and anyway, amazing or not, "What has it got to do with my daily life?" I intend to answer this frequent question, and to demystify intuition by clarifying what it is and is not, and wherein lies its greatest importance and usefulness. I hope and expect that the first two chapters will dispel this common misconception.

Readership. While this book in intended for a general audience interested in intuition and its applications, it will appeal mostly to those whose curiosity is oriented toward the *use* of intuitive capacity for worthwhile personal and professional purposes.

I suspect that most readers will be interested in learning about intuition for what it can do for them personally, not only as an information resource for external, practical accomplishments but as an aid to improve their own self-understanding and enhance their personal lives. This latter goal is addressed mainly in the first three chapters to follow. New intuitive information is best obtained through ones own ability, of course, but one may also rely on "expert intuitives" who are able to answer inquirers' questions. The chapters that follow focus on practical applications.

This book will also be useful to professionals seeking new information and understanding within their chosen field or specialty. It offers them a new approach to gaining whatever new knowledge they would like to acquire in their professional work. Those working in the particular fields and subfields covered in Part III—seismology, history, mood disorders, nutritional science, linguistics, AIDS research and a few others—may enjoy a head start. Both clinical and research psychologists will find here several useful discoveries about the workings of those portions of the unconscious mind in which the intuitive faculty is involved. Parapsychologists too may benefit, since intuition lies at the heart of most of the psychic phenomena which they study.

The only important requirements that readers need to satisfy are a well motivated curiosity and a willingness to embrace fresh new knowledge suggested by others' experiences and experiments. No prior background in psychology, parapsychology or scientific methodology is needed to understand, appreciate and utilize the findings reported herein. Some of the applications presented in Part III involve technical material, but the general reader not interested in these specialties may safely skip over these details.

This book is *not* intended for those whose principal interest is personal intuition development, a topic well covered by other sources. Still, the descriptions and explanations offered herein may help to motivate the learner and can enhance his learning process. Similarly, the scholar seeking to develop a theory of intuition will find in these pages valuable gems he can use, but he should not expect a rigorous treatment; this is not my purpose and is probably impossible at the present stage of understanding of the mind.

While the experiments described later provide abundant convincing evidence that intuition is a real capacity of the human mind, the reader who demands first convincing scientific proof of this fact will do better to seek it in the voluminous literature on creativity, parapsychology and certain writings in modern psychology. This historical evidence is sketched briefly in Chapter 1, and references and other resources are given in the text and Appendix. This introductory overview should be sufficient for most readers so they can shift their attention to intuition's important properties and its usefulness, and appreciate the contributions offered here, without being diverted by a the need to be convinced that intuition truly exists.

This book is not a "piece of scholarship," as some would surely prefer, and it should not be regarded and judged as such. The reader who is searching for a full, rational, scientific proof of the reality of intuition will certainly be dissatisfied. This is not because persuasive evidence is lacking, for it is abundant, but because the subjective nature of intuition precludes such rigorous proof. Science rests on certain assumptions about the real world that do not hold for human thought, perception, intuition and other mental processes. Moreover, scientific methodology, for all its value and power in the domain of logic, reason and materiality, is too narrow a means with which to investigate and explain most mental capacities, including intuition. When these human attributes are involved science is simply inapplicable, and one must turn elsewhere for "proof." Indeed, science can open doors and argue for the truth, but by itself it never truly convinces anyone of anything.

This book will also not be helpful to those whoso goal is to use intuition to impress others with their new powers, to make easy money or to obtain private information for the purpose of taking advantage of other persons. We will see later that, while almost any kind of information is available intuitively to the motivated seeker, certain broad conditions exist and must be satisfied if an inquiry and its subsequent application are to succeed. These conditions preclude purposes such as these just mentioned.

This author's role. I see my main role in this book as an informed guide, not a "teacher" in the customary sense of the word. My method of guiding is to share with my reader information and explanations he may not be familiar with, so as to remind him about matters he may have disregarded, forgotten or not yet appreciated. It is you, the reader, not the writer, who is the main actor here. You will hopefully be enabled to take advantage of whatever useful you discover among the information and explanations to which you are being exposed in these pages.

I also hope to inspire you to move forward boldly on your own inner path of discovery, whatever it might be. However, if you are looking for a perfect master who has all the answers, you will surely be disappointed. I believe I have some answers for you, but I know that if you enter any search with a surrender of your personal power to an external authority (or with an over-skeptical posture), you will experience only frustrations and delays. You can't find your own truth by blindly following someone else's path. You may learn much from others, but you must always forge your own path forward.

Best of all, I would like this book, along with the reports of others from whom you may hear or read similar accounts, to help you to expand your own vision of what is possible for you to achieve for yourself—your personal potential. Believe me, if you can: as this vision enlarges, what you think, believe and do will automatically expand to fulfill it. Your ability to imagine and vision for yourself are not fundamentally limited by your genes, your background or your physical environment. Nor are they imposed upon you by anyone else or by society. They are under your direct, voluntary control. They are well supported by your intuition, whether you are presently aware of this support or not. So envision freely! Prepare yourself for the positive changes that must follow!

I wish I were an accomplished writer of fiction, which in some ways would be a more suitable vehicle than non-fiction for communicating the essential ideas and even information about the novel discoveries reported in this book and about intuition itself. The realization and appreciation of these new ideas is blocked for so many readers by a solid intellectual wall, one that rests on a foundation of Western thought and language. To surmount this barrier is difficult for almost everyone. Nevertheless, this language that we share will have to do. It is all I have in my tool-bag for describing the rich inner experiences, understanding and potentialities I want to convey. I hope thereby to help my reader find a way around or through this intellectual wall. At the least, perhaps he will be persuaded to explore these matters further with his own mind, and discover for himself that the intellect, for all its value, is inherently limited for comprehending his inner world. He will then be compelled to seek beyond it for answers.

Several of the observations and claims of this book are challenging. They may stretch your beliefs so far that you find them difficult to accept. I can only suggest that you persist with an attitude of curiosity and openness.

Ideally I would prefer to let my message speak for itself, but this is impossible in a work of this sort because so much of the message deals with the very beliefs, views and expectations asking to be challenged and modified. I cannot expect you to embrace this message unless you know something about the person who is offering them to you. A short personal background is included in Chapter 1. Brief mention of several of my own experiences with intuition are scattered throughout the text, always identified as such, and a few longer accounts are boxed in italicized sidebars. Beyond this, the message will have to speak for itself.

The text is fully referenced. Credit is given when due and known, though many of the early contributions to present-day knowledge about intuition can no longer be traced to their origins. Patents and prizes aside, perhaps it is not so important who made the discoveries first. I remain grateful for all contributions to our present understanding, from whatever and whoever they may have originated, and I do not expect such acknowledgement from those who make use of the new material presented herein.

Finally, I must ask your indulgence to interpret the pronouns *he*, *his* and *him*, and the words *one* and *man*, as referring to both genders, except when a specific person is indicated. Alternative constructions to avoid this unfortunate deficiency of the English language (actually, most languages) are just too cumbersome to adopt here.

William H. Kautz
San Francisco, California, USA
Portnoo, Cty. Donegal, Ireland
Ocotitlan, Moreles, Mexico
Prague and Nachod, Czech Republic
Tucson, Arizona, USA

PART I

INTUITION AND INTU-
ITIVES

CHAPTER 1

INTUITION PRIMER

STEPPING INTO THE WORLD OF INTUITION

"Throughout history, human beings have had the experience of knowing more than what was given them by their senses....The existence of such a channel, operating outside the intellect and sensory pathways, seems impossible to Western science, because there is no place in its cosmology or psychology for any means of knowing other than rationality or sensation. We cannot imagine any other process at work....We have not been motivated to challenge scientific rationalism or to look for other avenues of knowledge. After all, what else is there? The answer to that question is intuition." [Arthur Deikman[1*]]

This book's message necessarily involves a personal story, so we will do well to begin with it.

It all began in the early 1970s when I was thrown into a few casual interactions with individuals called psychics, channels, clairvoyants and healers. I noticed that these persons sometimes brought forth pieces of information, both personal and technical, to which they could not have had prior or present access—or so it seemed. As a young scientist I found this incredible. All I had been taught said that such things were not supposed to happen!

---

* Endnotes are listed at the end of each chapter.
  An asterisk (*) indicates a comment .

I was sufficiently disturbed to try to verify that the information given was indeed accurate, and that these otherwise unexceptional individuals were indeed ignorant beforehand of what they had spoken. Also, I had to be sure they could not have figured out the information from what they already knew, and were not guessing and lucky. As a working scientist I knew how to conduct such an investigation, and did so.

I discovered from this effort that in many cases these unusual performances were indeed genuine. I was forced to conclude that *there has to be a means within the human mind by which information could be obtained outside of the familiar channels of reasoning. sensing and memory*, at least as these mental faculties are ordinarily understood. I decided to learn *how* these persons were able to perform such mental feats.

It did not take long to discover that my observation was not new. This capacity of "direct knowing," "spontaneous knowing" or "immediate apprehension" had been around for a long time—throughout recorded history, in fact; moreover, it is very widespread, universal according to some scholars. It is called *intuition*.

Why had no one ever told me about intuition? I had never learned about it in school. My scientific colleagues knew nothing of it. It was discussed only briefly in encyclopedias, and not at all in psychology textbooks. How was this possible, that a human capacity so central to the generation of knowledge could be missed? It's potential applications appeared to be huge: solving problems, making decisions, generating new ideas, forming new perspectives and feeding creativity generally—all of which activities depend on the acquisition of new knowledge. If intuition could be harnessed and applied, its impact on mankind's many knowledge-limited endeavors seemed fantastic! Was I missing something obvious? Was this omission a grand conspiracy? A social taboo? Or a heretical breakthrough? Perhaps I was just being terribly naive.

Apart from adjusting to the shock of this mystery, I began to try to answer the basic questions about the intuitive process itself. What kinds of information are accessible through intuition? How reliable, accurate and deep can the information be? Is the ability as practical and useful as it seems to be? Who is able to practice intuition—even me? Is intuition the same as "psychic" (whatever that really is)? What conditions have to be satisfied if accurate and relevant information is to be obtained intuitively? By what natural laws or principles is it working? I felt strongly compelled to understand these very basic matters. The resulting investigation took fifteen years—and is still going on.

The Center for Applied Intuition

The attempt soon led to the founding of The Center for Applied Intuition (CAI), a San Francisco organization that functioned from 1977 to 1991. A committed staff shared my curiosity and participated in developing various programs and projects: initially a few years of experimental and library research on intuition, followed by application oriented research, intuitive counseling for individuals, intuitive business consulting for companies, intuition training, and a series of public education activities. The latter included a membership program, a newsletter *Applied Psi* (later *New Eyes*), a magazine *Intuition*, four published books, a weekly radio program, many public lectures and demonstrations, and four national and international conferences on the role of intuition in professional fields such as psychology and education.

The work was not always easy. Funding was a continual limitation. Most of CAI's individual and educational services paid for themselves, but only a few of the research studies and applications were sponsored by outside organizations. There was much fumbling and many mistakes were made as we probed this nebulous area. Still, most of the efforts were at least moderately successful, and some very much so. We seemed to be the recipient of many synchronicities and epiphanies as the work progressed. We gradually learned much about how intuition functions within the mind, how it relates to other established areas of knowledge and especially how to work with it in practice.

The early applicational experiments, which involved only a few skilled intuitives, generated verifiable and potentially useful information in archeology and a few specialized topics in science. With practice our question-asking improved. The responses became more accurate, meaningful and applicable. Some portions of the new information could be readily checked by independent means, thereby lending confidence to the results. Further inquiries followed, mainly in science and technology, the field in which verification is easiest, but also in the social sciences where applications are more direct.

A multi-intuitive approach called "Intuitive Consensus" was devised to facilitate the inquiry process and (so it seemed at the time) to render it more accurate. Additional "expert" intuitives were found and integrated into the program. The investigations were deepened to access levels of information well beyond what was known at the time—even information that *no one* possessed—but such that at least part of the information received could be independently verified. Intuition was used as the means of acquiring needed information in each chosen field of application for which other methods of inquiry had proven inadequate or had never been attempted. The areas included conventional research topics (scientific, medical, philosophic and historical), the humanities and social sciences, the commercial domain and personal self-understanding.

This book is a first report on CAI's findings from these experimental programs on applied intuition. In the following paragraphs and chapters I will explain and illustrate with examples how this direct-knowing faculty called intuition (1) actually functions within the human mind, as a creative and productive mental process; and then describe how it can be used to (2) fill in and fill out present-day bodies of knowledge in various fields; (3) enhance the quality of human life through the acquisition of practical knowledge not accessible by conventional means; (4) help solve a wide variety of specific problems, both individual and societal; and later (5) to assist those who wish to undertake a program of enhancing their own intuitive abilities.

What Is Intuition?

> "If you have intuitions at all, they come from a deeper level of your
> nature than the loquacious level which rationalism inhabits. Your
> whole subconscious life…[has] prepared the premise, of which
> your consciousness now feels the weight of the result. And some-
> thing in you absolutely *knows* that the result must be truer than any
> logic-chopping rationalistic talk, however clever, that may contra-
> dict it. [William James[2]]

Before becoming involved in the applications of intuition it will be important to understand first just what it is and what it is not. We will spend most of this chapter defining it and scoping out its main properties and features.

In common parlance the term *intuition* is almost synonymous with a bright idea, a burst of comprehension or a spontaneous hunch that seems to occur outside the process of ordinary thinking: "I had a strong intuition to call my sister. Sure enough, she was in trouble again." "His intuitive breakthrough saved the whole project." "She just *knew* that the relationship was not going to work." And perhaps Archimedes' famous bathtub insight, "Eureka, I have found it!" when he discovered how to measure the density of irregular objects like a king's crown.

Electromagnetic Intuition

Robert Ornstein gives us the following delightful analogy on intuition:[3]

Suppose we say to a group of pre-technological people: "There is information available 'in the air,' so to speak, which you normally cannot receive. It is present in this room, on the floor, in the walls, above the ceiling. It exists where you walk, where you sleep, where you sit; but you do not yet possess the receptive capabilities to make use of it. If you work with us, you may be able to construct a piece of specially tuned apparatus, and you may then be able to receive these ever-present, subtle, ordinarily unseen signals. Among other things, there is music, special instruction, and diversion available to you on this new avenue of sensation. You will be able to perceive events in the past and events taking place at this moment at great distance. You can receive this information whenever you wish, if you possess the proper sort of receptive capabilities."

Now this sounds like obvious nonsense to most of these people, but to us it is simply a description of television. The TV signals are carried by high-frequency electromagnetic radiation; such radiation is present at all moments, right in the room in which you read and outside "in the air." Without a proper receiver *it might as well not be present,* for our normal sensory systems cannot receive high-frequency electromagnetic energy directly. But if the proper technology is developed we can tap into a dimension of knowledge which is almost always available and which is *already developed.*

These simple examples may not be true instances of intuition, for good ideas and insights can emerge in various ways. Anyway, they beg the question of where truly intuitive ideas and insights come from and by what process they are produced. Do they arise from unconscious rational deduction, induction or inference? Are they the result of subconscious association? A fragment of temporarily forgotten memory? A barely perceived sensory signal? Perhaps a combination of these processes, or something else?

The many great thinkers of the past who pondered long and hard about the origins of human knowledge acknowledged intuition and defined it either as "innate knowledge" or the retrieval of innate knowledge to consciousness. This seems more like a renaming than a definition, but what they are saying is that a portion of what we know as human knowledge *already exists in the mind* somehow, and only has to be coaxed out, or "remembered," to become known. Recent studies in philosophy and in human consciousness offer an equivalent, empirical definition based on exclusion—what the phenomenon is *not*. This is the definition we will adopt here, at least for the time being. Namely, *intuition is the mental process of acquiring information and knowledge directly into the mind, without the use of reasoning, sensing or even memory (in the usual sense of that word).*

The characteristics of television as a source of knowledge (see accompanying box) also apply to intuition. Intuition's unseen signals, ever-present and subtle, promise valuable instruction, entertainment and knowledge, from the remote past through the present to the future, to great depths and much more!. But first we need to acquire "the proper sort of receptive capabilities." Herein lies the opportunity for the intuitive explorer.

Intuitive information may manifest to consciousness in various ways. Most people who recognize intuition find it in their dreams, the hypnogogic state of consciousness just preceding sleep and the hypnopompic state upon awakening. It may also appear during day-dreams, reveries and properly conducted hypnosis. For some persons it works best through a partial or full trance state. Intuition may also be given the credit for many of the sudden bursts of insight that everyone experiences from time to time, either from a normal state of consciousness or during a "peak experience," emotional crisis, a physical accident or a moment of exhilaration or dissociation. These are all moments when the intellectual mind is at rest or otherwise diverted from its normal activity. The intuitive information that leaks through these non-ordinary states is not always clear, reliable and useful, but it is a reminder that the ability is always there. It may be taken as an invitation to remain open to the faculty, so at some point one may embark on the path of deliberately developing his intuition.

Most persons acknowledge the non-rational quality of some of their ideas and insights, but if asked about their source they attribute them to an undefined, mysterious and unaware aspect of the mind (which explains nothing). They may respect the phenomenon as a "gift" that manifests on special occasions and for a few privileged individuals, but not as a natural, common capacity everyone possesses—and certainly not something they want to probe into very deeply. Intuition has also been compared to the mental capacity to learn a language: it is innate, everyone can do it, but there has to be an intention or need before the development takes place. Others put intuitive insights into the category of religious revelation, mysticism or parapsychology, all of which are catch-alls for the unexplained and a pretty sure prescription to keep them unexplained.

To m any the lack of awareness of their intuitive ability leads them to the belief that it does not exist at all. They assume that whatever arises in the mind as a "thought" or idea is generated through one's reasoning faculty alone, partially unconscious, with a little help from sensory inputs and memory. This observation can be only a belief, not true understanding, since the reasoning capacity of the unconscious mind is not at all well understood; current explanations are at best limited and even doubtful. A primitive hunter might hold the opposite belief (also doubtful) that his familiar skills are due entirely to his natural, built-in knowledge—and what is this thing called "reasoning"?

Is intuitive the same as psychic? No, but they are related, for what is commonly regarded as "psychic" performance is *one* way in which intuition may manifest. However, the term "psychic" is vague. It refers to a range of performances, some of which have nothing at all to do with intuition.[4*] It is used most often to name an unexpected and seemingly impressive insight, or the performer who provides it, with emphasis on the phenomenon or the individual rather than the message being conveyed. In common usage the adjective "psychic" means little more than "mysterious" or "unexplained."

Intuition, on the other hand, refers to a capacity and a process rather than a kind of performance, just as reasoning is not the same as a logical deduction. It is the mechanism that enables and explains the best psychic feats, just as it enables the most revealing dreams, daydreams, reveries, peak experiences and hypnosis. Genuine psychic performance includes the main types of classical and proven ESP (extrasensory perception), namely, clairvoyance, clairaudience, psychometry and precognition, all of which can be valid manifestations of intuition.

Not many of the popular psychic performers function highly intuitively. A few may be powerful and even "expert" intuitives, though the typical neighborhood psychic is so fascinated with the process that he pays little attention to the relevance, correctness and value of what he is communicating. If a psychic's motives are confused or not fully positive, his performance can be a hindrance—even pathological—rather than a blessing,. Mentally ill patients often receive powerful psychic (and even intuitive) impressions by virtue of their heightened sensitivity or their diminished intellectual faculties.

The Mysterious Unconscious

"Man cannot persist long in a conscious state; he must throw himself back into the unconscious, for his root lives there." [Goethe[5]]

Intuition is an innate, fundamental and universal capacity of the human mind, coexistent with and parallel to the reasoning faculty. We will see in the following sections that both reasoning and intuition are essential components of what is normally considered "thought." The two work together intimately, mutually supporting one another, even when the individual is not aware of the partnership. The human mind cannot function unless both reasoning and intuition are working in balance. Occasionally one of them may function so strongly that the resulting thought appears to be purely rational or purely intuitive, and this may be. However, what one happens to be aware of and what one speculates about the partnership is a another matter, not necessarily valid.

My first clearly intuitive experience as a young adult happened when I was resting in the sun on the library lawn, right after lunch and before returning to work. The scene is still well embedded in memory. Just a few days earlier I had moved into a new apartment, and was waiting to receive a new phone number from the telephone company. I wondered what it would be, and at this instant four digits suddenly flashed into my mind. I was surprised and incredulous, but noted them down anyway so I could check them out later.

They turned out to be correct, as the last four digits of my new phone number. (I might have guessed the first three for my particular area.) I was excited and full of questions but also shocked for what had emerged from what I thought was a stable, rational mind. Such things were not supposed to happen! I felt the fear of knowing more than I felt I could handle, and the loss of some cherished beliefs.

It's probably just as well I didn't know then the many surprises in store for the coming years, or I might have backed away in terror!

Similar to the reasoning faculty, other recognized mental activities such as attention, imagination, dreaming and memory (storage and recall) all overlap intuition. Whichever one of these is active in the mind at any given moment may or may not be fed by intuition, though we will see soon that it often is, at least to a limited extent. Conversely, the active presence in the mind of these other faculties affects how intuition operates: each may aid it or impede it. Intuition pervades all facets of thought, and all thought affects intuitive functioning.

It should be obvious that these capacities, including reasoning, take place at least partially within the unconscious mind; that is, they do not reach full awareness. This partial obscuration means that we can never be certain that our conscious mind is fully informed of the roots of what actually manifests to consciousness as images, thoughts, desires, feelings, beliefs, speech and behavior. It also implies that we may be largely unaware of the intuitive component that is affecting these other mental functions and is affected by them. Of course, we prefer to believe that our consciousness has control over our mind processes and is responsible for them, and this is certainly true in a broad sense. Still, the fact remains that *we can never declare with full confidence what it is that we truly want, what we love, what we believe, what we choose, what we feel and what we know.* There is always more, and we must respect it. We must find a way to somehow accommmodate to this ignorance. Herein lies the deeper meaning of words like faith, destiny, will, courage, coincidence, soul, spirit and love, which to the conscious mind alone can appear unfounded and somewhat vague.

We all recognize that we *possess* an unconscious mind, simply because we know that much is going on in the mind of which we are not aware (dreams, at the very least). So how can we become aware of this unconscious self—how can we learn about it? Only by wanting and staying open to what it is trying to tell us, in every thought and act of life. Those who practice this art diligently have much to say about the marvels to be discovered.

Might intuition provide the missing channel for bringing the unconscious to consciousness? We will be exploring this question and seeking an answer throughout this book.

Intuition Relative to Other Mental Functions

"Unless there is a gigantic conspiracy involving…highly respected
scientists in various fields,…the only conclusion the unbiased
observer can come to must be that there are people who obtain
knowledge existing in other people's minds, or in the outer world,
by means yet unknown to science." [H. J. Eysenck[6]]

The mind possesses functions besides intuition, of course. How do they relate
to intuition?[7*]

The *memory process*, for example (as distinguished from the mind that holds it
and its content), can be thought of as having two functions or stages. The first
stage is the selection (usually unconscious) of which information and experiences generated by the rational, intuitive, sensory and other aspects of the
mind are to be retained. This discrimination is natural and automatic because
each of these inputs is typically incomplete and uncertain. It tends to be filled
out and integrated before being stored for later recall. The second stage of
memory is the recall: the searching and recognition that occurs subsequently
when information is retrieved. Everyone's memory contains an abundance of
irrelevant information and experiences, as well as many emotional and
somatic associations, along with the information being remembered at any
particular moment. The two stages of the memory process interact with the
flow of new intuitive information, both influencing it and being influenced by
it. They therefore govern the accuracy and reliability of information both as it
is stored and as it is recalled.

This recall process is actually very similar to the reception, apart from memory, of intuitive information alone to consciousness. Experienced intuitives
often testify that when they receive new intuitive information it feels like they
are remembering something they know but have forgotten. The difference now
is that *intuitive information arises from a different part of the mind than ordinary memory.* (We'll look at this other part shortly.)

Attention is a conscious function but is triggered into action, usually unconsciously, by any of a variety of signals: a sensory input, such as a sound, image,
danger or pain; by a momentary subconscious memory recall, which may be
either a pleasurable sensation or a fear; by a rationally based realization—or by
a signal from the intuitive part of the mind. Once triggered, attention may be

increased and focused by these same factors, though at this point conscious intention is able to intervene if the individual so chooses. Therefore, an openness to intuition may shift one's attention, and where one places his attention helps to create an openness to receiving intuitive information. Attention skills can be sharpened by meditation and similar practices, and these improve intuitive skill.

Imagination is the human creative capacity for constructing in the mind images and entire scenarios as substitutes for and extensions of actual experience. It also plays an important role in filling out incomplete rational thoughts, sensations, memory recalls, perceptions, feelings and impressions, including intuition itself, as part of overall mental activity. Intuition is intimately incorporated in the imaginative process for both the creation of scenarios and their corroboration against reality. A well functioning intuition can greatly enhance one's imagination. When imagination is used independently it may easily lead to fantasies and hallucinations, and a strong intuition is helpful in screening out such creations as unreal.

Dreaming is the one activity of the mind most strongly influenced by the mind's deep intuitive source, whatever that might be. Not only is dreaming a universal activity, because everyone dreams, but it occurs during sleep time when the most extensive integration of intellectual, sensory, feeling and memory activity is taking place. Most persons are in closest touch with their intuitive source when they are remembering dreams, just falling asleep or just waking up, because at these times the unconscious mind is more accessible to the conscious mind than during waking hours, and their intuition is able to function more clearly as well. Thus, dreams can be a rich source of ideas, new perspectives and improved understanding. Anyone may cultivate dreamwork as an active and practical intuitive facilitator.

Is intuition the same as *instinct*, or some aspect of it? The two notions share the traits of being innate and fundamental, but the term "instinct" normally refers to an unchangeable source of behavior (even in animals), or an inborn drive rather than a capacity one may deliberately develop. Intuition is not a physical characteristic, as instinct is usually assumed to be. As already noted, intuition might be said to be "instinctual knowledge," another way of saying that the knowledge is already present, not acquired or created.

Faith. The definition of intuition makes it sound somewhat like faith, at least in the meaning of faith as "belief that does not rest on logical proof or material evidence." This is what we mean when we speak of faith in God, or an unexplained trust such as "I have faith that it will turn out all right" or "Have faith in me, I will not let you down"—but not "She follows the Jewish faith," or "He is faithful to his aged mother." Religious faith and faith as confidence or trust *may* be intuitive, but they are not necessarily so. Intuition and faith have much in common, but to equate them is not correct. In any case, the word faith usually refers to a state of mind rather than a mental capacity like intuition.

Faith, like intuition, is often wrongly cited as a justification or defense against explanation. The rational mind is not comfortable with the notion of faith because the it seems to be demanding acceptance of a statement or idea without any reasonable basis for it. This is indeed true, because the validity of many matters cannot be based on reason alone. But it can rest on a deeper kind of knowing, such as intuition. Even though faith as belief without basis makes no sense, many persons appear to live by such beliefs. At the opposite end of the spectrum we find the deep religious faith exemplified by many saints from all religions, for their faith rests strongly on inner knowledge.

Both intuition and genuine faith allow one to just *know*, without explanation or justification, sometimes apparently contrary to reason and sensory experience. From a practical standpoint both intuition and faith share the useful function of nudging the mind off of an intellectual track, so it may discover other valid ways of knowing.

Information, Belief and Knowledge

"This term [intuition] does not denote something contrary to reason, but something outside the province of reason."
[Carl Gustav Jung[8]]

Beliefs are not the same as knowledge. Believing occupies an intermediate place between the receipt of new information, which is a kind of observation and requires no evaluation or judgment, and the subsequent step of incorporating it into *knowledge* that is solid, trustworthy and integrated into an existing knowledge framework. Beliefs constitute a temporary or tentative acceptance of matters that seem to be true but are still not certain, according to fully accepted past experience and the criteria of the inner mind.

When one states a *belief* about something he is acknowledging that he is not sure about it. Beliefs are always subject to challenge and examination. We find ourselves automatically drawn to situations in which our current beliefs can be tested and refined. Beliefs are like rough garments that enclothe and cover the "truth," which is still hidden and not readily expressible in words. The clothing of belief gets in the way, for it tends to obscure, confuse and distort the reality it is covering. Still, it brings truth closer and helps us make it more comprehensible and accessible to our waking consciousness. People spend entire lifetimes getting through and beyond certain unreal beliefs, yet they could consciously transcend these beliefs with a little courageously applied effort.

In contrast, *knowledge* is already accepted and incorporated into our ground of comprehension, our worldview. It is not up for question, argument or change, and it needs no defense. (A sure test of whether a person's notion is a belief, as opposed to knowledge, is whether he feels the need to defend it.) We do not *believe* in our feet, dogs or the sky; they simply exist. Also, when we love someone or something unconditionally, we *know* it and no doubt is possible. Knowledge is unquestionable and unquestioned because it is an accepted portion of deeper, innate knowledge.

Knowing transcends believing because it consists of personal truth. Its home is outside the realm of words, pictures, the senses, space, time and gravity. Knowledge may always be expanded, of course, because there is always more to be assimilated, but once a piece of knowledge is in place it is inherently unchangeable. Psychologist Carl Jung said it well:

> "People speak of belief when they have lost knowledge. Belief and disbelief are mere surrogates. The naive primitive doesn't believe, he *knows*, because the inner experience rightly means as much to him as the outer. He still has no theory and hasn't let himself be befuddled by booby trap concepts. He adjusts his life—of necessity—to outer and inner facts…. Whereas we live in only one half and merely believe in the other, or not at all." [Carl Gustav Jung[9]]

Beliefs are indeed useful, but only as *stages* along the path to valid knowledge, not as the final authority. They are problematic because of the human tendency to rely on them as substitutes for knowledge. Sometimes we seem to have little choice, but they cannot play this role well and our acceptance of this substitution leads to undesirable, sometimes painful consequences.

Beliefs have these effects because they are conditioned into existence by concerns of security, which feed a fear of what is presumed or imagined to follow, but rarely does unless the belief is allowed to create the feared consequences. The option is to choose to live with uncertainty and trust one's inner knowing as the needed guidance. This is a another way of saying that beliefs impose a barrier along the otherwise direct and natural path from personal experience to acquired knowledge. Beliefs are basically unnecessary. The best use of experience is to be led *directly* into knowledge, rather than solidifying the experience into an intermediate belief, then attempting later to convert or turn the belief into knowledge—usually a slow and painful process.

Intuition is a powerful force for the transcendence of beliefs into knowledge. At the same time there is no greater barrier to the reception of intuitive knowledge than beliefs waiting to be transcended. To enhance intuition is to transcend beliefs, and vice versa. The two mind expansions take place together.

Information lies between facts and understanding, but as the main constituent of knowledge (in its widest sense) it is closer to the former. Like facts, information can be packaged into verbal statements, though we use the term more broadly here to describe the elementary and identifiable elements of understanding, comprehension and knowledge, including those that cannot necessarily be expressed in words or pictures. Thus, information may be an impression or insight as well as a piece of data, a mental picture or a testable fact. It may be right or wrong. The mind's task is to screen it for validity before accepting it as part of knowledge.[10*]

It does not seem necessary to define *wisdom*, precisely here. We recognize it as a kind of practical, broad "inner knowledge," commonly regarded as lying at a level deeper than ordinary knowledge but not as deep as ultimate knowing or absolute truth. Wisdom is sometimes used as equivalent to intuition, but this is misleading. Intuition is an important component or agent of wisdom, but it is a mental capacity and process rather than an advanced state of the mind, a result of intuition and other faculties discussed above.

The Evidence for Intuition

"Do you believe that the sciences would have arisen and grown up if the sorcerers, alchemists, astrologers and witches had not been their

> forerunners; those who…had first to create a thirst, a hunger, and a
> taste for hidden and forbidden powers?" [Friedrich Nietzsche]

Not all properties of intuition are clearly understood and explained. Consequently, most past attempts at its application have been ambiguous, sporadic and not very successful. On the other hand, the accumulated evidence for just the *existence* of intuition as a real capacity of the human mind is abundant and a matter of widely recorded history.[11] Let's review this evidence briefly.

Evidence of intuition as a faculty of the mind or a kind of performance has arisen conspicuously through more than 6000 years of human history, in every major culture, with many kinds of individuals and in a great variety of contexts. In fact, intuitive activity was broadly accepted as "normal" in most of the major cultures of the world until the scientific-industrial revolution in the Western world, and even in cultures today that have escaped the influence of modern civilization. During the last two centuries intuitive performance has been generally regarded in the West as unexplained and suspicious magic. It has been largely disregarded by both science and the many professions that follow scientific principles and methods.

Philosophical deliberation, religious thought and recent psychological study have all made small but positive contributions to the collective recognition and understanding of intuition. While minor they have kept alive the notion of intuition as a natural and virtually universal attribute of the human condition. The perennial philosophy, the collection of ageless traditional wisdom common to all the major religions and philosophic systems of the world, clearly embraces intuition as either inherent, innate knowledge, or as an accessible knowledge reservoir residing deep in the human mind.[12] Also, intuition has undoubtedly played its part by contributing to philosophical and psychological understanding, as it has in various other areas.

While science has not been sympathetic, the creative breakthroughs of individual scientists were undoubtedly enabled by a strong reliance on intuition, as were many artistic accomplishments, numerous examples of truly exceptional human performance, a host of "inspired" literary works and the long tradition of deep religious experience. Many other advances probably had an intuitive source or trigger, but were not recorded well enough for us to be certain today. Wherever documentation in these fields exists, it shows that intuition was responsible for countless instances of inspiration, revelation, wisdom and insight. This record leaves no doubt that "direct knowing" was both prevalent and pervasive in many human creative activities in the past.

During the last 100 years the study of intuition, under various names, has been gradually taken over by the field of parapsychology, as it was being abandoned by the scientific disciplines. This relatively new field has documented many times over, according to strict scientific standards, that singular intuitive performances actually occur, at least under favorable circumstances. Still, little progress has been made in understanding just *how* the intuitive process works and the conditions under which it occurs. Both scientific and public acceptance of parapsychological findings have been improving in recent decades. The public is more savvy about intuition today but is still doubtful that it is relevant and useful.

One recent, very successful development has been Remote Viewing (RV), a form of clairvoyance devised by two scientists at SRI International in the 1950s. RV is an alternative approach to the kind of intuitive inquiry of the CAI experiments.[13] It involves the description of a specific target site, distant from the intuitive and unknown to both the intuitive and nearby experimenters. A second experimenter and a witness visit the site, selecting it by random means on the way. The intuitive viewer in the laboratory describes the site.

Hundreds of RV tests were highly successful. In some tests the viewing was conducted *before* the target was actually chosen. In others the targets were not visited but identified only by their geographical coordinates. RV was used only for physical targets, not to provide answers to personal or technical questions. This extensive research showed that almost anyone can generate correct and evidential target descriptions, though the most impressive results arose from a few very skilled viewers. The main purpose of the experiments was determine whether useful intelligence information could be gathered through RV, and this purpose was achieved. The researchers chalked up many impressive viewing successes. Whether direct applications to actual spying occurred has not yet been fully reported. (More comments on RV are included in Chapter 14.) As if this mass of evidence were not enough, we may turn to our own individual experiences. Everyone has had at least a few singular occasions in which his intuition functioned by itself for a moment, without rational or emotional interference. Modern surveys show that these kinds of personal experiences— insights, deja-vu, revelations, moments of greatly enhanced awareness and unexplainable predictions—are not at all rare but are so common as to be virtually universal. They may seem unsettling and even threatening at times, and are therefore easily forgotten, though they remain in memory and may be recalled with a little effort. They do not fit in well with the way modern society, with its pressure for consensus and its reliance on rational explanation and justification, conditions us to think.

Most psychiatrists and psychologists have had little experience and no professional training in intuition or intuitive behavior. They cannot explain intuition from the models of the mind familiar to them, so they tend to regard intuitive performance as a problem to be solved or an illness to be cured (and intuitive practice certainly has its pathological side). This limited view is understandable, since psychiatry, and subsequently psychology, grew out of Western medicine and took over its objectivist and reductionist framework, which had worked so well for materialistic science. Modern subfields such as transpersonal and humanistic psychologies have been breaking out of this narrow framework.[14] They welcome individual experience, including intuition, along with measurement and rationality as a valid ground of observation, and as valid data on which to build a more comprehensive, realistic and useful understanding of the mind.

The history of intuition has been varied and contentious, at times even violent. In the past those who admitted to having intuitive insights or claimed they were responding to an inner voice were variously honored as divine messengers and saints, or were persecuted as heretics, witches or agents of the devil. Fortunately, modern society has progressed in its acceptance of unusual abilities since those days. This significant aspect of the mind called intuition may now be experienced and practiced openly, studied by scholars and experimented with by researchers. Not everyone understands well what is going on, but you may now freely acknowledge your intuitive insights without fear of being either burned or sainted.

Purpose and Scope of this Study

What needs to be done next is to go beyond these occasional, spontaneous and largely uncontrolled instances of intuitive performance to a further stage: to find out how to work with intuition reliably and effectively. In other words, we must learn how to actually *use* intuition to generate new information and ideas on demand, to enhance understanding and perspective on matters of our own choosing, and hopefully to apply this new knowledge to help solve important personal and societal problems, reach good decisions and be generally nourished by this rich inner resource.

Specifically, we must find out how to *conduct intuitive requests for new information*—deliberately, under control, with focused intention and with the ultimate application very much in mind. To this end we must determine what kinds of knowledge that we ourselves, or the best intuitive "experts," can bring forth, and the particular conditions under which the flow of intuitive knowledge operates best. We may also need to work out how to *verify* intuitive information by non-intuitive means—that is, by other ways of acquiring knowledge—in order to convince ourselves and others that the new, intuitively derived information is indeed accurate, reliable and relevant to our needs.

Herein lies our charge as we explore the applications of intuition. The experiments described in the subsequent chapters of this book seek to provide a positive and informative response to this challenge.

This presentation is limited in that it considers intuition only as a *process and means for acquiring information and knowledge*. Actually, intuition is much more than this. Before going further let us look briefly at what is being omitted from the intuitive potential.

The broader notion of intuition arises from the well established observation that intuitive "information" consists not only of mere facts, statements that can be said to be true of false, but also more subjective ingredients of human knowledge: comprehensive understanding, perspective, accumulated experience and even feelings, as noted briefly above. These ingredients are not necessarily true or false, cannot be pinned down objectively and often cannot be described verbally. Intuition feeds each person's acquisition of knowledge, especially self-knowledge, as well as his perceived and evolving relationship with the greater reality of which he is a part. It inspires him as he passes the challenges along his path, and it does so by giving him "information" of a greater sort.

This broader notion of information arises out of intuition's role as the main communicative link between each individual's conscious awareness and the deeper and largely unconscious realm of his mind, his personal essence, heart and "soul," the realm that emerges in dreams, imagination, feelings and fantasies and that governs the overall "gestalt" of his life. This kind of intuitive knowledge cannot be comprehended second-hand through reading, the senses or instruction, but only directly through experience. Each individual must endure this process by himself, as lightly or deeply as he chooses.

While this deeper aspect of intuition is without doubt much more significant to human life, it is also more difficult to speak about effectively. I could talk around it, as many others have tried to do, and might eventually persuade you to explore it for yourself. (I might attempt this in a subsequent book). But to squeeze such an explanation into the confines of this report would be an unproductive compromise. It would dilute and distort the present message, and for most readers would leave a poor and inaccurate impression. The limitation lies mainly with the language, incidentally, not the experience itself, which is rich, rewarding and readily accessible to those who seriously seek it. We will touch again on this aspect of intuition in Chapter 15.

In contrast, the objective side of intuition is much easier to discuss and understand, even in the absence of direct experience. This will be the main focus in the chapters to follow. It is the preferred approach from which we may add to the convincing "evidence" that intuition exists. We will show that it is a valid, important and useful capacity in today's world, and that virtually anyone may learn to apply it. This applicational work is also a sound basis for personal intuition development, for those with this interest.

Another exclusion of this study is reflected in our pragmatic approach to learning about intuition, as opposed to theoretical research that would attempt to build up a body of solid understanding, step by step. The reasons for this preference should come as no surprise; namely, there is today too little psychological understanding of the human mind to serve as a foundation for growing a theory of intuition. The existing base of empirical data is very scanty, so much experimental data would need to be gathered. The major impediment, however, is that we would have to make use of scientific methodology. While this approach is well developed for the investigation of physical matters, it suffers from inherent limitations that prevent its direct use in the study of consciousness. A way will have to be found around these shortcomings before a "theory of intuition" can be developed.

The empirical, trial-and-error approach chosen for the present work involves a risk of wasted effort, of course, but it is more direct and will help provide the data, insights and hypotheses needed for the more scholarly study that will inevitably follow in due time.

Observations from Intuition Development

> "True intuition…is as much a part of the human as the senses of
> touch and taste and smell. However, few people are trained or even
> encouraged from an early age to explore, develop, or trust such an
> inner faculty." [Christopher Childs[15]]

Another restriction is that I will not be explaining how one may go about
expanding his native intuitive ability into a useful skill. This aspect of intuition
has been well explored and reported in several readily available books.[16*] and
taught extensively in workshops and classes in the U.S., Europe and elsewhere.
(At a later time I hope to add CAI's own contributions to this accumulated
experience.) It will be helpful now to cite only three discoveries about intuition
that have emerged from these explorations in individual development, as a
convenient way to begin to explain how intuition functions in the mind and
how it works when one employs it in practice.

First, whoever chooses to undertake intuition development soon realizes that
strengthening his intuition is not so much a matter of training a new skill, such
as learning to play the piano, speak French or drive a truck, but rather one of
removing blocks to the natural emergence of an existing ability, namely, his
intuition. The main effort required is one of abandoning or circumventing certain acquired beliefs, mental habits and emotional conditioning. Inother words,
it requires more unlearning than learning. The task is one of becoming aware of
these barriers, identifying them for what they are, confronting them squarely,
and then with firm intention and (usually) disciplined practice removing them.
This is the key personal process needed to open the intuitive gate.

There are many specific methods for carrying out this "clearing." The appropriate ones are unique to the individual student, since they depend on the particular obstacles to be dealt with. All approaches involve introspection and
inner work, however, and especially learning how to *deliberately set aside
rational mental activity.* The intuitive process is not an intellectual one; in fact,
an uncontrolled intellect is the major obstacle for most aspirants. It is similar
to learning to speak a new language, certainly not an intellectual task, for even
children and the ignorant can do it. As in any deliberate learning, the main
requirement is a clear intention or need, and a willingness to open oneself up
to new experience. For adults, relaxation techniques, along with meditation,
dreamwork and awareness enhancement are the most common and effective

prescriptions. These practices work to clear out the obstacles to the natural flow of intuitive knowledge, just as one cleans out his library or garage after acquiring too many unneeded items: old habits, beliefs and attachments in this case. Some find this effort difficult, others easy, though all may take pleasure in it when it is accomplished.

Second, the student of intuition development needs to enhance his sensitivity to the part of his inner mind that is the source from which intuitive knowledge flows. To communicate well with this portion of his mind *he must learn its subtle, internal, non-verbal language.* In this effort, which involves his feelings more than his brain, he must learn how to distinguish genuine feelings arising from his deeper mind and his heart, from those that are emotional reactions or intellectual intrusions from his subconscious mind. As this learning progresses he discovers he can listen better and better to his inner mind without being diverted, so he can begin to form a cooperative partnership with it. This is not an entirely a new activity. We all engage in this kind of internal self-communication automatically in the course of our daily lives, but normally only occasionally, inadvertently and rarely gracefully. In contrast, it is an active process during sleep. As we practice it consciously, more and more of the unknown (the unconscious) automatically and gradually rises into conscious awareness (consciousness). Indeed, this on-going "dance" on the boundary of the known and the unknown is what makes like challenging—and interesting!

Third, and most important from a practical point of view, highly skilled intuitives testify that *there is nothing to be basically feared in the learning process.* Like the true explorer of any unknown land, the student developing his intuition may proceed confidently with the assurance that there is nothing in this new territory that is inherently malicious and stronger than his own determination (will, intention, desire), and his capacity to overcome whatever difficulties arise. He is *never* a victim of dark, mysterious forces in his unconscious unless he believes himself to be, out of a self-created fear of what he imagines lies in these hidden depths of his mind. Such fears arise only from ignorance. His best defense against them is his serious intention to explore, to come to know and understand this new domain. In short, *the conscious mind is the director of the unconscious.*, not the other way around.

These three discoveries from intuition development practice are saying first, that intuition is an innate ability that manifests naturally when the intellectual and emotional barriers to it are identified, confronted and "unlearned." The barriers are largely cultural residues, not inherent or fixed but typically outside of casual awareness. The effort requires self-inquiry and a voluntary, internal cleaning out of these inhibiting portions of the subconscious mind. Second, the higher level of the mind from which we presume intuitive knowing comes communicates in its own language, which must be learned before an intimate intuitive dialogue can take place. It is a non-verbal language, based more on feelings than intellectual structures. Finally, the barriers to intuitive functioning can be transcended by virtually anyone, because the controlling agent, the conscious mind, is not at the mercy of unconscious forces but is free and able to do so.

Corroboration of Intuitive Information

> "True intuition comes from a deeper understanding that transcends evidence and proof and logic and reason, and all those tools with which we try to determine whether something is true or not—and thus whether it is important."
> [Neale Donald Walsch[17]]

Is intuition always correct and true? What people typically experience as intuition is certainly *not* consistently correct, for various kinds of errors can and do occur. Evidence is building, and it is almost conclusive, that intuitive knowledge is inherently correct at its source within the mind, whatever that might be, so that all errors that reach the conscious mind occur in the subconscious process of conveying, translating and interpreting it[18]. This is an exciting hypothesis, because, if true, it indicates just where one must apply effort to reach higher knowledge, perhaps even the ultimate level of "truth."

Even if intuitive information is inherently correct at its source, however, it cannot be assumed to be so when received and used. Moreover, if it is to be subsequently applied to a shared purpose it must be communicated to other persons and made credible to them. This further step can easily introduce additional errors.

Actually, this observation is true of new information from *any* source, not only intuitive information. Unless information comes from deep inside oneself, in such a manner that one simply *knows* intuitively that it is true, the mind demands that it be compared and checked with previously acquired human knowledge before it can be integrated with this knowledge and added to it. We have no right to expect others to accept our personal intuitive insights and revelations, and we should be hesitant to accept them ourselves, without some kind of corroborative "evidence." We would also be badly mistaken if we accepted others' such insights unless we can independently verify them.

Corroboration is a natural and necessary part of applied intuition. It is needed for all *kinds* of information: small fragments and large; varied collections; facts and explanations; new perspectives and ideas; interpretations of knowledge already on hand; and information sought both for personal use and for collective acceptance by groups, organizations and the public. Because of its great importance we need to pause here and examine the means available for carrying out corroborative studies or tests, and how effective and convincing these means might be.

Corroboration may be carried out by various ways, the choice depending mainly upon which *qualities* of the new information need to be verified. These depend in turn upon on the kind of information at stake, the particular application and who is going to be carrying it out. Some of these qualities can be checked directly, independent of already existing knowledge: its clarity (freedom from ambiguity), precision (exactness), specificity (non-vagueness) and self-consistency. Three other qualities, relevance, responsiveness and usefulness, are also relatively direct, for they require only that the information be compared against the particular need for which it has been sought.

Most difficult is the requirement of correctness, or *accuracy*: the information must be compatible with well accepted knowledge from other sources, or what can be readily deduced from this knowledge. Again, these criteria apply to new information from *any* source, though they are especially critical in emerging areas such as intuitive inquiry still on trial, so to speak, and struggling to prove themselves.

On very specific matters the best alternative source for corroboration is an objective discipline such as science, or one of the several fields derived from science. The huge volumes of scientifically derived knowledge are not perfect, but they are the most solid resource available throughout all history. Science also provides a well-tested methodology for checking new information for accuracy and for consistency with existing knowledge, and it may be used in many areas outside of science itself. Thanks to libraries, universities and Internet, this body of knowledge is readily accessible to those who wish to tap it for the corroboration of intuitive information, or just for their own edification.

There are serious limitations in both the applicability of scientific knowledge base and in its methodology, but they do not ordinarily arise when checking substantive, "factual" information about the physical world. Anyway, fitting or not, science carries the greatest public credibility in the modern world. It is widely accepted as the final arbiter between truth and illusion, even on matters not wholly scientific.

A second option for corroboration is the body of specialized knowledge that has arisen from traditional disciplines rooted in thoughtful consideration or expression of the human condition: philosophy, religion, history, education and even the arts. Peripheral areas such as psychology, anthropology and social science also belong here—despite their efforts, not entirely successful, to be considered as sciences in their own right.

On less specific issues one may fall back on the base of widely accepted knowledge, ordinarily regarded as "common sense," that has evolved from the long history of collective human experience. Portions of it are not sensible at all, of course, since they consist of widely held beliefs, not supported, verified or verifiable. While this source is not entirely reliable and is seriously limited as "truth," it is broad, pervasive and not often questioned, and its public credibility is fairly high.

There are also various "other ways of knowing" besides the conventional ones relied upon in the modern world.[19] While unfamiliar and controversial, they are unique and trustworthy on certain non-factual matters. Arising in cultures far from Western civilization, they have a limited but rightful place in validating intuitive information.

In certain other cases intuitive information may be validated experimentally, using specially designed tests, scientific or other. These tend to be time-consuming and expensive but can be very convincing. One form of this approach is prediction: to deduce a future consequence implied by new information, one that will occur if and only if the information is correct. One then need only wait for the consequence to occur. (There are pitfalls in making such predictions, since the outcome can be affected by the fact of the prediction, so one must be very careful.)

Sometimes new information may be corroborated by applying it directly, without any other verification. Its applicability is then its own test of validity as well as of its usefulness. Indeed, when direct application is the *only* goal of intuitive inquiry, then formal verification efforts such as scientific tests, protocols and experiments are unnecessary.

In certain situations one seeks assurance that a piece of information was obtained intuitively rather than from a non-intuitive source. This is usually difficult to do but is occasionally and fortuitously possible. One way is to demonstrate that the alleged intuitive information is totally new, not known to anyone and not derivable from existing knowledge by sensory or intellectual means. (Some predictions fall in this category.) Another way is to show that the intuitive who received it could not have had prior access to the information through exposure to television, reading, early education, childhood experiences or the like, even though it may be known to others. Such a thorough biographical examination is rarely possible. Fortunately, proof of intuitive origin is required only for certain parapsychological tests and perhaps to convince skeptics about intuition, not in most intuition applications.

Much new intuitive information cannot be formally corroborated at all, even though it may be valid, because no secondary source exists against which to compare it. This category of information arises, for example, when it cannot be adequately expressed in words or pictures. It also arises for certain personal information, which may strike home as true to the individual (whether received by himself or through a skilled intuitive) but is not necessarily convincing to someone else. In this situation relevance can be more important than accuracy since the value of the intuitive information lies mainly in its role as encouragement, inspiration, sympathy or a reminder, even though it may not be factually quite right.

Might corroboration be aided by requesting the same information independently from several intuitives? Perhaps so. We will examine this possibility in Part III .

The corroboration required to satisfy a single inquirer, rather than an application team, skeptical scientific body or the general public, has similar possibilities but it is usually not so difficult. Not only is the criterion of validity simpler for single inquirers, but only a single person needs to be "convinced"—a largely internal process. In intuitive counseling, for example, formal corroboration is not normally necessary, or even possible, since such personal information is usually subjective, explanatory, interpretative, not specific and not externally verifiable. (Partial external verification may occur through clients' personal testimonies on specific matters.)

At best, for the single, independent individual who has learned to tap and trust his own intuition well, accuracy is not so much a problem. External corroboration is not strictly necessary for him, though he might wish it if he is harboring residual doubts or wishes to share his discovery with others. When his intuition is working strongly and clearly, the acceptance of new, valid information into his base of prior knowledge can be direct and effortless, without rational argument or sensory verification. He *knows* it is valid.

Corroboration has pitfalls of its own, of course, whether the information is correct and relevant or not. Past experience with intuitive experiments, psychic readings and clairvoyant demonstrations shows that the receivers of new information are sometimes inclined to judge its validity by their erroneous expectations rather than whether it is correct or not. For example, they make unwarranted assumptions, have unjustified preconceptions or neglect to declare their desires clearly; they are then disappointed when they receive unsatisfactory answers. It is also common for clients to ask for personal information they could not handle if it were provided, or that would be harmful to themselves or others with whom they might share it (secrets, for example). Sometimes they ask questions whose answers they already know or could easily obtain, so the inquiry turns into a request for evidence instead of a search for understanding and knowledge. These kinds of mistakes have sabotaged many past inquiries and experiments, and they block meaningful corroboration. They serve here as a warning and a forecast of what could arise in CAI's own inquiries.

In addition, publicly accepted criteria for what constitutes valid evidence and proof are often unreasonable or highly restrictive, sometimes not even making good sense. This is because they depend upon widely held but mistaken beliefs, and complex subjective conditions that are far from the truth. Highly relevant and correct new information may appear threatening or have controversial implications in sensitive societal areas—religion, politics, commerce, education, etc. In particular cases any of these factors can complicate the corroboration process and render it impractical or ineffective. Thus, the corroboration of certain pieces of new, controversial intuitive information must be very strong before they could become publicly acceptable.

The issue of provable accuracy will certainly be a persistent issue in all future intuitive applications, just as it has always been for new knowledge of other kinds. For acceptance and application of intuitive knowledge in the public domain, one must struggle with the issues of evidence, proof, beliefs, credibility and expectations, all of which are barriers to be overcome on the route to successful application. Corroboration will be seen to be a recurring theme throughout the following chapters.

A Model of the Mind

> "Of all the hard facts of science, I know of none more solid and fundamental than the fact that if you inhibit thought, and persevere, you come at length to a region of consciousness below or behind thought...and a realization of an altogether vaster self than that to which we are accustomed....So great, so splendid is this experience that it may be said that all minor questions and doubts fall away in face of it."
> [Edward Carpenter]

The questions about where intuitive information comes from, and which factors influence its accuracy and other desirable qualities, are serious sticking points for almost all newcomers to the intuitive arena. This obstacle is best dealt with from the vantage point of a tentative *model of the mind*, which explains in simple terms how the mind works when it generates and communicates intuitive information. It also clarifies how intuition relates to the familiar mental processes discussed briefly above: reasoning, memory, imagination, thought, dreams, sensation and so on. Models like this are needed in every field as a framework or infrastructure on which to hang observations and facts and thereby build understanding. In well established fields these models are an inherent in the accepted knowledge and are no longer seriously questioned. In unexplored areas such as intuition they need to be created and spelled out specifically.

The simple model adopted at CAI evolved naturally out of our early research and direct experience with clients, though it turned out to be not original. It had been used off and on, and in one form or another, for at least the last hundred years. It is consistent with the picture of the mind already understood in philosophy, parapsychology and transpersonal psychology. It passed further tests later when CAI taught intuition development classes and conducted the experiments reported in the following chapters. Still, it is a *working* model, tentative and hypothetical, and not derived through formal theoretical study, experimentation, data collection and reasoned analysis. Such a refined model of the mind is not yet available, nor is it likely to be for a long time.

This model is based on a separation of the mind into three parts that are readily distinguishable through their recognizable functions. First, there is the *conscious* mind, which possesses awareness of itself and physical reality. It plays the role of a focuser of attention, a reasoning agent and a control center for managing itself, certain body functions and semi-conscious processes such as memory and imagination. The conscious mind has little memory of its own, drawing most of what it needs from the large memory banks within the unconscious mind.

All else is unconscious. What is known about the unconscious mind must be presumed indirectly. We have already noticed that intuition is a largely *unconscious* process, if for no other reason than it lies outside of awareness, except for occasional observable effects—such as the insights that rise to the consciousness from time to time.

Nevertheless, we may safely separate the unconscious portion of the mind into two parts. The first, called the *subconscious* mind, contains the memory, body control, sensory functions, conditioning and learning acquired from one's biological birth and all subsequent development and experience—those physical and mental functions that derive from genetic inheritance, past intellectual activity and interaction with the physical and social environments. The subconscious manages the signals received from the senses and generates those transmitted to the muscular and chemically driven organs of the body. It contains the "programming" for automatic functions and the memory bank for all personal experiences—major and minor, pleasant and fearful, rememberable and apparently forgotten. Many memories remain inactive but can be tapped when needed.

The other part of the unconscious is called by various names in the literature of philosophy, esoteric religion and psychology but is most commonly termed the *superconscious* mind.[20*] This portion too is defined by its function, namely, the direct knowing, intuitive phenomenon discussed above. It is the source of all knowledge that cannot be accounted for by reasoning, the senses

and memory. It has no recognizable connection with immediate past development, and cannot be explained by the subconscious properties just defined.

It is not even certain that the superconscious is confined solely to the individual. Evidence from many sources suggests that it is shared by *everyone*, has no
specific location in time and space, and functions outside of them. It may be
thought of as a *repository of all human knowledge*, past, present and potential,
innate and built-in, simply an attribute of humanness. Psychologist Carl Jung
attributed these features to it when he called it the "Collective Unconscious."[21]
In different religious traditions it is called The Book of Life, the Great Book,
the Akashic Records or The Book of God's Remembrance.

Many speculations have been offered on properties of the superconscious
mind and where might lie its boundaries with the rest of the mind, the brain
and physical reality. These help a little to explain its primary "all-knowing"
function in familiar terms. One view says that an individual's superconscious
mind holds the essence of his personal being, his true inner nature, what may
be called his "soul" (though this term also has various meanings not intended
here). It is also said to be the deep space in our minds where we may meet not
only our true individuality or Self, but also that of other persons—in fact, all
life in the universe, and "God" or "All That Is." It is the place, they say, where
"We are all One." These speculations suggest that the superconscious may be
the ultimate source of all existence, being and truth.

Further, according to many mind-explorers who claim to have gained deep
and intimate access to it, the superconscious allows them to *experience directly
and subjectively* whatever they wished to know, instead of acquiring the knowledge objectively, descriptively and through familiar means of communication.
They describe this kind of directly retrieved information as a personal and
intimate integration with "reality," that which transcends knowledge in its
usual informational sense and enables the inquirer to not only know *about*
something but to truly *know* it.

These speculations will probably turn out to be valid in some sense, but at the
moment they are too loosely defined and speculative to be either confirmed or
denied. We may hold them as exciting possibilities, but it would not be wise to
build our case on them. In terms of information and ordinary knowledge,
which is our main concern here, it will be sufficient to take the simpler and
more modest perspective that the superconscious is merely a huge *knowledge
reservoir*—even though it is surely much more than this. This mammoth "data

base" can be thought of as containing the answers to many of man's endless questions, if not all of them. If claims about it are true, it embraces all times and places, all topics and persons, those expressible in language and those truly ineffable. It even includes the inquirer himself. This breadth and depth of knowledge is conjectured to be the main property of the superconscious. We shall see in what follows how much of this conjecture may be true.

Figure 1 illustrates this model of the mind graphically. Each downward-pointing cone depicts the mind of a single individual. The dashed line across the middle of each cone separates the tip, which represents the conscious mind, from the subconscious region just above it. The dotted line separates the subconscious from the open-ended superconscious at the top.[22*] *Intuition*, shown in Figure 1 as the downward arrow, is the communication channel through which information, knowledge and certain kinds of inner experiences flow from the superconscious mind to the conscious mind.

This figure exhibits immediately several properties of the mind relative to intuition: the role of the conscious mind is the contact with physical reality; the location of the boundaries separating the parts of the mind vary from person to person (and in fact are not solid and fixed for one person); the superconscious is shared at least partly with other individuals, suggesting a common mind-basis and a "mind-to-mind" link; and the flow of intuitive information passes through the subconscious before becoming conscious.

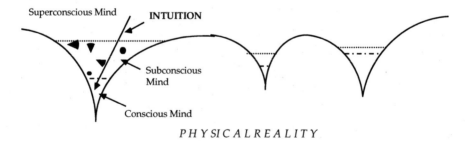

Figure 1. A Model of the Mind, Showing Residues

Obstacles to the Flow of Intuition

"As it [intuition] is a normal function of the human psyche, its
activation is produced chiefly by eliminating the various obstacles
preventing its activity."
[Roberto Assagioli[23]]

This last property indicates that it is the task of the subconscious to perform
any necessary translation of information from the abstract, non-verbal "language" of the superconscious into the familiar language of the conscious mind,
and to carry out the reverse translation when inquiries are made. Herein lies
the major obstacle to the intuitive process, for the subconscious sometimes
balks at its translation task. It may distort or block intuitive messages so they
are not properly conveyed to the conscious mind.

Generations of experience with creative performance, psychic functioning and
religious and other inspiration all indicate that these distortions can almost
always be traced to false memories, limited knowledge structures and conditioned patterns in the subconscious mind. These can be traced in turn to
unreal attitudes and beliefs held by the individual, or to neuroses or other
emotional obstructions he has built up in his subconscious and has not cleared
out. Further, it is known from psychology that such distorting memories
almost arise from early experiences that were painful or frightening when they
first occurred, and were repressed into the subconscious in an incomplete and
unintegrated form[24]. In this sense they had their origin in the conscious mind,
because this is where they were first encountered and were relegated to the
subconscious. These subconscious "residues" (shown as small black spots in
Figure 1) are emotionally loaded barriers to full mental functioning. They create disturbances affecting almost all mental activity—rational thought, perception, feelings, imagination, dreams, the formation of beliefs and especially
intuitive reception. If not cleaned out they become hardened over time and
difficult to remove.

Because these residues are not fully conscious they are not always seen clearly,
or at all. They typically reveal themselves only as errant attitudes, illusory
beliefs, anxieties, irrational behavior and confusion. They can manifest further
as bodily weaknesses, stress, blocked energetic flow, dysfunctional behavior
and disease. When severe these symptoms can be totallly preoccupying, and

the residues themselves become even less visible, are easily overlooked, are seen as unchangeable and are very hard to remove.

To the present point, when these residues are present in the mind they impede the flow of intuitive information so intuition cannot function on demand, accurately and appropriately. They interfere with the access to the superconscious, and the translation and conveying of inquiries and responses. In fact, these obstacles are the only real barriers to the intuitive process. Discarding them is the main task of intuition development. Not all of them need to be removed before intuition can function even highly skilled intuitives retain a few unresolved residues. (Perhaps some enlightened masters have eliminated all of them.) Indeed, every removed residue improves the intuitive flow.

This model of the mind is a reminder that everyone lives his life along the conscious-unconscious interface in his mind. His conscious territory, which rests on the knowledge he has already acquired, is so familiar that it is not a matter of great challenge or attention. His unconscious territory is also not a matter of conscious attention or concern: he is simply not aware of it. It is only in the border region where he is actively living and learning through life's experiences. He draws what he needs from both his conscious knowledge, incomplete as it is, and from the resources in his unconscious, mostly hidden from him; that is, subconscious memories and superconscious knowledge. The activity of his life, his inner growth, is a dance on this boundary, as he gradually brings more and more of his unawareness into awareness, the unknown into the known, the unconscious into consciousness.

Seen in this way, intuition is one of his greatest tools of man's personal growth because it is the main channel by which superconscious knowledge crosses this active boundary and augments his waking consciousness. The best news is that he may take advantage of this opportunity to control the reception of whatever he needs and wants to know. He is free to direct this transfer, using his intention, desires and curiosity, and to apply the results to his growth, happiness and fulfillment. He may open himself up widely to whatever he feels he can handle from the superconscious source.

Intuitive Inquiry

"Advances are made by answering questions.
Discoveries are made by questioning answers."
[Bernard Haisch]

In order to explore intuition as a means of obtaining new and useful knowledge, one must work out a way to deliberately seek this knowledge rather than to wait for it to emerge on its own. New knowledge never manifests automatically, of course, whatever may be the context; it must always be *requested* in some sense, either consciously or unconsciously, perhaps just as a quiet receptivity, surrender or a felt need. "Seek and ye shall find. Knock and the door shall be opened." This age-old counsel appears in all the world's religions and philosophic systems. It holds whenever understanding is sought, especially through intuition. Inquiry is the communicative aspect of intention.

We had to learn at CAI how to conduct inquiries, and this meant how to ask questions properly. The pitiful record of past attempts to obtain information intuitively showed clearly that

Relaxing on the south shore of Crete, overlooking the broad expanse of water on a warm and breeze-free afternoon, I was suddenly struck by the metaphor between this long stretch of beach, with its dozens of busy bathers on the sand and in the surf, and the boundary area between the conscious and unconscious minds, the in-between domain where we do our significant living.

The great sea, like the unconscious, mysteriously beckons and tempts one but doesn't letting him experience very much in terms he can handle. He can swim around a bit, but he can't walk and he can't go far or deeply into it. The land behind him, like the conscious mind, is familiar, supportive and safe, but it is also common place and predictable, sometimes boring to an eager swimmer.

But the beach region in between—this is where the real action takes place. Here he can dip into the unknown, see how far he can go, in the security that he can always return. He can play his games, discover his strengths, learn to let go and be nourished, and is free to explore his challenges. He may go slowly and carefully into the water, or he may dive courageously into the unknown. This beach land is where he dances the dance of life, on the edge between the known and the unknown, between safety and risk, control and surrender, outer and inner. And yes, between reason and intuition.

skillful inquiry is a key factor if good information is to be obtained. It also became apparent early on in the series of intuitive experiments that *the way in which the questions were asked was critical if the answers were to be responsive to our needs and be truly useful.* The requirements for effective inquiry turned out to go well beyond those needed for ordinary conversational requests, and even those used in interviews by experienced question-askers such as media reporters, police investigators and court attorneys. The reasons for this strict requirement, and how one should implement it, were not initially obvious but evolved slowly over the course of the program.

It will be best to postpone a full consideration of the approach eventually worked out until later, when it can be better understood in the light of the entire sequence of experiments. For the moment it will be enough to state four general conditions for carrying out successful inquiry sessions, as they were deduced from unsuccessful prior work by others and were worked out in the first few CAI experiments. We will then pursue a few of their implications and speculate on the reasons why they seem to be necessary. They will be refined later from the experience gained in each experiment, and generalized and evaluated in Chapter 14.

The four tentative conditions for successful intuitive inquiry are:

1. The inquiry must be conducted so no one will be harmed by any consequences that ensue.
2. The inquiry should be motivated by a positive personal purpose.
3. The questions asked should be precise, literal, specific and not contain biases, presumptions or unrealistic expectations.
4. The questions should be addressed only to *expert* intuitives.

These conditions demand that the questions to be posed to the intuitive (oneself or another) be created carefully before they are actually posed. The inquirer should decide what it is he most wants to learn from the superconscious source (#3), why he wants it (#2), what he intends to do with the results (#1) and whom he might ask (#4).

The third condition indicates that the inquirer would do well to acknowledge first his own ignorance in the area of concern, so he may better distinguish what he already knows for certain from what he does not yet know, is uncertain about and wishes to learn. He should be receptive to meaningful and truthful answers even though they may challenge his desires, beliefs and expectations. If the answers he receives pass his personal test of validity, he ought to be willing in advance to act on them, by applying the new information to his intended purpose. He must anticipate the consequences of the application as best as he can, assuming his questions will be answered correctly and fully. He should not ask questions for which he already has the answers, at least without very good reason.

His next step is to formulate these questions clearly and unambiguously, without biases or presumptions arising from his limited knowledge. Why this clarity and precision should be necessary was not initially clear. It appeared later to arise for a variety of reasons, which distinguish intuitive inquiry from ordinary conversational questioning. Here are three possibilities:

First, the base of knowledge in the superconscious mind is so huge that the inquirer's request for a piece of it needs to be specific and to the point—even more so than when asking for information from the Internet or the librarian in the Library of Congress, say.

Second, the superconscious apparently has no intention of its own, so its responses are largely a direct reflection of the inquirer's intentions. It seems to work rather mechanically and cannot be counted on to second guess what the inquirer wants but does not ask for. It will not argue with him, demand clarification or react emotionally to poorly stated questions as a human communicant might do.

Third, ordinary dialogue relies heavily upon a mutually understood and accepted *infrastructure* or *context* of language and knowledge which serves as a ground for the communication. The weaknesses of ordinary conversation are not commonly apparent to its speakers. We typically use words carelessly, make vague references, employ relative pronouns ambiguously and jump into subjects on the assumption that the listener knows what we are talking about and what we intend. Our dialogues with one another work well enough, despite these imperfections, because of the shared, assumed and unspoken context for the communication. In contrast, with persons we do not know, especially someone from another culture, our communications are obviously constrained.

In the superconscious mind this shared context also seems to be weak or missing. Its absence places an extra demand on the language used for communication. When conversing with the superconscious, we have to convert ordinary expressions into a form much more intentioned, precise and unambiguous than the mode used for daily conversation. Probably only particular aspects need to be improved, but until we know better what these aspects are, it is necessary to be unusually focused in our questioning, and avoid assumptions, preconceptions, unstated conditions and vagueness.

The first condition above may seem surprising since most other mental capacities do not have an immediate, built-in protection against misuse. When a person offends, causes pain or lies to another, it may take a long time for the consequences to return to him, if at all. The intuitive access process in the superconscious appears to be governed by some kind of harmlessness principle, so that information dangerous to the seeker or to others is difficult to obtain, perhaps impossible. Even curiosity is not always a legitimate motivation for intuitive inquiry because it can unintentionally lead to harmful consequences. This first condition is

You may prefer to reject intuition because it is a destroyer of wonderful mysteries, but I cannot agree. In retrospect, the only times in my life when I did not welcome new knowledge and understanding occurred when I was feeling protective of firmly held beliefs, or when I did not want the responsibility of handling new knowledge. In other words, I resisted the knowledge because I was afraid of the consequences of holding it. Yes, fear was behind the rejection.

Since then I have come to believe that everyone may come to know anything and everything he wants and is able to handle, later if not immediately, in the course of his individual life. I believe that the very nature of human life allows and encourages every one of us to learn as much as he can deal with. I'm still respectfully cautious, but I know that fear is my only obstacle.

Of course we cannot avoid responsibility when obtaining new knowledge. Knowledge carries power, and power can cause harm when improperly used. But no one can escape his responsibility by remaining ignorant. There is also the risk of arrogance: believing you understand something when you don't, and behaving as if you do. This temptation exists whether one is acquiring knowledge or not, and it need not be a barrier to acquiring more. Finally, many matters do not need to be understood but only accepted. It is so easy to get caught up in striving to know, understand and "prove" matters to oneself, rather than just acknowledging without doubt what is revealed to be true through deep knowing. Well, there goes much of science.

Anyway, has there ever been a mystery that, when revealed, has not led to yet greater mysteries?

admittedly vague at this point, but we will see later from the experiments to be described how it can be firmed up somewhat.

CAI's early experience with intuition, and that from others who reported their experience in sufficient detail, suggests that if an inquirer's "need to know" is sufficiently strong and positive, and if he has not imposed any barriers to clear reception, the knowledge he seeks will emerge in his mind all by itself, even bypassing ordinary awareness and language. If this is generally true, the requirement on questions preparation (#3) might be relaxed somewhat. Some kind of preparation is surely necessary, but exact formulation and his acceptance of the answers may all take place largely unconsciously, as if the unconscious mind is generating the queries and listening for the responses. In contrast, when one must rely on an intuitive other than oneself, spoken language must necessarily intervene as a communicative bridge between inquirer and intuitive. This places a burden on the transfer if it to occur without serious distortion or loss of content. Intuitive inquiry always appeared to work best when the inquirer relied on his own intuition rather than that of an skilled intuitive.

In some respects intuitive inquiry is similar to personal prayer which typically takes the form of a request. (Good prayer is much more than an appeal, of course, but this begging aspect prevails.) The similarity with intuition arises partly because of the key role played by the inner (superconscious) mind in the communication, and partly from the necessity for proper preparation if the effort is to be successful. Both prayer and intuitive inquiry demand a focusing of attention on one's purpose: clearing the mental space so that the desired response may come through, letting go of preconceptions and attachments to a particular outcome and developing trust in one's chosen source, whomever or whatever or it may be. In both cases sufficient preparation can sometimes (if not always) generate enough receptivity and clarity on the issue at hand that a formal request becomes unnecessary.

Summary

Our initial claim should now be clear and well established, namely, that intuition is an innate, virtually universal and powerful mental capacity for acquiring information and accumulating knowledge directly, without the intervention of reason, memory or sense perception. We have also seen that intuition interacts closely with other recognized mental functions, which aid its functioning and are aided by it. It operates like a direct channel from the higher, superconscious mind down to consciousness. The main barriers to its accurate reception lie in the intermediate region, the subconscious. The effort in individual intuition development is to remove these barriers, no more and no less, and highly skilled intuitives have done just this.

In trying to demystify the concept of intuition I have stressed throughout its practical aspects, and will continue to do so in the rest of this book as actual applications are described. First, however, we must take a closer look at the skilled intuitives who are going to be providing the information needed for these inquiries.

> "In the past, we've undervalued intuition. Today, intuition is increasingly recognized as a natural mental faculty, a key element in discovery, problem solving and decision making, a generator of creative ideas, a forecaster, a revealed ingredient of what we call genius. Intuition is also a subtle guide to daily living."
> [Philip Goldberg[25]]

• Endnotes—Chapter 1

[1] Palmer, 1998, p. 177.

[2] James, 1958, p. 72.

[3] Ornstein, 1972, pp. 162-3.

[4*] The term "psychic" also includes other kinds of paranormal performance, such as psychokinesis, for which intuition does not appear to play any role.

[5] See Whyte, 1962, pp. 119-120.

[6] Eysenck, 1984.

[7*] The explanations offered in this section on the workings of intuition relative to mental faculties well recognized in psychology are taken from a variety of sources, but are central to transpersonal psychology. See, for example, Vaughan, 1979, Palmer, 1998); Walsh & Vaughan, 1993, Grof, 1985.

[8] Jung, 1990.

[9] Jung, 1973, p. 5.

[10*] I am not using the term *information* here merely in the Information Theory sense, as that which resolves uncertainty in digital communications, despite the obvious overlap in meaning.

[11] Klimo, 1987, Mishlove, 1993.

[12] Huxley, 1945..

[13] Puthoff & Targ, 1976, Targ & Puthoff, 1977.

[14] Again, .see: Vaughan, 1979, Palmer, 1998, Walsh & Vaughan, 1993, Grof, 1985.

[15] Childs, 1997.

[16] See the Appendix for suggested texts on intuition development.

[17] Walsch, 1996.

[18] Vaughan, 1979.

[19] Broomfield, 1997, Walsh, 1999.

[20]* The superconscious mind is known and acknowledged in all of the world's major religious and spiritual traditions, and is a part of the perennial philosophy. See, for example: Walsh, 1999, Huxley, 1945, Jung, 1959.

[21] Jung, 1959.

[22]* Like the layers of the atmosphere, there are no known, well defined boundary lines that separate one level of the mind from the next. These terms—conscious, subconscious, superconscious—are qualitatively distinct but can be only a rough classification of the different "levels" of consciousness.

[23] Assagioli, 1965.

[24] Grof, 1985, Vaughan, 1979.

[25] Goldberg, 1983.

CHAPTER 2

ENTER THE PLAYERS

EXPERT INTUITIVES AND THEIR WORLD

"The power of intuition…requires the unfoldment of another faculty in man. Intuition is a function of the mind…and, when rightly used, it enables man to grasp reality with clarity, and to see that reality free from glamour and illusion." [Alice Bailey[1]]

Experiments in intuition must clearly rely upon individuals who have developed their intuitive capacity into such a refined skill that they can access requested information accurately, thoroughly and on demand. Such a person is called here an *expert intuitive*. The qualification "expert" refers both to the high caliber of the information received and the clarity with which it is communicated. CAI worked actively with fifteen expert intuitives over a fifteen-year period, and ten more occasionally. It is appropriate now to become acquainted with them and their work.

Unlike the previous chapter, the following description of them is offered from a present day standpoint, not as they were seen before the experiments began.

Characterizing Expert Intuitives

How to describe expert intuitives? There are few common personal qualities by which one can characterize them as a group, apart from their intuitive interests and intuitive skill. They came from all walks of life. They were little different from the general public in their personalities and activities: all ages, male and female, uneducated and well educated, wealthy and poor. They varied from unskilled laborers to highly skilled professionals, with and without a religious background, and with and without partners and children. A few were well known for their intuitive work, though most are not.

Looking more deeply, however, you would find a few distinguishing qualities. Most were unusually sensitive to their feelings, open and honest about themselves and not inclined to hide behind a persona of the self-controlled, well-behaved citizen as most persons habitually do. They tended to see themselves as continually changing, not static, and to be especially conscious of their personal growth.

While all those selected for work with CAI were amiable, easy to work with and worthy of high respect, some might strike you as a bit oversensitive, unusual or ungrounded. I have found this impression commonly arises from the expectation that anyone so tuned in to higher knowledge ought to be a highly evolved individual, one whose life is working perfectly. Sorry, wrong expectation. All expert intuitives I have known display a few of the same emotional anxieties, bad habits, challenging relationships and embarrassing hang-ups as do most persons. They are all competent, likable and caring, but they are not by any means perfect individuals (if such persons exist at all).[2*]

Several CAI intuitives began their intuitive work with the aid of numerology, astrology, the I-Ching, Tarot cards or another similar divinatory system. A few continued to make use their system occasionally as a kind of "warm-up" at the beginning of their personal sessions.

All these systems consist of rich, complex matrices of human characteristics and their possibilities. They seem to work by providing relevant concepts and terminology and at the same time overwhelming the intellectual mind, so that the intuitive faculty must step in to enable the necessary selections and interpretations. When the intuitive "reads" an individual, the system itself provides too little personal information to be objectively valid as a full description, but it can be very helpful for practice, and also for initiating the intuitive flow of information from the superconscious. The I Ching is a particular good for this purpose.

I don't want to overstate this strangeness, because all were very "normal" by ordinary standards. Still, their involvement with intuition had somehow imprinted them with a radiating quality that set them apart from others, at least in the eyes of anyone sensitive to such things. I have heard it described as a kind of wisdom, or possessing a deeper understanding of important matters than is the norm. Some observers would describe it simply as a spiritual attitude. Others would say that they had a capacity to emanate a feeling of love and trust, without requiring that others love and trust them in return.

The differences between them are also revealing, for they show the variations in how intuition operates in practice. Expert intuitives use various ways of communicating intuitive information, and they vary in the kinds they provide. Some tend to give short, concise answers to the questions asked of them, inviting further inquiry, while others prefer long responses that may go beyond what is specifically asked. Some like to to take every issue back to its underlying cause or origin, and others stick to the level at which the question is posed. A few prefer to engage inquirers in a dialog, and even raise questions themselves for the client to consider. Most are comfortable with stage work but a few avoid any public displays of their abilities. Almost all engage in modest promotion of their counseling or teaching as a service activity, though they do not seek public recognition for their work and have therefore not had to deal with the challenges of fame. (Only one of the CAI intuitives [KR] actively pursued notoriety, and he did so apart from his CAI work.)

Expert intuitives differ from one another most conspicuously in the *mode* with which they access intuitive information. About half work from a fully conscious state, just as in a normal conversation. Others operate from a full trance state, usually termed "channeling," and to a casual observer they appear to be talking in their sleep. Their speech and body mannerisms may appear like they are coming from a different personality. Several fall in between these limits: they speak in their own voice from a light trance and are present consciously, or partially so.

Trance channels claim they prefer a trance state because they do not want to be continually questioning and doubting the information as it comes through them. They usually provide technical information more directly and clearly than the others but the difference is small. The belief that a trance state enables the best information is not correct. In contrast, non-trance intuitives prefer *not* to channel, claiming they feel responsible and want to know what they are saying. Well, each to his own. Those who work consciously or in partial trance report that something seems to inject words or thoughts into their mind, speak to them soundlessly or impose pictures on their inner vision as the questions are asked. These are all subjective impressions, of course. They appear to be personal preferences rather than fundamental differences.

A few intuitives dislike scientific inquiries, saying they feel them to be less worthwhile than personal work, or they are anxious about providing specialized information accurately. Indeed, they do not perform well when confronted with detailed, factual questions, and were not employed for these studies.

Finally, we felt that channeling was not appropriate for business consulting because it carried less credibility within the commercial environment. In public demonstrations of intuition, however, channeling attracted the largest audiences. Personal counseling clients revealed no consistent preference.

Despite these differences all CAI's expert intuitives, including channels, were comparable in their competence at retrieving intuitive information in general. Our experience showed early on that, while they may differ in their manner of expression, their mode of working, their subject preferences and even (to some degree) in their intuitive skill, no one style was significantly more accurate, profound or credible than another. The differences appeared to be just the personal, particular ways of receiving information intuitively with which they are comfortable. They sometimes affected the dialog with the inquirer and the way matters were explained, but the content and accuracy of the information conveyed were not significantly affected.

Interacting with Expert Intuitives

Many people become uncomfortable in the presence of an intuitive because they think he is "reading their mind" or "seeing right through them." This is true in one sense, for expert intuitives certainly possess the capacity for such deep perception. Amateur intuitives sometimes cross this barrier of privacy, but a practicing intuitive soon discovers that this perceptive capability functions properly only when it is *asked for*—at least at some level—by those who seek the intuitive's assistance.

Since the superconscious mind behaves as if it has no will of its own, an external *intention* is needed before it returns information. Consequently, the expert intuitive's mind is not continually bombarded with unrequested information. It would not be helpful to himself or anyone else if he probed the minds of the others without their permission. A malicious intuitive, is such a person exists, might do so, but the qualities that must be developed to manifest intuitive ability make such misuse either impossible or very difficult. (This issue is discussed in more detain in Chapter 14.) The fear that an experienced intuitive will intrude into your mind without any kind of invitation is unfounded.

Channeling

> "What I find necessary is to remove my active mind from its domi-
> nant role....It's a willingness to simply say, I trust, I trust, I
> trust....The more I can simply surrender, which is my task, the
> more I can simply say the first words."
> [Pat Rodegast[3]]

Channeling is certainly the most bizarre mode of intuitive reception, but appearances reveal rather little of what is happening. The entire channeling process is only partially understood, even by psychologists who have studied it.

For example, sometimes the voice in trance appears to originate, and may claim to originate, from a personality or "being" that is distinct from the channeling intuitive. It may display its own speech style, mannerisms and personality.[4*] This "being" appears to make use of whatever knowledge, experience and language it finds inside the channel's subconscious mind. (Channeling language styles are discussed further in Chapter 10.) Despite several years of research by CAI and others, no one has a satisfying description in familiar terms as to who or what are these "beings" who appear to communicate through channels. They themselves claim to be genuine individuals who happen not to be based in physical reality at the moment, and they therefore do not have bodies, brains, personalities and names. Historically they have described themselves as angels, extraterrestrials, the disembodied spirits of those who have died, multidimensional entities or "collective souls." They might even be synthesized creations of the channel's subconscious mind, similar to those that emerge in dreams, or non-physical energies of some sort, though the evidence against this interpretation is now strong. Many unanswered questions remain, because it is not yet clear what is going on in channeling (see the accompanying box).

However, to explore and use the information that channels provide, one does not need to understand the process involved, adopt beliefs or theories about the source, or pass judgment on it at all—any more than one needs to know the details of how television works if he is to enjoy the programs and benefit from them. Much can be said about channeled information solely on the basis of many years of experience with it, from CAI and from others. We find we may dialogue with these beings, including their manufactured names and personalities and be good friends with them, just as if they are embodied. From a practical perspective we do not need to concern ourselves with channeling's phenomenalistic and information conveying aspect. We may leave it as a side question of theoretical interest.

Also similar to television, the quality of channeled discourse from unknown intuitives, may consist of profound information and useful wisdom, or meaningless entertainment or misleading pronouncements—with many gradations in between.[5*] Just as when listening to information from any source, *the inquirer must always discriminate for himself what is true and relevant from what is not*—whether he is himself the expert intuitive or is communicating with one. A source that is channeled, claims to be "spiritual" or speaks with cosmic authority does not in itself make the information more valid.

What does channeling feel like? Most expert intuitives who channel say their channeled personality feels like an "energy" or "presence" that gently enters their mind as they relax and release their consciousness into the trance state. The experience has the feeling of being in the presence of a loving and supportive friend or guide. Once in trance there is little or no awareness at all, just a feeling of contentment as in a pleasant, barely perceived dream, while the presence speaks through them. (Usually there is just one such "being," but occasionally two or more emerge.) Most are completely unaware of what they are saying and do not remember it on awakening from the trance.

Who or What Are These Channeled "Beings"?

It is admittedly difficult for a rational person to know how to interpret the experience of intelligible conversation with a personality he cannot see and who presents itself through an intermediate, the so-called channel. A typical initial reaction is to presume that the channel is either mentally off balance, acting or deceiving himself. Another interpretation is that he has somehow been "taken over" by an "evil spirit" who is trying to manipulate him, and perhaps the listener too, for who knows what terrible purpose. Less maliciously, the speaker may be seen as a "person" who is speaking from beyond the grave, or an extraterrestrial from the Arturus system. These views are all interpretations without little if any basis, no more than desperate guesses and certainly not explanations in familiar terms. It is not even known what is meant by "taking over," or what an "evil spirit" might be. There is rarely any indication that the intent, whatever it is, is really as malicious as supposed.

Our modern world offers no basis of consensual knowledge against which we may corroborate this phenomenon. Each one of us is left to his own resources to interpret and understand it, hopefully without preconceptions, biases and fears. The answer must ultimately arise internally, through one's own personal experience, common sense and intuition. We may accept suggestions and ideas from the experiences of others, including the channels themselves—their own explanations and those given by their sources or 'beings"; here we find a fair consensus:

These "beings" are indeed alive and real, they say, and they seek to communicate with us. Since they are free of the constraints of physical existence, including bodies, personalities, time, space and material concerns, they are truly "spirits" in one important sense of that word. Their connection with physical reality is limited to persons who are willing and able to cooperate with them. Communication must take place through the intermediary of a shared inner mind—the superconscious— rather than through the physical senses alone. These "beings" usually have positive intentions, but sometimes not; some have their own rather selfish agendas. The information given is usually valid, but sometimes not. Also, they can usually be trusted to be helpful, but sometimes not; indeed, a few of them have malicious intent ions and may even "take over" a disturbed and vulnerable person (possession). Most commonly, though, and always for expert intuitives who are channels, the partnership is a willing, productive and beneficial cooperation. These limitations and exceptions are created as much by the desires of the channel as the "being" itself, just as when earthbound persons form relationships, communicate and interact—not always to mutual advantage. In this respect a channeling partnership is no different.

I was often asked whether channeled personalities are arise from inside or outside of the channel's mind. To answer this question we would have to agree first on what we mean by "inside" and "outside"; that is, where lies the boundary that separates one's own mind from other minds and all else? It may be that there is *no* boundary, only a gradual blending of conscious into subconscious into superconscious—contrary to the assumed separating lines in the figure in Chapter 1. If this is so, then "outer" means only "not yet recognized" or "unconscious," and the inner-outer distinction is merely an unconscious-conscious distinction. We already know well that this fuzzy interface differs greatly from one person to another, and for each person is continually changing as he matures. Thus, the "I" each of us identifies with is only a very limited "I" The "I" that includes our subconscious is much larger, and there may well be an even greater "I," not yet recognizable, at superconscious levels.

Whatever these channeled entities might be, and wherever they might be located, they have certainly provided valuable gems of human-like intelligence, wisdom and compassion from time to time. Therefore, the only sensible choice is to take them seriously, listen, and discriminate.

The Backgrounds of Expert Intuitives

CAI's expert intuitives report nothing consistently unique in their early backgrounds to suggest they would actively engage in intuitive work as adults. Nor did they follow asingle, typical path in the development of their intuitive skill. Most relied upon a combination of approaches rather than just one: meditation or similar daily practice, attendance in a psychic development class, much reading and a disciplined experience in a spiritual community. Only a few followed an independent, self-directed path, alone or guided by a single teacher.

The most common preparation for intuitive practice was a great deal of personal work on themselves to clear out emotional and other obstructions. They did not ordinarily have intuition development in mind as a goal when going through these struggles, although they realized later that their intuitive skill could not have emerged as it did unless these obstacles were confronted and removed.

All of CAI's expert intuitives found their way into intuitive counseling, in which they used their intuitive skill to give personal assistance to other persons. Most also taught classes and workshops on intuition, meditation or healing. A few undertook professional intuitive activities such as medical consultation, corporate training or business consulting. About half worked full time in their intuitive activities while the others pursued regular jobs, fitting in their intuitive work on the side. One [RW][6*] worked full-time as interviewer and editor for a radio station. Another [CN] operated a large mountain ranch. An electronics engineer [JF] worked as a consultant and in his own home laboratory. Three were graphic artists [PP], [VB], [DR], and another a statistician for a government laboratory [NS]. One [LH] managed a mobile-home park and accommodated research and personal sessions into her spare time. Two have since retired from intuitive counseling and found their places in the ordinary working world, where they could make quiet use of their skills within a professional context, one as a psychotherapist [MG], the other as director of an alcoholics prevention center [DC]. Several wrote books about their intuitive work [PP], [SXS], [KR], [AA], [GB], [SSR] and [JR].[7]

Observers often express surprise at the wealth of information provided by expert intuitives. They presume incorrectly that the intuitive is relying on unconscious knowledge picked up directly from the inquirer or from previous life experience. This is not at all the case. For personal sessions in which the client is present, the intuitive might receive a few clues from facial expressions, body language and a few words of greeting, but these minuscule signs do not begin to account for the elaborate and often profound responses given. In any case, for sessions in which the client was *not* present (about half of them), the intuitive has no such clues at all. As explained in Chapter 1, intuitive knowledge arises not from subconscious memories, sense perceptions or cognitive deduction but from the superconscious mind, a much vaster resource.

In research sessions the inquirer only rarely offered supplementary information beyond the questions themselves—just a clarification of terminology, or a distinction that appeared to be important. It was also rare when the intuitive had any background at all in the topics of inquiry, many of which were specialized and technical. Even when he did, his previous knowledge usually turned out to be irrelevant or incomplete, occasionally even incorrect. Sometimes the intuitive information they relayed was totally new, not known by anyone, so it could not have been recalled from memory.

Prior familiarity with the subject matter—a technical background, for example—probably aided some intuitives' explanations for certain inquiries.[8*] A technically informed intuitive could use the correct terms and concepts when relaying specialized superconscious information. In contrast, most intuitives employed metaphors, analogies and images as they translated the information into non-technical language. The loss in communication in these cases was small, however. It turned out that all intuitives were able to relate the same message in their own ways, without recourse to specialized language. An intuitive's prior knowledge on the subject under exploration was never a significant advantage or disadvantage.

Expert Intuitives Speak

It's time now to let them tell their own stories. The following accounts from five CAI expert intuitives describe in their own words how they entered intuitive work, learned how to do it and chose to work with their skill, and what it has meant to them:[9]*

Charles Nunn:

Growing up in a Southern Baptist family in Georgia was not exactly what you would normally think about as the place to begin working with psychic and intuitive development.... I had difficulty relating to the people around me. I had feelings about things others didn't seem to understand or recognize. Even in the first grade I found I approached things with a much different point of view than my classmates. So I judged myself as somewhat deficient, and drew back. I hated homework, even in college....For years I felt very much separate and alienated. It was not because I wasn't loved, for my family was supportive, but we didn't communicate

A legal firm once asked me to testify on the subject of channeling at the court trial of an intelligent and respected school teacher. He felt his channeled guidance had given him a special mission that justified his taking what he needed from others or from society at large. Before the trial in question the court had already convicted him of stealing a large sum of money and a mobile home from a wealthy man he had befriended. He was serving time in jail for this offense. The state attorney was now accusing him of drowning the man, who had mysteriously disappeared from a lake resort where both were staying.

The body was never found, and it was not totally clear that the teacher had really killed the victim. His claim to supernatural guidance surely did not help his case before the conservative, rural jury. It found him guilty, and he was convicted of murder on circumstantial evidence. He is now serving a life sentence in a California prison.

It was not intuition that was at fault here, but his interpretation, acceptance and use of what he mistakenly presumed to be faultless guidance. What got him into trouble was his uncritical belief of his seemingly external voice as "the truth."

One must always check intuitively received information, from any source, with one's best knowing, conscience and common sense before accepting it and acting upon it.

a great deal about the matters that were so central for me. I felt I couldn't share the things that were deepest in me with the people around me....It kept turning me back to look inside: what was it that I really knew? For a while I developed a way of talking with myself.

Later, working in labor relations and personnel management I came to realize that the things that made me most successful were the intuitive resources I used, rather than the training I had received. But I kept feeling worse and worse.

Over a period of thirteen years, I've had a series of five near-death experiences, which resulted from illnesses that made hospitalization necessary....On several occasions I asked that I just be lifted out of this whole thing because I felt that I couldn't cope with the world....[These experiences] changed my entire attitude toward life. They made me realize with great force that life is extremely short, that I must not waste time by being overly cautious, but rather should simply trust and engage life....I entered training for a while, and finally came out of my rational box. To my delight, I found that relying on intuition made my life very much simpler, and I was able to grow farther as a human being.

In my consultation and counseling work the intuitive information is simply available to me as I speak. I never know what I am going to say until I open my mouth....Information just flows into my mind....No entity talks through me. I don't "channel". I simply take a few moments to become quiet and the information comes to me....I just have to trust the process, and trust that what I am communicating is exactly what the people in front of me need to hear....Trust is essential, for sometimes I have no frame of reference for what pops into my head. I might be addressing a problem in an area that I know nothing about.

I don't consciously gather information. On the contrary, I try not to do so. I find I do best when I know as little as possible about a company, so my intuitive reading of the situation is unaffected by my personal notions....I don't make a point of studying my clients' respective cultures either. When I began consulting in Japan, for example, I wasn't given enough time to be informed about Japanese culture and industry. I had to trust that the intuitive process would guide me through the complexities of foreign cultural patterns. It did, and it always has. [CN]

Penney Peirce:

I grew up with an absolutely normal childhood. Nothing weird happened to me....I was interested for many years in the mysteries...in psychic things, the only stuff I could get a hold of in the Midwest. I read books....Bit by bit I found I had ability in this area of giving counseling readings to people, and that I could study to learn how to do it.

I took meditation classes every week, and classes to develop my clairvoyant skill. What these classes were all about was learning to focus my mind. When I tried to meditate I was totally restless, so I just avoided it. The trouble was I was going at it from a very mental point of view. I was trying to be "mentally spiritual." You really have to let your body in on it. My main motivation was a voracious curiosity about how everything worked. I wanted to *know*. I sponged it up, and couldn't stop. Maybe I just totally subdued my mind, for eventually I was just forced into my body.

I learned firsthand that the intuitive process, or what I call direct knowing, is a natural human ability and not the realm of a special few. If I can learn to be intuitive, you can, too.

I see now how important it is to trust the pull of your interests....trusting the current to carry you to your destiny, or destination, is a big part of intuition. By doing this I learned that the process itself is the teacher....Eventually, to get answers that felt really right, I had to enter the intangible world of metaphysics. I wanted to know how consciousness, and the world, worked—from the inside out.

I work in [light] trance but I forget what I've said about five minutes after. While it's happening I'm aware that I'm merged with the process, but I'm not directing it, I'm not creating it out of will. Then [afterward] it's like waking up in the morning and the dream fades away.

I don't have any entities that I work with. Sometimes that feels lonely. I have to rely on my own self as God, as the vehicle to access things. I don't have a guru, I don't have a teacher, I don't have a guide. What I have is a *flow* I feel I am in. Everyone who comes [to me for readings] is part of my teacher. If I have a need, someone comes and answers it. It doesn't matter who it is—it doesn't have to be someone who is "enlightened." It is a humbling experience for me.

What works for me is to use my imagination first to create images and moods, actual scenes and feeling tones, a mood or space I can project myself into....It's tactile, I can smell it, there's fresh air and golden light, and so on. Then I merge into that, so my body gets that nice cozy feeling and knows that all is well, is at peace. When the body relaxes, the mind relaxes, and the spirit projects through the body back to the mind.

Psychic phenomena, as it turns out, are just the first signs of a much greater and all-encompassing wisdom....Intuition is not just about knowing who's calling you on the phone—it's about attaining crystal-clear perception....If you persist in the search for a more elegant, more efficient, more living, more uplifting way of knowing, you'll follow the intuitive way deeper and deeper into life....In the end, the intuitive way is truly a spiritual path.[10]

Everyone is intuitive. Everyone can do what I do. I just kept going with my curiosity. And if you keep going, you too will get to someplace where the correct form of service and self-expression for you will be natural and passionate—and fun. It doesn't have to look like anyone else's. [PP]

Lin David Martin:

For years I was involved in a center in Phoenix, founded by a man who was an outrageously gifted psychic. He could do absolutely anything....I was very interested in Edgar Cayce's work, and read everything about him I could get my hands on. I was involved in meditation and was interested in healing. But I had firmly convinced myself that I didn't want to be a psychic. I was the world's biggest skeptic about my own process.

Our "classes" were given from an Native American spirit teacher, through this founder of the center. They were about waking up, not about being psychic or being healers; that was comfortable for me....Over a period of many years I had dreams that were not dreams, but out-of-body travel, precognitive experiences, strong intuitions about others, etc., but I kept my mouth shut....I practiced doing healing, which I found comfortable.

Once, when observing the founder working, I found myself picking up things before he said them, and realized suddenly that I could be a psychic—just what I had convinced myself for so long wasn't for me. Later I had an insightful dream in which I was going around a room of 50 people giving them personal messages. (Some were later verified.) This showed me that the energy involved in this "psychic" work was the same as that used in healing, something I was already familiar with, and I knew I could do psychic work, too. This broke the ice, and I started doing it.

Two years of this passed, then one time I became conscious that this spirit teacher was talking through me; I was in trance. I've been doing it ever since, along with clairvoyance and healing.

As our intuitive self emerges, an important part is learning how to be in the body, to stay with the body. This means taking good care of it with diet, exercise, etc. Also, you must continue to love wherever you're at, because you're always striving for more and will never be satisfied with where you're at.
I was working with a weird New York lady once and found myself getting irritated, sucked into her consciousness. After about five minutes I slipped into that framework of unity where healing happens. My outer "monkey mind" was freaking out, for here was this divine being that I was dearly loving! It was such a powerful shift in consciousness, this transition from the ordinary mind to the deeper mind, that I was high for two weeks....I became so very aware of how limited our outer mind normally is, and how it creates judgments that keep us separated.

I think we're all trying to bridge this inner mind, which knows no separation, to the outer mind, which runs around feeling totally separated all of the time. Any way you can find to bridge the two—through meditation, healing, music, working with groups—do it. You will recognize that there is part of you that *knows*, even though the outer mind continues to insist that it doesn't. [LDM]

Mary Gillis:

I grew up in the South in an Episcopalian family. I feel I got support there—not energy support, but the sense of ritual and ceremony that gave me a protected feeling so I could go into that quiet place inside.... My intuitive skills were survival tools, growing up in this type of family where important things were not talked about. So it was really necessary to have my psychic antenna strongly tuned. I can remember talking with animals and plants, also seeing things in the air—my mother took me to the eye doctor! I quit talking about what I saw and what I heard and what I sensed inside. But I didn't let go of it.

When I was little and trying to go to sleep, but not sleepy, I would sometimes play with going in and out of my body. I especially loved some of the stages, like expanding out into the whole room. I studied art in school, and feel that working with this non-verbal part of myself helped me to use a part of the mind where words are not the means.

For me the process has definitely meant a tremendous amount of change. I went through a rigorous training program through a series of schools in the Midwest. I worked with strong concentrative

Late one evening I had asked the last question in a research session with an expert intuitive [LH]. As she responded her channeling voice suddenly began to speed up for no apparent reason. After ten seconds or so she stopped speaking very suddenly at the end of her final sentence. We looked at one another and laughed, puzzled at the strange performance, for which she had no explanation. I thanked her, retrieved my tape from the tape recorder (which was out of her sight) and found my way to the car.

While driving home I continued to wonder what had happened, and decided to replay the last part of the tape in the recorder on the seat beside me. The tape ended a fraction of a second after her last word.

and meditative exercises that go back to Tibetan Buddhism, raja yoga and kriya yoga. In the early part of my training and until recently [my task] was to go to the furthest reaches I could touch of the superconscious realm.

I began to have many dreams in which I would be working with people, and then they would come to me in real life, in physical life, and I would get to work with them again.

The way I work is to contact first the divinity in myself, and then the divinity in the other person, and find how that person is caught in separation, where there are strong polarities and where there is a battle going on. My role is to speak first to that divinity, and say what needs to be said and to be brought through. Then I try to articulate what is blocking that divinity, what is keeping up the experience of separation.

I'm pulling now much more into my body and working with my heart, so the energies can move through me and allow me to be changed in the process.

Sometimes we want to know intuitive things to protect ourselves from what we fear, from having to change. The main process is not to protect ourselves from change, but to open toward it in the living experience. [MG]

Richard Lavin:

At the end of high school I took a course in transcendental meditation. I started opening up, and learned a lot....Then I moved to California; everything changed after that! I got turned on to the Seth Material, from Jane Roberts—remarkable work, but it really scared me, coming from a source that was unknown. I was raised catholic, you see, and trained to believe in demons and devils, and that God was somewhere out there. And here's this "demon" saying, "No, it's inside."...But something felt very real about it, so I continued to explore....This exploration led me into training as a hypnotherapist.

I got to use an altered states of consciousness—these are *very* potent tools for transformation—and I learned how to get into deeper and deeper trance states....Once I felt a really benevolent energy around, really loving...and I got the impression that this energy wanted to drop into my body. So I said, "OK, why not." It felt like this personality came into the top of my body and my personality got compressed into the back of my body. And out of my mouth comes this wholly different personality, with a different voice, and it identifies himself as "Ecton." And here I am in the back of my body, thinking, "Hmm, this is interesting!"...Ever since them my life has been totally different.

This entity "Ecton" is profound in his love, in his awareness, and in the information available from him. He stresses that he is no different than us, but has just made a couple of different choices: he doesn't choose a body full time, like we do. He calls himself a traveler....I don't make any claims for what he is; I don't know what he is....When I work with people [for intuitive counseling] he travels through the deeper realms of their being in a really wonderful and unconditionally loving way.

So they [these "beings"] really love us, and they're trying to teach us unconditional love, which is real tough. It's OK for people to be just the way they are. That's unconditional love.

Is Intuition "Spiritual"?

CAI's experience with many expert intuitives shows that, to obtain information not accessible by ordinary means, it is not necessary to chant, go into seclusion, recite the fifty names of God, sacrifice a goat, fast for three days—nor enter a trance, for that matter. Nor are material artifacts necessary to make intuition work. Crystal balls, candles, incense, subdued light, icons and similar devices may be relaxing and inspiring, like soft music or a painting on the wall, but they are not an inherent part of the intuitive process. These practices and devices possess no power of their own, and expert intuitives do not depend upon them as an essential part of their work. Some begin with a moment of prayer or inner attunement, as one might do for any kind of sensitive work involving a degree of surrender to an agency out side of one's control. They prefer a comfortable, quiet and non-intrusive environment, but they can dispense with even this convenience when the situation demands.

There is nothing magical or mysterious about intuitive work, unless you want to argue that *all* life is magical and mysterious, which it certainly is. Intuition is completely natural. It becomes a strange or spooky phenomenon only when one chooses to regard it as such.

Similarly, there does not appear to be anything inherently sacred, holy or spiritual about the intuitive process itself, any more than is life as a whole. The human intellect is just as sacred and holy as its intuitive counterpart. Of course, intuition can be a powerful means for gaining spiritual knowledge— which we may define for the moment (without trying to be precise) to be the recognition of the true nature of one's inner self or essence and all the cosmos. All CAI's expert intuitives manifested such an orientation, and many of their communications contained messages of unquestionably spiritual content and value. But again, comparable messages have arisen from other, apparently non-intuitive sources, and even at times from intuitives who did not appear to be spiritually inclined at all. Intuition is also a refined and welcoming doorway into the spiritual realm of being, though it is not the same as this realm, and other doorways for those so inclined.

The means and modes for receiving intuitive information appear to as neutral as the telephone. Any observable spirituality or sacredness, as well as any negativity or evil qualities one may find, lie wholly in the mind of the beholder, or in the *content* of the messages as perceived and interpreted, not in the intuitive as a person or in the intuitive process itself. Also like the telephone (and like dreams, too), the information conveyed cannot be judged as more or less spiritual just because of its particular mode of reception, or because of a claim that it is coming from a highly evolved and benevolent authority, or because of accompanying phenomenal effects, or even if it includes pieces of very impressive information. Only a clear look at its *content* and *relevance* reveals its validity, accuracy and value.

And while we're looking so clearly, let's not forget our awe and gratitude for the sacredness of *all* life and all mind, intuition included! If there is anything sacred about intuition, it is in the *choices* each of may make in response to the abundant opportunities that intuition provides.

Doing this work has been alternately wonderful and grand and sometimes it's the hardest thing I can imagine doing. We're stepping into territories we don't know anything about. There are no road maps....To get to the truth I've had to dig through a lot of stuff—old beliefs, old ideas, old attitudes, things that just don't work for me any longer. Some of the journey has been very painful....But I know it doesn't have to be. And on the other side of the pain of the intuitive journey is a grand sense of your own self—your higher self! What else is there? What else is there? [RL]

Similar testimonies are available from several non-staff expert intuitives with whom CAI worked with from time to time. For example, Jane Roberts spoke eloquently about the various inner realities she was able to enter.[11]* Regarding her most common trance state she says:

For me, [it] is an accelerated state. I would compare it to a higher state of wakefulness rather than to the sleep usually associated with trance—but a different kind of wakefulness in which the usual world seems to be the one that is sleeping. My attention is not blunted. It is elsewhere....The trance state is characterized by a feeling of inexhaustible energy, emotional wholeness and subjective freedom.[12]

She dictated several books for "Seth," the name of the "being" whom she channeled:

> I am sure that Seth is my channel to revelational knowledge, and by this I mean knowledge that is revealed to the intuitive portions of the self rather than discovered by the reasoning faculties....As to who or what Seth is, his term "energy essence personality" seems as close to the answer as anyone can get. I don't believe he is a part of my subconscious, as that term is used by psychologists, or a secondary personality. I do think that we have a superconscious that is as far "above" the normal self as the subconscious is "below" it....It may be that Seth is the psychological personification of that superconscious extension of my normal self....I do not believe I could get the equivalent of Seth's book on my own.[13]

Regarding her inspired process as a writer of poetry, fiction and non-fiction, she says:

> When I am caught up in inspiration, writing a poem, then I'm 'turned on,' excited, filled with a sense of urgency and discovery. Just before this happens, however, an idea comes out of nowhere. It is 'given.' It simply appears, and from it new creative connections spring....I was not connected in this way with Seth's books, and had no idea of the creative processes involved.[14]

Her descriptions of these intuitive states reveal much about the capacity of the human mind to access non-ordinary states of consciousness. They could be the basis of a fascinating psychological study. She claims this capacity is not hers alone:

> I do know that each individual has access to intuitive knowledge and can gain glimpses of inner reality. The universe speaks to each of us in this regard.[15]

Channel and teacher Sanaya Roman devoted several books to the intuition development process and the direct applications of intuition in one's personal life. For example:

> Truth comes from the feeling level....The doorway to deeper truth is awareness. It is paying attention to, holding up the vision, of truth. Finding truth means holding every situation up to the light...to the heart, [with] a deep level of compassion.[16]

Intuition does not operate in the world of form and structure....It is the ability to know without words, to sense truth without explanations.... Intuition operates beyond time and space; it is the link to your higher self. It is not bound by the physical body.[17]

She warns about the risks of relying upon intuition and nothing else:

It's not enough to live in the world of intuition, for the person who lives there will do nothing with his life other than daydream and fantasize....You can be dazzled by future ideas, so that the present, in contrast, seems mundane and boring....If you want to translate your intuition into physical reality, develop the qualities of patience, trust, confidence focus and concentration.[18]

Accomplished intuitive and intuition teacher Sharon Franquemont also stresses that a developed intuition is not just a useful skill but pervades one's entire life:

Intuition does not emanate from consciousness, but consciousness is where it is invited and experienced....Intuition is more than a tool. It is a way of being in the world....It is the language of the soul, but it's not the soul itself....Intuition is not personal—i.e., of the personality. It is transpersonal....

Intuition does not lie.[19]

Carolyn Myss, an accomplished medical intuitive, believes that intuition is not the privileged gift of a lucky few but is a universal ability that may be practiced by anyone:

I firmly believe that intuitive or symbolic sight is not a gift but a skill—a skill based in self-esteem....Intuitive ability is present in everyone because it is a survival skill, not a spiritual intention....Clear intuitive impressions have no emotion attached to them. This is the main signal that they are correct.[20]

Selection of Staff Intuitives

CAI built up its cadre of expert intuitives by first locating candidates (not so difficult in California in the early 1980s), obtaining their agreement to participate (no problem) and then testing them for competence (more difficult). We knew that conventional testing, in which the answers to posed questions were already known by the inquirer, would be inadequate. This approach lacked sufficient motivation and correct answers might be explained as "mind-reading"—an interesting phenomenon but not what we were looking for.

Instead, a personal inquiry was conducted with each candidate to try to obtain three kinds of new but potentially useful information:

(1) Personal information about a volunteer—a "guinea pig"—whose life was so rich with challenges that additional guidance would always prove helpful.

(2) Personal information about an obscure person in history for whom an intuitive biography was in preparation, and with whom the candidate would be expected to be unfamiliar.

(3) Specialized information on a non-personal topic of on-going CAI research, as reported in Part III of this book..

The candidates' answers on these topics could all be checked rather easily. They were also reviewed for clarity, directness, ease of flow and self-consistency—all important qualities for any good verbal communication. They were compared with answers already obtained from staff intuitives, previous candidates, and (for a few of the questions) with available knowledge sources (e.g., an encyclopedia). Other criteria were applied that pertain when hiring anyone, intuitive or not: integrity, reliability, commitment, flexibility, willingness to accept criticism and emotional stability. Less than one-third of the candidates examined passed all of these "tests" and were qualified selected for a trial run as expert intuitives.

For research projects CAI worked occasionally with outside intuitives whose skills were well known from their work as intuitive counselors, consultants, teachers or research subjects. Some of these associates were considered "experts" without explicit testing.

It is difficult to believe that members of the CAI team were so unique and exceptional in their intuitive skills that equally competent expert intuitives could not be found almost anywhere—so long as there was a need for them and a positive intention to work with them constructively. CAI received many suggestions of candidates in Europe and Japan as well as the United States, but the need never arose to check them out.

Common Shortcomings

When looking for an expert intuitive for yourself you should be aware of the most common deficiencies of candidate intuitives who are not fully qualified. Their major failing is obvious: their answers to the questions put to them are poor or not responsive. Here are some other shortcomings, not always so immediately apparent, as they discovered during CAI's examinations:

> There was (and still is, I believe) a distinct need to assist those seeking intuitive counsel to discriminate the experts from the many who practice intuitively but are not fully capable. We at CAI would have liked to create a certification service in which we could evaluate practicing intuitives. Those who applied and passed the test could then assure prospective clients that they were truly qualified for intuitive work.
>
> Unfortunately, we were never able to find a suitable criterion that would be objective, effective and fair for the wide variety of persons who wished to be certified. Too little was known about the boundary between capable and incapable intuitive performance to set up a reliable test that could distinguish them properly. We had to drop the idea.
>
> Someday enough may be learned about the intuitive process to allow such a service to be set up.

- *"Here's what I'm getting"*: Some conscious intuitives are trained to work without questions. They consider their task to be one of passing on whatever comes to them, with little or no direction from the inquirer (client). They leave it to their "source" to determine what the client wants and needs to hear, and whether he is able to make use of it. Their source may have such concerns in mind and even be able to exercise them wisely, but this is rarely the case. Trust is necessary, of course, but for an intuitive to totally surrender accountability is not responsible.

- *Psychobabble*: Here the intuitive (or his source personality) gives the client a lecture on a particular topic, which may be interesting but is not responsive to the questions asked or to what is needed. A lecture format may be appropriate for group presentations but is rarely helpful in personal sessions.

- *The Manipulator*: It's sad to say that some trance personalities or "beings" are more concerned with carrying out their own agendas than serving the needs of those who come to them for help. They may take a sympathetic approach initially, gradually build up the listener's trust, and then give strong recommendations and commands in pursuit of their own purposes.

- *The Amateur*: These intuitives have little confidence in their intuitive abilities, so the session is dominated by their search for emotional support, reassurance and confirmation. Constructive feedback is always appropriate, of course, but a client has the right to expect genuine capability and emotional maturity before he trusts an expert intuitive for counsel—just as with any helping professional.

- *The Voice of Authority*: Finally, some candidate intuitives speak with such an attitude of authority and conviction that they do not seem to be sensitive to the confusion, fragility and even suffering that clients bring to their session. To be certain of one's knowledge and intention is surely a virtue, but insensitivity and dogmatism arise from uncertainty rather than certainty, and from a rigid position instead of firm knowledge. The intuitive and his source should not do the client's thinking for him.

These deficiencies are surely more serious for intuitive counseling and consulting than in requests for impersonal, factual information. At CAI there was never a need to compromise on quality when competent experts were available.

Locating an Expert Intuitive

It is not difficult today to find candidate intuitives if you live in the United States, Canada or Western Europe. Still, locating a truly *expert* intuitive is more difficult than finding a reliable dentist, lawyer or car mechanic. The telephone Yellow Pages may not be very helpful. However, most every metaphysical bookstore, new-age magazine, personal growth center and community bulletin board announces intuitive readings, self-help courses and counseling of some sort. Intuitives who announce themselves in this way are not necessarily well qualified, of course, but these notices can at least lead you to candidates with whom you may start your search, and practice evaluating them.

The main step involves screening and selection. An organization similar to CAI may be able to help you pre-qualify intuitives but in the end you must check them out for yourself. The advice of trusted friends may be helpful; still, you cannot rely solely upon such recommendations, since their enthusiasm for a candidate is not necessarily a good indication that he is right for your needs. Well known channels and other intuitives must have something going for them, but popularity does not guarantee accuracy, integrity and a sense of service. It is safer to assume that your personal requirements are unique, significantly different from the preferences of your friends and the public.

Your own intuition, in whatever might be its present state, is certainly your best guide when choosing candidates, examining them, evaluating what they tell you and then selecting whom you want to work with. Until your intuition is strong and trustworthy the following suggestions may help you assess candidate intuitives:

- Try to find articles, books, printed interviews or reading transcripts that your candidate has made available. Read some of these, and imagine yourself entering a trusting relationship with him. Does he "feel good" to you?

- Learn what you can about his background and values. Is the information he provides consistent with the highest spiritual and moral principles of which you yourself are aware? Is he living the values he espouses: does he actually "walk his talk"?

- Learn what you can about his motivation for offering intuitive counseling. Is he committed as an act of service to the positive use of his intuitive capacities, or does he seem to be interested mainly in making money, becoming famous or manipulating the lives of others?

- Try to discover other persons who have used his counseling help. Request interviews with them and ask discreetly if they found his counsel helpful, and why. Ask further questions so you may judge if these persons are themselves credible reporters whose opinions you value.

- In a trial reading with your candidate be skeptical but open and non-judgmental. Try not to conduct the reading as a "test" in which you ask questions to which you already know the answers, as if you are looking for evidence. Rather, ask questions of personal importance to you, and persist until the responses are clear to you.

- Check your trial reading against the common deficiencies of practicing intuitives cited above. Does your candidate display any of these limiting characteristics?

If a candidate fails on any of these issues you probably need to look further.

Summary

The main purpose of this detailed discussion of expert intuitives has been to demystify the intuitive process—especially channeling—by stressing its naturalness and the importance of content over means and mode. The world of expert intuitives is not a weird or strange one. They are all normal in spite of their unusual skill, they are the first to stress their normality and the act that anyone may do what they do.

This introduction to also explains the modes of intuitive access and what they imply for the inquirer seeking new information about himself or a topic of special interest. The intuitives' personal testimonies reveal how they originally developed their skill, how they became accustomed to using it and what it means to them. Also described is how candidate intuitives may be examined for expertness, and the most common shortcomings of those who failed.

The following eleven chapters (3 to13) describe specific applications of intuition. After Chapter 3 they may be read in any order that conforms to your particular interests, with only a minor loss of continuity.

> "To me the purpose of all this is to remember who we are. That's
> the greatest thing I get out of this work—really feeling it, knowing
> it, opening to it, with the fullness of my body and my mind." [Mary
> Gillis]

- Endnotes—Chapter 2

[1] Bailey, Alice,…5-25

[2]* Indeed, I have known a few trance channels who met all the requirements for an expert intuitive, including the skill for providing high-quality intuitive information, but they were obviously highly neurotic and had emotionally driven and disordered lives. They were deemed too unreliable to join the CAI staff.

[3] Klimo, 1987, p. 138.

[4]* The dividing line between channeling and non-channeling intuitive performance is

not sharp, and may turn out to be specious because it depends the notion of what "appears" to be beyond the intuitive's consciousness. See, for example Roman, 1987, Klimo, 1987.

[5*] The proliferation of practicing channels in recent years reveals (even on the Internet) large numbers who offer their services with questionably motivated appeals, incredible claims and an obviously poor understanding of the channeling process itself. While not a new phenomenon, it certainly does not help those who are truly expert and wish to carry out their work responsibly and with integrity.

[6*] The letters in brackets indicate the particular expert intuitives, identified by name in the Acknowlegement section at the end of this book.

[7*] Peirce, 1999, Franquemont, 1999, Ryerson & Harolde, 1989, Abrahamsen, 1993, Blackburn, 1983, Roman, 1986, Roberts, 1972, Richardson & Huett, 1987. Some of these writers have published other books as well, based on their work as expert intuitives.

[8*] Three staff intuitives [AA, JF and NS] had technical backgrounds, though only rarely in the particular specialties in which inquiries with them were conducted.

[9*] These five accounts have been transcribed and extracted from two panel presentations, one at the conference, "The Intuitive Process," held at San Francisco State University 18-19 April 1986, and the other at a special public event entitled "Intuition and Channeling," held in Palo Alto, California, on 6 February 1987.

[10] Peirce, 1999, p. xv, xvi.

[11*] Jane Robert's books were originally published by Prentice-Hall (Englewood Cliffs, NJ), then republished later by Amber Allen Publishing (San Rafael, CA). The entire Jane/Seth collection of published and unpublished material, including notes, is now held in the Yale University library.

[12] Roberts, 1977, pp. 15-16.

[13] Roberts, 1970, p. 293; Roberts, 1972, p. xv.

[14] Roberts, 1972, p. xiii-xiv.

[15] Roberts, 1972, p. viii.

[16] Roman, 1986, p. 79

[17] Roman, 1986, p. 79

[18] Roman, 1986, p. 127

[19] Franquemont, 1999.

[20] Myss, 1997, p. 33, 38

PART II

THE INTUITIVE ADVISOR

The three chapters to follow describe experiments in which CAI sought intuitive information to assist individuals, called here *clients*,* in response to their personal needs. The opportunities usually arose because these applicants were not able to obtain what they wanted through traditional means of acquiring knowledge or through their own personal resources, intuitive or other. Their motivation varied from the curious to the desperate, and the topics of inquiry ranged from personal issues (Chapter 3) to business matters (Chapter 4) to information for recovering lost or hidden items and missing people (Chapter 5).

In all of these inquiries the clients provided the questions, which were posed to a *single* expert intuitive. (Multi-intuitive inquiries will be taken up in Part III.) Some of the sessions were conducted face-to-face, some remotely and a few by telephone. The intuitive was not usually informed ahead of time about the subject of inquiry or the questions to be asked, and often not even the name of the inquirer.

While these sessions were similar in appearance to conventional psychic readings, they differed from them substantially in three ways. First, the intuitives were more capable (more expert) than the typical psychic. Second, the intention and motivation behind the questions was usually stronger. Third, the intuitive's comments were more responsive, to the point, sensitive and deep. The sessions were intended to be helpful rather than evidential, though evidence of the accuracy and relevance of the information usually manifested incidentally. Occasionally the intuitives interjected a piece of evidential information not asked for—and not useful to the client except to capture his attention and confidence.

CHAPTER 3

INTUITIVE COUNSELING
FINDING AND WALKING YOUR LIFE PATH

"Perhaps at times your burden will seem heavy and you will feel as though you have passed the same way many times. Yet, in reality, you are on an ascendant path which spirals gracefully upward and onward." [Kevin Ryerson[1]]

Of all of the applications of intuition, intuitive counseling is the most interactive, personally involving and potentially beneficial for the inquiring individual (referred to here as the *client*). This is surely because the information being sought is not substantive, intellectual or about a scientific topic, business problem or field of knowledge; rather, it concerns the client's own inner life. The experience of receiving intuitive information about oneself, whether from an expert intuitive or through one's own intuition, is the most personally convincing of all demonstrations of intuition. It reveals. better than any words can convey. the depth to which intuition can go in providing meaningful and helpful information.

Over a ten-year period (1981-91) CAI carried out more than 1200 "life-path readings," or simply "life readings," for persons in the United States, Japan and other countries as part of its Intuitive Counseling International (ICI) program. Each 45- to 90-minute session took place with one of the fifteen or so expert intuitives on the CAI staff. Each reading focused primarily on three areas: the life purpose of the individual, action he could take to achieve this purpose, and answers to his questions on matters of his own choosing. The latter typically included the challenging aspects of his life: family and other relationships, career, health, personality issues and emotional problems.

These aspects typically took different forms with different clients. For example, he may have felt his life was "stuck," not going anywhere, but he did not know where to turn. Or perhaps he was active and moving but running out of control, his behavior dominated by his emotions. He may have felt closed up and insensitive to other people, or he may have been trying to overcome low self-confidence or was having difficulties in close personal relationships. Perhaps he wanted to enhance his sensitivity, develop his creativity or release hidden or blocked potentials that he knew he possessed. There were often health problems. Some clients felt an emptiness or meaninglessness in their lives. These and other personal difficulties were the order of the day. They ranged from the practical and obvious to those so barely on the edge of awareness that they could hardly be named and talked about at all. Some had just recently arisen though most were long-standing or chronic, even incapacitating.

This chapter describes in detail the history of intuitive counseling, its typical content, how CAI arranged and conducted the counseling sessions, how clients felt about the information given to them and how they utilized it. Also explained is how one may select an expert intuitive and prepare for his own life reading. Finally, the life reading is related to other kinds of counseling.

The Background of Intuitive Counseling

The practice of counseling was set in place thousands of years ago by political advisors, shamans, priests, astrologers, fortune tellers, and even wise grandparents. All relied upon common sense and wisdom gained from years of life experience—and sometimes intuitive skill, a little or a lot. They sought to advise those who came to them for help, were willing to listen to counsel and perhaps act upon it. Over the last two centuries clerics, consultants, psychologists, psychiatrists and others have formalized the practice into accepted professions. Western society now educates most of these counselors through formal training and has established standards and credentials for maintaining a verifiable level of expertise. Specialized versions meet specific needs: counseling for relationships, grief, employment, investment, rape victims, refugees, alcoholics and so on. Non-professional forms have survive, too: astrologers, graphologists, numerologists, card-readers and others who practice without imposed standards or publicly accredited training. Some of them do excellent work but as a group these semi-professionals command much less respect.

Intuition has undoubtedly played an significant part in much past counseling, though the intuitive portion is not normally identified and is only rarely recognized for its contribution. At the opposite extreme, clairvoyance, mediumship and psychic readings are primarily intuitive and are acknowledged as such. They have the longest history but (as just noted) a shaky reputation. While honored at times in every culture, they have stepped into respectability in the West only during the last century.

Intuitive Edgar Cayce gave many health readings and more than two thousand "life readings" in the 1920s-40s. He set a higher standard for intuitive counsel, both in the specificity and accuracy of the information he provided and in its compassion and depth[2]. His readings dealt with the psychological and spiritual as well as the physical life of the counseled individual. They discussed the purpose of his life in its broadest sense, how this purpose was manifesting in his present life, often some pertinent excerpts from "past lives" and the specific steps he could take to bring his present life into better alignment with his life purpose. He also gave most of his clients detailed information on health matters, including corrective remedies, dietary changes and inner practices such as prayer and meditation. He also proposed various ways to strengthen the client's connection with what he termed the "creative forces." His work was carried out with unusual humility, in the finest spirit of selfless service, and with a strong spiritual element.

In the decades following Cayce's work hundreds of intuitives in the U.S. began to offer intuitive counseling. It was an exciting time of experimentation and discovery. Many of these latter-day counselors worked consciously or semiconsciously, not in full trance as did Cayce. Their readings varied greatly in their depth, accuracy, specificity, credibility and compassionate concern. The best of them were comparable in quality to Cayce's, and in some respects were more communicative in their language and style. (He was a devout Christian, and this preference influenced his channeled language style.) His readings initiated a surging wave of popular interest and openness in self-development, including intuition—all part of the now familiar "new-age movement."

How Life Readings Were Carried Out

Like other practicing intuitives we adopted at CAI a standard life-reading question format, similar to what Cayce seemed to be following. It was modified to fit the different client of the 1980s and to accommodate the styles of the several CAI intuitives. This question format, shown in the accompanying box, was maintained throughout the ten active years of the ICI program.

The use of standard questions may suggest that clients played only a passive role in their life readings. This was not at all the case. Each client was invited to add five or so questions of his own. We encouraged him to think carefully ahead of time about what he most wanted to know from the intuitive source, and what kind of specific information he could best apply in his life. The purpose of this preparation was to induce him to ask better questions, to listen more attentively to the answers given, and to be more willing to apply the intuitive's suggestions afterwards. It also helped stimulate his own intuition and soften the otherwise unilateral quality of the communication.

Most important, when anyone seeks the counsel of an expert intuitive—or any counselor or advisor, for that matter—he must obviously rely on his own individual judgment, common sense and intuition to interpret and evaluate the advice given him before he accepts it and applies it in his own life. We all know that if we follow someone's advice blindly, as if "he certainly knows better than I do," and if we neglect to screen this advice against our own knowledge, beliefs, preferences and insight, we may be worse off than if we never sought advice at all. *Each client is inherently an active participant in his own life reading.*

When applying for a life reading the client indicated on the application form three preferences for an intuitive counselor, out of several available at the time. The descriptive brochure included for each intuitive a photograph and a short resume that described his background, viewpoint and any special emphasis he placed in his readings. When scheduling the reading itself CAI selected one of the client's three choices, based on timing, availability and location. Occasionally we were influenced in this choice by our own (intuitive) impression of which of the three could best handle the client's questions.

About half of CAI's life-reading sessions were "in-person"; that is, the client traveled to the intuitive and was physically present with him during his reading. These sessions took place in the CAI office, the intuitive's premises or at another location if he was on tour. In in-person readings the client posed his own questions and followed up on the responses in dialog with the intuitive.

The other half of the sessions, termed "remote" or "distant," took place without the client being present. He submitted his questions to CAI by mail and a CAI *conductor* sat in for him. At the beginning of the session the conductor announced the client's name, address and date of birth—just enough information to identify him uniquely from all other persons alive at the time.[3*] He then posed the questions in turn, first the format questions and then the added questions, following up on each response until it was clear and complete. Before closing he asked for "any additional information that the client should to be aware of." CAI selected its conductors to be sympathetic, sensitive and intuitive in their own right.[4*]

Each client received a tape recording of his life reading, and a typed transcript was prepared and mailed if one had been ordered. Duplicates were retained of all mailed materials to guard against loss. All sessions were treated as confidential. For a few years CAI sent a follow-up evaluation form to each client a few months after his session, to help keep track of client satisfaction and solicit suggestions for improvement.

Standard Question Format for a Life Reading

Please give a brief discourse on the life dynamics of this individual, including his/her life purpose, major life lessons, purpose of the current phase of life experience and the mental and spiritual patterns. Specific questions will follow.

- Give a description of the individual's true essence and capabilities, and any beliefs, attitudes or conditions that may be blocking the full expression of these qualities.

- Give suggestions to assist this individual to accomplish his/her life purpose.

- Give information on predominant "past lives" having a current impact on his/her personal life, and indicate any karmic patterns still to be worked out.*

- Describe any significant astrological or numerological conditions that may be important to this individual at this time.*

> • What steps are recommended to help improve this person's physical body, so it may better serve his/her mental and spiritual development? Give specific suggestions to assist this individual in harmonizing the body, mind and spirit—especially regarding spiritual practices and tools that may be helpful.
>
> • Please describe a life seal or personal mandala which symbolizes this individual's present life pattern.
>
> * *Note*: Past-life, astrological and numerological information is normally provided, but only when it will prove beneficial to the applicant.

Some intuitive counseling clients preferred a deep-trance channel over one who functioned fully or partially consciously. When asked why, they said they felt that a trance personality could provide better information. As described elsewhere this belief is not generally correct. Many years of experience showed clearly that if an intuitive is qualified to provide life readings at all, his personal mode of operation is not important to the accuracy or relevance of the information given. Some clients may have felt more secure in discussing their personal issues in the privacy of the intuitive's unconscious state, though this preference also seems groundless. Perhaps they would heed better the seeming authoritative advice of a trance channel. Some clients were probably attracted to trance channeling just because they wanted to experience its unusual nature, and to converse for the first time with what appears to be a "non-physical being."

More than five hundred readings were conducted for Japanese clients. At least 90% were carried out remotely and required transcripts to facilitate accurate translation into Japanese.[5*] The remaining 10% took place in-person, using interpreters, when CAI staff members visited Japan and during two tours of Japanese to the San Francisco Bay Area, (arranged by CAI so they could experience intuition related activities).[6*] Two intuitives [PP, RL] continued to visit Japan over the decade following CAI's program, in order to give lectures, teach classes and perform life readings for Japanese clients.

The Content of Life Readings

> "Most intellectuals are to a certain extent afraid when an intuition intrudes into their thought processes. They are diffident and treat it

very generally. Consciously or unconsciously, in most cases they repress it." [Roberto Assagioli[7]]

Before examining excerpts from typical life readings it will help to be aware of the kinds of information and guidance they provided. There were three sorts.

First and most obviously, each reading supplied answers to the prepared questions. The intuitives' responses were usually direct and to the point, though sometimes they answered "the question behind the question," provided background explanations or responded indirectly—probably because the client was not yet ready to face the full truth of his situation. They sometimes described why and how particular problem situations had arisen and relevant factors that may have been already known but had been forgotten, repressed or disregarded.

Second, their responses occasionally included short speeches or "discourses," with the apparent purpose of appealing to the client sympathetically and intuitively rather than trying to persuade him with facts and reasons—just as one might speak to a troubled child to give him reassurance and support rather than explanations. As far as we could tell after examining hundreds of transcripts, these discourses served mainly to put the client at ease, lessen his defenses and elicit his trust of the more directly relevant words to follow. Such a discourse may also reassure him that he was on the right path, expand his awareness and understanding on a particular matter, or direct his attention to an important issue of his life to which he was not paying sufficient attention or was in denial. In other words, it attempted to prepare him to confront the obstacle that was preventing him from generating his own answers.

A third and less common component consisted of a single, specific piece of information that was useless in itself but impressive and evidential, something the client would not expect anyone to know but could immediately verify as true. Examples would be a secret he had carefully kept from anyone else, a question he was about to ask, an almost forgotten memory from his childhood or a future action he had privately planned. To judge from the obvious mindset of those who were given these little surprises, I believe they were included to help the client overcome a skepticism that would have hindered his attention and receptivity to the guidance that followed. Ample evidential information normally emerged naturally in the course of life readings. Still, sometimes an extra bit seemed to be needed at the beginning to allay residual doubts the client may have harbored about expert intuitives and the intuitive process.

Finally, while these kinds of personal information were obviously relevant and usually directly useful to clients, the most outstanding feature of life readings was the compassion with which they were given. They virtually radiated a quality of sincere consideration and care toward the client. They were always honest, candid and intimate, never solicitous, patronizing, judgmental or condescending. Most had a calm, light touch or a sense of humor, even in the face of tragedy and pain. These qualities, which lay behind the factual information and actual words spoken, seemed to be the main factor responsible for winning the client's attention and trust and for rendering useful the specific counsel. Without this trust the reading could easily be regarded as just another display of a bizarre phenomenon, or an intellectual demonstration of little personal significance. Indeed, a few disappointed clients saw their reading just this way.

This persistent compassion was all the more remarkable because the issues brought up in life readings were typically very sensitive, and could easily be taken as threatening. They were the very issues one might hesitate to raise with even one's closest friends, yet they were being discussed openly and frankly. The expert intuitive appeared to be reaching into the client's unconscious mind just beyond the boundary where his own thinking, contemplation and conscious attention stopped, but not so far as to threaten him with his unacknowledged fears. As far as we at CAI could tell as observers, most clients accepted and trusted this gentle intrusion, felt safe with the process as a whole and could experience a measure of healing in which they themselves had participated.

To stress again three points: First, these results were achieved with expert intuitives. The same qualities and results cannot be expected or claimed for intuitive counselors who are not properly qualified for this type of work. Second, in almost every case the client was completely unknown to the expert intuitive. In over half of the life readings he was thousands of miles away. Third, the life readings were cooperative ventures between client and intuitive, not one-way therapeutic treatments, or problem-solving sessions for which the intuitive must be given full credit.

Questions Asked by Clients

In practice, clients' individual questions varied considerably. They typically dealt with the full range of problematic issues mentioned above. The best questions were well thought-out: they focused on important personal issues; they were clear, unambiguous and to the point; and they asked for understanding, suggestions and specific information.

The descriptive brochure accompanying the life-reading application form included instructions on how to prepare personal questions for the expert intuitive. Despite our admonitions, however, many questions were very poor: superficial, badly worded or too broad to be answered within a single session. Some clients were obviously quite confused. They asked vaguely for reassurance against a perceived fear, or babbled on without acknowledging their problem or asking questions about it. Many obviously wanted the intuitive to make decisions for them. Some sought pointless predictions. Others wished new arguments to justify their petty resentments, rigidly held beliefs or chosen role as victims. A few were tricky, as if they were trying to test the intuitive.

The intuitives handled poor questions in various ways. Their answers were invariably given with attention, concern and patience, as a loving parent responds to the persistent questions of a young child. I never witnessed expert intuitives become cross, impatient or condescending toward a client, even when the client behaved badly: resistant, skeptical, stubborn, demanding, facetious, angry or accusative. They corrected errors firmly and gently, turning aside accusations with a soft, humorous or amusing suggestion.

A few of the questions submitted were strange indeed. A life-reading application from a physician included four single-spaced, handwritten pages of personal background, his current life situation, unsolved problems and pet theories; yet, he never asked one question for which he wanted an answer. CAI returned his application with a reminder: we require only the questions to which you seek answers; no background, explanations or justifications are necessary. We also pointed out that it would have taken over half of his reading period just to read his treatise to the intuitive.

It was common for questions to contain implicit and invalid assumptions that rendered them meaningless as stated. For example, one woman asked how to deal with her husband who was cheating on her. But was he? The intuitive said no, he was not unfaithful, and suggested she examine her own jealousy, doubt and suspicion. A physician wanted to know what drug to use to treat one of his patients. A non-drug treatment would be safer and more effective. In cases like these the intuitive politely pointed out the mistaken assumption, though occasionally he sidestepped the question and discussed the basic issue behind the belief.

"When will I marry?" asked a young Japanese girl, presuming first of all that she will indeed get married, and second, that the date and the man were predetermined for her and not her own choice. (There is a long tradition in Japan for arranged marriages, though they are not so common today.) The intuitive pointed out a few matters that were more important to her than getting married, and encouraged her to look at the origin of her concern whether she was acceptable to a man.

Over the many years of work with intuition I have been greatly enriched by several counseling sessions for myself from CAI staff intuitives and a few others. These readings were very valuable, not just because they provided experience in interacting with different kinds of intuitives and learning to ask good questions, but also because they showed me how to utilize intuitive information to manage my own life better. Some were highly insightful indeed.

I discovered that taking advantage of intuitive guidance is both a skill and an art. It meant I had to figure out how to interpret, screen and integrate new and sometimes disturbing information from the intuitives. When processing their counsel it was often hard to strike a happy balance between my critical posture and my need to test their information, on one hand, and my own inner sense and gradually expanding intuitive insight, on the other. It took a long time to develop an appropriate balance. Actually, the effort is still ongoing but I feel now that the process is working quite well now.

I can't help but feel that everyone who works with intuitive information, in fact with any kind of internal plus external guidance, for that matter, must go through a similar struggle and find his own balance.

"Tell me about my mother," asked a middle-aged man. A ten-hour lecture could be given on that topic. So what did he want to know? Another woman wanted to be told how she could make her husband stop his abusive language. Sorry, my dear, it is his choice to stop, not yours, though perhaps you could examine why you feel it is up to you to change him—and learn how your own attitude may be provoking his abuse.

A few clients sought information about stock investments, currency markets and real estate. In a few of these cases the intuitives provided the client with abundant, substantive and specific information. More often, though, they gave only a nugget he could check out and use, as if to demonstrate that intuitive information is indeed available and can be accurate, then they dealt with the inquirer's motivation: Why was he trying to make fast money without due effort? What was he going to do with the money if he received it? From whom was he taking it? Was his attempt really the best use of his abilities? Making money was not in itself criticized, but the means employed to acquire it and the purpose served by possessing it were the key issues.

Often clients seemed to be more curious than serious about actually making use of the information they requested. Some had obviously not thought ahead about the consequences that would ensue if their questions had been fully answered by the intuitive. In any case, the intuitives typically encouraged clients to learn to use and trust their own intuition rather than rely heavily on intuitive counsel.

Some clients asked questions about other people in their lives but expressed little interest in facing their own issues. A few wanted to locate a lost object or a missing member of their family, but did not seem to have considered whether it was a good idea to find them (see Chapter 5). Two clients (perhaps there were more) were secretly conducting parapsychological tests. The intuitives caught both at their game, gave them a small piece of impressive and evidential information and gently sent them on their way.

Many clients sought medical advice, sometimes with an obvious expectation of a quick fix—a pill, a simple shift in diet or a change in environment. The intuitives readily provided diagnoses, and sometimes proposed treatments, but they usually took clients back to the negative mental state that had generated the symptom in the first place: anger, resentment, bitterness, guilt, lack of self-love, victimhood, deep distrust of life, lack of openness to new experience, a holding back of personal energy that was trying to express itself, or others. More often than not the suggested action lay in attitudinal changes rather than physical treatments alone. (This emphasis on the non-physical origin of physical disorders was a recurrent theme in Cayce's medical readings.)

Many clients wanted to know about the future: forthcoming personal changes, new business opportunities, political or social developments, natural catastrophes, etc. Everyone is curious about the future, of course, but some are preoccupied with it as a security issue. Some of the experiments (mentioned in Chapters 5, 9 and 13) demonstrated that intuitives can indeed predict much of the future, though it is not always truly helpful to do so. The intuitives typically offered reassurance, but specific predictive information was not usually given.

Judging by the way clients' questions about the future were asked, the main issue was almost always one of personal security, not a desire for constructive action or for someone else's benefit. The intuitives usually handled these questions by reminding the inquirer of the origin of his concern about the feared event he felt might occur in days to come. They also pointing out that his future is never fixed, but is the result of the choices he is continually making, both consciously and unconsciously, in the present moment. They reassured him that his future would indeed be "safe," then proposed that he focus his attention on the present, the only point in time when he can consciously make the choices. This kind of counsel is a reminder that the main value of a prediction lies less in how precise or accurate it may be, and more in its capacity to induce the listener to change the direction of his life for the better.

When there seemed to be a genuine value in knowing about the future, the intuitives indicated opportunities, options and occasionally probabilities. They might describe the consequences to be expected from choices already made, and those that would follow from choices that could still be remade in the present. Encouragement to follow a particular path might be suggested, but I never heard a competent intuitive make an unqualified assertion about what must occur in a personal future.

Some clients were seeking reassurance from their fears of natural catastrophes. During the '60s and '70s, for example, rumors were spreading about cataclysmic events, predicted by several popular psychics (including Edgar Cayce) that would occur in California, Hawaii and Japan: great earthquakes, volcanoes, tidal waves, entire coastlines and islands sinking into the Pacific Ocean![8*] As is typical in such cases, these concerned clients, by accepting immediately and literally these prophecies about earth changes, were projecting onto them their individual fears. They were *not* asking about the conditions under which the predicted events would occur, from what sources the predictions had arisen, or whether it was at all likely that they would really happen—all relevant questions before believing any new information. CAI's intuitives assured them that the presumed catastrophes were extremely unlikely, and tried to redirect their attention toward the character and source of their fear, which was the prime issue to be dealt with.

Typical Intuitive Counsel

Just as with non-intuitive medical, business and other advice, intuitive counsel is often not shocking or unusual, just "common sense." It would be obvious to everyone except the recipient, who had been overlooking or blocking what he needed to hear again from a source he could respect. Nevertheless, the intuitive counsel given in life readings typically went far beyond common sense. It contained insights that were centrally meaningful to the client's situation and state of mind. These insights would not necessarily be immediately obvious to a casual observer, but they could be detected in individual cases if the observer examined the entire tape or transcript and then interviewed the client—which we on the staff did on occasion. Even better, an observer could win this appreciation for life-reading counsel by directly experiencing a reading for himself.

In reading the following excerpts, do keep in mind that that are completely out of context. They do not include the particular issues about which the individuals were inquiring, the specific information they were seeking or any indication of the kind of counsel they were able to hear. Such background would be much too voluminous to include here. What may be appreciated from these samples is the type of counsel given to clients: informative, candid, sometimes stern, but consistently patient and compassionate. Note that it is devoid of programming, fortune telling or any interference with the client's freedom of personal choice. The intuitive gives what is true, relevant and (apparently) acceptable, even though it may not be profound or dramatic.

> "The time is coming to take some risks in relation to your career, love and marriage. Put yourself on the line instead of hiding behind a shield of safety. You can't do this any longer, for the cost is very high. The cost is your integrity." [ICI-1060]

> "The individual has been born into this life with many diverse talents, including an acuteness of intellect and both a sensitive and spiritual nature. This natural sensitivity…works both for him, and, when over-extended, against him,…appearing as stress both in the body and in the mental capacity….His happiness is linked to the balancing of these capacities, through a certain spiritual resiliency [then described in detail]." [ICI-805]

> "You need to change very desperately. Let the fear go. It is not necessary. You have quite a few years left yet and you cannot stay in the prison you have been in. You must make a dramatic stand for your own goodness and

your own love. As you do...your ability to express yourself fully will manifest for you." [ICI-72]

"Are you willing to touch all facets of yourself? Are you willing to share with people all of your feelings? Are you willing to be naked in a world that finds nakedness appalling? Are you willing to step out on a limb and experience the danger of preparing to fly? You know the mother bird will push her children out of the nest even though they would not go of their own free will. And as a bird is pushed, it experiences the most extraordinary primary care. As the bird falls, feeling its mortality coming closer with every inch, it realizes it has something it forgot it had. It has wings!" [ICI-1055]

"During this particular time, over the last several years, there have been elements of sadness, doubt, and questioning. Now shall be the turning point in opportunities. These will come forth fully and completely. It will also be the forthcoming of love. This will entail going deeper into the soul search and releasing old attitudes, finding ones which provide love and joy." (ICI-1141)

Many life readings, when discussing the non-physical origin of health problems, encouraged the applicant to take advantage of his poor health as a motivation to examine and change his attitudes.

"Understand that the reason for this high blood pressure in due to the fact that you are such a passive person, that you do not allow yourself to cleanse the angers, anxieties and frustrations which have occurred in your life. Instead of the negative energy being released, it has been stored in your body. Now there has been some permanent damage, but as you align yourself with love more clearly and fully, you can lessen the effects that this circulatory difficulty has had within your life." [ICI-175]

"If you continue to try to pack all of you into this balloon, not only will you gain an excessive amount of weight but you run the risk of having some of this emotional devastation turn into a physical ailment. Right now there is a manifestation of this in your circulatory system. Your little box cannot hold you anymore, my friend. You are afraid to come out and play because the child within is so wounded....Well, let this child lick his wounds, for if you continue to protect the child, you prevent him from healing himself. Let this child breathe fresh air, and look at his pain." [ICI-178]

"You have wrestled in the past with the issue of judgment. You have worked especially with ways of protecting what is between you and the world, as if the part of you that the world would wish to see, this part of you that can truly assist [others], as you now want, has been denied you. Therefore, it has been necessary [for you] to create several significant negative thought forms in your life pattern—[which manifest] particularly in the chest area and in the solar plexus. This is to remind you that, if you continue to protect, to judge, if you stop this flow of energy any longer, you will have to deal with these things internally and directly." [ICI-1121]

"Now there is a danger that you might choose to depart physical reality much earlier than you think, for right now there is a health difficulty, which, if not addressed, you will die from in your early fifties. What I'm sensing is a tremendous blocking of energies right there is your intestinal region. There is already somewhat of a difficulty with your digestive workings, a danger of colitis, and beyond colitis, rectal cancer." [ICI-189]

"At this point in your life you have some choices to make....Much inward-looking is necessary now, and examination of your beliefs....Go through them, one by one, write them down. [Much specific advice followed]...For you have reached a point in your life at which you know deeply that you must act. .. If you choose not to do this re-thinking, then your health will become worse, your relationship with individuals will become worse, your feelings about yourself will become worse." (women, age 63, with many health problems) [ICI-1102]

(Why was I born into U.S. society?) "You chose a country as progressive as your own nature....Your country was discriminatory against persons of your persuasion, yet...was being forced to be progressive and accepting of those persevering in their basic rights as human beings." (Client was an outspoken homosexual.) [ICI-805]

Many life readings dealt less with problems than with opportunities:

"Many of the things you have worked for in the past are changing. Many of your beliefs are changing as you move into a realm of awareness beyond anything you imagined. You might identify this as what we call a middle aged syndrome. You might think you are merely restless, but in reality you are preparing to change everything in your life, preparing to discard what does not work for you." (ICI-1060)

"Allow all the facets of yourself to manifest completely, to rise to the surface so that you might be in a more conscious position to choose the realms of your personality that you wish to keep and those you wish to discard." (ICI-1056)

"When you begin to see your creativity in motion, you will not be harnessed infinitely to the concept of aging, which is a belief, a rampant belief, upon this planet. So is the belief about death. It is an illusion specifically manifested to help mankind move beyond the illusion of being out of control of his or her own reality." [ICI-1074]

"We would suggest that to be driven to the point of ecstasy and of complete alignment with all of life, is to move oneself beyond one's limited will, beyond one's ego, to push oneself into complete surrender. This means uniting the personal will with the divine will, uniting the personality with spirit. Surrender means coming into divinity rather than losing oneself to outside forces." (ICI-2003)

The Life-Purpose Issue

"The average man sleepwalks his way through life, and seldom questions his motive and intention. He is driven by his unconscious and conditioned mind. This man does not know the purpose of his life, or why he was born or what he is doing in the world. He thinks he can think a thought, but actually his thoughts think him. His life is driven by thought forms until he awakens." [Reshad Feild[9]]

The format question about life purpose is admittedly a loaded one, and it was central to the life readings. I think it is safe to say that most persons are resistant to examining the purpose of their life. They rarely confront the issue directly, even in their later years. Some go so far as to reject the notion that their life has any purpose at all, and if it does they suppose it is unknowable and comes from outside of themselves as an imposed destiny within which they are being fatefully manipulated. I was shocked to discover that many persons consider human life, including their own, to be a series of random biological accidents and other chance events, some pleasurable and some painful, leading only to a meaningless death. (Unto middle age I understood very little of how the life process works, but even in the absence of any religious or spiritual education I never doubted that my life was governed by an overriding but barely visible personal purpose, largely of my own creation and responsibility.)

These beliefs in purposelessness are not at all consistent with the view presented by the expert intuitives. Everyone's life has a deep, essential purpose, they say, and this purpose is a reflection, a stepping-down or particularization of a common, universal purpose that applies to everyone. His individual life purpose is largely self-created from a deep unconscious level. It is held safely in his inner mind, ready to emerge when his conscious mind is ready to acknowledge, examine and accept it. Even apart from intuitives, there is no lack of witnesses who can testify that this is exactly how it has worked for them, at least past a crucial turning point in their lives. Support for this view is also abundant in the in-built spiritual traditions of the world's major religions. Literally correct or not, it is at least a possibility that has to be taken seriously, not sloughed off as irrelevant nonsense.

It should be obvious that ignorance of your life purpose is a heavy burden to carry. Becoming aware of it and accepting it relieves you of the plague of confusion, vagueness, uncertainty and indecision that naturally follows when you do not know where you are going and why you are going there. A knowledge and acceptance of your purpose automatically provides an ongoing discrimination between matters relevant to this purpose and those that are not. This discrimination directly shapes all desires, thoughts and activities, so that clarity and certainty emerge naturally and eventually. All external circumstances can then be interpreted and responded to much more effectively. Most deep decisions follow effortlessly, and fears of insecurity (based on what one imagines *might* happen) tend to be diminished. This directed state also allows one's intuition to flow more freely.

Judging by their elective questions, the majority of counseling clients had only the vaguest notion of why they were living and going through the difficulties of their lives. Indeed, the term "life purpose" meant quite different things to different people. Many clients thought of their purpose, if they thought of it at all, solely in terms of a professional, career or family goal. Some found it in service to others, but had little awareness or concern with their own self-development. Others saw their life task to be one of overcoming emotional or neurotic obstacles and little else. Many were obviously hanging on to childhood beliefs and were confused by the contradictions between these beliefs and what they were experiencing in everyday life. Relatively few perceived their life purpose in terms of any kind of inner growth or spiritual fulfillment, who saw themselves on a definite, self-chosen track and sought an improved understanding of where it was headed, what they might expect to accomplish in their life and how they might best focus their energies to achieve it.

The answers offered by the intuitives respected with sensitivity this broad range of possible interpretations of "purpose." Their approach always appeared to be one of nudging the client to discover this crucial piece of self-knowledge for himself, rather than just feeding it to him outright and in full detail (though this seemed to occur occasionally). In response to this variation in purposes, their answers to the life-purpose question varied considerably from one client to another. While the counsel invariably contained specific information and suggestions, it also preserved a sense of mystery about the client's life and encouraged him along the path of self-discovery.

As far as could be determined from reviews of dozens of cases in which we were able to observe both the client and his reading, the depth of counsel given was a direct reflection of the client's present state of awareness of his life and his openness to hear what could help him. In other words, the intuitive's response was aimed to a level of self-understanding just beyond the level he already possessed and with which he was comfortable. Depending on the client, therefore, the response might consist of a discussion of specific behavioral obstacles, or his personality and character, or the growth of his inner being or "soul." One's very deepest purpose is truly ineffable, of course—it can't be explained in words without greatly distorting it—but there were many cases (including my own) in which the discussion of purpose in the life reading touched very deeply.

Here are a few examples of individual life purpose as presented in intuitive counseling sessions:

> "The dynamic here, the life purpose and the life lessons, all relate to growing into your own power. We mentioned before working through an "ownership' difficulty with your husband, a dependence difficulty with your mother and a power difficulty in your job. On a deeper level all of these relate to the same issue: understanding that *you* are the controller of your own destiny. Your primary purpose is coming to the awareness of yourself as a god, as a powerful being who can affect change in your own life. As you come to recognize your own power and wield it justly, then indeed you fulfill your life's purpose. All your life dynamics revolve around this one point." [ICI-441]

Talk about life purpose! Surely the wisest, most comprehensive and deepest life purpose for all of us is the need to learn to love—to love everything and everybody, and to do it unconditionally and without qualification, hesitation or excuse.

But who can live up to this grand ideal? And ideal it certainly is. We all need ideals to keep us moving in the right direction, though it's not very wise to set them up as goals to expect to achieve. But it's so hard to just identify fully with this ultimate purpose as we are learning the lessons life is offering us. We cannot even <u>see</u> our own non-loving incompletenesses, even when they're right in front of us, let alone accept them gracefully and begin to work on them deliberately. Moreover. it's so very easy to blame the difficulties resulting from our blindness on our life situation, the environment, other persons or just "bad luck.".

We are such contradictory creatures in how we choose to love and not love, are we not? The same man who loves his wife with such great devotion goes off to his 8-to-5 job to help design weapons systems for the government's Department of Destruction. The gifted artist abuses her children but would be crushed if life took them from her. The doctor who has given his life to serve the poor and oppressed loves to play with young boys. An accomplished political leader is unfaithful to his wife and lies about it. The list goes on. If we are at all truthful with ourselves we are all like these (admittedly extreme) examples. The opposing facets of our capacity to love and not love can exist, side by side with one another, in the same human being.

[ICI-1102]

"The individual's purpose in this lifetime is to master the high creative energies that come through spiritual service, and various unusual means: meditation, examination of personal life affairs in autobiographical format, and perseverance in creative endeavors." [ICI-805]

"I sense a tremendous creative ability for your life to be as you wish it and as you see fit...but also a great deal of anger, of blockages, of resentment and bitterness....For deeply within you have allowed your life to be one of suffering,...of non-fulfillment of the deepest purpose in your life. You have allowed your life to be led by others, to be misled by the essence of what you thought to be true.... Your purpose is to fulfill this creativity by removing the obstacles you have built up."

Let's face it. We are all students in this huge earth classroom for learning how to love. We are not yet complete, not yet finished, not yet graduated. Today's lesson is to learn to love a bit better, in one of our incomplete areas, using whatever situation we find ourselves in to help us. There's just nothing else to do, nothing else worth doing.

If you can't find a specific purpose for your life, start with this one grand purpose, and work back from there to a goal you can get your mind's teeth into. Ask yourself, am I doing right now what I want to do, and what I need to be doing, toward this single end—to love everyone and everything?

"Your life's purpose is to come to terms with all of these lessons [just described] and to allow your face, at last, to be disclosed to the world. Your ability, then, is to be a leader, to be one who would draw others to you, who would stand strong and allow others to revolve around you. This might not seem possible or even available to you at this moment but this is, indeed, your life purpose. You are the one who may soon clear the path, so to speak, and create the opening for those who would come behind you." [ICI-1121]

"Your life purpose is to come to a final realization that you are a loving, giving being. There is nothing evil in you. I say this because down deep there is a belief that you were or did something very wrong at some point in your past, and that you are having to make up for it. But, you see, God does not want you to sacrifice yourself, but to *be* yourself, *fully....*" [ICI-1036]

Past Lives in Life Readings

* "Reincarnation is part of the larger framework in which any individual's health and well-being must be considered....[It is] not nearly as rigid as many believers in the concept think." [Seth[10]]

Many life readings contained brief descriptions of two or three so-called "past-lives" of the client: his presumed existences in other cultures, prior time periods and life situations prior to his present life. This notion of "past lives," karma and reincarnation is a problem for almost everyone. It is almost impossible to understand the idea, beyond mere intellectual appreciation as a theory in which to believe or not believe, without a direct personal experience of it. A past life is not even what most persons think it is. The notion therefore requires some explanation. (See the accompanying box.)

This popular rejection of the concept of reincarnation in civilized societies is in spite of the fact that at least one-third of the population of our planet accepts the notion, not only as a religious or intellectual idea but as an obvious aspect of human existence. That is, they actually *live* by it, or at least hold it as an accepted religious belief. Reincarnation was an integral part of Christianity for several hundred years before being discarded from the doctrine of the early church. When coupled with the concept of karma—roughly, the enduring accountability for one's behavior—the idea certainly makes good logical sense as an explanation for the apparent injustice of human suffering, and for persons entering life with strong interests and capabilities that cannot be explained genetically or by family environment. What could be more fair than for each of us to have multiples lifetimes in which to reap the rewards of virtuous action, to experience the consequences of one's errors and to have the opportunity to correct these past mistakes? Moreover, other common explanations of these mysteries do *not* make much sense: "It's all pure chance" or "God wills it this way" or "Those who suffer are just ignorant or primitive."

Once a direct experience of past lives has been gained, however, it is no longer a matter of belief but of certain knowledge. Like the taste of strawberries, intense physical pain and falling in love, there is then no longer any doubt about it—and also no adequate way to describe it to others who have missed it. Demonstration, persuasion and argument will never convince the doubters, though they might be induced to welcome such an experience on the basis of another's testimony. For this reason an intuitive reading covering one or more of one's past lives can provide an initial eye-opening and positive exposure to the possibility of reincarnation.

The value of a past-life lies entirely in its connection to present-day issues. Intuitives' descriptions of these prior existences *always* emphasized to a client that, regardless of his belief in and even fascination with his past lives, their relevance and usefulness resides only in the self-understanding they may contribute *in the present*. Sometimes the intuitives did not answer the past-life question at all, or if they did their comments were only cursory. Again, they seemed to be matching their remarks to what the client could accept and utilize. In other contexts (apart from life readings) the intuitives explained that many persons cannot make good use of past-life information because their main need is to focus their full attention on current issues and their principal path of growth. Information about past lives would only divert them from these matters.

Past-life reports from non-CAI intuitives, including psychics, astrologers and others, as well as individuals' reported past-life experiences "remembered" from their dreams or hypnotic induction, are very varied. They range from relevant and helpful information to the most absurd accounts—those that only a credulous subject would accept as a valid past life.[11*] Listen to typical remarks from those who have accepted alleged past-life information—it may or may not be valid—from their favorite psychics. For example:

- self-importance: "I was a famous queen in ancient Persia, you know."

Prior Lives? Sense and Nonsense

Most people find the notion of past lives and reincarnation an interesting idea but just too impractical and abstract to take seriously for themselves. Unless they can find something in their own experience to substantiate it, it must remain in the area of speculation, opinion, belief and theory. But what we find is a matter of what we look for. Not everyone is seeking an explanation for where he came from, why he is enduring his current life with its various pleasures and difficulties, and why there is such confusion and suffering among certain family members and friends, and among people all over the world for that matter. Even those who say they *believe* in reincarnation and past lives do not necessarily *know* it as a personal truth; they are still unwilling to take the idea a step further and embrace it as a reality in their own lives.

It's not hard to identify some of the specific barriers to the recognition of reincarnation. For one, there is the limitation of your memory: you cannot remember much of your childhood, such as what you were doing on the fifth day of your fourth year at school, so why should you expect to remember an earlier event in a context even less familiar? In addition, we can never trust memories fully for they are sometimes "false." What we regard as memory is not necessarily what really happened in the past, since the recalled event could have arisen from imagination, a mistaken thought or a dream. Even if the "'core" of a past-life memory may be valid, the mind may be superimposing its own images, forms and words on it to make it seem familiar (as in dreams). Anyway, are we sure we are remembering our own past lives, and not someone else's?

Second, there is a deeper issue: just *who* is having these supposed past lives, anyway? Is it your present conscious self? Certainly not, or you would know about it. So it must be a deeper aspect of yourself, perhaps down at the level of "soul" or "essence," we may say. To validate the notion of past lives for yourself, you will have to get to know this essence better.

Third, there is the confusing issue of *time*. Are past lives really "past"? Those who claim to have "been there" remind us that, at the level of our deeper being, the level at which intuitive information originates, time does not exist in the familiar way. Each event belongs only to the moment at which it is experienced, as in a dream. "Past" lives, they say, are parallel and timeless experiences, a part of one's greater existence. They belong no more to the past than to the future. Moreover, they are irrelevant as history until a point of growth is reached at which they become important and useful; then they arise to awareness on their own, just like other spontaneous memories. It is not necessary to strive to reach for them, and it may be unwise to do so.

Finally, what use would a past-life memory have for you today? If it is not relevant to the challenges you are facing in your life at the moment, it is only a distraction—perhaps a serious one.

What all this adds up to is that reincarnation is a real and useful notion for those who can relate to it constructively. Detailed information about past lives is, for most persons most of the time, useless, irrelevant and possibly distracting. If approached at the right moment, however, with openness, readiness and a sincere desire for self-understanding, reincarnation and the recall of specific past lives can be an enlightening step on the path to self-knowledge and fulfillment.

- irresponsibility: "I can't help this neurotic habit because of the hard life I had in China."
- resentment: "No wonder I hate my wife—she was once my executioner!"
- guilt: "I'll never make it up to my son, whom I sold off as a slave in that life in Peru."
- romance: "I'm spending the summer in Greece so I can explore where I once lived."

- career: "I've decided to give up nursing and become as astrologer, like I once was."
- relationship: "I'm so excited! I'm marrying the man who was my teacher in Atlantis."

If you are told about one of your past lives, or feel you intuit such information by yourself, how can you tell if it is valid? I know of no external, objective criterion one can apply to test if it is genuine or illusory. You will know for yourself only if it "rings true" with your self-knowledge, your critical sense and your own intuition. Even the inclusion of previously unknown but verifiable information (such as a previous name, the location of your tombstone or the name of the ship you sailed on, for example) does not validate the entire report, since a good intuitive can retrieve such specific information without having had the past life. If external assurance is desired it would be best to rely upon a qualified intuitive and seek confirmation from multiple, independent sources.

It is certainly valid and safe to *wish* for past-life memories, and to welcome them into your life when they come. You can be certain that, if heeded, they will bring you added understanding, and probably new challenges of their own. But to *force* their emergence before you are able to discriminate their validity and are ready to handle them can be confusing, disruptive and even dangerous. Emotional obstacles may induce misinterpretation and amplify the underlying fears.

Here are some typical examples of past-life information as expressed in individual CAI life readings, showing their connection with the clients' current life situations. (Again, the overall context of the information is necessarily omitted in these brief excerpts.)

> "…The next major lifetime was as a scribe in the library in Alexandria in approximately the time period of 100 BC. where the individual [spent] many long hours of retreat and studies as a highly scholastic fellow.…He mastered meditation and knowledge of past lives. He was born in Cairo to an Egyptian father and Grecian mother.…Many lifetimes were spent in esoteric groups or monasteries…. In this [present] lifetime he seeks at times a cloistered existence among individuals of either a common degree of philosophy or an interest in spiritual pursuits, but these retreats are not serving him fully." [Special]

"Let me suggest that you look at a lifetime in which you were a pioneer woman in the late 1800s in Utah, north of Salt Lake City. You lost your husband when you were 22 years old and spent the rest of your life alone. You were not powerless, however, because you could plant, you could take care of yourself. You were the only person you could rely on. You lived a very strong and healthy life even though you were lonely....This translates to your life right now, when you have forgotten how to do this. You forgot how to satiate and fulfill loneliness in yourself. You might wish to even meet this individual in a past life regression for instance, so she can give you more information, so you can more fully understand how you may pull out of the prisons and chains of your life at this time." [ICI-1022]

"There was one [lifetime] that took place in the time of Christ, a period of tremendous upheaval and change. The lesson you learned there, as a woman, was that this change, this way of understanding the world, would come again and you would then be ready to accept it....At your death, you decided that your life would end in a way that helped others, that you would will a certain inheritance not to your family but to the beginning church at that time, for writing down the words of Christ....This was of great benefit, but you saw later...between incarnations...that the money had been misused. There is yet within you a certain regret toward family members. Your willingness to share with them often comes from guilt rather than the true way, of love." [ICI-1032]

"From an early age you have worked to please other people, to be a "good girl," not to make waves. At the core of your being you have a very strong desire to serve and to help other people. You have had quite a few lifetimes in which you learned how to give of yourself....[Now] is the culmination of that lesson....I feel a strong sweetness about you, a delicacy, a poetic quality, for creating an environment to heal people—physically, emotionally, mentally." [ICI-1036]

These samples convey some of the wisdom conveyed in a full life reading, albeit an incomplete impression. Better, if you feel you are ready for this kind of personal counsel, why not prepare for a life reading for yourself, and seek out a competent expert intuitive to provide it for you?

Results of the Life-Reading Program

Many clients responded to the follow-up questionnaire or wrote to CAI later on their own, explaining what their reading meant to them. Most spoke about how much the reading had enhanced, and in some cases transformed their lives. Among clients who were present for their reading there were often tears, not so much of pain, I think, but of the joy that arises from a felt connection with one's deeper being—as sometimes happens to al of us at births and weddings, for example. A few clients whom I already knew personally testified that their life reading was the first occasion in their adult life when they were truly *seen* and accepted for what they were, without judgment or criticism. They were obviously deeply moved, even though they may not have listened all that well to the words of the intuitive's message. This kind of trusting experience obviously has value in itself, whether it arises from counseling or in some other way.

In fifteen life readings—about 1%—the clients expressed disappointment: "The reading was too general," "It could have been said about anyone," "My questions were not answered" (the way I expected) or "Some of the facts were in error." We examined all of these cases in detail, listened to the tapes and discussed most of them with the clients by telephone to try to understand what had gone wrong.

In most cases we were able to trace the difficulty either to unusually poor questioning or to an inaccurate expectation of what intuitive counseling offered. It was as if the client had not read the descriptive brochure sent along with the life reading application. The errors some complained about invariably arose from poor questions; indeed, these clients received what they asked for, either through carelessness or perhaps because they were not yet willing to face their own issues. A few clients expected the reading to confirm certain of their beliefs and were disappointed when they didn't receive what they wanted. Some were obviously looking for a quick fix, one not requiring personal effort and not threatening to their fixed way of life, and were therefore disappointed. Three of the disappointed parties received their readings as gifts from enthusiastic friends, but it became obvious that were not really very interested—at least not at the time. (We discontinued the gift-reading offer a year after starting it.)

Six of the dissatisfied clients wrote us six to ten months after their complaint to thank us. It seems they were not ready at the time of their reading to accept what they could accept later. Several satisfied clients also reported that pieces of information given in their reading seemed irrelevant or wrong when given, but became true and meaningful several months later. (I have experienced this delayed reaction more than once myself.)

Others may have been disappointed but did not complain, of course, and still others who complained may have later found value in their reading but did not tell us so. Ten or so clients with whom we remained in close contact, and others who responded to the follow-up questionnaire, were enthusiastic about their life readings and very grateful for them: "It really changed my life!" We too were pleased, but must remain humble in the face of these compliments, for we know that there is no way we can take sole credit for the results. After all, people change by themselves when they are ready to change, not before. All someone else can do is to be present to encourage them and perhaps trigger the change when the time for it is ripe.

The availability of life readings was announced through CAI publications (a membership newsletter and the magazine *Intuition*), in a few published magazine articles and at CAI and other conferences and public presentations. Many clients first heard about intuitive counseling through personal referrals. Some clients returned months or years later to update their earlier life readings and to seek answers to further questions.

Preparing for Your Life Reading

If you have chosen to seek the counsel of an expert intuitive to assist you with your personal life issues, you should first understand clearly what a life reading is and what it can do for you. To begin, review this chapter with your particular goals in mind.

The next step is to formulate the questions you want to ask the expert intuitive. It is essential to take the time to *prepare your questions carefully*, a point already stressed repeatedly. Your questions should be clear, unambiguous, unbiased and not resting on questionable assumptions. Whenever you probe from what you know into the not-yet-known, you need to ask your questions from a firm base of personal knowledge, not speculation, shaky beliefs or what someone has told you. In other words, your ground of inquiry should be solid. Also, the quality and usefulness of the answers you receive will be in direct proportion to the focus or pointedness of your inquiry, the seriousness of your intent and how open you are to hearing the "truth" about yourself. This does not mean that they should be narrow (like yes-or-no), over-specific (like asking for an exact date, name or location) or irresponsible (like asking for a decision you need to make for yourself). Just ask for knowledge that, when obtained, will enable you to take a positive step toward whatever purpose or goal you see for yourself. Finally, check your questions for the potential value of the answers. Try to anticipate how you are going to make use of the kind of responses you expect to receive.

After you have prepared your questions carefully and are satisfied with them, don your intuitive hat and try to answer them for yourself. Set your own intuition to work in whatever contemplative manner works best for you: through meditation, when day-dreaming, in seeded dreams, on falling asleep or awakening, or during a walk in quiet natural surroundings. Do this in a free, playful manner, without "thinking" to find the answers and without a sense of obligation, responsibility or urgency to do so. Just be open, calm, unhurried and receptive. Listen to your inner mind uncritically, non-intellectually and without judgment for whatever answers try to float upward to your conscious mind. Several clients reported that when they stepped out of the preparation mode and examined what they had written, some answers appeared by themselves.

By reviewing your questions in this way you will be practicing with your own intuition and learning to trust it better. You can also check your personal insights against what you learn later from the expert intuitive. This is always the best way, for life readings are intended to provide timely assistance and stimulate self-reliance, not to encourage long-term dependence on external sources of help. They may be profitably used as a short-term substitute for your own growing intuition, which is presumably not yet so well developed that you can fully rely on it.

Intuition and Psychotherapy

"There's nothing that the public at large…would more like to learn from psychologists than what makes for behavior change.
Thus far researchers haven't gotten very far with the question."
[Huston Smith[12]]

Psychotherapy is a counseling modality in which the therapist catalyzes a client's healing and growth through a conversational dialog aimed at self-discovery[13]. At its best it is an effective process for dealing with common neuroses, many emotional problems, some mental illnesses and personal development in general. Like all successful healing, psychotherapy is not something the therapist *does to* the client; rather, the therapist guides the client to effect his own changes. He does this by taking advantage of the client's motivation, values and strengths, and by creating a safe space for honest confrontation and growth.

Many people think erroneously that psychotherapy is for the mentally ill or the obviously non-functional, not themselves. They see it as a repair process, similar to medical intervention, and their image of it is distorted by their fear of external pressure to force them to make changes in themselves they do not want. This view may have been true at some point in recent history, but it is not at all justified today. The purpose of psychotherapy is growth, even in the absence of observable symptoms, and growth is a process we are all involved in.

Intuitive counseling and psychotherapy are complementary counseling approaches. Both are client initiated, though in the former the intuitive leads the process while in the latter the client leads. The intuitive form prefers a somewhat "healthier" client, or at least one who is reasonably self-responsible, open to self-examination and ready to accept help. Psychotherapy, on the other hand, is most appropriate when the changes that are necessary call for more persistent, day-to-day internal work than can be facilitated by even the deepest and most compassionate intuitive session. There are also persons who find psychotherapy preferable because they distrust the intuitive process, just as there are those who prefer intuitive counsel because they distrust psychotherapists. However, there are many exceptions to this rough dichotomy.

Intuition plays an important part in effective psychotherapy because the therapist uses it to perceive more clearly the basic issues, blocks and strengths in the client's mental world than he can do efficiently by conversation, observation and analysis alone. When the dialog is properly managed the therapist may constructively and indirectly reflect this deeper understanding back to the client. He need not declare that he is using his intuition, or even be aware of it himself. Frances Vaughan, scholar on intuition and an accomplished psychotherapist, reminds us that the therapist's role is not to inform his clients what he sees intuitively or to otherwise show off his intuitive talents. "My task in psychotherapy is to listen to people," she says. "When it's finished it's not something I can say *I* have done." Rather, the therapist's task is to stimulate and support his client's self-responsibility, knowledge, insights, trust and, of course, his intuition[14]. He may even have to resist short-cutting the process if the client insists on knowing what his therapist "sees" about him.

I was fortunate to be on hand when one of CAI's expert intuitives [DR] met for an afternoon with a group of psychotherapists at the Counseling Center of the Institute of Transpersonal Psychology, then in Menlo Park, California, to discuss their difficult cases. She described accurately the particular issues of several of their clients, after being given only their names, and then offered practical suggestions for how the therapists could be more effective. For two of the therapists she described their personal issues that had been blocking their efforts. While we had arranged the meeting to lend practical assistance, not to demonstrate intuitive powers, the therapists present were obviously very impressed with her intuitive performance.

For many years Anne Armstrong [AAA], not on the CAI staff but an expert intuitive with whom we worked occasionally, met monthly with groups of psychotherapists in a similar fashion. This work sought not only to benefit their clients, albeit indirectly, but also to help the therapists refine their intuitive skills.

This kind of collaboration between intuitives and therapists holds much promise for enhancing therapeutic practice in the future.

Intuitive counseling seeks to achieve the same goals as psychotherapy but in a different manner. While both counseling modes are non-intrusive and respect the client's free will above all other considerations, the intuitive counselor displays his intuitive skill conspicuously and relies on a single intensive session. He does most of the talking, providing insight and information in response to the client's acknowledged needs, within an inquiry mode. In the psychotherapeutic dialog the client does most of the talking, within a framework guided by psychological principles.

Each approach has its own domain of effectiveness. Preference of one or the other depends upon the client, the particular therapist or counselor and the issues at stake. In fact, the two can work very well together when all parties are comfortable with the three-way partnership. There were a few occasions (and there were surely more) when issues raised in an ICI reading became the main focus in a client's psychotherapy.

Other Types of Counseling

Astrologers, card readers, palmists numerologists and graphologists may have a dubious reputation as a group but the best of them can provide excellent guidance for their clients. *To do so they must rely mainly on their intuitive skills.* This is known because too little objective information is contained in their horoscopes, cards, palms, birth dates and writing samples to enable these scanty sources to serve as more than a starting point and a framework for counsel.[15*] When their intuitive skills are strong enough, these counselors may perform as effectively as expert intuitives. It matters little what modality they use or what they choose to call it, so long as their clients are not put off by it. These practitioners often do not see themselves as "intuitives" at all,. They may even deny they are using their intuition and give full credit to their chosen device, their analytical abilities and their common sense. Several CAI intuitives began their counseling careers with one or more of these approaches, but eventually dropped them when they seemed no longer necessary.

The procedure for checking out these practitioners is the same as other candidates, as discussed in the previous chapter. The odds for success may be less, but you may be lucky to find an astrologer or a similar practitioner who qualifies as an expert intuitive.

Counseling in Emergencies

CAI sometimes received requests for emergency counseling sessions: "I'm in a terrible situation and am really upset. I must see one of your intuitives as soon as possible. Can you arrange an appointment this afternoon?" Sorry, probably not.

An emergency situation presents a fine opportunity for effective counseling because the client, being desperate, is better motivated to listen to, accept and follow valid guidance. They may also be closer to a personal breakthrough. On the other hand, a crisis is often the best time for *independent* personal change, even transformation, without the intervention of someone to whom credit for the change can be attributed later. With or without help, anyone in a psychological or other crisis must work with his own inner resources when solving his problem. We are all inclined to offer help first, of course, and consider only later about the kind of help that might have been the best. Since the information most needed for a truly sensible decision is not ordinarily available when the decision must be made, each case has to be decided on its own merits, often intuitively rather than according to fixed guidelines.

While there is no set formula for how to achieve the right balance in assisting this process—aside from the broad one: compassionately!—CAI took the position that intuitive counseling serves best when it helps to prepare the ground for change rather than when it intervenes in the midst of change. Therefore, we did not plan the counseling program to provide life readings on immediate demand, and we refused almost all requests for emergency intuitive help by referring the petitioners to other counselors. In any case, we were often heavily booked so could not react quickly. Even when exceptions were made they did not appear to be helpful; they amounted to little more than hand-holding, which may have been valuable but could have been done just as well by others.

Intuitive Counseling at Work

This chapter reported on CAI's experience in conducting more than 1200 "life-path" sessions in which expert intuitives assisted individual clients in their personal growth. The readings were structured around a standard set of questions on the life purpose of the client, recommended action he could take to achieve this purpose, some related topics and elective questions he had submitted. The intuitives' answers were normally thorough, detailed and encouraging, always compassionate and occasionally profound. The complaint rate was below 1%, and half of these reversed themselves later. Many clients returned for follow-up readings.

We may conclude that intuitive counseling is a positive and effective application of intuitive skill. At its best it provides a transformative boost to clients, by encouraging them toward greater self-understanding and appropriate life-choices, suggesting solutions to individual problems and enhancing personal development generally. Intuitive counseling can be a significant factor in healing difficult life situations, especially spiritual crises, because of its capacity to work deeply and compassionately with clients.[16]

Of the several applications of intuition explored and reported in this book, intuitive counseling emerged as the most humanly significant and the most broadly applicable—that is, potentially useful for almost everyone. In this sense this experiment on counseling was the most successful of all applications attempted.

Nevertheless, this success depends strongly upon the cooperation of the client. Intuitive counseling is *not* a one-way treatment in which the client is a passive recipient of the counselor's efforts (as in most medical treatment, public services and auto repair). The client must be ready to take a step of personal change, be motivated to engage in the counseling process, and be reasonably clear about his intention. His intention is perhaps best expressed through the questions he asks, though this specific form is not always necessary. The intuitive process works at his leading edge, wherever it may be, and handles well even very sensitive matters that would normally be disturbing.

Intuitive counseling is representative of and central to the entire range of intuitive applications. It is subject to the same requirements of harmlessness, positive motivation, clear questions and expertness of the intuitives, just as for other applications. The first two conditions are satisfied implicitly by the client's self-declared interest. Because intuitive counseling involves such intimacy in the client-intuitive interaction, dealing as it does with highly personal issues, it forces these conditions to be satisfied without circumlocutions and other language difficulties that can so easily arise in other kinds of inquiries. Intuitive counseling makes strong demands upon the intuitive process, pushing to the limit its capacity to access and then communicate appropriate information for the client. Finally, the client's questions demand at least the same attention as if he were asking about non-personal matters, and the inquirer still needs to check and validate for himself all information received, before accepting and using it.

Evidence for the accuracy, relevance and practical usefulness of intuitive counseling information cannot be obtained by conventional scientific means but was otherwise abundantly evident in the testimonies received from many of the clients. Besides their personal benefits they occasionally referred to specific information in their intuitive sessions that was evidential to them or directly helpful. It may have been valuable to collect such fragments and verify them, but this would have been hard to carry out thoroughly because the subject matter of the sessions was subjective and confidential. Even when a "healing" occurred as claimed, we could not assign cause and give credit among the contributing factors: healer (intuitive), healee (client) and setting (the reading).

The intuitive form of counseling compares favorably with other forms, such as conventional psychotherapy (including psychiatry) and specialized counseling (such as for grief). It is far superior to sessions with typical psychics, astrologers and similar practitioners. It is especially effective if carried out in conjunction with psychotherapy, because it introduces substantial depth and trust, both of which qualities are usually difficult to achieve.

It was clear from this experiment that the quality and usefulness of the intuitive's answers increased directly with the seriousness, directness and clarity of the questions asked. This valuable lesson was reinforced in the other intuition applications.

> "Life is a whole journey of meeting your edge again and again. That's where you're challenged. That's where, if you're a person who wants to live, you start asking yourself questions like, 'Now, why am I so scared? What is it that I don't want to see? Why can't I go further than this?'...Sooner or later, everybody meets their edge."
>
> [Pema Chödrön[17]]

• Endnotes—Chapter 3

[1] Ryerson & Harolde, 1989.

[2] Stearn, 1967.

[3]* Date of birth was requested not for astrological purposes but to discriminate among family members having the same name and address. Two mistaken identifications actually arose before birth data was required.

[4]* Some life readings were conducted over the telephone, a practice that increased near the end of the 1980s.

[5]* Most of these readings for Japanese clients were arranged through the Comet Research Institute in Tokyo, under the direction of Mr. Minoru Kodera. He and his staff carried out the translations and all arrangements with Japanese clients.

[6]* Two of CAI's expert intuitives [PP and RL] were still (in 2002) making their own annual trips to Japan to provide life readings, lectures and training seminars for Japanese clients.

[7] Assagioli, 1965.

[8]* These "prophecies" first emerged in modern times in the readings of Edgar Cayce, and subsequently with several other intuitives. They may have had some probabilistic basis, but the events never actually occurred at the predicted dates. Their appearance from sources that proved otherwise to be so reliable and accurate raises some basic questions about the nature of intuitive prophecy.

[9] Feild, 19xx, p.. 1983.

[10] Roberts, 1988, p.160.

[11]* For published reports of past lives, see for example: Grant, 1969; Haich, 1974; Bernstein, 1956; Oliver, 1974.

[12] Smith, 1989.

[13] Vaughan, 1986.

[14] Vaughan, 1989.

[15]* This is not to say that the device used does not somehow carry some relevant information, but only that the intuitive skill of the reader is needed to interpret this information properly and relate it to what the client needs and is able to hear. For example, it is still an open question how much personal information is actually contained in an astrological birth chart (horoscope). All but a few of the dozens of the careful research studies conducted to date to uncover such information have turned out negative. Still, every generation of space research is revealing new radiative effects from the planets and the sun that may someday be shown to influence the human psyche. And, of course, the alleged "influence," if it exists, may not be physical at all.

[16] Grof & Grof, 1990.

[17] Chödrön, 1991, p. 53.

CHAPTER 4

INTUITIVE CONSULTING[1]*
INTUITION IN THE COMMERCIAL WORLD

"In the future, intuitive leadership will not be a luxury or a passing
fad; it will be at the heart of business. The underlying requirements
of efficiency, productivity and profitability will not disappear, but
the means of attaining them will no longer be the sole product of
the intellect." [Barbara Schultz[2]]

With every decade since the 1960's intuition has become more widely
acclaimed as an important and even essential aspect of creativity and decision
making in business and other functional organizations. In the United States,
Great Britain and other Western countries articles on intuition have appeared
in prominent magazines such as *Fortune, Forbes, Entrepreneur* and *The Wall
Street Journal*.[3] Training seminars in decision making, creativity, "personal
effectiveness" and intuition development have arisen at all levels of the commercial world, from sales teams and departmental managers to vice presidents
and CEOs. A few major universities have added courses on creativity and the
intuitive arts to their MBA (Master in Business Administration) curricula.[4]* Intuitive consultants to businesses are finding their services more in demand. Old jokes about "female intuition" are gradually giving way to discussion on what its male counterpart might be.

This burst of enthusiasm about intuition in organizations is all very well, yet it's quite clear from their speeches and writings that many of these outspoken leaders do not understand what intuition is, other than a vague term for their insights, smart decisions and good guesses. These insights and decisions may be highly intuitive, or they may be due to more familiar mental faculties: an active imagination, a refined reasoning ability, a subtle sensory signal or just a good memory. All these non-intuitive skills may function partially unconsciously, of course, and a lack of awareness of them does not magically transform them into intuition. Like many a scientist or artist amazed by his creative breakthroughs, it is especially easy for an excited businessman to label his accomplishment by the exotic title of "intuition," thereby defusing any serious attempt to explain how his effort led to a surprising result.

Nevertheless, the fact remains that some of these businessmen's decisions and ideas could not possibly have been obtained by rational or sensory means alone, based on the data available to them at the time.[5] Intuition must have played am essential role.

After a few words about this emerging glow on the business horizon, this chapter describes CAI's efforts to bring expert intuitives into the executive boardroom. We will then look at a few issues peculiar to the application of intuition in the business environment, followed by comments on the future of intuition in organizations.

The Changing Business Environment

Intuition is still not widely accepted or understood by the organizational-business community at large, as just noted, even though the ice has been broken by the publications and training programs mentioned above.

More and more leaders in business are realizing these days that the aggressive, hard-nosed, competitive posture of the traditional businessman does not work well, and are gradually dropping it in favor of a "softer" stance. The prime drive in the corporate world is shifting from its traditional, primary goal of "making money" to one in which profitability is seen as only one of several essential elements for success. They are realizing that financial viability is a natural and automatic byproduct when due priority is given to the welfare of human beings within and without the company, and to the responsible nurturing of society and care of the outer environment. Good business decisions require more than volumes of statistical data, market analyses and clear reasoning. Executives who measure their success only in financial terms are working contrary to the natural laws by which organizations function; they can expect obstacles to arise.

Besides these emerging pragmatic, outer changes there is also the inner one. Leaders are gradually coming to understand that good business practice involves a deeper aspect of the mind, something akin to a "gut feeling" or a "hunch," which must be allowed to function if the visioning, decisions, ideas and human interactions are to be correct, wise and effective. They are appreciating that this inner component, which we may interpret as an inner knowing or intuition, is the hidden factor that marks the difference between a successful business leader and the many who don't "make it," despite their other outstanding qualities, such as intelligence, education, confidence, reputation.[6]

The articles extolling intuition cite several personal qualities of competent leadership that are believed to be enhanced by the practice of intuition:

- holding a realistic and positive vision
- making wise decisions
- being alert to new opportunities
- generating good ideas
- maintaining a clear perspective over an overall situation
- being responsible toward the environment
- respecting regulatory social institutions
- establishing healthy relationships with clients, superiors, peers and employees.

Testimonies of businessmen about how they regard intuition in their work as managers, executives and consultants may not be as immediately convincing as those from scientists and artists, but they are abundant and enthusiastic. The accompanying box cites several recent examples.

Decision Making in the Commercial World

Why do these executives speak out so strongly about the importance of their intuitive experiences when other professionals do not? This is partly because the context in which ideas emerge and decisions are made in the corporate environment are so complex that it is almost impossible to attribute positive results to a single source: good reasoning, an outstanding memory, exceptional sensitivity, common sense—or even intuition alone. The situation is difficult to assess fully because businessmen do not ordinarily document the reasons for their decisions and actions as do scientists; thus, the bases of their claims cannot be inspected and criticized. We must accept or reject what they tell us. Without better evidence than their enthusiasm we must look elsewhere for solid support of the importance of intuition in business.

Intuition at Work in the Business Environment

- E. Douglas Dean and John Mihalasky at the New Jersey Institute of Technology spent a decade studying the relationship between executive intuition and profitability. Eighty percent of those who did well on a simple intuition test had also doubled company profits within the previous five years.[7]

- Professor Weston Agor at the University of Texas in El Paso formed the 7500-member Global Intuition Network (now headed by Jeffrey Mishlove—see the Appendix), and has written a number of books on intuitive decision making. He found in his studies that 2000 managers scored higher on intuition than those ranking lower in the organization; also that 70 top executives acknowledged privately that they were using intuition in their work.[8]

- Professor Michael Ray at the Stanford University School of Business has a long waiting list for his unusual course, "Creativity in Business," in which intuition development is a major component. In his textbook he writes, "The secret of creative decision making is deciding from your essence, particularly your intuition."[9]

- Chester Carlson, inventor of xerographic copying and founder of Xerox Corporation, believed that the information for his development of the photocopying process "came from the spirit realm."[10]

- In 1986 the International Management Institute in Geneva, Switzerland issued its report for the year 2000, which specifically called for increased training in intuition. It convened an international conference on this theme the following year.[11]

- According to John Naisbitt, author of *Megatrends*, "Another shift I see that really impresses me is a new respectability for intuition in corporate settings. In the 50s, 60s and 70s, everything was done by the numbers. Now people are willing to say, 'I just feel this is going to work.'"[12]

- Jagdish Parikh, conductor of a recent international survey and author of the book, *Intuition: The New Frontier of Management* interprets the trend this way: "The advent and availability of electronic data processing to analyze vast amounts of information [etc.] added up to a remarkable edifice of systematic knowledge in the area of business management...a highly analytical approach....During the last decade, however, there has been a growing perception that there was something incomplete about this modern paradigm....Experienced practitioners began to suggest that there might be inherent flaws in the tendency to treat the economy like a huge machine, working like clockwork."[13]

- Henry Mintzberg said, "To my mind, organizational effectiveness does not lie in that narrow-minded concept called 'rationality'; it lies in a blend of clear-headed logic *and* powerful intuition. [Society] has paid a terrible price by rejecting intuition over the course of almost a century in organizations, the study of organizations and behind that the field of psychology itself."[14]

Intuition in Government

Intuitive insights have played an important but subdued role in the U.S. government. Many leaders, even presidents, have remarked after leaving office how they relied upon their intuition at critical times.[15, 16] In recent years Washington has shown a few signs of opening up to the importance of intuition, but in this domain the wheels of change turn very slowly. It is not hard to see why. The lines of responsibility in government are well defined but long, slow and conservative. In contrast to business they are open for all to see, for government leaders are accountable and are expected to be visible examples of responsibility and respect for authority, fine qualities in themselves. Intuitive insights are not honored as a basis for decisions and are rarely cited. Personal intuitive experiences and successes with intuition may be widespread, but they tend to be kept quiet and are not openly shared.

CAI's Experiment in Intuitive Consulting

In the period 1985-89 CAI provided 24 intuitive consultations to 20 Japanese companies, varying from small family businesses to firms having thousands of employees. The contacts were provided through a large Japanese consulting company whose president had utilized CAI's services previously for both business consulting and personal counseling.[17]* He set up the appointments for us and provided a competent interpreter.

While on a visit to Washington, DC. in the mid- 1980s I visited several "closet supporters" of intuition in the U.S. government. These visits were set up by C. B. "Scott" Jones," an advisor at that time to Senator Claiborne Pell (D, RI). I was eager to learn how these government managers were using their intuition as they carried out their work and administered their departments, and especially how they related to their colleagues when intuition was involved in a decision.

They reported unanimously that they felt their insight helped them in their work, though they had little opportunity to speak out on their views and experiences or even to collaborate with one another. In the conservative government environment they were not encouraged and remained isolated as far as their intuitive activities were concerned. In fact, they felt they had to operate inconspicuously just to preserve their credibility and remain effective in their positions.

The consulting procedure was always the same. CAI's expert intuitive [CN] and this author entered each company with no prior information about its products, market, management or policies. After personal introductions to the company staff—the president or CEO and usually a few board members, vice-presidents or project directors—the meeting opened with our brief orientation on how intuition functions, what we were offering and how to make best use of the services of the intuitive. I explained that their questions should be direct and simple. It was not necessary to explain why they wanted the information they sought, what had already transpired in their thinking or planning or other background information on the topics raised.

For the next two to six hours the intuitive answered the clients' questions. Occasionally he volunteered information not specifically requested.

The accompanying box lists the most common kinds of questions asked: the range of issues and situations for which these clients sought intuitive information and advice. The following examples illustrate how the intuitive responded to particular companies.

Typical Questions Asked by Consulting Clients

- Why is a particular product (or service) not selling? What can be done to make it more successful?

- Where should we locate our new sales outlet (research center, manufacturing facility, administrative office, etc.)? Should we build or buy? When to do so?

- How can we best deal with particular government regulations: tax laws, import-export restrictions, licensing, security requirements, tax laws, etc.?

- What is the best way to market a particular new product or service? (Where to sell it and to whom, best timing, best packaging, how to present it, type of advertising, sales effort, etc.)

- How can we best cooperate with external collaborative partners such as subcontractors, ownership companies, suppliers, members of joint projects, etc.?

- Which of our current company officers would make the best next company president (and similarly for other positions and candidates)?

- How can our company accommodate to future social changes: in the national market, within the evolving international situation, in public tastes and preferences, in the labor force, in financial markets, etc.?

- How can we best work with various employee groups such as unions, women, unproductive workers, near-retirees, dissatisfied or unappreciated teams, etc.?

- What particular opportunities and challenges are coming up in the future for our company?

A nationwide green tea company. The company's questions dealt first with the status of the tea business in Japan and especially how the company should deal with confusing fluctuations in the consumer market. For each of four or five types of teas being produced, the intuitive provided information about forthcoming shifts in consumer tastes and how the competition would be responding to these changes. Also covered were: a strategy for achieving their sales goals; the best timing and location for opening a new retail store; where and when to relocate the corporate offices; some development options for management personnel; an opportunity for international expansion; how to respond to a growing market for herbal teas; and unrecognized medicinal values of certain of their tea products. Finally, he dealt with personal issues for the company President.

A diversified longshoremen company. Board Members raised a broad assortment of issues in a full-day session. The intuitive helped them determine which of three sites under consideration for major new construction would work the best for them, in view of a complex interplay of external factors. He also provided information on how the company might market a poorly positioned product they had bought in large quantity and were "stuck with." For handling labor unrest among longshoremen he offered an unusual approach involving an internal safety program. He also discussed ways to redefine the president's role within the company; some preferred locations for future branch offices; and how to procure a certain government license normally difficult to obtain.

A life insurance company. Company officers posed questions on a variety of financial, management and health issues. The intuitive indicated (in 1987) that there would be an economic recession in Japan, U.S. and Europe in 1989-91, including a dramatic drop in the value of the yen: first to 130¥ per U.S. dollar, then to 120¥ in two to three months, and in the next year to near 100¥. He described the impact of the recession on this company. He also answered several questions about a large multinational project in China in which the company was involved with the Soviet Union. He described future changes in the positions of the other project partners over the next few years and how to prepare for these changes. He also offered counsel on setting up a Life Extension Institute the company was considering as part of a long-term expansion program; the possible use of pharmaceuticals employed in Chinese medicine; and a strategy to deal with government resistance to a certain new technology for handling patients' medical records.

A kimono manufacturing company. This old family-run business was having difficulty accommodating to changes in the market for kimonos. Young Japanese women are no longer so interested in these traditional, costly items of dress; also, kimonos are now commonly made from plastic fabric instead of silk, and these require different methods of manufacture. The intuitive proposed several alternative fabric products that would soon become profitable in Japan, ideas that had not occurred to the owners. He also described how their existing products could be marketed to appeal to young Japanese women. Finally, a tricky family problem was addressed: the young daughter, soon to inherit the business from her aging parents, had a different career in mind for herself. Her disinterest and immanent departure seemed to threaten the company's survival.

A large department store. Two all-day visits with the Board of Directors of the largest retail store in Tokyo permitted the intuitive to advise on many issues in strategic planning, branch store locations, finances, personnel and topics similar to those already mentioned for other companies.

Other Japanese organizations for whom CAI consulted included three discount retail stores, a large real estate and property management company, three health food manufacturers, an Alaska fisheries firm, a biochemical research laboratory, a computer software company, an electrical appliance wholesaler and a seaweed producer.

Again, the intuitive was given no information about the company prior to the visits and little or no background information as questions were asked.

Unrequested Information

For three of the Japanese companies the intuitive provided unrequested and unexpected confidential information.

In one of the discount retail stores the intuitive described an employee who was embezzling company funds. The president recognized the embezzler from the description given, and admitted he had suspected the man but had found insufficient evidence to accuse him.

Second, the intuitive told the skeptical president of a large computer software company that his company had a secret contract with the U.S. agency NASA (the National Aeronautics and Space Administration). The president was shocked but admitted it. The contract agency was actually NSA (the National Security Agency), not NASA, but he mentioned later that NSA was routing the funding thorough NASA. He was noticeably attentive for the balance of the session and had many questions.

Third, during the meeting with the insurance company involved in a large international project, the intuitive sensed that one of the four men present at the meeting was a spy, and that the meeting room was bugged. When the meeting was over he quietly asked the company president to call him from a pay phone in the evening at his hotel, so he could speak with him further. On the way out of the building we noted that a Soviet cultural exchange office occupied the floor immediately below the meeting room. We were both a bit nervous until safely on board our flight out of Japan.

Remote Consulting

CAI received a mail request to advise the research and development laboratory of a major cosmetics company in Japan. The scientist who wrote wanted to create a line of cosmetics that were organic and "alive" instead of relying on traditional chemicals, so as to treat the skin as a living part of the human body. The CAI intuitive [JF] provided detailed descriptions of the ingredients that should be used for this purpose, and others to be avoided; also, how these ingredients should be prepared and applied to the skin. For example, he recommended that certain preparations be exposed to sunlight during manufacture. He also explained that many person's skin disorders arise from certain unsympathetic attitudes, and how one may correct these disorders through a combination of cosmetic preparations and mental exercises.

This information was sent to the client, but we received no response. She wrote us later to say that she found the suggestions fascinating and was anxious to try them out, but was not yet able to persuade her management on the novel approach. The lesson we learned here was that, when arranging intuitive applications, it is important to work with those who are not only motivated to seek the intuitive information but are also in a position to actually apply it.

Why Only Japanese Clients?

CAI was often asked: why were your consulting clients Japanese and not U.S. companies? A simple explanation would be that CAI's connections arose through our fortuitous Japanese contact, as mentioned above. However, the real reason lies behind this good fortune. Two factors seem to be key.

First, unlike U.S. companies, Japanese firms tend to function "top down"; that is, they operate with a strong base of authority from the company president.[18*] Japanese management staff tend to listen well to their staff and employees, but the final decisions come from the top. The president's directives are accepted and followed to the letter. Thus, if he decides to call in an intuitive consultant, his board can be expected to politely accept his decision as "a fine idea." This typical Japanese attitude toward its leaders has a long tradition.

Western management functions differently. The American CEO still has the ultimate authority, of course, but he relies much more heavily on the support and agreement of his management staff. Relations tend to be more openly interactive, candid and outspoken. The game is more one of persuasion and argument than patient, polite discussion and unquestioned authority. A typical CEO who proposed to hire an intuitive consultant would probably be confronted, perhaps ridiculed, by his colleagues, though he might quietly arrange a private session for himself. (Indeed, CAI provided several such combined counseling-consulting sessions for individual executives.)

The second reason for "Why Japan?" lies closer to the intuitive process itself. The Japanese have the tradition of being a very intuitive people, meaning, in comparison with Westerners, they tend to rely on their inner sense of matters more than their intellect. In ordinary relationships they are not so inclined to provide reasons for their choices or to defend them. If reasons are offered they are often only the polite ones, not even correct, and the listener understands this. In Japanese business meetings a kind of "group intuition" is the norm. (I have watched this process in a dozen technical meetings.) When individuals offer their ideas and insights they tend to present them to the group deferentially, so they appear to emerge naturally out of the discussion as collective creations. I never observed anyone seek personal credit or be praised for his contribution.

There is also a long-standing tradition in Japan to honor leaders who have strong intuitive insight, without demanding reasons and arguments. This characteristic can be seen in the high respect given her wisest leaders and visionaries, along with a tolerant acceptance of seers and fortune tellers. While a Japanese businessman would not normally seek sidewalk counsel under any name, he is quietly tolerant of such practices—"they might be right"—and remains respectful of their place within his cultural tradition. From a Western perspective we would say that the Japanese are credulous, but this is an unfair and excessively broad judgment.

In Japanese business meetings the participants' remarks tend to be brief, modest and slowly spoken, typically interspersed with long silences. In contrast, the American is accustomed to the more pushy practice in which participants compete for talk time and seek to advance their own views persuasively, not always listening so well to their colleagues. Western businessmen attending Japanese meetings are often surprised at this polite "listening" mode, and become impatient at the slow rate at which agreements are reached.

I am told that the scene painted above is not as widespread nowadays as it was a generation ago, or even in the 1980s when CAI's visits took place. Western modes of group interaction have been invading Japanese business practices over recent decades and are gradually being incorporated.

Corroboration

An intuitive consultant can expect few opportunities to verify intuitive business information for himself because he does not normally have access to company records and the full context of his consultation. In any case, company matters are normally held private. Also, because consulting information is so complex and advisory rather than factual, it is difficult by its nature to assess fairly its accuracy and value. The client's expression of satisfaction, for whatever it is worth, is usually the only measure of success.

In CAI's consulting work we knew at the start rather little about Japanese society, its business world and its economy. We could not tell if some of the intuitive's statements (especially the predictions) might not have been reasonably anticipated by our hosts. In fact, they might have already known the answers to some of their questions and were just testing the intuitive. We were not in a position to detect such testing, to follow up on information to confirm its accuracy or even to verify that predicted events occurred.

In spite of these limitations the company representatives often corroborated before the meeting was over several factual portions of the intuitive information. Also, we were able to confirm later a few fragments of predictive and precautionary information from news reports from Japan and from return visits to a four of the companies. For example, the intuitive's statement about the declining value of the yen (mentioned above) surprised our hosts and us when it was given, but it proved later to be correct.

Even though most of the intuitive information given these twenty four clients could not be verified, no portion of it was revealed later to be was downright wrong. Perhaps most significant, in all but two visits the company officials said they were satisfied and pleased with the information they received. The first exception was a hostile company president who asked very few questions and gave no response at all to the intuitive's counsel. The second, the president of a large Alaskan fishing concern, utilized the visit to give us a 90-minute lecture on his company but he asked no questions at all. There was apparently a misunderstanding about the purpose of our visit.

The expert intuitive [CN] who performed all CAI business consulting in Japan had prior past experience in his own small U.S. business, and had consulted for U.S. companies on his own, apart from CAI One might claim he was relying on his previous, non-intuitive familiarity with the commercial world as he providing new information, perhaps in ways that were not apparent to anyone else or even to himself. Having witnessed his performance in all sessions, I can attest that his background may have helped him a little, but only very little. At best it allowed him to be more at ease and acceptable to his hosts. He had never been to Japan before our first consulting trip, and he knew virtually nothing of Japanese language, culture or business activities, no more than what anyone might pick up casually from Western newspapers or television. Finally, it would be ridiculous to presume that he was familiar with the specific issues raised by the officials in these several Japanese companies.

Intuitive Consultants Speak

This intuitive [CN] offers the following comments about his intuitive consulting.[19]

> Usually there is an individual…in the company who has a certain resonance with intuition, creativity, psychic phenomena or spiritual ideas…one who feels I might be able to offer insights into or even solutions to problems his or her company is facing—problems for which conventional approaches may not have been too successful.

> Occasionally I walk into a board room realizing that, initially, only my contact person will be receptive to what I have to say and that other board members are skeptical or downright hostile. However, their reactions don't concern me much. I simply focus on the task before me.…Usually it doesn't take long for everyone to become curious, especially when they hear information from me that I couldn't possibly have known beforehand or that confirms their own private thoughts, which for whatever reasons they

hadn't dared to air themselves....The encounter is not merely mind to mind, but primarily heart to heart....No one leaves the boardroom quite the same.

My intuitive responses to whatever problems are presented to me all spring from the same source. This guarantees that my answers...are not merely local but also global. For this reason I refuse to consult on matters I feel are at odds with the welfare of people and the environment in general.

Meliton V. Salazar, once Executive Vice President of a large appliance company in the Philippines and now Professor at the Asian Institute of Management, tells the following story. He had called a meeting of his department managers to take place at noon. One hour before the meeting, he suddenly asked his secretary to cancel it. He could give no rational explanation for his decision; he only had a sudden urge to go home and eat lunch there, although he had earlier called his wife to tell her he would not be home. Before he left the company premises, he passed by the office of the Medical Director, and asked him to have lunch with him at home.

When they reached the executive's home they found his wife sprawled unconscious near the kitchen in a pool of blood. She had had a miscarriage. The doctor quickly administered first aid to her, declaring afterwards: "If we had been late even for a minute, your wife would have been dead for loss of blood."[20]

Another CAI expert intuitive [PP], who has consulted with businesses on her own, describes her work this way:

My work incorporates yet goes beyond normal psychological perspectives, to address the causes and possible solutions to everyday problems. The information comes from the combined superconscious minds of counselor and client, using heightened intuitive perception resulting from empathy and 'conscious communion.'

In business, the process of direct knowing can shed light on the underlying unconscious agendas interfering with success, help define the most comprehensive, accurate and current vision statement, and assess prospective business partnerships. It can also identify trends in pertinent markets, pinpoint timing, project sales figures and create and double-check strategies. Since 1977 I have been collaborating in this way with many leading professionals, executives, scientists and government officials.

Possible Abuses

The practice of intuition, like any powerful competence, opens up opportunities for abuse. If we project into the future when hundreds of company staff and employees may be trained to develop and use their intuitive skills, the risk appears to increase because a single instance of misuse could be very damaging in an environment which relies so heavily upon openness and trust. Any of the following misapplications of intuition might occur:

- spying on management for the purpose of blackmail or other personal advantage
- obtaining "insider" information about investments, coming price changes or stock sales • gathering information about other companies to gain a competitive advantage[21]*
- discovering opportunities for sabotage or embezzlement
- collecting valuable technical information to sell to competing companies

It appears that these offenses could be committed either by a member of the management staff or by an employee, for personal gain or to benefit the company itself, within or between companies, and in behalf of one's own nation or a foreign government.

Of course, ethical issues such as these arise with the development of *any* powerful personal skill, not just intuition. Such potential abuses as these come not from intuition itself but from how the intruder chooses to apply it.

A strong intuitive sits in a position of invisible personal power. If he is able to use his intuitive skill for malicious purposes at all (and there is a question about this—see end of Chapter 14), he is in a position to gather confidential information and then apply it in a manipulative manner. Such an intrusion leaves no trace, so he cannot be directly identified, apprehended, accused and convicted. In some situations the offense may go unnoticed until long after the damage is done. The risk may be small, but the possibility may induce companies to adopt special safeguards to protect their interests, just as they do today to counter thievery, embezzlement and more serious security violations.

Fortunately, the attitudes and practices required to develop intuitive skill make it difficult to maintain an unethical posture as one's capability improves. The limits of intuition's natural self-protection against harmful application are not known. Many novels, movies, legends and even respected historical reports create the impression that intuitively skilled but badly intentioned persons can use their intuitive skills to harm others. These accounts are entertaining but I know of none that is factual and fully believable. It may even turn out that the conjectured offenses using intuition are simply impossible. Until this issue is resolved, caution must be observed.

Intuition in the Commercial World

Business has proven to a valuable test ground for intuition. It is a domain of human activity in which one *must* operate intuitively to be successful, yet the businessman, unlike the psychotherapist and the archeologist, is in a conspicuous and respected power position in his society. He manipulates needed goods and services, and especially money, the medium by which the value of so many things (surely too many things!) are measured. His work is inherently practical. He has much freedom to do his job in his own way with a minimum of external constraints. He is rewarded for making crucial actions actually happen, utilizing his ambition, will, authority and material resources. The successful businessman also has high credibility in his society: others listen to him when he speaks. When he acknowledges that his intuition has been helpful to him, his listeners tend to believe him more than they might believe most persons.

What can the development and practice of intuition do for the modern company? We may identify four specific areas of benefit:

- Intuition can provide a strong impetus to *creativity*, both in the research laboratory and also in the generation of new business ideas, the development of broader perspectives on important issues, the recognition of new business opportunities and the creation of novel solutions to specific business problems.
- Intuition can aid individual and group *decision making*, by clarifying available options, indicating the consequences of various choices, identifying the proper timing of critical actions and making the actual decisions.
- Intuition can be utilized to obtain specific technical, economic and procedural *information,* by means of focused inquiries to assist scientific

and market studies and to learn more about the social and environmental context in which the company is operating.

- Finally, the personal development of intuition by executives, staff and employees can have a significant impact on the *operation* of the company, because it leads to positive changes in individual lifestyle, in attitudes toward work and career and in relationships among workers. As a result a company under intuitive direction and operation will tend to be less driven by competition, financial gain and security issues, and more by cooperation, harmony and collective understanding.

Here are three ways in which company leadership (administrators, executives, responsible officers) may accomplish this shift of direction:

(1) They may develop and utilize their own intuitive skills. This is certainly the most effective effort, since it requires personal participation and automatically supports whatever else is done.

(2) They may bring in expert intuitives from outside the company, as exemplified by the consulting work described in this chapter.

(3) They may inaugurate internal programs to encourage staff members and employees to expand their individual intuitive capacities—perhaps first for a few promising individuals, then for working teams and departments, and later for the entire staff. Incentives and rewards can be set up to encourage individual interest and accomplishment.

When we translate these actions from the company as a whole down to the level of the individual leader, we can see that his challenge is:

- to discover and acknowledge the role played by intuition in his own life, so he may become more aware of how it functions;
- to take deliberate steps to enhance his own intuitive capacity, so it may function more strongly and reliably;
- to learn how expert intuitives can assist him, both personally and for his company; and
- to work out the best balance between his own developing intuition and his already well practiced and trusted intellectual faculty.

Several analysts have already predicted that both business management and industrial research will be significantly enhanced in the future by a wave of widespread acknowledgment, development and utilization of intuition.[22]

Summary

The several examples of consultations sketched in this chapter demonstrate that an expert intuitive can assist various types of businesses significantly on a broad range of issues, situations and specific topics. There is every reason to believe that other types of organizations—in other countries and for many kinds of issues—could benefit similarly: trade unions, professional groups, political parties, private clubs, foundations, philanthropic institutions, governmental bodies and even religious organizations.

Reliance on intuitive resources within and without companies is now expanding throughout the world, and will very likely continue to do so over the next few decades. Intuitive consulting has been well tested within the business environment and found to be not only possible but practical and helpful. The benefits begin with useful factual information and sound advice affecting important decisions. They continue with innovative ideas and new viewpoints. Finally, they include implicit encouragement to all parties involved to develop, practice and rely upon intuitive resources in the future. These benefits apply to executives, managers and workers, both those who are utilizing their own intuition and those who choose to rely on the services of expert intuitives.

There are no known obstacles to accessing needed intuitive information for commercial purposes so long as the four conditions stated in Chapter 1 (and refined in Chapter 14) are satisfied. When an expert intuitive consultant offers his services he should present the credible image expected in the business world, but no special familiarity with business language, customs and practices is necessary. Hindrances from the client's side such as skepticism, poor questioning and unrealistic expectations seem to be dealt with easily.

Finally, I would like to emphasize that, while we at CAI were pleased with the benefits we were able to bring to our client companies, our goal was not merely to enable them to make more money or to make money for ourselves. As in CAI's other programs, we functioned as a non-profit organization; our purpose was research and education. We sought to demonstrate convincingly the value and potential of intuition to an ever wider audience of persons, especially those in leadership and power positions in society.

Moreover, our effort focused not so much on the companies as commercial entities as the individuals with whom we interacted. We know that at least some of them benefited personally from the eye-opening performance in which they participated, and which they would probably never have chosen to attend outside of their work environment. Some of them held influential positions in the larger Japanese business world, so their positive impressions of the intuitive consulting session may have spread beyond their own companies. This involvement with individuals was for CAI a much more satisfying outcome than the financial returns.

> "Managers skilled in the use of intuition tend to possess particular decision-making skills that most people lack. Specifically, these managers have a sense of vision of what is coming and how to move their organization in response to that vision. They are particularly adept at generating new ideas and in providing ingenious solutions to old problems. They also function best in crises or situations of rapid change." [E. Zehnder[23]]

• Endnotes—Chapter 4

1[*] Portions of this chapter have been adapted from a preliminary version published in 1996 in the Korean journal Create.

2 Schultz, 1995.

3 See, for example, Cook, 1984.

4[*] The program at Stanford University, conducted by Michael Ray, is perhaps best known. See his book, Ray & Myers, 1986.

5 Weber, 1992, Brown, 1977, Rowan, 1986, Pondy, 1984,; Mihalasky, 1976.

6 Schultz, 1995.

7 Dean, 1974, Schroeder & Ostrander, 1974.

8 See, for example, Agor, 1989; Agor, 1986, p. 9.

9 Ray and Myers, 1986.

10 Berger, 1991, p. 61.

11 Schultz, 1995

12 Naisbitt, 1994.

13 Parikh, 1994. pp. 11-12.

14 Mintzberg, 1994.

15 Friedman, 1995; see also accompanying articles on intuition in government.

16 Friedman, 1995.

[17*] CAI is pleased once again to acknowledge its indebtedness to Mr. Yukio Funai, President of Funai Consulting Company in Osaka and Tokyo, Japan, for his introductions to these Japanese companies and for providing a interpreter and other assistance.

[18*] I learned about these features of Japanese companies through several years of technical, non-CAI consultation with three Japanese computer firms: Hitachi, Fujitsu and the research laboratory of NTT, the Japanese Telephone Company.

[19] Feuerstein, 1993, Sullivan, 1992.

[20] Licauco, 1991.

[21*] If the principle of harmlessness is literally valid, such spying would be limited by the wishes of those spied upon, which would have to be respected. It is not clear at this point whether and how this principle applies to organizations.

[22] Rowan, 1986.; Parikh, 1994, Schultz,1995, Agor, 1989.

[23] Zehnder, 1987.

CHAPTER 5

THE INTUITIVE SLEUTH
LOCATING BURIED AND LOST OBJECTS AND MISSING PERSONS

"For seven years I have been doing this [locating mineral deposits] and nobody knows anything about it....Big businesses are beginning to listen to people who think they can deliver something with their sixth sense." [Uri Geller[1]]

An attractive candidate area for intuitive application is the task of finding an object or person that is buried, lost, stolen, missing or otherwise hidden from the seeker's awareness. The motivation for conducting such inquiries would appear to be positive, since there is almost always a legitimate need to find whatever is lost or hidden. The task is specific and well defined. The recovery automatically verifies the intuitive information.

CAI conducted several such inquiry projects in the 1980s, most of them to assist individuals or organizations who were seeking help after they had exhausted other means of locating what they were seeking. A few of these clients were prepared to conduct a major search effort if they could obtain sufficiently definitive information.

These searches can be grouped into three classes according to what was being sought: lost objects and people, oil and minerals and archeological items. Each category had its own peculiarities and each taught its own lessons about how best to apply intuition to find things whose location is initially unknown. There were indeed a few surprises.

Other persons and institutions besides CAI have carried out intuitively aided searches in the past, both before and after our own. This chapter includes mention of some of their attempts.

The Search for Lost Objects and People

Requests for assistance in locating lost objects and missing people are usually more personal, and are therefore more clearly motivated, than commercial endeavors and academic searches. All but one of CAI's attempts utilized a single expert intuitive. Most led to actually finding the object or person sought, but sometimes both CAI and the client had to modify their notion of what constituted "success" in the search. Still, almost all were beneficial in their own way.

In most cases the intuitive provided directly the location of the lost object, and it was recovered without difficulty. A lost ring was found in the back of a drawer, for example, and a missing briefcase was located. In others the intuitive located the lost object, but it had been damaged, destroyed or otherwise made inaccessible. Occasionally the intuitive information was

One evening I accidentally left my briefcase in a parking lot, and by the time I came back it had disappeared. I asked three intuitives to help me recover it. Two from CAI agreed independently that the police had picked it up along with a criminal suspect, and it was being held in the "evidence room" of the local police station. I tried to retrieve it from the police, but they refused to cooperate on the basis of what they considered merely "psychic speculation." In fact, they were suspicious that I might have had something to do with the crime. So I was not able to recover my briefcase, and could not even verify the intuitive information.

Most interesting, though, the third intuitive, not on the CAI staff, gave a detailed but different description. She said the briefcase was in the trunk of an old car which was parked on the San Francisco waterfront. She described the car and the nearby buildings. I could not act on such meager information, and was in any case doubtful of it. Several weeks later an out-of-town stranger called to tell me he had found my briefcase: someone had put it into the trunk of his car, he said. I was naturally delighted and agreed to meet him at a parking lot next to his work—on the San Francisco waterfront!

We met as planned. The local buildings and car matched the intuitive's description. He opened his trunk and gave me the briefcase—but it wasn't mine! It belonged to a business colleague who did not know about my loss and had not mentioned his own loss to me. The only identification information inside it was one of my business cards. My colleague was pleased to get his briefcase back, but as for my mine —well, it may still be in the evidence room of the Palo Alto Police Department.

disregarded by the client, despite his initial interest, so there was no way to check the accuracy of the information. In a few cases the intuitive gave an explanation of what had happened to the missing object or person, and then offered the inquirer a choice: to receive more information about its location so it could be recovered, or to reconsider if it might not be better if the object were *not* found. In one case the request was refused by the intuitive with the explanation that more harm than good would result if the object or person were retrieved. Let's look at three of these problematic cases.

A retired San Francisco violinist sought to recover her valuable violin, which had been stolen from the trunk of her car.[2*] She was informed by the expert intuitive [JF] that it had passed through several hands, one in Ohio, and had finally come into the possession of a promising young girl student in New York, who knew nothing of its origin. The intuitive reminded the violinist that she had already turned down earlier opportunities to let her instrument pass into younger hands. (She confirmed this.) He offered to provide additional information to help her track down the missing instrument, but asked her to consider first if she might now be ready to give up the instrument. She deliberated for a week and finally chose to surrender the prized violin, collect the insurance and use her "picnic" violin for teaching. She visited CAI a year later to thank us, and explained how her whole life began to change positively after this decision.

Two "lost" people were handled similarly. The concerned mother of a missing 17-year-old girl was assured that her daughter was safe. The intuitive [JF] said she had run away with a man and gave details: the city in which they were staying, the kind of car they were driving and part of its license plate number. He then offered the mother details if she wanted them, but suggested a delay to give her time to consider if perhaps it wasn't time for the girl to leave home on her own, and to let her go. The mother balked but accepted this counsel. The daughter called in a few weeks later, as the intuitive had predicted, to say she would be visiting her parents soon. She confirmed the information about the car and her location.

In another case the expert intuitive [LH] provided directions about how to find a missing five-year-old girl in Eugene, Oregon; the police had no clues. She said the girl was kidnapped by a young man and hidden in a local cave: "She is scared, but alive." She described the man's physical features and his car. She gave directions to the area of the cave, naming the villages, road junctions and a rail crossing through several miles of country roads, so I was able to follow the route easily on a map hidden on my lap. Her description stopped one-half mile before the cave with the words, "The parents will know how to find the particular location." I typed up the intuitive information and sent copies to the Eugene police and the girl's parents.

A Treasure Hunt

CAI was asked to assist in an organized search for a cache of gold bars, which legend said lay buried in the ground on a U.S. Army base at Fort Huachuca, Arizona. We agreed to consult on the endeavor. This search occurred in 1975, in the early days of our experiments with intuition, before we had a full staff of expert intuitives and had developed an effective method of inquiry. The search team never found the treasure but we learned important lessons from the effort.

I met with the technical leader of the team and we prepared a rough map of the search area, choosing a few distinctive features to serve as reference marks. I took the map to nine intuitives of differing capabilities, and posed to each of them the key question about the location of the treasure. Eight said that the bars were indeed there, hidden in an underground cavern. They agreed with one other on the approximate depth of the cache and its location to within about 30 feet, relative to the chosen reference marks. Two of them described how the gold came to be buried there, and their stories were the same. Three mentioned that the motives of the searchers were not as benign as claimed, since they really wanted the gold for themselves, with no intention to return it to those who would be considered its rightful owners. Two intuitives said without being asked that the project to find the gold would not succeed; arguments would arise among the team members, leading to delays and expiration of the Army's search permit.

This intuitive information was passed on to the team leader. Despite the warning, the search effort proceeded just as these two intuitives had predicted: after a week of searching a disagreement arose on how to proceed; this caused a delay and the team had to leave the site before significant digging could begin. The gold may still be there. We were left with very little confirmation of the consensual portion of intuitive information, but also no reason to doubt it.

> This early experience showed that an intuitive inquiry for assisting an anticipated search should cover not only the factual information needed to make a discovery, but also the capabilities, motives and intentions of the search participants, as well as the consequences which would follow from a successful discovery. It also taught us the importance of working only with *expert* intuitives. These lessons were helpful in later years as CAI assisted in other searches for lost objects and missing people (see text). We never again chose to take part in a treasure hunt, despite a number of invitations to do so.

Obstacles arose, however. Triggered by the local publicity on the case, dozens of amateur astrologers, psychics and dreamers had bombarded the police with conflicting information about how to find the missing child. The police had no way to assess which of these dozens of messages might be helpful, and there were too many to investigate individually, so they disregarded all of them, including CAI's. I was passing through Oregon ten days later and stopped in Eugene to check out the local geography, and perhaps find the girl myself. There were indeed caves in the target area named by the intuitive, but they were on private property. It seemed unlikely that I could arrange a search warrant on the basis of the intuitive information. I visited the parents and found them confused, still in shock and dealing with marital problems, with the result that they had taken no action. The girl's body was found a few weeks later in a nearby river.

Several famous psychics have successful finds to their credit: Peter Hurkos, Jeanne Dixon and Kathlyn Rhea, for example. Parapsychologist Jeffrey Mishlove has documented many practical applications of psychic abilities. One interesting case that he researched and verified involved an elderly man who had disappeared from a California campsite.[3] A two-week search by 300 persons failed to find him. Six months later the man's wife, still unable to collect his death benefit, called on Kathlyn Rhea, a psychic who has an excellent record in working on more than 100 police cases. Rhea described what had happened to him: he had wandered off, become confused and had a stroke. She indicated that his body lay behind a bush near a path to a certain small cottage. The sheriff recognized her description of the site, walked there directly and found the body.

"Another case involving Kathlyn Rhea, which I have personally verified, involved the murder of an Ohio woman," writes Mishlove.

"Rhea provided...a detailed description of where the body could be found....The detective visited a site where he thought the body might be found and was not successful....He provided Rhea's description to the police. Simultaneously, some local Boy Scouts uncovered the body at another location which matched Rhea's description in major details. The sheriff's department, which had assumed jurisdiction over the case, took note that an accurate description of the body's condition and location had been turned in by the detective prior to the body's discovery. They detained him as a suspect....Additional information...from Rhea was that the local police chief had actually committed the murder. Rhea suggested that fibers from the victim's clothing would be found in his police cruiser. Acting on this tip, investigators searched the car and did find the fibers. The police chief was convicted of the murder and is now serving time in prison."[4]

Several detectives and other criminal investigators have gained a reputation for solving crimes through hunches that appear to go well beyond rational analysis and critical thinking, but it is difficult to distinguish the source of their ideas as intuitive or otherwise. However, psychics such as Kathleen Rhea have a outstanding track record of successes in intuitive sleuthing, and this leaves no doubt that such an intuitive application is possible when the conditions, not fully known, are right.

Oil and Mineral Exploration

For centuries individuals called "dowsers" have been locating underground water for customers wishing to drill wells. Several well-drilling companies work regularly with dowsing consultants to assist them in their choice of good drill sites. Data that would verify that their successes occurred by a special mental ability rather than by foreknowledge or chance (water exists almost everywhere if you drill deep enough) are not abundant, but there are enough to provide solid evidence that dowsing actually occurs. Henry Gross, perhaps America's most famous dowser, has an excellent record of success, not only for water but also for minerals, oil and even lost people.[5] Like several others he dowses on a map as well as in the field. Soviet scientists have also reported similar successes with what they call the "biophysical effect."[6]

Many of these dowsing efforts are fine examples of intuition at work. One cannot explain these successes by claiming that the forked wooden stick or a metal rod, as ordinarily used by dowsers, is somehow picking up electric or magnetic fields around the water or minerals, as suggested by some investigators. Successful map dowsing with a pendulum, in an area new to the dowser, can be explained only as an intuitive act.

Scientific exploration for oil, gas and mineral resources is financially risky because they are very expensive, yet scientific knowledge about the complex crust of the earth is too incomplete for exploration companies to know for certain where to drill or dig, how deep to go and what they can expect to find there. On the other hand, the financial payoff from locating a new oil or gas field or a large mineral deposit can be huge. These companies are willing to conduct risky speculative experiments in spite of the high cost.

Intuitive information can be very helpful in such circumstances. It is difficult for outsiders to know what is going

I once gave a lecture to the local chapter of the American Society of Dowsers on the role of intuition in finding lost and hidden objects. It was an open-minded and jolly group. They asked many questions and were eager to share their own experiences at discovery, some of which were very amazing. It was clear that the practice of dowsing, as I had learned about it years earlier, had advanced far beyond the use of forked sticks to find underground water. These folks were locating oil and minerals, dowsing on maps and even diagnosing disease in ill people, with at least partial success. Outwardly they attributed their accomplishments to the devices they were using—rods, pendulums, etc.—and gave credit to them in glowing terms, but this seemed to be a polite cover for what they saw with pride as their own "gift."

Some were defensive about this notion of intuition. It seemed they preferred to regard their abilities as a kind of personal magic about which one should not inquire too closely or try to "explain" in familiar terms. I had seen this same reaction in several scientists, both by their writings and known personally. They had made unusually insightful discoveries, obviously through intuition, but were reluctant to examine the source of their new knowledge. They didn't want me or anyone else to suggest how they had have made their breakthroughs.

on within these companies, since they operate privately and competitively and are not eager to reveal the methods they employ to select good sites. Nor do they reveal how their experiments have worked, so the records of successes and failures in intuitive exploration for oil, gas and minerals are not public. Even when all the facts are known the successes are not necessarily evidential of intuition, because it is so hard for one to know to what extent scientific field data were used as well. A successful oil or mineral discovery is sometimes just a lucky hit.

Nevertheless, a few persons inside the industry acknowledge unofficially that several exploration companies have quietly but successfully employed dowsers, "professional psychics" and other intuitive individuals to assist them in locating natural resources. According to the testimonies of a few of the intuitive consultants, they were chosen because they had a fine track record on simpler dowsing tasks, such as finding well water or buried pipes. The companies hired them to augment the interpretative work of geophysical experts who analyze the engineering field data. Not all attempts with intuitive consultants have been successful, but there have been enough successes to justify the consulting arrangements. They're not talking much about it, so we don't know just how "expert" were their intuitives, or to what extent the intuitive information was crucial to the final choice of the site.

An effort in oil exploration was carried out by a team that relied on the renowned channel Edgar Cayce, for the purpose of raising money for a hospital. The effort failed despite persistent effort.[7] The explanation provided later through Cayce's channeling indicated that the exploration team was unsuccessful because it was not strongly enough committed to its acclaimed purpose. The joint effort would have collapsed later.

Uri Geller, famous for his psychokinetic and clairvoyant demonstrations, both on the stage and in the laboratory, reports that he has worked successfully for several mineral prospecting companies. (Note his quoted comment at the beginning of this chapter.) He also claims considerable success with a number of oil companies, though "they do not want their names to be linked to the psychic, to the paranormal."[8]

A few published reports of prospecting sessions provided by Cayce and other intuitives reveal that the questions asked were typically ambiguous and not specific, and the answers received were equally vague. It's not obvious that this deficiency was responsible for their failure, but it certainly confused and retarded the effort. Perhaps the poor questioning was itself a reflection of the lack of a suitable commitment by the searchers.

CAI turned down two requests to participate in intuitive oil exploration, mainly because we were not comfortable with the limited capabilities and questionable motives of the entrepreneurs. Both found help elsewhere and later failed.

Archeological Exploration

Archeology would appear to be another excellent area for intuitive experiments. The motives for archeological searches are usually unselfish, academic and non-commercial. Unlike most areas of science the information being sought is simple, specific and directly verifiable. Under appropriate questioning the intuitive simply tells the archeologist where to dig, how deep to go and what will be found there, or where in libraries or old museum basements he ought to look to find the desired item. He needs only to follow these instructions, corroborating the information as he goes.

The record of successes in intuitive archeology is quite good. There exist at least ten documented reports over the past century in which intuitives provided the specific information needed for discovery, and for which subsequent exploration proved them correct. In all but one of these cases the intuitives themselves were not archeologists or specialists, and it may be safely assumed from the circumstances that they had no significant prior knowledge that could have given them essential clues. In some cases the objects discovered were so unusual that they could not have been expected from reasoned analysis or even informed guessing. These successes are summarized in the accompanying box. Taken together, they provide a convincing demonstration of the possibilities of intuitive archeology. Still, most intuitive discoveries in archeology were limited to modest, poorly funded efforts on home territory, and they involved only a single intuitive.

In the 1970s CAI participated as an informal intuitive consultant to an exploration team that was attempting to find unknown passages around the Sphinx at the Giza plateau in Egypt. Three intuitives reasserted what Edgar Cayce and other modern psychics had stated a few decades earlier, namely, that there exists an underground tunnel running northwest from the front paw of the Sphinx toward the Great Pyramid and that it leads to a "Chamber of Records" where important discoveries could be made.[9*] (It is possible that some of them already knew about Cayce's statements.) However, they claimed that (1) the tunnel extends from the *left* paw, not the right as Cayce had said (perhaps he was looking from the opposite angle); (2) the tunnel is not empty but filled with debris; (3) it extends not in a straight line to the pyramid, but leaves the body of the Sphinx at a right angle, then bends northward after 200 feet or so; and (4) the planned effort to find the tunnel from the Sphinx and the Chamber would not succeed. Two of them went on to explain that while the Chamber of Records exists, the records in it would be misunderstood and not properly cared for if they were discovered at the time of the exploration. They said it would be many years before it would be discovered.

Discoveries in Intuitive Archeology

Here are brief summaries of a few of the best documented cases in which intuitives assisted archeological research.

- Frederick Bligh Bond, a British amateur archeologist responsible for the excavation of Glastonbury Abbey, the first Christian church in England, was directed by psychic John Bartlett to the exact location of the "Edgar Chapel" and other archeological features at the site. Bartlett's descriptions were precise, and excavations proved him correct.[10]

- Stefan Ossowiecki, a Polish psychic, provided detailed and precise descriptions, later verified, of ancient artifacts, in a long series of carefully controlled experiments spanning the four-year period 1941-45. His examiners included a team of professors from the University of Warsaw[11].

- The late Professor J. Norman Emerson, then Head of the Department of Archeology at the University of Toronto, employed psychic George McMullen to locate various buried Indian objects in Ontario.[12]

- Anthropologist Dr. David E. Jones conducted several psychometric and cultural reconstruction experiments in psychic archeology in the Southeast U.S. and Mexico in the 1970s. Some of his findings were evidential. He worked with four intuitives.[13]

- Jeffrey Goodman, working with intuitive Aron Abrahamsen [AA], was directed to a specific remote piece of land near Flagstaff, Arizona, and told what he would find if he dug there. Following this counsel, Goodman subsequently excavated at various levels a large number of artifacts dating back 30,000 years, just as Abrahamsen had predicted.[14]

- Writer Christopher Bird reports that a Russian anthropologist Pushnikov has successfully used psychic dowsers to probe the remains of the Borodin battlefield, where Russia battled Napoleon in 1812..[15]

- Stephen Schwartz conducted underwater explorations near Catalina Island west of Los Angeles. Working with psychic Alan Vaughan and remote viewer Hella Hammid, he was directed in 1987 to the discovery of the wreck of a merchant brig that had sunk in the early nineteenth century. It was three feet below the sea bottom, with only one small part sticking out of the sand.[16] Schwartz conducted other intuitively based explorations near Alexandria in Egypt[17]

The 1977 exploration team from SRI International (Stanford Research Institute), in cooperation with Ain Shams University and the Egyptian Department of Antiquities, was adequately funded and technologically equipped with various devices: magnetometer, underground radar device, ground resistivity meters, acoustical sounders and a bore-hole camera.[18] They surveyed the underground area around the Sphinx, using various instruments as were appropriate. They detected weak anomalies just to the left of the left front paw, in front of both paws and at the very rear. (The team's findings in and around the Chefren pyramid and at other sites in Egypt were more successful.) A year later (1978) they drilled two test holes under the *right* paw but found no cavities or tunnels.[19] Subsequent explorations around the Sphinx in 1987, 1991, 1992 and 1996 by other explorers, using similar technology, found evidence of small irregularities but no open underground cavities.[20] These surveys were repeatedly compromised by cracks and natural discontinuities in the rocks, and must be judged as largely incomplete and inconclusive. While a small part of the intuitive information was confirmed, and some of it now seems unlikely, but the search cannot be said to be finished.

CAI's intuitive inquiries about undiscovered chambers within the Great (Khufu) Pyramid at Giza were encouraging, though little opportunity arose to explore these monuments. A quick survey around the Great Pyramid detected no passage entering from the Sphinx, though if filled with debris is could have been missed. Two intuitives said that an undiscovered room could be found near the Queen's Chamber, one of the four known room-like spaces inside of the Great Pyramid. The SRI team found a slight anomaly near this chamber in 1977, and French and Japanese explorations reported in 1986-87 that they had located a cavity off the horizontal passageway leading to the Queen's Chamber and not far from it. Drilling through the wall confirmed an abnormality filled with sand. Again, these discoveries lend a little support to the statements of the CAI intuitives. One intuitive [LH] said further that another chamber can be found above and to one side of the King's Chamber, but no such space has yet been searched for systematically or found. It will be interesting to see what future explorations of these monuments reveal.

Despite the success and promise of intuitive archeology there are practical problems. One is that major archeological explorations must be carefully planned and formally approved by sponsoring foundations, professional bodies, landowners and foreign governments and institutions before an actual expedition can be undertaken. A major exploration is risky, expensive to carry out and must compete for limited research funds.

There is also an ethical issue as to whether the past should not be left alone, out of respect for those who have lived before and for their beliefs about what is sacred, or because recovered objects cannot always be preserved properly, despite the searchers' intentions and the best technological means. (Recall the damage done to the Dead Sea Scrolls after their discovery, for example.) This issue is familiar to archeologists and historians but in the absence of a higher authority they continue to probe into the past.

Further, while cooperating intuitives could surely make a great difference in the success of these operations, not everyone on the team is likely to believe so Some members may be openly hostile to the idea. Professionalism and rigid adherence to scientific standards are important to archeologists. This position leaves little room for reliance on unproven and still controversial approaches, such as intuitive consultation. Most intuitive discoveries in archeology have been limited to modest, poorly funded efforts on home territory, and they involved only a single intuitive, not necessarily expert.

A Redefinition of Success

CAI experience with these several intuitive search cases, along with similar results from others, shows convincingly that intuitives can help in locating oil, gas and minerals, in exploring archeological sites and artifacts, and in finding lost and missing items and persons. However, if whatever or whomever is being sought is to be actually found, the *entire context of the search must be taken into account*. This includes the motives of the searchers, who is likely to benefit from the discovery, and the consequences that may follow from actually recovering the missing item. That is, if the search is to be successful it must be conducted in the best interests of all concerned. In the case of lost persons, this includes the desires of the person himself.

In contrast, we had naively assumed at the start that it would *always* be worthwhile to find natural resources, lost items and missing people. This assumption turned out be naive and unjustified. "Success" in an intuitive search does not always and does not necessarily imply that it is best for the buried, lost or hidden item or person to be actually recovered. Sometimes it should remain unfound in order to protect one or more parties, or, in exceptional archeological situations, to prevent the destruction of discoveries before they can be appreciated and preserved, as just noted. This principle may also explain why many past attempts at intuitive exploration have failed[21]. (Unskilled intuitives could also be at fault, of course.)

This occasional lack of "success" encountered in intuitive searches is certainly not the result of relying upon intuition. It could arise in any attempt to find buried, lost or missing items or missing people, whether conducted intuitively or by any other means. One might also expect it to occur in a search is for abstract ideas or the hidden "secrets" of nature, instead of the substantive items sought in the examples described here.

The main obstacle to the further application of intuitive skills to archeology and mineral and oil exploration continues to lie in the sometimes unwilling attitude of the responsible individuals to trust an intuitive approach to discovery. In their attempt to be conscientious and objective in their work—and this intention must be respected—they often neglect to give free rein to the very creative process that is responsible for their best ideas and discoveries. This situation will surely improve in coming decades as intuitive applications come to be better understood and more widely accepted, and as demonstrable progress is achieved through intuitive methods in fields other then archeology itself.

> "Gold was in the world from the beginning. How many men pass
> where it lies hidden, until one digs and finds it? Wisdom was in the
> universe from the beginning, but only those whose minds are open
> it can deduce the truth from what they see."
> [Talbot Mundy[22]]

• Endnotes, Chapter 5

[1] Comment by Uri Geller on his work for Anglo Transvaal Mining Co; quoted by J. Mishlove in Cook, 1984.; see also Geller & Playfair, 1986.

[2]* This case is described in more detail in Kautz & Branon, 1987, Chap. V .

[3] Mishlove, 1993, pp. 262-3.

[4] Mishlove, 1993, pp. 262-3.

[5] Roberts, 1965, Schwarz, 1965, Bird, 1979.

[6] Bakirov, 1974.

[7] Cayce, Hugh Lynn, 1971.

[8] Mishlove, J. loc cit.; p. 266.

[9]* Cayce, Edgar, 1999.; Cayce, Edgar Evans, 1968. Cayce's main assertion reads: "'References and clues [which] indicate Egypt as a repository for records—records of Atlantis and ancient Egypt during the time of Ra-Ta, which may some day be found...that a vast underground repository was established containing a library of wisdom from the lost civilization of Atlantis: 'This in position lies, as the sun rises from the waters, the line of shadow (or light) falls between the paws of the Sphinx...There is a chamber or passage from the right forepaw [of the Sphinx] to this entrance of the record chamber...'"

[10] Bond, 1918, Kenawell, 1965,

[11] Schwartz, 1977.

[12] Emerson, 1974., Emerson, 1975.

[13] Jones, 1979.

[14] Goodman, 1977.

[15] Mishlove, Jeffrey, 1993 p. 228.

[16] Schwartz & Edgerton, 1980.; see also: Schwartz, 1983.

[17] Schwartz & de Mattei, 1989.

[18] Barakat et al., 1975., Dolphin et al., 1978. see also www.ldolphin.org.

[19] Dolphin, 1978.

[20] Yoshimura et al., 1987, Yoshimura, 1988., Dormion & Goidin, 1987. Esmael, 1988.

[21]* McMoneagle reports his experience that remote viewing does not work well for finding lost items, based on his several years of success as a remote viewer for the Cognitive Sciences Laboratory of SRI International and for the Defense Intelligence Agency. His approach is somewhat different from the inquiry method described here, though he does acknowledge that the wishes of the lost people or the losers of objects must always be respected when searches are attempted. See McMoneagle, 2000, McMoneagle, 1997.

[22] Mundy, 1924.

PART III

THE AUGMENTATION OF KNOWLEDGE

The chapters in this Part describe ten experiments in which information was sought intuitively to extend knowledge in particular subject areas.

The broad purpose of these experiments was to learn how to conduct intuitive inquiries so as to obtain information to help solve *knowledge-limited* problems—that is, problems that had not already been solved because of a lack of specific knowledge or information. These studies sought specific solutions, answers to questions, understanding on a confusing issue or merely exploration of an interesting subject. Topics ranged from the theoretical to the practical, and from broad, poorly defined areas to those requiring specific technical facts. The inquiries varied in their breadth and depth, and also the extent to which they were novel and speculative as opposed to resting on a solid base of well-established knowledge.

The results from these experiments, as you will see, displayed different kinds of information from the expert intuitives. Some experiments yielded information that was specific, detailed and practical while others were interesting but not as useful as we hoped. These failings usually occurred because we were either overwhelmed by the magnitude of what we were seeking, or because we were not well prepared in our questioning. More was learned about the intuitive process itself from these ten experiments than from the preceding three.

All of the studies were incomplete in one sense, for the answers the expert intuitives gave to our more prepared questions invariably generated still more questions that begged to be answered. Nevertheless, taken all together, they provided much useful data for subsequent investigation or direct application. Most important, they revealed how to conduct future intuitive inquiries on knowledge-limited topics.

The experiments in Chapters 6 to 13 are presented in roughly the same order in which they were conducted, though they overlapped considerably in time.

Intuitive Consensus

All of the explorations described in Part III employed a method of inquiry called *Intuitive Consensus*. Stated simply, it consists of posing the same set of questions independently to several intuitives, compiling and comparing their responses, and then collecting the common portions into a set of (hopefully) correct answers.[1*]

The inquiries employing Intuitive Consensus were carried out as follows. In these studies CAI always employed three or more expert intuitives who did not communicate with one another during the course of the investigation. (In retrospect I doubt if this imposed isolation affected the results, though it may have weakened their credibility in the eyes of ultimate users.) In most cases the questions to be posed were worked out carefully in advance. For each session the interviewer—usually myself, sometimes assisted by an interested specialist, an associate or a small group—posed each prepared question in turn and pursued the responses in dialogue mode until the answer was as clear and complete as the situation allowed.

Every session was tape recorded and the tape was transcribed and checked for accuracy. We then cut up the several transcripts and pasted together the several answers to each question asked. (In later years a computer assisted with this step.) We then compared the various answers to each question with one another and with well established knowledge on the topic when it was available and relevant. This step uncovered any downright contradictions (rare), new viewpoints or lines of inquiry not thought of originally (occasional), and information offered by one team member but not the others (fairly common). We sometimes undertook a second round of inquiries with some or all team members in order to fill in gaps and resolve ambiguities. The supplemental responses were integrated with those from the first round.

Finally, we assembled all the consensual information and identified opportunities for validation. We also looked for any new perspectives on the chosen problem and formulated hypotheses for further study. In some cases we published an article on the findings, or a summary report if a sponsor required it.

Three experimenters not with CAI have employed their own versions of Intuitive Consensus. Two were done for explorations in psychic archeology (see Chapter 5): Stephen Schwartz and his Möbius Group in Los Angeles,[2] and Norman Emerson at the University of Toronto.[3] More recently, Remote Viewing (RV) was developed and applied to military intelligence by the Cognitive Sciences Laboratory at SRI International.[4]

• Endnotes—Part III

[1*] The Delphi Method used in futurism studies is similar to Intuitive Consensus in that it makes independent inquiries of multiple sources. However, these sources are not selected to be intuitive, only "well informed" in the area of inquiry, and no distinction is made between intuitive information and that obtained by rational means, memory or informed guessing. The method has proven to be sometimes useful, though the overall success rate is poor and the types of issues on which it works best are not well defined.

[2] Schwartz, 1978, ; Schwartz & Edgerton, 1980; see also Schwartz, 1983.

[3] Emerson, 1974a, Emerson, 1974b.

[4] Puthoff & Targ, 1976, Targ & Puthoff, 1977, Puthoff, 1996, Targ & Puthoff, 1977, Targ, 1996, McGoneagle, 1993, Morehouse, 1996.

CHAPTER 6

THE INTUITIVE HISTORIAN[1]*
RE-CREATING THE FORGOTTEN PAST

"History has been preempted by other forms of storytelling because
of its claim to objective truth. The historians are trying to be scientific by standing outside of what is happening and looking at it.
This is all changing now. Objective truth, if it exists at all, cannot be
reached with words. History is an art, not a science." [Ursula
LeGuin]

Can intuition be used to recreate lost history? In this chapter we will see that,
by asking expert intuitives carefully posed questions about what occurred in
times past, historical information can be recovered, including verifiable facts
and other details never to be found by the best methods of conventional archeology or from old written records.

This first experiment on the application of intuition consisted of the reconstruction of the lives of two individuals in ancient Egypt, both at the edge of
history: the early physician *Imhotep*, around 2700 BCE, and the controversial
pharaoh *Akhnaten*, about 1375 BCE. In each case we will review first what is
already known about the person (not much), present and examine the intuitive findings and then compare the two. Next we will look at the interpretation of history in general and discuss how to verify intuitive historical
information when this becomes necessary.

Who Was Imhotep?

Historical data on Imhotep are
sparse. Records from his own
period declare him to be "chan-
cellor of the king, high priest,
chief sculptor and administrator
of the great mansion" for the
Third Dynasty pharaoh Dzoser

(Zoser, Djoser) about 2650 BCE.[2, 3] Later records cite him as "vizier, overseer of public works, chief ritualist of the king, and scribe of God's books." These grand titles may be literally questionable, but they leave no doubt that he was a highly esteemed person. Other records cite him as architect and creator of the first temple at Edfu and the Step Pyramid complex near Sakkara. Imhotep's parents have been identified; his father Ka-nefer is known to have been a respected architect.

Such are the solid facts about Imhotep's life; all else has arisen from later writings as part of an expanding legend. There is no hard evidence that he was ever a physician, but he was worshipped as a demigod of healing starting a century later. The historian Manetho credits Imhotep with instituting reforms in writing and the design of the first building using hewn stone (hard to believe). References to Imhotep's accomplishments as sage, astronomer, writer and man of medicine date from the Middle Kingdom (20th to 17th century BCE), and temples of worship, healing and teaching were erected to him over these centuries and those to follow. Imhotep shows up still later as a demigod worshipped by the Greeks, who identified him with Asklepios, their god of healing. He was deified in the 26th dynasty (6th century BCE).

Several dozen statuettes and mural paintings, most of them dating from the 22nd Dynasty (10th century BCE) have turned up in various parts of Egypt, but they disagree on his physical features. Egyptologists conjecture that his tomb is at Sakkara, near the pyramid he is supposed to have built, but it has never been found.

Clearly, Imhotep is an individual at the bare edge of history. There is no doubt that he really existed but biographical details about him are sparse and the later legends are factually unreliable. Even his Third Dynasty Egyptian culture is mysterious, for scholars know rather little about how people lived at that time. Thus, we may expect to check part of the intuitive information against known history, but most of it will have to be totally new. This historical time period is so distant that it is unlikely that all expert intuitives in the inquiry team would be familiar with it. For these reasons Imhotep seems to be a fine candidate for intuitive inquiry.

CAI conducted this early intuitive study with seven expert intuitives and a few others in the late 1970s and early 1980s. The questions posed were those anyone would ask when collecting material for a biography. They dealt with the man's personality, his physical appearance, interests, accomplishments, childhood, growth and development, family, position within society, character strengths and weaknesses, creative work, health and manner of death.

As in all of CAI's Intuitive Consensus studies, the questions posed to the expert intuitives were prepared in advance and the inquiries were conducted separately from one another. A good consensus resulted on almost all points. What follows is a condensed summary of the intuitives' responses to these questions. (To present the full record would need an entire book!) Included at the beginning are a few redundant excerpts to illustrate how the several intuitives communicated similar information.

So fasten your mental seatbelts. Here we go on a journey across time!

Imhotep: Physician and More

General picture. The consensus confirmed Imhotep's well established accomplishments and added a few more. The most outstanding are discussed below. They depict him as a gifted "Renaissance man" of his day. Most striking is the picture presented of his character: his personality, his beliefs and values, his strivings and struggles, and his relationships with others. Also covered are the main events in his life, from childhood and adolescence to maturity and death. These personal facets have never been accessible from archeological and historical sources, and probably never will be.

Character. As a youth Imhotep manifested two outstanding qualities that were to set the pattern for the rest of his life; namely, his strong determination and his curiosity:

> He was always considering his fellow beings. He was considering how he would help them, how he could administer and minister to them. [AA[4*]]

> He listened a lot and was a deep thinker. Once he had risen to a cause there was no yielding or bending—sometimes to the point of stubbornness. [LH]

> Basically, he was a very optimistic individual. When there was a problem which everybody said, "This is impossible," then he knew there was a possibility. He used people as his point of calibration. When there was a consensus

that something could not be done, then he knew it could be done. And so he left himself open to the possibility for an expansion, for a development. [AA]

He was also very bright:

> He knew exactly what he wanted. He had much going for him on the intuitive side. But on this same point, he was a very gentle individual. [AA}

> He had a fantastic mind, full of ideas and enlightenment. [AM]

> These qualities found for their development a keen mind, a prodigious memory, a strong intuition and much determination: He is one of these people who has assimilated everything he ever inquired about, learned and saw. He has a tremendous memory, and constantly dwelled on all aspects of life that he has stored away. His mind is very keen, sharp and not limited to the area that he is most interested in. [GB]

> Knowledge was easily obtained by Imhotep. The mind was quick and precise. Memory was profound, and execution of knowledge was effective as well as creative. He could easily have been a scholar. [BR]

> His outstanding nature or quality is his curiosity, his inquiring. I don't think he ever stopped asking questions. With that quality of not accepting everything he is taught, he wants to find things out for himself, to investigate and see what is true. He has so many things that he wants to do, to work on, to investigate. He's bubbling with it, bursting with energy—all potential ideas that he wants to do. [GB]

> Now here we find also that this individual knew how to ask questions. He did not beat around the bush when there were answers that he needed. [AA]

Imhotep was humble and unattached:

> He has a very ambitious schedule, but he did not seek too much for himself. He did not seek high position, high power. But when he received high power, when he received authority, he used it to the fullest advantage—for himself, as well as to promote the good will of whomever now he served, or whomever had his services. He was not a seeker, *per se*, for selfish reasons. He was a seeker of truth. [AA]

On the other hand, these strengths led him into an independent and lonely life, largely separated from his fellow man:

> Lonely. Though surrounded by people and constantly involved with people, Imhotep was most lonely. His communication with the Gods restricted in part his communication with man. Much he could not relate and was required to keep it within himself. This led to caution, which led to a great silence and loneliness. [BR]

> He didn't like crowds. He liked to remove himself from things to gain a better perspective. He lived ninety percent of his life in his own mind; the other ten percent was family life and other matters. [LH]

> He spends lots of time by himself. [AM]

Family life. A rewarding relationship with a woman was apparently not his destiny:

> His family life wasn't all that good. He could have been better at that. He knew also that he had a weakness when it came to other women, other than his wife. [AA]

> I don't find a woman that is close to him that he cares about. I'm going back briefly to see if there was one he might have lost or whatever, but it's almost as if he had no time. [GB]

> [Did he have a wife and children?] Yes, but they are way out of the picture, except for one son that he hoped to pass things on to. [LH]

Negative traits. He also had a driving impatience, which sometimes burst forth in anger:

> At times, when he became impatient—and he *did* become impatient, especially when his experiments failed or when people would die or when that which he had planned did not work out—so did he begin to blame himself for mistakes or failures....Sometimes he was a quiet and silent and innocent as a lamb, and at other times he was a roaring lion. [AA]

He had lots of control over things, though not himself, for he had a temper, and experienced frustration and roughness at times. [AM]

This gentle man had also a temper that was profound, caused largely by pain suffered most of his life. [BR]

Another weakness in his character showed up later in his life as he received awards and recognition:

He had all that he needed, and he did not want very much. Except when it was given to him—that is, positions, authority, responsibilities—then he held onto it for dear life. Though he knew that it was through his own efforts that he had achieved, he also felt that now these rewards belonged to him and no one was going to take them away from him. And so it was like a dual personality. [AA]

He was cautious at times, especially when he knew that in a few weeks hence he would be receiving a great reward or a promotion or an assignment. He was very cautious; but when he attained to that position, he was almost like a different personality. People became afraid of him for a while. But then everything calmed down, and after the newness of the position or assignment had worn off, then he returned to his own self again. This happened a number of times. [AM]

Physical appearance and health. The intuitives agreed that Imhotep was tall, slender and fair-skinned in comparison with his contemporaries. His build was square and stocky, somewhat hunched. He looked to be non-Egyptian. He had a high, protruding forehead (some said it was bald), large hands and large, beautiful eyes. An accident to his leg or hip in his youth (one said at age nine) left him with a limp and caused him pain throughout his life. In other respects he was fairly healthy until old age.

Education. In his younger years his father educated him in both medicine and statesmanship, the latter as a "backup" trade. Early on, however, he showed ability not only in these two fields but in music, mathematics, architecture and astronomy (i.e., astrology) as well. He eventually became very capable at understanding people, especially in diplomacy and what we today call psychology:

He had a very penetrating personality. And though his eyes could see right through people, he withheld information from people that he knew about them, for fear that they would not be able to take it. In short, he could even "psychoanalyze" people quite quickly. He was able to work as a mediator, as a fact finder, even. [AA]

He could have been a diplomat; he could have been a statesman; he could have even been a premier, an ambassador; but instead he chose to go into the field of being a physician, the field of medicine. [AA]

He also taught himself several languages.

Religious orientation. Imhotep was described as an irreligious but spiritual person:

I don't see him so much as a religious man, following the religion of the times.... He couldn't be bothered by what was prescribed: the prayers, the concepts, and so on....He found ways to leave the priesthood alone, so to speak. They did make demands on him, but he didn't have too much to do with them....The priests always wanted drugs, herbs from him, potions for work with the neophytes, for the psychic out-of-body state to bring them information. He had no patience for any of that. He preferred to deal with the facts. The body was mystery enough for him. [GB]

He had a peculiar relationship with his God, namely, that God was his guide. He felt—and he said so to his close friends—that he could talk to God. These people thought that he had gone just a little too far, but they kept it quiet. But he was quite an outspoken individual in having a relationship to God. The creative force was an idea which he also had come upon, which proved to be right. [AA]

Man was a wondrous creation to him. He had an understanding of many of the other forces that could affect him, such as the sun and moon and the stars. However, he was not totally aware of the inner workings of man, though he did realize that he was more than just a happenstance being on the planet. He had the awareness that there was an almighty force that directed each being on earth. There was a spiritual understanding, yet it was not something that he tried to change man's thinking about. [LH]

Imhotep was a man of healing and a very spiritual man. He was a man very much in favor of the Gods of that time. [BR]

He had a far greater grasp of the universe, the healing effects and the uniformity and expansion of the universe, than anybody else at his time. He did not write much of that down, but he thought it, he spoke it to his close friends. [AA]

Contributions to medicine. Imhotep's greatest accomplishments by far lay in medicine, we are told: the use of herbs and potions, anatomy, the nervous system and the circulatory system:

[What specific contributions did he make to medicine?] In this case, the anatomy, pertaining now to the bone structure. He specifically came out with the anatomy which is written in one of your classical books. And he also began to understand the nervous system....He knew also another major contribution, which people are just beginning to touch upon in your present lifetime, that illnesses are not with the physical body, but that the source is with the mind. He knew the connection [distinction?] between psychosomatic illnesses and those which were truly a physical defect. He knew the differences. And when people complained, he could quickly go to the source. [AA]

Perhaps his greatest knowledge was in curing fevers, which overtook men and ravaged the body and mind, causing sweats and then dehydration. His knowledge of herbs was comparable to your best chemists today. His knowledge of the organs enabled him to deduce much in regard to troubled areas of the body. He was aware that water caused fever but not how. His contributions to medicine were extensive, yet were not recognized or acclaimed to a great extent. His ability as a healer was, however, acclaimed. [BR]

His special interest and study seem to be centered around the brain and the spine, the central nervous system. I think he feels that everything stems from that, almost as if all other systems are dependent upon the spine, brain and nerves....He is particularly fascinated with paralyses, all injuries resulting from the spine, even mental derangements. [GB]

Blood flow and internal organs....He knew of the meridians, though not the pressure points. He had a faint knowledge of the nervous system. He was familiar with the use of herbs, a skill he learned from others. He did some direct healing. [LH]

He performed surgery, but only a little and under duress.

Imhotep also founded an unusual school for male medical students, passing on to them much of what he had learned. He was not always a good teacher, however. He preferred students as bright as eager as he had been, and was impatient with those less motivated or less intelligent.

Architecture. The intuitive team did not support the historical picture of Imhotep as a pyramid builder. While he was fascinated with pyramids, especially the Great Pyramid of Giza, it was their use for healing that most interested him. He participated in the design of the Step Pyramid and was given credit for it, but he was not its architect or chief engineer, as is commonly supposed:

> He and a friend who was a mathematician discussed and worked between themselves, confirming the energy that could be there [in the pyramids], the potential. The friend worked on the precise mathematical point of view. He was very keen on what the friend told him the energy could do. They ran experiments together, building them as models....What they are doing is planning the perfect pyramid, like a great dream, a vision—the mathematician through preciseness and him more through intuition—for that was one of the outstanding features of this physician. [GB]

> The Great Pyramid was built by the time he lived there...Yet, the most significant work that he did as far as building pyramids was so it could be used in the area of healing, in the area of instructions, and also as an observatory for looking at the stars and so forth. [AA]

> He had knowledge of them [the pyramids] and of the engineering and math, but this was not his profession....He was not there to build the pyramids. [BR]

Death and entombment. We did not explore this topic deeply or thoroughly, but the intuitives who addressed it agreed that Imhotep was buried in a fairly simple wooden box under a pyramid-like structure, now completely covered by sand. One source gave his manner of death: cancer in the abdomen at 73. There was disagreement regarding the entombment itself. Two intuitives mentioned that the public burial was a mock one, while his friends secretly put his boxed body in another tomb to protect it from thieves. In any case:

[Anything buried with the body?] There is a case, and his arm has gold on it. There is blue lapilus [lapis?]. There is a long shape inside the case, something like you'd keep papers in. It is cylindrical with an alligator-skin-like pattern upon it. There are papers inside that refer to guiding people in healing ways, also to potions and energies. [AM]

They placed in the coffin several scrolls about medicine, about architecture, about diplomacy, so he could have them in his next life, in his next journey. [AA]

There's some important medical information with this man, Imhotep. That's what's to be discovered, more than his body. It would be useful and practical now. [SF]

Most of the intuitives agreed that the body is still in identifiable condition, though one part has decomposed. Three said that his tomb lies northwest of the town where he lived (Sakkara), at a distance from 5 to 15 miles in what is now dune-like desert. There are no obvious landmarks in the immediate vicinity. The "casket" is 10-20 feet below the present ground level.[5*]

We might have questioned further to pinpoint the location of the tomb with enough precision to allow an exploration, but it would have been premature to do so until means were created to carry out such a search. One source had this to say about such an expedition:

It could be a very rewarding project but there will not be any big treasures in there, such as were found in other tombs, you understand. It will make an impact upon the medical community, inasmuch as they will now begin to realize there is more to the field of medicine than has originally been thought. Also, you will begin to realize that this man was a highly spiritual person, and he gained his strength from his encounter, his fellowship and guidance with his God, you see....There will be some difficulties in the unearthing of this crypt, for you will find remnants of waterways below the crypt itself. And so, you need to show a little caution. [AA]

The Credibility of Intuitive History

Can we believe this account of Imhotep's life?

Without any higher authority to rely upon, the credibility of the information given here must rest first on the consistency of the consensus—namely, the fact that the seven intuitives' independent reports agree well among themselves; second, with few exceptions they agree with what is already known from established history, where available; and third, as will be obvious in subsequent chapters, because the same intuitives have provided accurate and well corroborated information on many other matters about which no prior knowledge was available to them.

We see too that this intuitive biography of Imhotep presents a reasonable story on its own. It is fairly detailed, plausible overall, self-consistent and consistent with human nature as commonly understood. (One cannot make this claim for most of the channeled history published in recent years.) The intuitive picture supplements and fleshes out in a reasonable way the established historical picture of Imhotep, modifying it only on a few points—his limited role in pyramid construction, for example. It contradicts the legendary history on several points, more on matters of interpretation and emphasis than substance. Most interesting, the story extends beyond established history in describing Imhotep's personality and other facets of his personal life, none of which is accessible from archeology and recorded texts.

It would be interesting to explore even more deeply into this unusual man's life, drawing out other aspects of his personality and character and especially his inner qualities. These could provide an intimate look at how one ancient human being saw himself in relationship to his social and cultural environment, and more about the cultural worldview prevalent in his time. A search for his tomb might also be an worthwhile project. Judging by other successes in intuitive archeology (discussed in Chapter 5), an intuitively supported exploration ought be able to locate his tomb easily. If the intuitives are correct, a successful discovery would prove to be significant.

Akhnaten, Heretic Pharaoh

CAI conducted a more extensive experiment in intuitive history a few years later, this time on another Egyptian individual: the 18th-Dynasty pharaoh (king) Amenhotep IV, also known as Akhnaten.

According to well documented history Akhnaten ruled Egypt from 1379-1362 BCE. He is most renown as the "heretic" pharaoh for defying the firmly established priesthood (church and state were combined in those days) and for establishing a new, more liberal state religion. He also introduced a number of progressive changes into his society in art, literature and court lifestyle, and his policies affected relations with neighboring countries. He even moved the capital from Thebes to a remote site down the Nile, near what is now El Amarna, and named it Akhnaten.[6]

More is known about Akhnaten's family members than about this peculiar ruler himself: his wife, Nefertiti, whose classic beauty graced a famous bust found intact in the sands of El Amarna; his father, Amenhotep III, for his military accomplishments and a proliferation of huge statues of himself; and the boy Tutankhamon ("King Tut"), probably Akhnaten's grandson, whose famous tomb was discovered largely intact in 1924.[7]

Knowledge about the life of Akhnaten himself is fragmentary. History records him as shaped strangely in body, a bit unstable mentally and more of a visionary than a practical leader. His peaceful diplomacy did not work well, for the extensive Egyptian empire began to contract under his leadership; the 18th dynasty ended a few decades after his death. His religious revival did not endure, for the old priesthood regained control only 17 years after he assumed the throne. They deposed their strange king and destroyed most of the material evidence of his era. He vanished into relative obscurity until discoveries in the 19th century revealed these few details of his reign. His actual significance in Egyptian history also remains controversial. His life has been the subject of several scholarly books, a few popular biographical novels and an opera.[8] The latter fill out the sparse factual account with modern interpretation and imagination.

So we have in Akhnaten another enigmatic individual at the edge of history, and therefore a suitable candidate for intuitive inquiry. Sufficient archeological artifacts and documents exist to allow an intuitive biography of him to be partially corroborated.

CAI conducted nearly thirty sessions on Akhnaten with fifteen intuitives, six of them expert. They generated a voluminous, informative and detailed description of his life and culture. Just as with Imhotep the consensus was very good, almost entirely consistent with the solid historical facts about him, and contradictory only with some of the legend. It extends well beyond known history in personal details about the man.

This is not the place to report in detail on this large intuitive experiment, for the information is too extensive to be related and appreciated in a limited space. Suffice it to summarize briefly some of the unusual and novel features of his personal life.

The intuitives report that Akhnaten's childhood was lonely and isolated, not only because his family overprotected him as a royal heir but also by his very nature. He felt (later) that he came to Earth as a stranger with a mission, but did not really belong here. His health was poor from childhood onward. He had several wise teachers whom he respected and loved, but the greatest was his influential and ambitious mother Tiye, who seeded in him the progressive ideas he was to implement later as a ruler. As an adult he had broad interests, embracing art, education and philosophy—what we would call science today. He also sought to improve the practical professions (such as medicine) which at that time were disorganized and without accepted standards of competence.

Akhnaten was independent, moody and unpredictable, even somewhat unstable mentally. His emotional life was wild. He was less of a crazy religious zealot than history has painted him, however. His personal inner world was very real to him, and his spiritual understanding ran deep. He understood at an early age his destiny as a unique social transformer, but he had difficulty executing it well. History credits him with introducing a new monotheistic religion to his country, but the intuitives say it was not really new, for the concept of monotheism was already well known; he simply brought it forward, set up the sun as its symbol and made it central to his country's existing theocracy. Nor did he inaugurate a "new religion" in the modern sense; he merely shifted the emphasis and values of the existing religion, albeit somewhat dramatically, as an outer statement of his inner convictions.

Akhnaten had several marriages and sired many children, including children of his own children (a frequent practice for ancient royalty), and he cared for some of them deeply. He and his wife Nefertiti loved one another initially, though (as suspected by historians) became estranged later. She was supportive of his social and religious reforms until his death. His efforts to actualize these reforms were not very effective, for he made many mistakes before being deposed. Nevertheless, he left a significant legacy through his attempts to realign and restructure Egyptian religion and society. The seeds he planted in his short reign gradually and subtly set philosophical thinking in the Middle East on a new course.

The intuitive consensus greatly expands the historical picture of Akhnaten as painted by historians and Egyptologists and provides a wealth of personal detail. There is sufficient material here for an interesting biography. We made arrangements with a writer, a literary agent and a publisher to prepare a novel based on the intuitive readings. After long delays the project foundered for lack of agreement among the participating parties and was dropped. Someday, when a qualified writer arises to undertake the task, and the time is right, perhaps the envisioned biographical novel of Akhnaten may be written.

CAI's original expectations in carrying out these two studies in intuitive history were for the most part realistic and fulfilled, but a surprise lay in store when the problem arose of what to do with the new information after collecting, analyzing and corroborating it. We were able to locate only a few historians interested in Imhotep, and none were interested in new intuitive information about the man. The situation for Akhnaten was little better.

The Limitations of History

> * "A large part of our time is spent remembering the past. Only we
> don't realize that what we are remembering is not reality but rather
> images fabricated by our internal dialogue concerning what happened to us. We don't remember facts, but interpretations of facts.
> We are unaware of our real past because we are too involved in
> repeating to ourselves a mythical history that our ego has developed
> to justify its existence." [Carlos Castaneda]

Historical reconstruction suffers from basic limitations that arise not from the use of intuition but from the nature of history itself. This obstacle needs to be understood before intuitively derived history is interpreted and evaluated.

It must be appreciated first of all that, by definition, the term "history" refers not to what occurred in the past, but only to the selective written (occasionally oral) *record* of what occurred. A piece of history is a document or a memory, not an event.

Second, historical records are fragmentary; they represent only a fraction of what truly happened at the time they were written. This is especially the case for ancient history. Thus, the fraction of the past to which we have access represents only those events that fortuitously left a recognizable physical trace—a painting, mummy, potsherd, inscription or document—while the majority and often most significant events did not leave any detectable trace at all. It is the task of archeologists and historians to try to fill in these gaps through their extensive studies. They report to the rest of us what they believe "really" happened, but much that we would like to know is missing.

Third, and even worse, the scenarios reconstructed by historians and scholars rest strongly upon their *interpretation* of the fragmentary data. These data typically include political and religious writings, often composed long after the period under investigation. They constitute only a dilute embedding of facts within a much larger body of speculation and supposition, based in part on superstition, legend and mythology. Indeed, portions of the past exist only in the minds of historians, and cannot be said to be real except as all thoughts are in some sense real. They have helped to "create" a past the rest of us have accepted as real.

Modern professionals who carry out reconstructions accept and understand this limiting aspect; it is an inherent part of their noble efforts to try to regenerate a comprehensive and reasonably accurate picture of life in prior times. However, those who translate these scholastic reports for popular consumption often fail to distinguish this interpretive and speculative component from solid facts. In order to make history interesting and meaningful to the rest of us, they create "historical fiction" in the form of literature, popular texts and films. They use their imagination freely to fill out the stories in attractive ways. We may be grateful that they entertain us, educate us and awaken our interest in the past, and they often portray a valid side of history that the scholars dare not present. Still, it is easy to forget that their pictures constitute a distorted and incomplete packaging of factual history, not the real thing.

A fourth factor distorts the historical picture even more, namely, the "coloring" imposed by each age's particular culture and language on its writing and rewriting of history—the broad problem of interpretation or *hermeneutics*.[9] The ancient Greek's picture of life in his own country, for example, cannot be fully trusted, nor can we trust the succession of histories of ancient Greece as later historians saw it in the Middle Ages and the Renaissance, say. We know too that the historical report of nineteenth century America, for instance, as seen by those living at that time, was not very "objective" by present-day standards. Even nowadays we are writing our own history in ways that will surely disturb future historians. Every age insists that the accessible past be rewritten from its own perspective, for the past is always seen from the continually evolving present—sometimes with an improved perspective, sometimes with less, but usually different.

As a result, history is as much a mirror of the age in which it is written as it is a spy-glass view into times past. We can only accept the fact that there is no single, correct "history," and that no history ever exists apart from its historians, and the societies from which they came and within which we live at present.

These four factors pose a serious limitation on intuitive historical reconstructions such as those reported here. When we inquire intuitively into a fragment of the past and obtain answers, through whose eyes is the superconscious mind "looking"? Which of the various possible versions is being returned by the intuitives? Even if we are obtaining from the superconscious a truthful and undistorted intuitive picture of past events, can we understand, accept and appreciate it from our present-day perspective? Where can we find an ultimate authority on what transpired, to allow proper corroboration?

The expert intuitives provided no direct answer to these questions, and their remarks on how they perceive and receive historical information revealed only a little. Even some trance channels qualified their responses with the preamble, "This is how I see it," which suggests that there may be other ways to see it. Those performing consciously sometimes expressed doubt of what they heard themselves saying, because it appeared preposterous to them—though not necessarily to the inquirer. Published non-CAI intuitive histories of the same people, culture and time period do not always agree.

On the other hand, the descriptions of Imhotep and Akhnaten certainly displayed a broader and consistent perspective than typical ancient historical accounts. Their information about these individuals contained many novel pieces and their accounts are less colored and distorted than other histories of them. Moreover, as mentioned earlier, the consensus was very good and was consistent with historical information that is already known solidly about them. Finally, the high accuracy of the non-historical information obtained from the other CAI experiments, reported in subsequent chapters, adds to the credibility of these historical accounts and demands that we take them seriously at least.

These arguments may be persuasive but they certainly do not *prove* that the historical intuitive information is absolutely correct. In the absence of firm external corroboration we can only learn from this information what we can, be inspired by it, remain open to chances to verify it, and try to put it to use if and when opportunities arise to do so.

The Verification of Intuitive History

> *"Everyone automatically assumes that the present is the result of the past. Turn it around, and consider whether the past may not be a result of the present. The past may be streaming back from the now, like the countryside as seen from an airplane." [Alan Watts]

Verification of intuitive historical information is not always necessary, of course, but those who want to rely upon it (archeologists, for example) may demand some corroboration before they will accept it and use it. If a researcher wants to provide only an evidential example of the intuitive reconstruction of history, then he may select an area and time period for which partial checking is possible, as was done here for Imhotep and Akhnaten. Alternatively, if he chooses to assist on-going historical research or a field exploration with specific information, ideas, new viewpoints and hypotheses, he may wish to design the inquiry to generate first a few readily verifiable facts, then follow these by a larger body of useful information.

If the goal is only to verify that a piece of new historical information was received intuitively, and not by ordinary non-intuitive means, then the task may be more difficult. It is virtually impossible to rule out completely the possibility of incidental memories. for this would require that the intuitive's full past be examined in detail. To avoid this situation one might choose a portion of the past that is so distant from present-day knowledge that information about it is very unlikely to have reached the intuitive—or anyone else. This was the case in the study of Imhotep and Akhnaten. An even stronger example will be presented in Chapter 11: the intuitive recovery of a dead language.

For more complete verification one may try to "dig up" supportive evidence through actual archeological excavation, though this option can be expensive and time-consuming. Alternatively, intuitives can assist in locating lost or forgotten documents that confirm portions of regenerated history. Some intuitive information about the past will probably never be verified—for example, descriptions of presumed prehistoric civilizations in the Gobi Desert, Antarctica and the legendary Atlantis.

Several prior attempts at intuitive history have been published, though none is as consensual and credible as this one reported here. For example, there are several widely varying channeled accounts of what happened to Jesus during the years of his life not reported in the Bible (ages 12 to 30).[10] Unfortunately, they disagree greatly with one another. Too little is known about the conditions under which they were obtained to say which might be right and what might be responsible for the discrepancies. Individual "past-life memories" of historical periods (see Chapter 3), while not necessarily intuitive, are another conflicting source of historical information, not usually credible.

"The Urantia Book" is a 2000-page "history" of the entire universe (!), from the big bang to the creation of Earth (Urantia), to the growth of civilization and modern times.[11] This fantastic intuitive (channeled) account is so novel and unique that only a fraction of it can be corroborated against already available knowledge. Still, it is self-consistent and does not obviously contradict what is presently known, so it merits attention and study. A few portions have been incidentally confirmed by scientific discoveries made after its publication. It also includes (Part IV) an inspiring, highly detailed and apparently thorough biography of Jesus: his birth, background, daily life, death and interpretation, including his childhood and the 18 adult years not covered in the Bible. If more of the Urantia Book could be corroborated with independent sources it could be a prime example of intuitive history, and a valuable historical resource.

Evaluation

This experiment showed that historical knowledge can be extended and expanded with intuitive inquiry. Further intuitive reconstructions should be able to provide interesting and plausible scenarios of the past, and it is not appear to be difficult to carry them out. They offer the hope of a more meaningful and presumably more accurate view of man's past than is possible by purely empirical-rational means, and would allow historians to avoid much of the guesswork and subjective interpretations that characterize so much of recorded history.

This investigation of the lives of Imhotep and Akhnaten provided valuable experience that aided later Intuitive Consensus studies. It was an important lesson toward learning how to carry out intuitive inquiries in order to obtain clear, accurate and potentially useful information. It confirmed that the phrasing of the questions is especially important when accessing superconscious knowledge. While no requested information was denied in these two studies, a few important factual details were not immediately offered. The consensus was very good, as noted above, and there were no significant contradictions with well established know-edge. A few portions of the new information were amenable to partial verification.

Our failure to bring intuitive history to the stage of actual application was an early difficulty, soon to be encountered in some of the later experiments as well. We discovered that whose who might use the new intuitive information preferred to rely on their own resources rather than on information arising by unfamiliar means. This "not invented here" syndrome is a common charge against scientists, who are often seen as rigidly protective of their chosen turf and closed to new approaches, which they perceive as diversions. (I blush with shame at my own such attitude when working as a young scientist.) Reluctance to inquire too far beyond one's territory is understandable, of course, for it dilutes the effort toward one's goal. Also, in this age of overabundant information one must guard against overwhelm (like overeating at the buffet). Just the same, real difficulties come from common pride and arrogance: the unwillingness to remain open to outside ideas, information and even the best counsel. In the present case resistance also arises from the widespread bias against intuition, a faculty most people (notably scientists) do not understand well and cannot accept as having much if any validity.

This study gave no clues about how far one may go in obtaining intuitive information about the remote past. Perhaps this is not so important, since means for corroborating new historical information are very limited. Nevertheless, one could generate credible intuitively derived scenarios for study by contemporary historians and for public consumption, and these could well trigger increased appreciation and acceptance of alternative versions of history, just as is commonly done in modern historical reconstructions historical persons and events through popular novels and films.

Studies similar to this one could well lead us to the deeper, underlying and eternal messages that human history is urging us to recognize and understand: who we are as humans, individually and collectively; what we are doing on this planet; how our values and ideals express themselves in our actions over time—and indications of where we are headed. Herein lies the real value of history, whether derived through intuition or by some other means.

> "History, as you think of it, represents but one thin line of probabil-
> ities in which you are presently immersed....Reality is far more
> diverse, far richer and unutterable than you can presently suppose
> or comprehend....There are many other equally valid, equally real
> evolutionary developments that have occurred, and are occurring
> and will occur, all within other probable systemsof physical reality.
> [Jane Roberts/Seth[12]]

• Endnotes—Chapter 6

[1]* This chapter is adapted from Kautz, 1980.

[2] Hurry, 1928, Foucart, 1903, Sethe, 1902, Gauthier, 1918.

[3] Breasted, 1933, p. 112ff, Budge, 1904, Gardiner, 1962, pp. 72-73; Erman, 1971.

[4]* The initials in brackets refer to the particular intuitives, who are listed in the Acknowledgements section at the end of this book.

[5]* An alleged tomb of Imhotep, believed by some to be in an area of the Saqqara necropolis, was systematically excavated in recent years by the late Walter B. Emery of the Egypt Exploration Society. No positive identification was found.

[6] Aldred, 1988, Giles, 1972, Redford, 1984, Aldred, 1973, Silverberg, 1964.

[7] Cone, 1976, Carter & Mace, 1930.

[8] Drury, 1976, Waltari, 1949, Glass & Jones, 1987.

[9] Gadamer, 1976.

[10] Cummins, 1937, Cummins, 1949, Dowling, 1972, Caldwell, 1977, Anon2, 1955, Prophet, 1984, Bailey, 1937.

[11] Anon2, 1955.

[12] Roberts, 1972, pp. 226-227.

CHAPTER 7

EARTHQUAKE TRIGGERING[1]*
NEW LIGHT ON AN UNDERGROUND PUZZLE

"Four o'clock happened at the earthquake
A funny way to tell time.
Do events describe the moment?
Is the moment but a sign?
What can be thought of the present
If the past is in the mind
And he who sees the future
Is looking from behind?"
[Marsha Adams]

Encouraged by the success of the experiment on intuitive history, CAI under-took a larger and more technical investigation into the physical process responsible for the triggering of major earthquakes. We already knew that geo-physicists have very little understanding of what sets off earthquakes, so this seemed to be an excellent opportunity to apply intuition to an important and outstanding issue. This chapter describes the results of this first experiment on the use of Intuitive Consensus to solve a scientific problem.

I am not speaking here of the long-term cause of earthquakes. It is well known that they result from an erratic scraping and breaking of rock that takes place along the boundaries of the dozen or so "tectonic plates" that make up the thin crust of the earth. These plates gradually drift around relative to one another (roughly one inch per year), carrying the continents with them.[2] This movement defines roughly the regions where most earthquakes occur: along the boundaries between plates. More than a hundred years of records show their rate of occurrence in each region. But that's about all. These data do not begin to provide the information needed to forecast where and when the next large shock will take place and how big it will be. Practical earthquake prediction requires an improved understanding of the physical "triggering" process that occurs just before the built-up stress is released by a sudden sliding or fracture of the rock, or the foreknowledge of a measurable indicator of sudden movement.

The broad purpose of this intuitive study was to gain this missing knowledge about earthquake triggering. Its specific objective was to attain enough information about the triggering process so that seismologists could decide which on-going measurements ought to be made, where to make them and how to interpret them, so they could create a practical warning network for predicting damaging earthquakes.

Why Earthquakes?

There exist hundreds of outstanding and important questions in science. We chose the topic of earthquake triggering for an intuitive study for four reasons. Before becoming caught up in details it will be helpful to look at them.

First of all, the issue is humanly important. Earthquakes take a tremendous toll in human lives. The 1556 shock in Shensi, China killed 830,000 people, and the 1923 Tokyo earthquake and resulting fire took the lives of 120,000. Recall, too, the tremor that leveled Tangshan, China in 1976, burying more than 200,000 people (some reports claimed 600,000, though both figures are truly beyond comprehension).[3] In terms of fatalities, the only competitors to earthquakes are certain severe diseases such as the plague and AIDS, and, of course, mankind's seemingly endless wars.

Second, as just noted, present-day seismology has no answer to the earthquake triggering question and none appears to be on the horizon, at least for the next few decades. (Progress in seismology seems to advance as slowly as the tectonic plates themselves.) A practical solution is needed much sooner. Funding for earthquake research is pitifully small when compared with the damaging consequences when a large shock strikes a populated area. Even though standards for new construction are now quite tight in the United States, urban centers with many old buildings are still at great risk. The magnitude 6.7 shock in Northridge, California on 17 January 1994 destroyed 3000 homes, killed 60 people and resulted in an estimated $20 billion in damages.[4*] If the famous earthquake in San Francisco (18 April 1906, magnitude 8.3) occurred today the loss of life would be huge, and the estimated loss at least $150 billion. In most earthquake-prone countries the situation is much worse since construction practices are lax.

Third, practical action is feasible if only we could *understand* the earthquake triggering process. With this understanding

> *As a long-time California resident I had become accustomed to earthquakes and was no longer afraid of them. The most interesting one occurred under unusual circumstances: I was visiting my brother-in-law in Riverside, California. The small house was crowded with family, so I opted to spend the warm night in the backyard in a sleeping bag, directly on the ground. It was just after daybreak when the ground began to heave, waking me up and tossing me around. I knew right away what has happening, but also knew I was in the safest of positions, away from any falling buildings or other objects. Well, I thought, now this is the way to experience an earthquake!*
>
> *My first impression was the creaking sound of dozens of nearby houses as they wiggled on their foundations and strained under the shaking. I was prepared to witness a catastrophe, but the quake was not a large one and there was no obvious damage. The most surprising effect was a loud roaring sound, as if a powerful storm were blowing through the area, which was obviously not happening . This roar is very fresh in my memory, and to this day I still cannot explain it.*

the existing network of monitoring stations in earthquake-prone portions of the planet could be greatly expanded in number and type so as to watch for the telltale signs that a shock was imminent. These signs would enable society to take appropriate preparedness action: evacuate communities, alert fire departments, turn off public utilities, lower water levels in dams and so on. Today's of instrumental networks are intended for research purposes only and are trivially small. This is because no one knows which physical quantities to measure, so the instruments are of various types and are spread in small clusters over wide areas. They are not of much use for prediction purposes.

Thus, unlike many scientific problems, the earthquake prediction problem might be solved practically if only one could obtain a specific answer to a single scientific question: what are the measurable signs on the earth's surface of an impending earthquake?

Fourth, the problem remains unsolved only because of a lack of *information*. In this respect it differs from many social problems, such as homelessness, overpopulation and war, for which it is well known what to do but the necessary political will and public consensus for appropriate action are lacking. For earthquake prediction, however, the only need is for specific information that will indicate when and where the next large earthquake will strike. Intuition ought to be able to supply this information.

Enter the Intuitive Team

CAI began its intuitive exploration of earthquake triggering in 1975. By the end of 1977 five independent intuitive sources had provided the main body of information. Three follow-up inquiries took place during the following year to expand on the first explanations and to resolve residual ambiguities. None of the intuitives on the team had any personal or prior technical expertise in geophysics.

The eight intuitive sources were unanimous in attributing the triggering of major earthquakes to a certain complicated physical process. They varied in the completeness with which they described the process, and in their assignment of relative importance to the roles played by the various factors involved. Still, they agreed on the major ways in which the process manifests as physical changes that could be directly measured. The central message was consistent and clear. While more details would have been helpful, to obtain such thorough information would have enlarged the study beyond the means and time available to us.

The following paragraphs summarize the consensus of the intuitive hypothesis. Included here are selected verbatim excerpts from the transcripts of the inquiry sessions. They communicate the main explanations as well as their flavor. These samples are representative only. They reveal some of the consistency of the responses but exclude the mass of repetitive material supporting the consensus. (Again, this would require a full book.) Following the intuitive information on each topic is a discussion of which portions were not already known in geophysics at the time of the study. Some technical concepts and terminology have been retained to show the level of detail, but the non-scientific reader may safely pass over these if they are not immediately clear.[5*]

Primary Findings: the Underlying Forces

The consensus indicated that the triggering mechanism for moderate to large earthquakes is a complex physical-chemical-electrical process that involves a variety of interacting physical energies in combination:

> There is no one particular final [triggering] force except that which would be considered as the content [combination] of electromagnetic and vibrational energies upon the molecular level within the earth crust itself....It is the combined forces of gaseous pressure, electromagnetic activity—which must be elaborated upon[6*]—the pressures of centrifugal forces, combined with the normal expansionary pressures of any heated matter. When all of these reach a critical point, the final triggering of the quake [takes place through] the electromagnetic charge that has been built up. [KR]

The Earthquake Prediction Game

In past generations earthquake predictions came only from religious prophets, astrologers and seers. Even today we are occasionally hear these pronouncements of doom that appear in the tabloid media. Such popular predictions are usually loosely stated. Some forecast events almost certain to occur anyway, though both predictor and listener may not be aware of the likelihood. Only rarely are they accurate. There is not usually any follow-up on them; failures do not make interesting news. Some of them may contain an intuitive component but responsible intuitives do not engage in such work. Popular predictions cannot be taken very seriously.

In recent years a number of amateurs have achieved notoriety for their prognostications based upon sun-moon alignments, geomagnetic storms and tallies of lost cats, to name three popular ideas. A few predictions have been correct but their predictors waited until after the shock to announce them— which raises the question of how many unsuccessful guesses they never bothered to reveal. None of these unusual means of foretelling earthquakes has ever shown itself to be consistently correct over time. The predictors typically disclaim any reliance on intuition, yet we know that when the means is sufficiently complex it is difficult for anyone to know whether or not he is using his intuition.[7*] We are left wondering why these persons are so zealous to publicize their shaky predictions.

On the scientific front the predictions offered are more credible, but they are fewer, more conservative, highly qualified and apply only to small earthquakes.[8] Based on a great deal of collected and analyzed data, they are stated as probabilities rather than certainties, and usually pertain only to broad areas, well researched over long time periods.. They are not practical for public warnings. In the San Francisco Bay Area, for example, an anticipated magnitude-8 earthquake is long overdue, extrapolating from a 300-year-long record of large shocks every forty years or so, but no one has any good notion about just where and when it will occur.

China has been the tragic scene of many large earthquakes. It has an extensive monitoring system in place and a few impressive predictions to its credit. One in 1975 resulted in the evacuation of Haicheng, a town of 90,000 people, two days before a large shock destroyed the town. However, the Chinese have also had many failures. They have missed large ones and predicted several that never occurred. Perhaps it is easier in China to order repeated evacuations.

(What kind of forces are acting upon the rock at the point of fracture or sliding?) These are static pressures that come about from electrostatic, electromagnetic and nuclear pressures. The electrostatic and electromagnetic forces act not directly on the epicenter [hypocenter?[9*]], but in the surrounding area, while the nuclear force acts directly on the epicenter [sic]. [AA]

Ninety to ninety-five percent is electromagnetic, and yet there are other variations which also play a part in this. [LH]

When there is a concentration of the plasmic field, when it becomes exposed to the earth's magnetic field plus the earth's centrifugal force, [then there] is this critical force that causes a transference of energy from the kinetic level to the molecular level of the earth's stable crust. This is the setting-off factor that, in its own right, actually triggers the quake. [KR]

Current scientific understanding recognizes that ordinary pressures due to heat and mechanical action are at work in the final fracturing that sets off earthquakes.[10] At the time of the intuitive study the electromagnetic and nuclear phenomena mentioned above played no part in geophysical understanding.

The centrifugal forces apparently refer to solid-earth tides. Similar to ocean tides, this flexing of the earth results from the gravitational pull of the sun and moon upon the earth. It had already been partially investigated in connection with earthquakes at the time of the study, but they were not believed to play any role in earthquake triggering. (See more on this factor below.)

The rocks themselves are under great strain from activity deep within the earth:

> The main energy for earthquakes comes from the central core of the earth. This energy is very powerful and can take any form. It releases particles of energy, and these create tiny fissures and a great deal of pressure in the upper layers of rock, with the result that [the upper] part of the earth cannot sustain itself any longer. This energy has a very high vibration....[It] is like atomic energy, and has some electrical and magnetic properties. [AA]

> The principal triggering action is coming from changes in the internal radiation which originates in the central core of the earth. This core is neither solid nor liquid, but more like jello. It throbs and pulsates like a powerful human heart, and is continually changing its shape. These changes affect its radiation accordingly. [BR]

> The centrifugal force of the 's rotation causes movement of the magmas along the cooling crust, [producing] rarefied or heated forces from the expansion of these molten materials seeking release into the atmosphere;...also the electromagnetic charges building up beneath the earth's surface,...and hydrothermal forces—simply, steam. [KR]

Geophysicists have roughly mapped the core of earth through calculations based upon the way seismic waves bend as they pass through it.[11] They are aware that "dry" rock becomes stuck and then releases itself in the jerky motion associated with large earthquakes. They acknowledged the earth's state as solid, "jello-like" and liquid at increasing depths, but had only conjectured the dynamic character reported here.

Upper and Lower Energies

Most surprising, and totally new, the actual triggering process was said to begin near the surface of the earth, as energies from both below and above the surface come together:

> There is a combination of the forces within the earth itself, within the molten part of the earth, together with the electrical forces from the outside which are coming together and joining, even as you would see a discharge of energy between clouds. Here you have solid clouds. And there will be an eruption when these two meet, an explosion. That's the mechanism of it, for the earth is charged and so are these forces. They are charges, particles of charged energy. [AA]

> The trigger is not one thing but a combination—one factor in one case, another factor in another. Mainly, though, external energy is coming in from two sources, one external to the earth and the other inside of the earth, and there is an interaction between these two. [BR]

The lower of the two triggering components is a combination of, first, electromagnetic radiation, mainly of a low frequency and emitted from deep within the earth itself; and second, heat energy radiated and conducted from the core, plus various gases that leak upward through fissures and porous rock.

> The earth energy is less than 50 kilohertz....Metal deposits within the earth are concentrated in certain peculiar shapes and forms, and when gases of a certain nature reach these, they create an explosive effect that causes changes to come about.... [Did you say gas emission from the ground?] Yes. Now this does not seem to be as general as these other conditions. It is a definite factor in some areas. [LH]

> There will be radon, xenon, some .. argon, and also increases of hydrogen and oxygen...in proportion, as normally found in the aqueous state of water. [KR]

The intuitives go on to say that the internal radiations emanate from the earth's core in all directions, though their intensity is not uniform and even vary significantly between points one mile apart on the surface. There are large variations in time, over periods of hours, from one sector of the earth to another. Near an earthquake fault the intensity is higher and the wavelengths are shorter. These waves change their character as they come through the mantle (the layer below the crust) like "people emerging from a doorway get lost in a crowd."

In the 1970s geophysics did not recognize most of these internal radiations, and none of them except heat as relevant to earthquakes.

The upper component originates as high-frequency electromagnetic radiation emanating from outer space and modulated by the ionosphere.[12*]

The upper energy is in the infrared, almost visible. [LH]

(Describe these ionospheric changes that you mentioned.) In this case, there will be changes both in the pressure and in the particles themselves, such as there will be gases being changed from one state to another, or there will be a changing in the gases or pressures themselves. But as a whole, the ionosphere acts as a storage device, as a condenser, for the earthquake before it strikes. Lowered, it begins to release the energy, and then it rises again…within a few miles of the epicenter. It ascends as a balloon that has lost its baggage. There are changes taking place over a long period of time, but when the energy is released, the changes take place very rapidly. [AA]

(What parameters of the ionosphere are relevant here?) It has something to do with the lower layer. The height and density…vary, anyway. And it will be changes that you detect in this lower layer that will help to indicate it. (What kind of changes?) I see almost silver, like aluminum foil or that type of thing, as though the way it reflects seems to be the changing factor that indicates what the change is going to be. [LH]

[The critical] focal point can be detected by ionospheric disturbance, which will vary in size like a hole and travel over the atmospheric sheath like the shadow of the moon. You can detect it coming, and if it falls on a vulnerable spot, the earthquake occurs. [MA]

Many radiations from outer space are known and the properties of the ionosphere are fairly well understood. However, the thought that ionospheric changes could be causally involved in earthquakes had never been proposed by seismologists.

Extraterrestrial and Atmospheric Effects

The planets also play a role, acting partly through the sun, though the interaction is complex and indirect:

> Gravitational forces from both the planets and heavier activities [affect] the release of many radiations from the surface of the sun. All these activities indeed are integrated with the phenomena. [KR]

> It is when the earth comes in the area of a focal point of energies of the planets. This may involve some or all of the planets at any given time, for these focal points are coming into and out of existence as the planets change positions with reference to each other. It is the earth crossing one of these focal points that draws in the energy to start an earthquake. *Where* the earthquake occurs depends upon what has been going on in the earth. [MA]

Science recognizes no direct interactions of the planets with processes on or within the earth. Some evidence suggests that the combined and varying gravity forces of the planets acting upon the sun (these are readily calculated) modulate sunspot, solar activity and thus solar radiations.[13] It is well known that solar radiations, acting upon the earth's magnetosphere and ionosphere, cause aurora at high latitudes, affect power grids and long pipelines, and disturb radio propagation, cellular phone communication, Loran and satellite communications. It is conceivable, therefore, that the changing positions of the planets could have indirect effects upon the earth, including earthquakes. The causal link is tenuous, however, and has never been firmly established.

The intuitives explained that when cosmic radiation reaches the earth it is converted at the ionosphere into an "almost visible" frequency (surely infrared, largely heat) before it reaches the earth's atmosphere. It increases the concentrations of certain kinds of ions (i.e., electrically charged atoms)—one source said hydroxyl ions—in the upper atmosphere. This infrared radiation and these ions affect in turn local weather conditions:

> (Does the ionospheric activity you mentioned affect the earth directly or only through the weather, when triggering an earthquake?) Only by the weather. It creates the atmospheric and electrical discharge that completes or causes other changes…. The heat and dryness of the earth's crust is that which is the final catalyst after the pressure buildup has reached a certain

point...even though the particular time of the occurrence is not dry per se....The dryness seems to cause an electrical spark. [LH]

The building of gaseous forces, observable within at least a 50 to 100 mile radius of the quake;...high degrees of positive ions in the atmosphere;...a release of negative ions close to the ground;...observable cloud structures, bulbulous [bulbous?] and towering in nature, up to 50 to 200 miles from the center...a great release of quantities of water from the atmosphere. [KR]

There is a general atmospheric disturbance involving highly charged air. [AAA]

There is often the attraction of certain cloud forms to areas of quakes, and even the stilling of the atmosphere. Researchers have come to understand that the triggering of electromagnetic forces that account for atmospheric conditions of storms (even the triggering of lightning) are grounding principles involving the electromagnetic fields of the earth, and not simply the aqueous and gaseous dynamics of the atmosphere itself, not even explainable by the centrifugal and thermal dynamics of the atmosphere, but are more directly related to the earth's electromagnetic energies. These phenomena are interconnected and not independent of each other. [KR]

These last statements are saying that atmospheric science needs to take into account electromagnetic effects for a proper understanding of how the weather is created and moves about. Atmospheric science has paid little attention to such effects, apart from lightning, and certainly not in a causal role. Seismologists too have paid no attention to atmospherics as a possible causal factor for earthquakes.

Combined Triggering Effects

One source (LH) described a particular cause-effect sequence as an example of what may occur, though it does not happen in every earthquake. When atmospheric conditions are just right, a down draft brings ions from the stratosphere down to the earth's surface. If the air near the surface is dry, thus able to support high electric fields (static charge conditions), and if no strong winds are present to disperse gases seeping from the earth, a electrochemical reaction occurs between these atmospheric ions and certain earth gases. This reaction propagates down into the earth, somewhat like a fuse, thus triggering the earthquake.

In most cases, however, the triggering within the earth occurs through the interaction of atmospheric and internal electromagnetic changes, along with internal gases, both of which act upon the physically stressed condition at the earthquake's hypocenter:

> There are two forces which would account for triggering the final activities of quakes. In the centermost [part] of tectonic plates the centrifugal force of the planet in its axis of rotation combines with the thermal expansionary forces of the molten masses beneath the surface, to [cause] movement along the inner structures, toward the outer surfaces of the tectonic plates, wherein there is the gaining of the highly charged magnetic and electromagnetic forces and the accumulation of both gaseous and aqueous forces. [KR]

The intuitives also said that the solid-earth tidal force (mentioned above) sometimes contributes to the final nudge that sets off the earthquake. Earth tides, similar to ocean tides, cause the surface of the earth to flex and heave up to 18 inches, twice every day.[14] Since early in this century a few seismologists have conjectured that these earth tides, perhaps augmented in coastal areas by water loading from ocean tides, might be triggering earthquakes. However, most of the statistical studies that tested this notion were either improperly conducted or failed to reveal a connection.[15] But two more careful investigations recently yielded positive results.[16] The intuitive information on this point is clear:

> [Did you say tides in the crust of the earth?] They are responsible to a minor degree. [AA]

> The forces of gravity would be minor upon the earth's crust. The alignment of both the moon and the sun [may]...cause an upset in the earth's own ability to balance these forces electromagnetically. [KR]

> Earth tides aid the triggering process. [AAA]

Summary of Triggering Mechanisms

In summary, the intuitives report that earthquake triggering is a complex process involving not only massive physical activity, part of which is already known to be taking place in the interior of the earth, but also various electrical, electromagnetic, chemical and centrifugal activities not presently recognized as significant to earthquake triggering. Some of the latter forces operate within the earth, while others take place above the surface of the earth, even in outer space, the ionosphere and the both the upper and lower atmospheres. These forces come together at and below the surface of the earth, combining in a complex manner not yet fully explained, to create the final trigger.

The surface indications cited in the consensus might serve as timely predictors of the earthquakes they are helping to trigger. These quantities change more rapidly than do internal earth processes, most of which vary more slowly. Moreover, presently available instruments are capable of measuring all of the above-ground quantities that were mentioned, though few are actually positioned in the field.

Checking the Intuitive Findings

To set up a monitoring system for predicting major earthquakes based on the intuitive findings would be a major task. It would require much financial support and involve dozens of scientists. If all parties are to cooperate on such a project, the intuitive claims must first be validated according to accepted scientific standards. To this end, verification tests must be conducted.

There are several possibilities. The intuitive team suggested the following specific quantities as candidates for possible measurement as short-term earthquake indicators:

- Collect information on abnormal animal behavior. Many common animals are excellent detectors of one or more of the precursory energies cited, and modify their behavior in an observable way.
- Detect changes in the chemical composition and electrical state of the lower atmosphere at the time and place of earthquakes.
- Note particular changes in local weather conditions around earthquake epicenters.

- Use radio-sounders from the ground or from satellites in space to detect variations in the reflectivity of the lower level of the ionosphere around the time of earthquakes.

- Use chemical "sniffers" to record the concentration of certain gas emissions from the ground: hydrogen, radon, methane, helium, and perhaps others.

- Employ appropriate types of antennas and radio receivers for monitoring the strength of very-low-frequency (VLF) electromagnetic radiation emanating from the earth's core.

- Look for correlations between earthquake activity and cosmic radiations from deep space, electromagnetic radiations from the sun and sunspot activity.

A few of these quantities, including solar activity and weather conditions, have been measured widely and carefully for many decades for other purposes. These data could be compared directly with existing records of past earthquakes (also abundant) to try to establish a direct correspondence. Ionospheric activity has been monitored only intermittently and in limited regions, but these records may turn out to be useful. Earth-level electric activity and the chemical composition of the lower atmosphere have not been consistently monitored in earthquake-prone areas and would have to be newly measured, then compared against future earthquake reports. Still others, such as the chemical composition of the upper atmosphere, could also be measured, but only at considerable expense.

The claimed relations between planetary positions and earthquakes are fascinating, but the spatial configurations and physical mechanisms to be considered are too numerous and complex for easy exploration. Verification studies are not warranted without further intuitive inquiry.

Verification through Historical Observations

The explanation of earthquake triggering given by the intuitive team does not so much contradict existing geophysical theory as it supplement it. Where there is overlap with present-day knowledge of the earth's interior no contradictions were apparent, but the intuitive picture goes well beyond what is commonly accepted in geophysics.

Geophysical researchers have understandably focused their attention on the earth itself as the natural domain for understanding the cause of earthquakes. They have simply not been looking to the atmosphere or outer space for the triggering source. Moreover, most seismologists are not trained in electromagnetic theory or meteorology, nor are they particularly familiar with what is already known in geophysics about electromagnetic phenomena around the earth as a whole. Even the subterranean radiations and chemical reactions cited in the intuitive description are unfamiliar topics to most of them and they have not seriously considered them as possible explanations. Consequently, there exists very little geophysical theory with which to directly compare the new intuitive hypothesis and check it for agreement or disagreement.

On the other hand, over the past 100 years both the scientific literature on earthquakes and the popular press contained many observational reports of phenomena that may be associated with earthquakes. Almost all of these reports were simply published and then forgotten. Some of them now lend positive support to the intuitive hypothesis:

* There are many anecdotal reports, plus several from professional sources, that cite unusual animal behavior just before earthquakes.[17]

* Reports of dramatic changes in the reflectivity of the ionosphere emerged from ionospheric sounding stations that happened to be operating near two large earthquakes in the Pacific basin: one in Hawaii (26 April 1973, Mag. 6.3/6.1) and the other in Alaska (28 March 1964, Mag. 7.9/8.6). In both cases an unusual non-reflecting hole appeared in the ionosphere 15-20 minutes before the earthquake and disappeared shortly after.[18] More similar reports from Asia reinforce this association, although in some cases the ionospheric disturbance was detected only after the shock and was interpreted as a reaction to ground motion.[19]

* The technical literature contains numerous reports, without explanation, of strange electrical activity in the atmosphere near the epicenter of large earthquakes: bright glows in the sky ("earthquake lights"), sparking in the air, fluorescent light bulbs flashing spontaneously, and crackling sounds typically associated with electrical discharges.[20]

* Popular reports of strange "earthquake weather" are legend, though most are questionable.[21] One study from Nicaragua associated a series of prior earthquakes with long dry spells. A scientist issued a prediction

on this basis in 1972, one day before an earthquake destroyed all of downtown Managua, the capital city, causing 5000 deaths.[22]

* Several widely separated radio astronomy receivers in the Northern hemisphere recorded unusually large electromagnetic emissions six days before the catastrophic Chilean earthquake on May 22, 1960.[23]

* A Japanese scientist found atmospheric electric field variations on the occasion of a long swarm of small earthquakes in Matsushiro, Japan in 1965-66.[24]

* In the tradition of astrology earthquakes are associated with the planets Uranus and Mars. Several statistical studies (most of them unpublished) demonstrated such an effect but all were erroneous. Careful analyses have failed to reveal any significant correlation.[25]

* Odorous gases have been reported near the sites of several large earthquakes.[26]

Besides these early observations, newer reports emerged after the Intuitive Consensus study was conducted. It is very unlikely that they were stimulated by our findings:

* Methane, hydrogen sulfide, hydrogen and other reactive gases, as well as the inert gases radon and helium, were detected in shallow ground or in the lower atmosphere shortly before a number of moderate-sized earthquakes.[27]

* Chinese scientists reported measurable pre-earthquake changes in readings from a variety of geophysical instruments, and also many human observations of ground gases, well-water levels and abnormal animal behavior.[28]

* Observers reported fireballs and related electrical activity in the atmosphere before a number of earthquakes.[29] (These phenomena are known to have occurred without earthquakes, but such reports are not common.)

* Tests on rock samples under stress have generated spontaneous emission of electromagnetic radiation at a frequency of about 1 MHz.[30]

* Reviews of biological literature on animal sensitivities (apart from earthquakes) revealed several sensory mechanisms not known to be possessed by humans. These include, among many others, senses for detecting weak electric fields, low-frequency sound, very low concentrations of gases and

weak magnetic fields. One or more of these sensitivities could explain the anomalous pre-earthquake behavior of animals.[31]

* An Italian geophysicist reported evidence for both unusual animal behavior and strong electric fields before an earthquake in Friuli, Italy, on 6 May 1976.[32]

* A Stanford scientist recently noted strong variations in the intensity of ultra-low-frequency (ULF) electromagnetic radiation near the epicenter of the Loma Prieta earthquake (Mag. 7.1) near Santa Cruz, California on 17 October 1989.[33] (Again, the observation was fortuitous; he was not looking for earthquake signals.)

* Since 1990 there has been a flurry of interest among geophysicists in electrical, magnetic and electromagnetic phenomena surrounding earthquakes. Over 100 scientific papers have been published in the 1990's alone. This work strongly supports the association of earthquake triggering with both ionospheric and solar radiation. Two surveys summarize this work.[34]

Taken together, this collection of findings provides considerable support to the intuitive hypothesis on earthquake triggering mechanisms. It is strong enough to suggest that other aspects of the hypothesis could be successfully verified as well.

Verification by Experiment

Encouraged by these findings two research products, both sponsored by the U.S. Geological Survey, were undertaken at SRI International in the late 1970s. The first collected and evaluated data on pre-earthquake animal behavior throughout California. The second monitored atmospheric electric field changes in a particular area prone to small earthquakes.

As noted above, the intuitive team suggested these two tests, and both seemed to be good candidates for immediate experimentation and verification. It was not hard to find substantial reasons, apart from the intuitive one, to justify the animal study, which was initiated by myself and Dr. Leon Otis, an SRI biologist.[35*] The second project was carried out independently by another SRI team, also not aware of the intuitive suggestion.

Might Earthquakes Be Prevented?

At first thought this question seems ridiculous. For how could man possibly prevent a physical event originating so deep in the earth (up to 700 miles) and involving a tremendous release of energy? (A magnitude 8.3 earthquake releases the same energy as 750 A-bombs.)

Nevertheless, a chance observation in 1966 revealed that fluid being pumped into wells near Rangely, Colorado, appeared to be provoking small earthquakes in the region. A three-year research project undertaken by the U.S. Geological Survey demonstrated conclusively that, under the right conditions, clusters of small earthquakes can be turned on and off as water is pumped into and out of the ground near where the shocks are occurring.[36] It is understood now what is happening. The presence of the water increases the so-called "pore pressure" in the subsurface rock, allowing it to slip or fracture more easily. (You might say they were lubricating the fault.) This action converts a large impending shock into a series of many smaller ones, most of them too tiny to be felt.

The favorable conditions of this experiment are a long way from those that exist where the most severe earthquakes shake our planet. The latter are usually deeper, the subsurface temperature and pressure are much higher, and who knows what kind of rocks and fractures lie at these depths. Moreover, a magnitude-8 shock is not merely four times as large as one of magnitude 2, but releases a *billion* times as much energy! Thus, it would take a billion barely felt earthquakes, and maybe several that are not so feeble, to balance off one large one—not a very good bargain.

But the more important issue is the reliability. Even if man could devise a technology for converting a large earthquake into many tiny ones, how would this technology be used? No technology is perfect. If such a pumping system were installed along the California coast, say, it might accidentally trigger off the large shock it is attempting to prevent— the awaited and long overdue San Andreas quake. No one wants to be responsible for triggering such a catastrophe.

Clearly, neither science nor society is yet ready for this approach to the prevention of earthquakes. If they are going to be stopped, a better solution will have to be found.

Animal behavior: This project, undertaken in 1978, set up an active network of 1500 volunteer observers of pets, farm animals, zoo animals and others—eventually a total of 200 species—in selected seismic areas throughout California.[37] The observers followed a fixed reporting protocol, which required that they report all instances of unusual behavior seen in their animals on a telephone "hot line" set up especially for the purpose. We recorded and transcribed for later analysis all their telephone reports, including the times the calls occurred. When analyzing the data we counted only those calls made before any associated earthquake. This requirement was crucial for the study because post-earthquake recollections of unusual animal behavior were known to be inaccurate and unreliable as data.

A sophisticated statistical analysis was applied to all data collected during the project. These four-years were an unusually quiet period for the shaky state of California, but they included 13 moderate earthquakes within the confines of the observer network. Positive results were obtained for seven of these shocks. One of them, a magnitude 4.3 tremor near Fremont, California on 3 March 1981, was a truly impressive "hit." We calculated that the large number of reports preceding this earthquake would have occurred by chance with a probability of only one in 20,000.

Other likely explanations for the high call frequency in the few days before the quakes had to be ruled out: local fires (for which the fire-truck sirens would have aroused every dog in the neighborhood), county fairs, storms, a weekend effect (when many observers were home and more likely to notice their animals), etc. We concluded that the animal population near Fremont was responding to an unidentified precursor, one detectable by the animals but not detected by any of the geophysical instruments monitoring the epicentral area at that time.

Atmospheric electric field: This second project was a straightforward measurement using electric-field sensors and data recorders.[38] These were deployed at chosen sites near Hollister and San Jose, California, both of which communities regularly experience small earthquakes. Despite instrumental problems the scientists obtained positive indications for two of the three medium-sized earthquakes that occurred in the selected areas over a two-year period. Both showed strong electric-field increases during the 15-minute period just preceding each quake. Similar changes occurred at a few other times as well, apparently due to anomalous weather conditions or dust raised by trucks leaving a nearby quarry. While the results were not fully conclusive, they were nevertheless encouraging and partially supported the electrical part of the triggering hypothesis.

Two other projects were proposed but not funded or carried out: (1) automatic collection of samples of ground-gas emissions in earthquake prone areas, and (2) examination of historical meteorological records for correlations between earthquakes and weather patterns.

Intuitives for Earthquake Prediction?

One might well ask: Why not let intuitives predict earthquakes directly instead of trying to understand the physics of earthquakes, then convincing skeptical scientists that a new technological approach is valid and building an expensive monitoring system?

CAI experience indicates that intuitives can indeed predict earthquakes accurately, at least under suitable conditions. A brief inquiry with one expert intuitive [LH] sought to find good sites in which to place monitoring instruments to "capture" the next five forthcoming earthquakes in California and Nevada. She provided the locations, dates and approximate magnitudes of the first four of them. All were substantially correct. The fifth was said to be unusual; there was a sinking of the ground and the date was uncertain within a few days. Its location and magnitude turned out to be correct, though it occurred two days late—from an underground nuclear test!

Intuitive predictions from other sources were occasionally accurate but most were completely wrong. Analysis of a few dozen of them revealed first of all that those from CAI intuitives were more precise and accurate than the others; those for unpopulated areas were more likely to be correct; and those predictions conducted for private use rather than for release to a wider audience or to the public were more accurate. The latter two observations suggest that the difference lay in the purpose for which the prediction was sought. Those intended to help individuals protect or reassure themselves and their families, to gather scientific data or as a reasoned response to a real danger (rather than a fearful reaction) tended to be the most correct. Those that were volunteered and not sought and those intended to warn society at large were almost all either vaguely stated or totally wrong.

This conjecture needs to be verified, of course, but history shows that when non-authoritative and uncertain predictions of catastrophes are released to the public, they m ay create confusion, irrational mass behavior, even panic, and this may result in more damage than the predicted event itself.[39*] This response can occur whether the means of prediction are rational or intuitive, and whether the event is an earthquake or some other catastrophe. Storm, flood and tornado warnings are accepted regularly because their progress can be tracked on television and the public trusts authorities who provide warnings and the instructions for appropriate response. But earthquakes occur without warning and they cannot be tracked. If an earthquake prediction is announced—especially an intuitive one—public confusion can only be expected.

When the word spread that I was interested in earthquake prediction, several budding intuitives and amateur seismologists began to contact me with their personal predictions. Their methods varied greatly, from a professed use of intuition to complex planetary calculations, tracking sunspots and tabulating the number of newspaper ads for lost pets.

As might be expected, most of the specific predictions were wrong. Others were so vague that I couldn't tell ahead of time what kind of an event would be considered a success and what would count as a failure: "A big earthquake is coming south of Mexico City this fall." In other cases they were predicting near certainties, though they apparently did not know it: "There will be a magnitude 7 earthquake in Alaska this year." Still another problem was that they often reported their predictions only after the earthquake had occurred: "Oh, I forgot to tell you,…". To be fair, though, I must admit that some of these amateur predictions were specific and accurate, were provided in advance, and foresaw quakes not likely to occur anyway.

I finally printed up a stack of self-addressed postcards, with blanks provided for the essential predictive information (date, location, magnitude), and distributed them to the eager prophets, with the announcement that I would not count post-earthquake reports at all. This move put a quick end to the experiment.

It is clear that the general public is not yet ready for intuitive earthquake prediction. Society must continue to rely upon its scientists, perhaps augmented discreetly, privately and occasionally by intuitive inputs. We may conclude that intuitive earthquake predictions are best sought today for personal use only and to aid small research efforts, where they are more likely to be heeded.

Does Mankind Cause Earthquakes?

On several occasions the CAI intuitives described (without being asked) how in a limited way mankind is actually creating earthquakes. Now here is an interesting, albeit fantastic, notion! For, as noted above, how could man's puny activities have any effect at all upon these massive natural events, commonly regarded as "acts of God?" The intuitives' remarks stimulated us to check out this idea in case it might be true in some way.

First of all, examples of man-caused earthquakes, albeit only small ones, are already known: the control of small shocks by pumping water into and out of wells[40], filling new dams and reservoirs with water[41]* and setting off atomic bombs.[42] Such examples show that, if conditions within the earth are just right, human activities might trigger an earthquake.

When first asked to explain how people could cause earthquakes, two intuitives mentioned that it is more of a collective process then an individual one, and its roots lie buried within the human unconscious. An independent intuitive [JR] with whom CAI consulted from time to time, spoke most clearly about this effect:

> Your feelings have electromagnetic properties…There are what I am going to call "ghost chemicals"—aspects of normal chemicals that you have not perceived so far—which are changed into purely electromagnetic properties, and energy is released that directly affects the atmosphere.[43] [JR]

We have here an interesting clue, though not an explanation. This intuitive explained further that there is also an individual component because each person "decides," normally unconsciously, whether to live in an earthquake area or not. That is, everyone makes his own deep choice as to which area will best meet his inner needs for certain life experiences. One person may seek a quiet locale that will not place too many demands on his own growth, while another will choose to live within an energetic environment, including political unrest, wars, tornadoes—or earthquakes. This inner urge not only tends to collect together those who seek challenging drama. It interacts with the environment and encourages the earthquake itself:

> Natural disasters are brought about more at an emotional level than at a belief level, though beliefs have an important part to play for they generate the emotions…Those in earthquake regions are attracted to such spots

because of their innate understanding of the relationship between exterior circumstances and their own private mental and emotional patterns. The qualities of such individuals...*en masse* affect the deep electromagnetic energy of the earth....Obviously, there have been earthquakes where there are no people, but in all cases the origins are to be found in mental properties rather than exterior ones.[44] [JR]

If this is literally true, then earthquakes are not just random geologic events but are to some extent the consequences of the collective preferences of thousands of unconscious minds that "choose" to gather together around an epicenter. Our own private tremors are consonant with and interact with those the earth produces.

Further, apart from whether and how man, individually or collectively, is responsible for creating natural catastrophes, he certainly has the intuitive capacity to sense when and where they are about to occur. He can therefore avoid them if he "chooses" (perhaps unconsciously) to do so. When he disregards such inner knowing he may find himself experiencing one disaster after another—not merely earthquakes but also accidents, poor job choices, unworkable relationships, risky investments and inappropriate moves to other areas, to name just a few common personal catastrophes.

Finally, it has been shown that man possesses a number of largely unused physical senses, apart from intuition, just as many animals do.[45*] These sensitivities function subtly to protect him from danger, including forthcoming natural events such as earthquakes.

On other than conscious levels, simply as creatures, you are well aware of impending storms, floods, tornadoes, earthquakes and so forth. There are many hints and signs picked up by the body itself—alterations in air pressure, magnetic orientation, minute electrical differentiations of which the skin itself is aware.... Unconscious material is admitted into consciousness according to the beliefs an individual holds about himself, his reality and his place in it. Those who want to use their own unconscious precognition of such an event will take advantage of it.[46] [JR]

I carried out tests of two persons who claimed to possess this kind of physical sensitivity. Both were successful, though I do not know at this point how to distinguish this physical sensitivity from a strong intuitive faculty.

In summary, we are being told that people "cause" earthquakes in four ways: first, collectively, through their thought patterns, which physically affect the atmosphere and the earth in ways not yet understood; second, individually, by unconsciously choosing to place themselves in the way of earthquakes; third, as they disregard relevant intuitive knowledge about where and when an earthquake is about to strike; and fourth, by not responding to subtle sense-based indications of natural pre-earthquake changes.

Evaluation

Can intuition be used to obtain useful scientific and technical information? The answer is a clear *yes*, but the full conditions and limitations are still not fully known.

This second experiment in Intuitive Consensus was satisfying in the abundant flow of new information, its plausibility, its clarity, the level of technical detail provided and the fact that several partial verification efforts were supportive of its accuracy and relevance to the triggering issue. The consensus was good, though the proportion of information contributed by one intuitive and not the others was greater than for the previous inquiry. There was no indication that the information sought was being denied. In contrast, it seemed that much more was available but was not able to fit itself through the minds and speech of the intuitives without more specific questioning.

On the other hand, it became apparent very early that the problem under study was bigger than could be adequately explored in just a few intuitive sessions. This difficulty, soon to plague several later experiments as well, forced the inquiry to be more superficial than was desired or expected. The result was that the new information was fragmentary and could not be pulled together into a single, integrated hypothesis, one that might be explained in familiar terms and verified as a whole. Only certain fragments could be validated. While the results were all positive and supportive of the intuitively derived information, total verification was not possible.

The next logical step would be to fill in the missing portions, through additional intuitive inquiries, to create a full hypothesis, which may then be tested in a larger corroboration effort. The testing should be done not just for a few small earthquakes but a variety that represents a full range of magnitudes, depths and subsurface rock conditions—obviously an expensive and time consuming undertaking. Unfortunately this is how scientific research, including verification studies, must be carried out. Even so, the cost in time, money and effort to verify hypotheses is typically much less than the cost of searching for good hypotheses in the first place, without intuitive help.

Further intuitive inquiries could also be very helpful at this later stage for aiding in the fortuitous placement of instruments, and for understanding better how the triggering process actually functions in physical terms, not just as a set of measured phenomena.

When scientists are able and willing to trust and use their own intuitive capacities more directly and intentionally, they will be able to create better hypotheses, and research progress will surely accelerate. This deliberate reliance upon intuition could also guide future scientific endeavors into more creative and beneficial directions, by identifying in advance the technical and societal consequences of new discoveries.

> "This we know: the earth does not belong to humans, humans belong to the earth. This we know: all things are connected, like the blood which unites one family....Humans do not weave the web of life, they are merely a strand in it. Whatever they do to the web, they do to themselves."
> [Ted Perry[47*]]

• Endnotes—Chapter 7

[1*] Material in this chapter is adapted and extended from Kautz, 1982.

[2] Bird, 1972.

[3] Anon5, 1976.

[4*] Earthquake sizes quoted in this chapter use the new moment-magnitude scale, which measures the total energy released by the earthquake, instead of the old Richter magnitude scale, which is calculated directly from the strength of vibrations measured in seismographic records.

[5*] Geophysicists interested in working with the technical content of the findings reported in this chapter should contact the author.

[6*] The reference to "electromagnetic" forces requires elaboration, for these include in their definition all known forms of radiation, from radio, infrared, light, ultraviolet, x-ray and microwaves, to cosmic rays and even the fundamental particles of physics, which have both particle and wave properties. The distinguishing feature of all these forms is their frequency (equivalently wavelength), which varies downward from many miles to billionths of a millimeter and farther. Ordinary magnetism is essentially a field of zero frequency.

[7]* I had personal experience with such an individual: Reuben Greenspan. He had several successful and significant predictions to his credit: 15 in the 1930s, as well as the San Fernando, California, earthquake of 1971. He claimed for many years that he based them on earth-tidal calculations, unaware that the technical article on which his "theory" was based was seriously in error. He later admitted to me he had dreamed his predictions.

[8] Geller, 1997.

[9]* The *hypocenter* of an earthquake is the point within the earth where the rupture or slippage first begins; the *epicenter* is an imaginary point on the earth's surface, directly above the hypocenter. The location of the region of strongest ground shaking may be neither of these, since it depends in a complex way upon rock structures in the surrounding area.

[10] Bolt, 1993.

[11] Bolt, 1993.

[12]* The ionosphere is a multilayered, wavering electronic sheath known to lie 50+miles above the earth's surface. It protects the earth from harmful cosmic radiation, and radio stations use it as a reflector for bouncing medium-wave radio signals around the earth.

[13] Dean, 1977, pp. 496-502, Eysenck & Nias, 1984, pp. 143-162.

[14] Darwin, 1962.

[15] Knopoff, 1969, Simpson, 1938, Shlein, 1972.

[16] Heaton, 1975, Mauk & Kienle, 1973.

[17] Evernden, 1976, Kerr, 1980, Lott et al, 1981, Lee et al., 1976.

[18] Davies & Baker, 1965, Leonard & Baker, 1965; see also the references cited in these articles.

[19] See, for example, Calais & Minster, 1995, Zelenova & Legen'ka, 1989, Sharadze et al. 1989, Kim & Hegai, 1997.

[20] Derr, 1973, Ulumov et al, 1971, Davison, 1937.

[21] Santos, 1973.

[22] Rikitake, 1976, Wood & King, 1977.

[23] Anon1, 1980.

[24] Kondo, 1968.

[25] See, for example, Gauquelin, 1977, p. 500, Eysenck & Nias, pp. 143-162.

[26] Moulton, 1980, Gold, 1979.

[27] Moulton, 1980, Lee et al., 1976, Wakita et al, 1980, King, 1978, Teng, 1980, Rikitake, 1976.

[28] Jennings, 1980, Earthquake Reseearch Group, 1980, Zhu & Shong, 1980, Lee & Wang, 1976.

[29] Lee et al., 1976, Oike, 1978.

[30] Nitsan, 1978.

[31] Buskirk et al., 1981.

[32] Tributsch, H., 1978.

[33] Fraser-Smith, 1990.

[34] Parrot & Johnston, 1989, Park et al., 1993.

[35]* Both Otis and the sponsor were supportive of the hypothesis though neither was aware of its intuitive origin.

[36] See, for example: http:/www.loki.stockton.edu/~hozikm/geol/Courses/earthquakes/Lectures/

[37] Otis & Kautz, 1981.

[38] Adamo & Enns, 1980.

[39]* Experience with similar sudden catastrophies in foreign countries reveals a scenario that could also occur in the U.S. if an unofficial prediction is issued. While some authorities will deny the prediction, others will call for action. Controversy will ensue on whether to close up downtown areas, shut off utilities, evacuate communities, alert hospitals and lower water levels in dams. Some but not all businesses will choose to close. Some citizens will leave their homes despite the danger of vandalism. Traffic jams will build up on exit highways. With sufficient advance notice one can expect panic purchase of earthquake insurance and speculation in real estate.

[40] See ref. 22 above.

[41]* More than 20 such instances have been reported, including Hoover Dam (U.S.), the Aswan High Dam (Egypt), Hsin-feng-chiang Dam (China), and reservoirs at Kariba (Zimbabwe), Koyna (India) and the Arapuni River (NZ).

[42] Bolt, 1976.

[43] Roberts, Jane, 1972, p. 362.

[44] Roberts, Jane, 1972 pp. 362-3.

[45]* Several animals are known to be sensitive to the earth's magnetic field: pigeons, honey beas, tuna, salmon, dolphins and turtles, for example. Magnetite in the cells of certain bacteria are known to enable them to orient to the earth's magnetic field. Human red blood cells also contain magnetite, which may be responsible for a subtle human sensitivity to do the same.

[46] Roberts, 1972, pp. 364-5.

[47]* Seed, 1988; adapted by Perry from a speech by Chief Sealth.

CHAPTER 8

SUDDEN INFANT DEATH SYNDROME[1]*

EXPERT INTUITIVES LOOK AT CRIB DEATH

"A woman with babe said, speak to us of children. And he said:
'Your children are not your children. They are the sons and daughters of life's longing for itself. They come to you, but not from you.
Though they are with you, they belong not to you."
[Kahlil Gibran[2]]

In this next experiment we take a bold look at an unexplained human tragedy: Sudden Infant Death Syndrome, commonly called "SIDS," crib death or cot death. SIDS is the unexplained sudden death of an apparently healthy infant during its few months of life. In the United States one in about every 1000 births results in a crib death. It is the leading "cause" of infant deaths during the first year.[3]* The rates for other Western countries are about the same. (Useful figures are not available for most non-Western countries.[4]*)

While SIDS strikes relatively few people, its very existence is a shocking reminder of a aspect of human life most of us would prefer to ignore: children die, too, and seemingly well before their allotted time. Here is an open invitation for us to examine the meaning of our own lives, and those of our children, hence the deeper purpose of life—and death. The fact that established medical science and other accepted authorities of the Western world do not know the cause of SIDS adds a special motivation: it asks all of us to seek an answer to this puzzle within ourselves.

We began this study, and will begin here, by examining what is already known about SIDS. This preparation defined the domain of ignorance and generated a good set of questions. Described next are the results of CAI's Intuitive Consensus inquiry on SIDS. The main questions are addressed: What is the cause of SIDS? Is there a way to detect SIDS in advance? Can it be prevented? What happens in a child's body when it dies by SIDS? How may one interpret and deal with SIDS when it occurs (an issue mainly for the parents)? What does a SIDS death signify? What can SIDS parents—or anyone, for that matter—learn from the loss of a infant? Finally, we compare the intuitive findings with known medical knowledge, such as it is, and suggest their principal implications for future research, public policy, and especially for each of us as individuals.

What is SIDS?

Dozens of studies have generated speculations about characteristic symptoms accompanying SIDS deaths, but none that might explain it has been confirmed so far. Autopsies of thousands of SIDS babies (required by law in the U.S.) revealed no medically significant abnormalities that could conceivably account for these deaths.

Statistical studies have shown a slightly higher frequency for male children, twins, infants born with low birth weight, those not breast-fed and those whose mothers are very young, smoke, take drugs or receive less than normal prenatal care.[5] No ethnic group of infants is free of the syndrome, though the percentages are less or Orientals in the U.S.. Crib deaths almost always occur between the ages of 2 and 8 months, during sleep and a little more frequently during winter months. Otherwise no significant pattern to their occurrence is known.[6] None of these tendencies is strong enough to imply a cause of SIDS or to allow even partial prediction.

The Official Position on SIDS

A recent news item in a national Irish newspaper[7] announced the government guidelines on crib death. First acknowledging that, "Sadly, of course we do not know the cause of cot death,"...the Minister of Health goes on to recommend "that babies should be placed on their back or side to sleep, that babies should not be allowed to become too warm, that expectant mothers should not smoke nor allow anyone to smoke near the baby during the first year of life, and if at all possible, mothers should breast feed babies for the first few weeks...because it might reduce the risk of infection." This counsel given in the U.S. is essentially the same.[8]

The unfortunate aspect of this advice is that there is no medical evidence to support these factors as causes of SIDS, but only as "risk factors," a term that means only that they are statistically associated, or sometimes occur together, with SIDS death. For example, according to the research, one is no more justified in assuming that the mother's smoking causes the death than to assume that her unconscious awareness of the forthcoming death somehow induces her to smoke. Or that both the smoking and the death are the result of one or more unknown factors. No one knows what are the hidden connections—causes and effects—between a child dying of SIDS and the four factors cited. More likely, like the rest of life, there is a host of interconnecting influences at work, and the crib death is just one very conspicuous and painful one. There is no implication that changing the circumstances, such as placing the baby to sleep on its back or breast feeding the baby, is going to *prevent* the death. Of course, these suggested actions may be wise for *any* mother and child, but according to present understanding the reasons for them have little or nothing to do with SIDS.

If the intuitive information reported in this chapter is correct, these associated factors have to do only with the *manner* in which the infant dies, and are not the cause of death.

The Impact of SIDS

The most conspicuous impact of SIDS is upon the parents, especially the mother. Grief over the loss of any child is normal and understandable, but it is made worse when no cause can be cited to which the death can be attributed.

It is common for heavy guilt to set in: "I must have done something wrong." A physician's assurance that "no, you are not to blame" is a weak consolation when he can offer no explanation of who or what really is to blame. Occasionally uninformed police, friends, relatives or even a spouse will accuse a parent of negligence, which further exacerbates the guilt. There are even cases on record in which SIDS parents were jailed on suspicion of killing their infant. Sometimes the guilt or an inability to accommodate to it has triggered a collapse of the marriage. Even when there is ample sympathy and support, the unanswered question remains, "Why has this happened to me?"

The SIDS enigma is obviously a sensitive subject for many. There is probably nothing in normal life more mentally painful than the death of one's own child. The entire SIDS phenomena is full of unknowns so there is much space for imagination, rumors and fear to have free rein.

In offering here CAI's findings on SIDS, I do so with full respect for those who have already suffered from a SIDS loss or will suffer from it in the future. Indeed, it was the awareness of this suffering that motivated this study in the first place. Please understand that when speaking of infant death so volubly I am not taking the issue lightly or regarding it merely academically. I do believe it is essential for all concerned to discuss SIDS openly and freely, so we may defuse the pain, understand better what it really is and learn why we suffer so greatly from it.

What follows is not a superficial collection of opinions and speculations, but a serious, in-depth inquiry into the deeper cause, significance and appropriate handling of SIDS. We are inquirers here, not self-appointed authorities eager to provide unsubstantiated beliefs and unproven solutions. Therefore, consider the information provided in the following sections not as authoritative, well established facts but rather a fresh perspective on how to interpret crib death. Regard the intuitives' statements as a stimulus to thoughtful consideration and shared concern. You will find the truth about SIDS in your own heart.

At the practical level the intuitive perspective reported below offers several specific hypotheses, some for personal examination and experimentation and others that could be tested formally and scientifically, using accepted methods. At the least this account deserves the attention of anyone who is trying with an open mind to understand the puzzling enigma of crib death—and death in general, for that matter.

The Intuitive Inquiry

The first step in preparation for this Intuitive Consensus inquiry was a review of the medical and sociological literature on SIDS. It provided the statistics mentioned above and confirmed that the basic cause of SIDS has never been found, despite more than seventy years of committed research. We then compiled a list of medical, psychological and social questions to be posed to the team of five expert intuitives, collaborating with several SIDS parents to enrich the list. We conducted the inquiry with these questions, plus a few more that arose during the sessions. None of the intuitives on the team had personal or particular prior experience with SIDS, and none had a medical background.

The intuitive inquiry generated a great deal of specific information. As in most other Consensus studies the answers to the main questions were in good agreement. Individual intuitives contributed additional insights on particular matters. We obtained personal information on family circumstances surrounding a few specific SIDS deaths.

Again, we include here only representative excerpts from the inquiry sessions on SIDS, not the entire set of responses.

The Cause of SIDS: The Big Picture

The intuitive team explained that the general "cause" of crib death—actually, any infant death—may be regarded on two levels: the physical and the non-physical. Both are valid views but the physical is a consequence of the non-physical, which is therefore the root cause.

First, at the physical level there is no simple explanation of SIDS:

There is not one isolated cause of crib death. [BR]

Every case is different. No case is typical. [AAA]

Any body is susceptible to this peculiar set of events. It is not a virus, not a disease or an illness. The nervous system triggers this, but it is not a response, for SIDS is not a nervous disease....I look through the body...at the heart, the liver, the kidneys and all the different parts, and they all fade together. [LH]

It's not coming out of a physical defect. [SR]

They go on to say that the life force or vital energy withdraws from the physical body, which then dies from whatever bodily function happens to be a bit weaker or more susceptible than the rest, depending upon the child's overall constitution. If the infant is already ill, even with a disease that would not normally be fatal—a cold or a minor case of pneumonia, say—the body will appear to succumb through this illness. This category also includes certain readily avoided "accidents"; e.g., gagging on a foreign object, suffocating on a pillow or falling out of bed. But none of these conditions is the true cause of the death.

At the non-physical level SIDS was said to result from *a voluntary withdrawal of the infant's consciousness from its physical body*. In other terms, the life essence or "soul" of the child simply leaves on its own. It was pointed out that babies, like animals, can enter and leave life rather easily. One may correctly say that the child "chooses" to leave, for any of a variety of reasons (presented below), and it makes this choice out of its own kind of consciousness. The intuitives explained that the infant state of mind is similar to what adults experience in a dream, reverie or similar state of consciousness. Such voluntary withdrawal also occurs commonly with the aged as they approach the end of their life. The physical body then dies from whatever part is weakest.

The actual death of the SIDS infant is not usually in anguish, they say; it is just like falling asleep. The child's act could be said to be a suicide, though this may be stretching the meaning of the term, which normally refers to a *conscious* decision to end one's life.

Why should a child choose to leave? There are diverse reasons:

Many of these children are coming in without the background of experience with bodies that others have had. They need to learn rapidly what bodies are all about....Sometimes it's too fast. for them...[DF]

The soul simply decides to leave, for unfavorable conditions have happened after the soul has entered. [AA]

Sometimes a soul comes in just to touch base with reality, most commonly if it has undergone a violent death and is still hanging onto the physical world. [AAA]

The soul is not [always] trying to leave the body. It is simply…a calling back to realize it made a wrong decision. It's just a natural consequence. [GB]

[The departure] may be because of the body situation; or because the parents' will has changed so the entity does not…have the full situation it anticipated; or because the entity has learned in another manner what this lifetime was to provide; or because the parents have chosen to study death, and the entity is coming in to create a body and then die so they can examine their beliefs about death. [LB]

An interesting case illustrates one way in which SIDS can occur. CAI conferred with a mother a year or so after she lost her baby girl. We spoke about the possibility of consulting an expert intuitive to try to learn what happened from the girl's point of view. The mother agreed.

In the session the intuitive [AAA] (who had only the mother's name and address) reported that the girl had come into life in this particular family to have a strong interaction with the father. In fact, this relationship was to be a main focus of her life. However, during the pregnancy he became upset by the diversion of his wife's attention to the forthcoming child, and began to be moody and drink heavily. By the time of the birth he was well on his way to becoming an alcoholic. The girl, who had then lost the greatest interest in her new life, left at four months of age.

The mother confirmed the events in the intuitive's report from her own experience: her husband's jealousy, his drinking and her feeling about the girl's connection with her father. His alcoholism continued and the marriage broke up a year later.

What is recognized medically as the "cause of death" by the attending physician and is duly recorded on an infant's death certificate is quite another matter. The standard practice is to attribute the death to any detectable abnormality or medically identifiable disorder that could conceivably account for it. When none is found, and if there is no evidence of mistreatment or any negative indication from the infant's medical record, the cause of death listed tentatively as "SIDS," to be later confirmed on autopsy. This designation allows that the death may have arisen from an unknown virus, trace-level environmental poisoning, inconspicuous malnutrition or some other influence beyond what a superficial examination can detect. Consequently, some deaths classified as SIDS would properly be attributed to a physical cause if they were medically investigated more thoroughly.

Conversely, some deaths attributed to a physical cause (like a cold), and *not* classified as SIDS, may actually be due to a voluntary withdrawal of the infant consciousness. The term "SIDS" is merely a convenient and not very accurate medical classification. It describes not the presence of an internal condition but the absence of easily recognizable symptoms. It does not necessarily designate the cause of death.

In retrospect it would have been more correct to name this study "voluntary infant death," since this is what the intuitives allege to occur in most SIDS deaths and any other infant deaths. They say this "voluntary" aspect is where the true cause lies. Nevertheless, we will continue to use the accepted term "SIDS death" in what follows, despite its imprecision.

To confuse the situation further, the intuitives indicated that at a deep level all infant deaths, classified as SIDS or not, are in one sense "voluntary" for the child. This is because every person, including infants, holds deeply within his unconscious mind a foreknowledge of his own departure: when, how and under what conditions. Only very rarely does an adult have conscious access to this knowledge. (Sometimes it emerges to consciousness shortly before death.) In an infant this awareness is closer to the surface, so he is more likely to just "know" when it is time to leave. (More later on this deep level of what seems to be a kind of destiny.)

It should be clear now, if the intuitives are correct, why fifty years of research based on autopsies of infants classified as SIDS have not revealed any consistent pattern in either the physical symptoms or the presumed causes of death. Until medical science acknowledges a non-physical origin of SIDS it is unlikely it will do better in the future.

Immediate Implications

"Human beings have an idea they are very fond of: that we die in old age. This is just an idea. We don't know when our death will come." [Katagiri Roshi[9]]

How may one interpret this intuitive finding in the light of current medical and psychological knowledge (or lack of it), or even just from personal experience?

This explanation of SIDS clearly declares that an infant actually *has* a consciousness, even at a very early age; moreover, that this consciousness is capable of making decisions, even (perhaps especially) life-and-death choices. Such a picture clearly contradicts the popular view that an infant mind is an undeveloped bodily organ not yet capable of thought, yet alone making decisions. It appears that we are being asked to believe that a just-born baby, who seems to function entirely by instinctual physical needs, whose senses are not yet working well, whose brain is not fully developed and who cannot even speak, is *thinking*! Is this indeed the case?

At this point we must go back and ask where we acquired the notion that a newborn's mind is totally blank. This idea has its basis in contemporary Western physiological and psychological understanding of the mind. The models adopted in contemporary medicine and psychology assume that consciousness arises from a developed brain, not the other way around, and they disallow the type of infant mental activity claimed by the intuitives. If we question further what is the basis of this view, now widely accepted, we find that the contradiction arises not because there is any clear psychological or physiological evidence that such deep mental activity does not occur, but rather because psychology has not yet found acceptable evidence to support the notion that it does. This is a significant difference, because what appears to be a contradiction in the popular view is just an "unknown" in the psycho-physiological view. After all, lack of evidence for something does not mean that it does not exist, but only that it has not been found. And whether it has been found depends on who is looking, where, and how.

If we probe even further back to the psychological criterion of what constitutes "acceptable evidence," we find much unquestioned tradition and a strong reliance upon a convenient set of basic assumptions about the world. These assumptions are axiomatic, unsupported by either experience or experiment, and good evidence is showing now that they may indeed be quite wrong. Nevertheless, the field of psychology (and medicine as well) has already rejected many new models and explanations, such as the one presented in this chapter, as unscientific—especially those that are not so easily explored in purely physical terms, using physical methods and measuring instruments.

The information provided by the intuitives does not oppose the basic observational data of psychology, nor does it disagree with the results directly derived from these data by formal study. It does not even contradict the solidly based portion of existing knowledge about the infant mind. It offers instead to extend this knowledge and these results by filling in an important gap.

The Physical Process of Death

If we cannot find a physical cause of SIDS death, perhaps we can learn something about the dying process itself. When a healthy child dies by withdrawing its consciousness, what actually takes place within his body?

The intuitives described this physical process as beginning in the brain, then moving through the rest of the nervous system, some of the endocrine glands and other organs, finally reaching the lungs. The sequence ends with a cessation of breath and beating of the heart, the signs normally considered by medicine to signal the termination of life. The overall process is complex, they say, for it involves many closely interacting parts of the body. Moreover, it varies considerably from one infant to another, for each has its own pattern of susceptibilities.

> I'm drawn to several physical areas. There is a general physical collapse, but there is an earlier event...the nervous system, and this includes the spinal cord. [SR]

> The deaths are...epileptic in nature, in that there are imbalances between the left and right -brain hemispheres. Over-stimulation of electrical activities in the brain patterns or synapses between the neurological tissues causes a mis-coordination in the breath....Also, [there are] dysfunctions within the kidney and over-stresses in the metabolic response within the forming infant metabolism. Higher quantities of toxins are found in the bloodstream, related to the stresses placed upon the kidneys. [KR]

> The metabolism lowers, the hypothalamus misfunctions. [BR]

> [An]other area of physiological response may be caused by two critical collapses in the endocrine system synonymously with each other: the pancreas and the adrenals, due to over-stimulation of insulin within the system. This causes a rapid blood sugar drop within the physical body. [KR]

The imbalances finally reach the pulmonary system:

> This brings about a shortness of oxygenation to the brain tissues and complete brain death....Physical results would be the collapse in part of the lung tissues, and exhaustion of oxygen in the blood cells of the brain tissues, liver and intestinal tract—even in red corpuscles exiting through the lungs' capillary action. [KR]

> A brief struggle. There is a blockage in the base of the lungs, so the infant can't expel its breath. A pressure occurs. It's just the one breath, but that's its last. [GB]

> There appears to be a confusion in the lung system. The oxygen ratio changes. It's as if they [the lungs] have forgotten what they are supposed to be doing. A spastic condition develops in the upper part of the lungs. [AAA]

> It seems to be something in my lungs or breathing apparatus, but I don't choke or strangle. If air could rush out of my lungs at the same time as I'm trying to breath in, this feels like the impasse....It has to do with the oxygen and the blood....There doesn't seem to be any obstruction, other than air against air....It is a reflex action, an uncontrolled spasm, a lack of coordination in the body processes that is not detectable. It is sudden by nature. [LH]

There are various ways in which the chain reaction may progress. Some of the paths of the collapsing system may be affected by bodily weaknesses brought on by external factors such as nutritional deficiencies, ingested toxins or environmental poisoning. Here are three possible scenarios:

> The collapse of the kidney's tissues is in response to the functions of the liver, and may come about due to the misassimilation of micronutrient levels of zinc, vitamin C and vitamin B....At times there may be allergic reactions to the mother's own specific milk, as toxins stored through many years of use of unclean foods, as well as from the atmosphere, are stored directly in the fatty tissues of the mother. These may then impress themselves into the fatty tissues of the fetus during its development, particularly if there is nursing upon the mother's milk. [KR]

A SIDS death can result from...a rare, distorted molecule of the antidi-uretic hormone, which is produced by the posterior pituitary,...two to three hours before the death. It is amplified [?] in the hypothalamus, where it acquires a fuzzy antibody, one which originally arose from residues of certain medication the mother received. (Later: It's not the medication itself, but...a contaminant, potassium acetate, in the filler, common in aspirin and soft drinks.) [It then] goes in a direction that is abnormal for this hormone, and works through the respiratory center of the brain to cause some erratic, hiccup-like signals in muscles in the solar plexus area....There are also other factors. It is a matter of timing. It is a chain reaction....This same encased hormone can be present in others and flow through all right. [LH]

You will find that a high proportion of crib deaths [occur with] parents who have worked in a highly toxic chemical environment. These both stim-ulate genetic imbalance [and] contribute to the development of allergic states...also a high degree of fluoridations and sulfurs contained within drinking waters, perhaps for temporary periods of time due to changes in underground water tables. Also...concentrations of electromagnetic pollu-tants, produced both naturally in the environment but also produced through industrial magnifications such as underground transportation devices. [KR]

Keep in mind, however, that these various contributing factors are all second-ary to the primary, non-physical cause of SIDS. They describe only *how* the body dies, not the basic cause of death. Their variety and intricacy are interest-ing, but they offer little hope for intervening in the process to stop it, if that is possible at all.

Anticipation of SIDS Death?

Might infants who are about to die of SIDS be identified hours or days in advance? The intuitives indicated that there are no consistent, universal physi-ological signs to watch for, or tests that might be conducted prior to death, that could signal that a SIDS death is imminent. For some SIDSs, however, a few minor symptoms might be identified:

You will find that [on] the scanning of brain wave activities, [using] a normal unit of measurement, there would be detected, in part, mild neurological over-stimulation between the synapses of the right and left brain hemispheres. [KR]

Gradual changes in body acidity could be picked up with frequent blood tests a day or two before [the death]. [LH]

At the physiological level you may consider the blood pressure. Take it an hour before a crib death. It will have a sudden increase, a sharp rise, but it will not stay very long—just two and a half to three minutes....The other thing is the temperature, which will fluctuate quite rapidly, not necessarily in accordance with the blood pressure....The perspiration will increase....It will go to 102° but not much beyond that. [AA]

I keep getting the feeling of two spots here [pointing just below the front of the neck]....I begin to hurt and have trouble breathing....It's a thyroid imbalance. It's not a matter of a malformed thyroid gland, but thyroxin...T3 and T4., instead of staying on the same level are on a teeter-totter...[changing] every five minutes. It goes out of balance in the last hour-and-a-half before death. [LH]

Since these indications are all irregular and inconsistent they are not very useful. Obviously one cannot monitor all infants continuously. Neither is there any known basis for selecting those few who are at risk and might be monitored carefully. In general, continual monitoring of infants, even just during sleep, is not practical.

Anyway, so long as SIDS death is not known to be preventable, even a sophisticated warning system could do no more than reduce somewhat the surprise element, by giving the parents a few extra moments in which to prepare for the shock. Unless the monitoring device were highly reliable (which such technology never is), it would also give false alarms. The parents would hardly be put at ease when they are woken at night by loud signals that send the dire message, "Perhaps *this* time your child is really dying." Monitoring devices for infants have actually been devised, built and used in homes to detect breathing irregularities and heart problems. For some disorders they are surely helpful, but for SIDS the psychological impact, plus the fact that no preventative action can be taken, makes their use very questionable.

SIDS Prevention

According to the expert intuitives SIDS is not preventable at the physical level since its fundamental cause is not physical. At the non-physical level we might reason that it might be prevented, or at least delayed, if the infant consciousness is "undecided" about whether to leave or not—that is, if it has not yet fully chosen to stay or to depart. If this happens perhaps it could somehow be persuaded to stay around.

This is a real possibility, the intuitives say. They explained (in a separate Intuitive Consensus study on conception, pregnancy and childbirth) that a consciousness or "soul" about to enter the body of an infant at birth is sometimes afraid of being born, just as elderly adults are often afraid of dying. The birth nevertheless proceeds, just as death does, and the fear usually dissipates shortly after the birth. Occasionally, though, it persists for several weeks, months or even longer. (This fear can also retard the birth itself, they say, which is the main reason for exceptionally long labors.) Because the consciousness of a child is not as firmly attached to its body during the first few months of life as it is later, it is relatively easy for it to leave. If the postnatal consciousness is overwhelmed by fear, it may vacillate about whether it wants to stay around. A concerned parent who is sensitive to this condition might find a way to intervene.

How to detect this vacillation? It seems the best we can hope for is that, if a child is indecisive about whether to leave or not, there may be some physical or psychological signs of its wavering. He might provide to an alert observer a subtle behavioral clue that it may be leaving soon, a sign that a sensitive parent could pick up to indicate a possible departure. Alternatively, an expert intuitive might be able to identify in advance such an infant, apart from any physical signs.

If the indecisiveness can be detected, the question then becomes: how should the parents let the child know it is truly wanted? One way might be direct communication:

> Talk to the child, make yourself a close friend of the child....Speak positively to the soul, saying, "You don't need to leave." [AA]

The intuitives report that dialogues with the minds of infants and the unborn are not only possible, but caring parents commonly do so unconsciously. We did not ask for an explanation of how all this works, and how one might learn to do it deliberately, but it is well known that pregnant women often feel they are in communication with their unborn children.

An Experiment in Prenatal Communication

Five pregnant women volunteered for a small CAI experiment to see if expert intuitives could communicate with their unborn children. We tracked each case from the beginning of the third trimester, when an intuitive session was held with the mother present, until two months after the birth. The main focus of each session was to listen to what the infant might want to say to the mother, but I also asked several questions: What was the child anticipating for its coming life? How did it feel about entering the family in question? What were its main concerns? Did it have any messages or special requests? What was its sex to be? I hoped to be able to confirm some of the intuitive information with the mother after the birth. I hoped too that the mother might find the information helpful even if confirmation was not possible.

This experiment was not systematic in its conception, execution or follow-up and I did not expect any hard proof of contact with the unborn children. It proved to be interesting, nonetheless. I can say generally that the information given in the five sessions seemed to match very well each mother's feelings regarding her child, both its character and her expected experience in taking care of it. Whether the statements would turn out to be literally accurate or not, I certainly had the subjective impression that I was actually talking with the child through the intuitive. All five of the mothers appreciated the "contact" and felt it was genuine.

Some pieces of information provided by the intuitives were evidential, though the majority could neither be confirmed or denied. The sex of the baby was stated correctly in four cases; in the fifth it was wrong but had been given with uncertainty, as if the child wasn't sure about it or didn't much care. For two of the mothers I was in a good position to corroborate information with the infant's behavior during its first few months of life. In one case the child was unusually peaceful and cooperative, just as predicted. In the other he was very restless, with incessant discomfort, spasms and crying. This outcome had not been specifically mentioned in the session with the mother (perhaps understandably), though the intuitive provided several broad hints that big problems were forthcoming. For example, the boy

---

seemed very reluctant to enter life at all. The delivery was late and difficult, and for two months the mother was thoroughly exhausted in her attempt to take care of her continually screaming boy.

I found myself wishing afterwards that all mothers could experience this kind of communication with their unborn children. I have since come to believe that, with proper preparation, any mother can establish an intimate connection with her unborn infant by herself without the necessity of bringing in an expert intuitive.

A few of the CAI intuitives reported occasions when they felt they were able to "tune in" on an infant's consciousness, report its state of mind and wishes and sometimes experience two-way communication. (See the accompanying box for a related experiment.) Such a communication practice, if extended and refined, might also be able to provide a warning of an infant's departure, and perhaps other helpful information regarding the infant's "state of mind" as well.

On the other hand, persuasion may not always be called for. The situation might be compared with trying to convince a confused teenager not to leave home or an elderly person not to die. Sometimes such urging seems appropriate, but at other times it may be just a selfish desire to cling to someone instead of letting him go his self-chosen way. In the case of an infant, where one cannot persuade with words and arguments, and there is no way to elicit a direct spoken response, it is harder to know what to do. It may be in the best interests of all concerned for the infant to leave, even though the parents desperately want it to stay, based on their own needs, their beliefs or their reasons for what they feel is right. In contrast, the child may be feeling unwanted (in its own way) and just waiting for a bit of loving encouragement to stay around. How can a parent know? It sounds like an intuitive decision is needed.

In short, to try to prevent a SIDS death through persuasion is not always and not necessarily the best solution, though sometimes it may be called for. The intuitive sources recommended that, instead of trying to *persuade* an infant (or teenager or dying person) to stay, one should simply focus on transmitting unqualified love and support, without imposing personal needs, just to let it know it is loved and wanted. In this way its fear may diminish and it may make its own decision without external pressure. The universal principle that applies here is the same for infants as it for all persons: each person's freedom to choose for himself must be respected, even the choice to live or die. All one can do is to provide loving care and genuine protection may be appropriate.

Western society puts an exceptionally high value on the preservation of human life. It dictates that virtually any action to keep a person alive is proper and justified, regardless of his wishes and needs. Indeed, it is becoming more and more difficult to die when the time comes to do so. We lack a principle that would tell us how to balance the effort and cost of life saving against letting the natural life process take its course. The existing formula, for all its positive value, is very limiting because it does not acknowledge any form of "life" other than the purely physical one. Herein lies the root of the widespread misunderstanding of death, including SIDS and two other contemporary and controversial societal issues: abortion and euthanasia.

If the resident consciousness of an individual can be seen as the basic "life" to be honored and protected, and its uninterrupted existence before birth and after death is accepted, the entire picture clarifies. A basis for choosing to extend life or to terminate it must be found elsewhere than just the physical body. This view does not mean that physical life has no value—quite the opposite, in fact—but it places physical life within a larger context, offers a higher definition of what life actually is, and gives it a clearer purpose. It provides a more fundamental—we may say spiritual—basis for establishing the real value of human existence. In practice it calls for deeper questioning and examination of each individual situation, rather than just the blind application of a simplified moral rule, before a wise decision is made. Expert intuitives can assist in this examination, of course.

Accommodating to a Child's Death

"We love, we join. We separate, we hurt. Belonging and attachment die,
but true love survives and is nourished. Herein lies the great lesson."

Finally, after a child has died from SIDS, we may ask: what counsel can be offered to the parents to help them better adjust to their loss, and perhaps to learn something of value from the experience?

The parents need to understand the fairness of what has happened to them—that they are not being discriminated against. [AAA]

...Only to help them to understand that they have fulfilled their part....It is necessary that they understand that life is an ongoing force, and their infant is part of the total plan....When they have been released from the burden of their sorrow, they in turn must take their place to help others, even as they have been helped. [LH]

Separate them from the guilt of responsibility....Bring them together with other parents, particularly those who have had second and third births [after losing a child to SIDS]...[so they may] channel their psychological states into socially constructive labors...restructuring their desire for further births. [KR]

While conducting this intuitive study we came across several SIDS families who had committed themselves to helping other parents deal with their losses. Indeed, members of "SIDS Parents Clubs," which exist in most large U.S. cities, routinely contact new SIDS parents with offers of help.[10*] Some SIDS parents have gone on to raise large families. Grief counseling is commonly offered by psychotherapists and priests/ministers, some specializing in this particular form. Modern teachers such as Elizabeth Kubler-Ross, Steven Levine and Ram Dass have spent much of their lives offering counsel to the grieving and the dying, and showing in their workshops and classes how one may work through the death process to deeper understanding.[11]

Parenthood As Stewardship

"First of all, think of [your children], not of yourself, their lives and not yours. And don't use the word 'my' when you refer to them."
[Krishnamurti[12]]

The intuitive explanation for crib death can be helpful because it suggests a way for SIDS parents—indeed, for all parents—to come to a clearer understanding of the true nature of their responsibility toward their children. If they can fully and honestly face in advance the possibility that they may lose their child (a difficult visualization, to be sure), they may then find it possible to give it their full care and love without the continual fear that they will lose it, and with less of a shock if they do. With this attitude they are also less likely to become dependent upon the child, "possessing" it as a way of meeting their own emotional needs. By persisting with this visualization they can eventually come to regard themselves as the child's privileged caretakers or *stewards*, into whose care it has been given as a gift to teach them love without attachment.

This posture of "loving detachment" is admittedly not an easy human lesson, but it is a time-honored and fundamental one. To be attached to things or people is an almost universal human trait, yet it is not something we fundamentally need on our path to self-knowledge and wisdom. The great teachers of all ages and cultures remind us: to the extent that we are attached to others (both children and adults) and are dependent upon them for our sense of identity, well-being or security, then to this same extent is our capacity to love ourselves and others reduced. After all, we are here in life to learn how to love, not to learn how to be dependent. Children and partners are our best teachers.

This is also a challenge for teachers and practitioners who deal with young parents, especially pregnant women, for they are in an excellent position to encourage the parents to envision and appreciate the reality of their child's existence apart from its physical body. They can help them understand that parenthood actually begins before conception, not at the child's birth; that the child has in a real sense a "mind" of its own, its own kind of consciousness, and the ability to make some of its own deep decisions.

These days increasing numbers of young parents (and many older ones too) are adopting this more enlightened perspective on parenthood. To learn this lesson is certainly easier when our children remain alive and healthy, yet most parents refuse this option. They may have an opportunity to learn it only when they lose a child. The resultant suffering may be severe indeed, coming as it does after the joyful anticipation of conceiving the child, several months of growing it, the struggle of birth and succeeding months of personal devotion and loving care—only to lose it.

Validating the Non-physical Basis of SIDS

Validation of the non-physical explanation of SIDS presented here is beyond the capability of present-day science, which is ill suited to such research. Not only is its methodology not applicable to non-physical, unmeasurable data, but it offers no model or framework within which their analysis and evaluation can be carried out. Further, in this case there exists no other reliable source of knowledge against which the intuitive explanation of SIDS can be corroborated and validated. Even if it did, the validation would not fall within the accepted scope of institutions that support SIDS research and medical journals that publish such "unscientific" findings. There is simply no way to conduct and publish an effective, legitimate, scientific study to validate the intuitives' non-physical explanation for SIDS.

Sometimes independent but professionally qualified individuals work through cracks in the scientific establishment to conduct their own kind of research, then announce their findings to the general public through popular publications and at semi-professional conferences. This approach bypasses ordinary peer review and the other mechanisms for assuring high quality, with the result that valid and important findings are mixed with reports of poorly substantiated results. Most of the new knowledge we have today about alternative medicine, for example, emerged into the public domain through just this means. If the underlying cause of SIDS as described here is to achieve popular acceptance, then this alternative approach may be the only way to go.

Over the past few decades a dozen or so studies on prenatal infant consciousness were announced in this manner. The best of this alternative work offered convincing examples of children who reported detailed, verified memories of specific events in their prenatal environment, such as a mother's emotional crisis, physical abuse to the womb, a serious family dispute, music played during pregnancy, abnormalities in the birth (e.g., a caesarean or inverted birth) and moments of intense communication with the mother.[13] These reports provide ample evidence that some children possesses sensitivities and memory *in utero*. It is difficult to imagine how memories such as these could be merely imprinted on the developing fetus unless there was also an underlying ability to experience and translate their essential qualities. It is not such a big step, then, to suppose that the infant also has the kind of consciousness claimed here.

Validating the Physical Aspects of SIDS

On the purely physical side, reports published in the medical literature, independent of the intuitive study, corroborated two of the physical factors the intuitives indicated are sometimes associated with SIDS death (though not causal to it). All such medical studies are necessarily based upon autopsies, the only alternative for collecting data on SIDS, since there is no practical way to identify in advance which live infants are going to succumb to SIDS.

Good Grief

Grief has its origin in the loss of someone or something we care about and feel we need for our own feeling of wholeness, self-worth or security. While some of our tears at a death may be shed for the momentary connection with strong life energies, as at a marriage or a birth, others arise from the deep fears that underlie the loss. We recognize our own grief through the intensity of the emotion, and others' grief because we perceive it as a common human response, one that cuts across all ages, cultures, genders, levels of intelligence and walks of life. We honor it as evidence of caring, and wonder about those who do not display it when it seems they ought to.

We are sometimes a bit ashamed of our own grief as we try to hide our tears. It is as if we know deeply that grief is somehow an unnecessary and unintended aspect of life—if only we could rise above the situation at hand and see these major life events in clearer perspective. Indeed, people who suffer loss differ greatly in how long they remain in a state of grief—perhaps for a few weeks, often for years and sometimes until they themselves die. There are many questions. While grief is almost universal, are we to regard it as a human capacity to be encouraged, or a human weakness to be overcome? Is grief at death inherently different than that from other sources? Does grief increase or decrease with true compassion?

We feel that death should not happen to a child, but in fact it does. From the typical perspective on life it seems terribly unfair that we should be punished for loving. In the case of SIDS it is the worst: there is no one to blame as there is for murder, war and other so-called accidents. We can find no "reason" behind our suffering, and this mystery can easily lead one into grief and guilt. Either we give up and adopt the extreme belief that life, the universe and God are unfair and uncaring, or we continue the search for an explanation that honors both our painful experience and our faith that life is inherently just and compassionate. What has gone wrong here? Has someone (God?) made a mistake? Or have we misunderstood something about life that somehow led us to expect constant security, and freedom from change and loss?

In parents' experience with SIDS we find much grief, but occasionally some hard-won understanding about why a child comes into our life, we love it and then lose it. In this way grief teaches us deep lessons about the overall purpose of life: why birth and death occur at all, what is our individual place in the greater scheme of things and especially the design or plan that ties together all human experience and gives it meaning. Some societies hold this kind of life-knowledge collectively and pass it on to each succeeding generation, so everyone knows and accepts it in the course of growing up.[14] In our fragmented Western societies we do not preserve this knowledge widely or effectively. A few persons pick it up early in life but most never acquire it at all. A few more learn it painfully through the direct experience of loss during adulthood.

We can be encouraged in our search for answers to these fundamental questions by the fact that there are still individuals, wise by any reasonable criterion, who claim they have suffered, persisted and eventually won this understanding. If we could somehow reach the same awareness as they acquired, without the misery they endured, then we could open ourselves to transcending and transforming our own attachment, confusion, guilt and grief, yet not surrendering our capacity to love unconditionally.

So what are these teachers trying to tell us? They say, in a few words, that their suffering was a persistent nudging and invitation by life to surrender to a broader and higher perspective; that it was only their *resistance* to take that step that produced the suffering; and that this higher perspective, once achieved, is so grand that it justifies fully whatever they stubbornly endured to attain it. They then go on to describe, as best as they can, their own experience of this perspective. Seek out their words for yourself, for they are well worth listening to, whether you are experiencing grief at the moment or not.

- Two of the intuitive sources mentioned that erratic changes sometimes occur in thyroid activity shortly before death in SIDS cases. Medical research reported in 1981 confirmed the presence of usually high levels of the thyroidal hormones thyroxin-T3 and -T4 in a group of SIDS infants.[15]

- The consensus indicated that neural anomalies can be expected in most SIDS infants. One intuitive source [AA] pinpointed (in the mid-1970s) a particular area at the base of the brain and near the top of the spinal cord, and mentioned that important work on this defect was in progress at a medical laboratory in Cleveland, Ohio. D. Lonsdale and others from the Cleveland Clinic reported (in 1979) that they had observed abnormal auditory evoked brainstem potentials in infants they suspectedwere at high risk of SIDS.[16] In addition, medical research elsewhere implicated the adrenals and brainstem receptors as trouble spots. A recent report from Harvard Medical School and the Children's Hospital in Boston revealed that abnormalities were found for SIDS infants in two receptors in the area of their brainstems believed to be involved in the control of breathing.[17]

The intuitive team also indicated that SIDS is associated with poor family dynamics, lower socio-economic status and poor prenatal nutrition. It is well known that poverty low socio-economic status, absence of breast-feeding and the mother's habitual use oftobacco, medicines and other drugs is associated with SIDS.as trouble spots.[18]

An epidemiological study conducted by Dr. James F. Ransdell, M.D., and this author in the mid-1970s partially supported these correlates. This study analyzed statistically the data recorded on the birth certificates of all SIDS cases (917) in Alameda County, California, for a 16-year period—the longest and largest collection of SIDS infants ever examined. An equal number of live births (the "controls") were included with the data to provide a basis for comparison.[19*].

- The epidemiological study revealed that a disproportionate number of SIDS infants arose from families with low income and crowded housing; both of these factors are well known to be related to poor dietary and health habits.[20]
- This study also revealed a significant weekly periodicity in the occurrence of these SIDS deaths, peaking on Friday and Saturday nights. The reason for this cycle is not known, but it is certainly connected with the community or the family—not to the natural environment, which contains no weekly cycles. Perhaps it is related to the fact that parents are more likely to be away from home on these two evenings.

These research findings lend some positive support to the physical portion of the SIDS hypothesis from the intuitive team.

SIDS has come to be called the "theory-a-month disease," a reflection of the dozens of well intentioned research studies that claim to have found physical conditions that are associated statistically with the syndrome but are not strong enough to hold generally or to qualify as possible causes. In the 1960s and 1970s most of the many medical reports on new factors allegedly associated with SIDS used only small samples of cases and did not always employ control cases for comparison. Recent research, conducted for the National Institute of Child Health and Human Development, consisted of a comprehensive epidemiological study of 757 SIDS infants. It was conducted more carefully then the previous studies, but still "none of the dozens of risk factors uncovered in the study is strong enough to enable prevention of SIDS in vulnerable infants."[21]

Much of the public confusion about SIDS has arisen from inaccurate media reports that interpret each newly reported risk factor as a "breakthrough discovery" that will soon enable the disease to be prevented. Equally irresponsible are the unreasoned hopes of some SIDS researchers and volunteers who lead desperate parents to believe uncritically what they read about the syndrome. Many doctors, wanting to be helpful but not trained in research, have joined in the delusion. Part of the program of today's national and international SIDS organizations is dedicated to reeducating the public about the realities of SIDS.[22*] The long awaited and expected solution to the problem of SIDS is still not available, and none is in sight.

Possibilities for Future SIDS Research

According to the intuitives medical science can do virtually nothing towards solution of the SIDS problem unless the non-physical aspect is taken into account.

In its on-going struggle to find a physical cause for SIDS, medical research may incidentally learn something of value about the way in which the human bodies die, whether from SIDS or from other causes. Such efforts may expand medical knowledge on physical ailments such as cancer in adults, even though the withdrawal of consciousness is not so sudden as it is for SIDS. They may also provide clues on how to sustain life more effectively in the face of other illnesses that take the patient very gradually to the threshold of death's door. New knowledge about how breathing is controlled from higher centers in the brain could be helpful in treating disorders such as apnea, asthma, certain allergies and lung damage due to disease or accident.

These kinds of investigations may lead to a better understanding of just where in the nervous system resides the principal centers at which consciousness regulates the physical system. Eastern philosophy suggests that these centers are the seven energy foci called "chakras," whose locations correspond to some of the endocrine glands (pituitary, pineal, adrenal, etc.), though the glandular association may be coincidental. Research may lead eventually to evidence that the crucial energies that feed human life are non-physical, and in fact constitute the individual's essential "life force," the withdrawal of which is responsible for crib death, and probably for adult physical death as well.

It would be particularly helpful for future research to explore the psychological characteristics of SIDS families.[23]* A 1975 report by a social worker observed that psychological factors are very much at work in SIDS families,[24] but this approach has not been seriously pursued by others. Such studies could serve as a bridge between the physical and non-physical viewpoints. Some therapists and counselors who interact regularly with grieving SIDS parents say they have a "gut-level" impression of the psychodynamics at work in these families, including which families are susceptible to SIDS. They do not ordinarily speak or write openly on this sensitive matter, but their measured remarks suggest there are psychological signals of impending child loss. A carefully designed study could survey these therapists for psychological indicators that could then be formally tested.

Summary and Implications

> "When someone you love dies, let them go into the next step of
> their evolution. Give them a hearty 'Bon Voyage' and give comfort
> to others like yourself....Then enjoy a grand celebration, and go
> about the business of your own lives." [Emmanuel]

This intuitive experiment aimed at understanding Sudden Infant Death Syndrome explained that the root cause lies not in a physical malfunction but in a "decision" by the infant consciousness to leave physical life, in the fashion of a suicide. The parents may see the death as a catastrophic chance event, without explanation, but to the infant who dies it is merely a return to where it came from, usually without anguish. The physiological consequences that follow the departure of the infant's consciousness do not form any single or simple pattern; they represent only a natural collapse of body function as the life withdraws, in a manner largely unique to each individual. Physical symptoms may or may not manifest at the time of death, but they do not "cause" the death.

If the intuitive findings are to be believed, medical research on SIDS over the past fifty years and still in progress today has been misdirected, since it rests upon the mistaken assumption that there is a particular physical cause (or causes) of SIDS, such as a disease, virus, congenital defect or environmental influence waiting to be discovered. If this research approach continues it will at best uncover only some acausal physical correlations with SIDS, not of any use for prevention and probably not even for prediction. It would be preferable to use available research funds to educate parents about the true nature of the syndrome, their appropriate role as parents and how to avoid or alleviate the grief and guilt that typically ensues after a SIDS death.

A few side benefits and several hypotheses emerged from the inquiry, and some of these could be pursued in future medical research. The principal outcomes and implications lay in the area of consciousness studies. Some of these outcomes are amenable to advanced psychological research, the findings from which could then be used to help in the education of parents, teachers and physicians about the deeper nature of SIDS.

There is no scientifically acceptable way to check the non-physical explanation of the cause of SIDS, which is largely consistent with Eastern wisdom teachings though not with Western medicine or traditional psychology. Some of the specific intuitive findings are amenable to validation. A few physical associations that were pursued were confirmed, but they are only partially supportive of the findings.

The errors of procedure made in the two previous intuitive experiments (Chapters 6 and 7) were corrected in this one, which was simpler and more direct with no negative consequences. The motivation and questioning were generally satisfactory, and there was a good communicative flow with all five intuitives. The substantive information was clear and unambiguous. The consensus obtained was excellent: no contradictions or inconsistencies arose among the expert intuitives questioned. The main questions asked were all answered. No contradictions arose between the consensus and the facts about

SIDS that are specific and well established. Differences emerged with the direction of current medical research, findings from poorly conducted research studies and official SIDS policies.

On the other hand, our initial expectations were not entirely correct. We had assumed a physical cause for SIDS and sought its explanation, along with appropriate strategies for prediction, prevention and treatment. Instead, we were given a deeper cause, which turned out to be not physical at all.

We will return in Chapter 12 to an intuitive look at another kind of death.

> "Dying is absolutely safe....The fear of death is the fear of letting go. Once the fear is laid aside, death is a joyous and exciting adventure, just as with other fears in life." [Emmanuel]

• Endnotes—Chapter 8

[1] This chapter is adapted from an earlier article: Kautz, 1984.

[2] Gibran, 1951.

[3*] More accurately: the SIDS rate in the U.S. has been about 0.2% for the past several decades, but gradually dropped in 1999 to a current value of less than 0.1%. The reason for the decrease is not known, though the criterion for classification of a death as "SIDS" has been tightening as more infant diseases have been medically identified as "causes of death."

[4*] No statistics on SIDS frequency are available for many of the world's cultures, since the medical examination required to distinguish SIDS from other causes of death is not carried out everywhere. Also, as just noted, the criteria for what constitutes a SIDS death differ somewhat from one country to another.

[5] Kraus & Bourbon, 1972, Peterson & Chinn, 1977.
[6] Beckwith, 1973, Valdes-DaPena, 1980, Kraus & Borbani, 1972.

[7] Anon4, 1991.

[8] Task Force, 2000, pp. 650-656.

[9] Katagiri, 1993.

[10*] For further information see later endnote of this chapter for a list of organizations.

[11] Kubler-Ross, 1969. Ram Dass, 2000, Levine, 1982.

[12] Krishnamurti, 1985, p. 20.

[13] Verny, 1975, Klaus, 1975, Klaus, 1996, Odent, 1989, Chamberlain, 1988.

[14] Sögyal, 1992.

[15] Chacon & Tildon, 1981.

[16] Orlowsky et al, 1979.

[17] Panigrahy et al, 1997.

[18] Naeye, 1976.

[19]* This unpublished study was carried out privately by Dr. James F. Ransdell, M.D. and this author. Further information may be obtained from this author.

[20] Brooke et al, 1997.

[21] Kraus et al, 1989.

[22]* The primary organizations, which cooperate closely, are as follows:
- Global Strategy Task Force (http://www.sidsglobal.org)
- SIDS International (http://www.sidsinternational.minerva.com.au)
- National Sudden Infant Death Syndrome Resource Center (http://www.sidscenter.org)
- American Sudden Infant Death Syndrome (SIDS) Institute (http://www.sids.org)

[23]* David B, Cheek (d. 1996) was one of the most effective pioneers in recognizing the importance of psychological factors in all aspects of childbirth. See, for example, Rossi & Cheek, 1988.

[24] Friedlander & Shaw, 1975.

CHAPTER 9

BIPOLAR DISORDER[1]*
THE MYSTERY OF MANIC DEPRESSION

"I am not a mechanism, an assembly of various sections. And it is not because the mechanism is working wrongly that I am ill. I am ill because of wounds to the soul, to the deep emotional self. And wounds to the soul take a long, long time [to heal[2]]."
[D. H. Lawrence]

We all know people who are sometimes depressed. Indeed, almost all of us have at some time in our lives experienced at least one such occasion: life was confused, heavy, uninspired and seemed without meaning. We felt empty, unsupported and alone but eventually pulled out of it. For some persons, however, such "downers" are not temporary but recurrent, severe and even incapacitating. The cycles may persist for years or their entire life. Sometimes the depressed episodes alternate with periods of extreme excitement and activity, to the point of uncontrolled and irrational behavior.

What is behind these so-called mood disorders? What is causing them? Why are some people so afflicted and others not? They seem to be uncontrollable, but are they really? Is there a way to prevent them from occurring, or at least to predict them or soften them when they occur? Is there anything others can do to help—family, friends or a professional such as a psychiatrist or minister?

Psychologists and psychiatrists have confronted these questions for decades. A great deal of effort and experience in working with mentally depressed patients, both clinically and as research subjects, has generated only a few partial and largely unsatisfactory answers. It was the lack of good solutions to this problem that motivated the Intuitive Consensus study reported in this chapter.

Background on Depression

Mental depression is a chronic disorder that manifests as sadness, low self-confidence, lethargy, inhibition, lack of initiative, inordinate stress, general despondency and sometimes reduced mental speed and inhibited speech. It arises for males and females about equally, a bit more frequently among close relatives, and usually occurs in recurrent episodes of varying duration. The most severe cases can be so incapacitating that the individual needs on-going care, cannot work and is forced to lead a socially limited life. They can even lead to suicide.[3*]

Appropriate treatment of depressives was almost non-existent in earlier times. Severely depressed individuals were either left with their families, roamed the streets as homeless or ended up in a care facility if they were not able to function by themselves. If disruptive or dangerous they were confined in a prison or mental facility, usually without treatment. As with other mental disorders, society preferred to hide its depressives out of sight instead of caring for them openly and compassionately. Later, barbiturates or electroconvulsive therapy was prescribed for mania. Such treatments were often given to render patients easier to handle rather than for their own good. In any case, these various means were very limited in their effectiveness, and were certainly not curative.

There are actually several medically distinguishable forms of depression. Some are primary, while others are secondary reactions to other medical conditions or life situations. The topic of the studies described in this chapter is a primary form, namely, *manic-depressive illness*, in recent years renamed as *bipolar affective disorder*, or simply *bipolar disorder*. (We will use these terms interchangeably.) Individuals who suffer from this disorder experience not only periods of mental depression but also episodes of manic excitement: high energy, extravagance, grandiosity, sleeplessness, heightened and rapid mental activity, speeded speech and movement, impulsiveness and easily aroused anger. Bipolar disorder can lead to burnout, irrational behavior and sometimes even violence, requiring confinement.

Earlier reports assumed that about 1% of the US population is affected by bipolar disorder, but recent systematic studies point to much higher numbers, over 5%.[4] In the first half of the twentieth century manic depressive episodes were difficult to treat and impossible to prevent.

In the 1960s it was discovered, however, that ingestion of the simple chemical lithium carbonate in proper dosage could moderate both manic and depressive episodes.[5] By 1980 its use as a prophylactic treatment, even over long periods, was widespread. It does not cure the disorder but has allowed uncounted numbers of depressives to function socially and to live reasonably normal lives. Possibly harmful side effects are still being tracked but when proper dosages are administered they appear to be minimal, at least physiologically.

In spite of this fortunate advance in treatment it is still not fully understood just how lithium works in the body. Nothing like a cure for bipolar disorder is in sight. Most important, there is no real understanding of the disorder at all; its true nature remains a mystery. For example:

- Is depression the result of an external influence (environmental, social, perinatal), or perhaps something the individual has done to himself, or due to some other cause?
- What are the mechanisms by which bipolar depression works within the body/mind (neurochemical, biological, psychological, etc.)?
- Why do some persons suffer from bipolar depression and others do not?
- Is the disorder, or a predisposition to it, inherited?
- Can the times of manic and depressive episodes be predicted? (They are typically repetitive but appear to be quite irregular.)
- Can the disorder be controlled through of nutrition or drugs?
- Can it be regulated or moderated through the individual's personal efforts?
- What is the deeper psychological/spiritual significance of bipolar depression?

The broad objective of the investigation reported here was to obtain answers to these questions and to generate ideas, new perspectives and actual hypotheses that might be corroborated and applied later. A subsidiary goal was to identify the salient aspects of bipolar affective disorder so as to reveal lines of inquiry that might be explored more deeply in the future. It was suspected in advance that the subject was somewhat large for an exploratory inquiry, so the questioning was more broad than deep and more exploratory than definitively focused.

The following sections summarize the resultant consensus, which arose from inquiry sessions with six expert intuitives. We examine the disorder first broadly, then present the intuitives' information about causes and mechanisms: where the disease comes originates and how it works its way through the mind and body to appear ultimately as depressive or manic-depressive behavior. Described next are the tests and measurements needed to better manage the disease, and various approaches to treatment. Considered last are possible steps for future clinical practice and research, and a summary of what was learned from this intuitive experiment.

The Origins of Manic Depressive Disorder

"Depression comes from a sense of separation, of being deprived of something you want and do not have. The spirit within has the power to heal all sorrow, loneliness, pain, fear and loss, because it heals the mind that thinks these things are real." [ACIM[6*]]

As in many human afflictions the descriptive term "depression" has more to do with its manifestations than with what is causing it. Different causes can lead to the same symptoms, and a single cause can lead to different symptoms, at different times and for different people. The cause or causes of bipolar depression are not known. The known origins of similar disorders suggest a few possibilities—heredity, early family environment, childhood abuse, physical environment, diet, etc.—but none of these factors has been found to be a predominant cause of bipolar depression.

In general terms, the intuitive team revealed that bipolar disorder is a complex disorder that lies hidden behind a relatively simple pattern of symptoms; that is, it is a collection of disorders that manifest similarly. It arises from different

origins in different individuals, and there are many interacting factors that influence whether, how and when it manifests. To describe these origins properly and fully, they claimed, would require a more refined model and a deeper understanding of the human body-mind system than is presently available. It is some-what like asking for the cause of cancer; we know today that no straightforward answer can be given to such a question, in view of its multiple causes and forms and the many ways in which it reveals its presence.
For example:

> [Manic depression] is not of one specificity, although it is put into one category....There are various causations and various treatments....The circumstances and conditions vary greatly from person to person. [VY]

> There are several possibilities in which rather similar symptoms can be manifested...that would have different sources. But the primary one is a miscommunication, so to speak, between the being and its environment. The root of the difficulty is a vibrational non-interaction of the various subtle bodies of the individual with one another and with the environment. [JF]

The most basic cause of mental depression was said to be non-physical, beyond body and brain, in the domain traditionally regarded as deeply mental or spiritual. (Recall the investigation of crib death in Chapter 8.) We did not initially inquire about this aspect of the disease but it arose spontaneously from all the intuitives consulted. Moreover, even at this non-physical level the "cause" of depression is not single or simple.

Briefly, this deeper cause originates in the inner essence or "soul" of the individual, which is non-material, timeless and indestructible. It is not fundamentally created by the body and brain but their underlying source. It predates birth and continues after death. The personal conditions that precede one's earthly life, usually termed "past lives," and the present-life residues of these prior conditions, designated here "karmic factors," are at the heart of the depressive's struggle. For example:

> The roots of depression [manic depressive disorder] are found in the spiritual life of the individual. They come from inabilities of self-expression. The frustrations arising from this deficiency work through the seat of consciousness that governs the sympathetic functions. These inabilities and the resultant frustrations can originate from past-life experiences in which the

person was either abusive of meditation, or who suffered extreme degrees of guilt from having manipulated knowledge to their personal advantage. [KR]

Many persons suffering from primary depression have had strong spiritual backgrounds. This is not really the cause of their present condition, but a strong spiritual orientation can often help them out of it. Unfortunately, the illness tends to block much spiritual understanding. As for past-life origins of primary depression, those who have this particular malady in this incarnation have many times helped to serve as executors or persecutors in past times. [LH]

Karmic factors are very significant, but not very much can be generalized in these terms. Sometimes the individual has experienced a relatively small number of incarnations and is still experimenting "to get the pattern right," so to speak. In such cases the depression is more superficial; there is rapid learning, and the theme will always be the opening of the heart:, a dropping of resistance to the love energy, close physical bonding, and the need for maintaining a proper mineral balance. On the other hand, beings who have not come to terms with violence in their pasts will typically experience severe cellular disruption,…as if the cells are not growing together properly. [JF]

The Genetic Component

It is difficult to even imagine how treatment or even diagnosis might proceed at this deep level. To return to the physical, the intuitives said that there is a limited genetic basis, or at least a predisposition, for manic depressive disorder:

Genetically inherited chemical imbalances can also occur, though the genetic contribution to primary depression varies greatly (from 20–80%). Your research has a long way to go before even the simplest genetic codes are sufficiently understood to be helpful. Also, such studies take attention away from the karmic origins of the malady and the soul's choice in selecting the genetic material in the first place. [JF]

The role of heredity is a chicken-and-egg issue. Indeed, the tendency for manic depression is in the genetic code, but one must look at where the code comes from, and how a particular case of manic depression arises within a given genetic code. It is more profitable to study the family patterns, since these are the areas where the healing can occur....The choice of family situation is the child's, and resides at the inner levels of the child's consciousness....As soon as there is healing, this is not passed on in the genetic code. [MG]

The reference to selection of genetic codes is the choice of body, and all that goes with it, made by the incarnating soul. Current research on the genetics of bipolar depression is yielding some positive and encouraging results (more on this later).

Manifestation through the Emotions

Bipolar depression is strongly associated with a depletion of emotional and physical energy, feelings of extreme separation from others and a low view of the self:

A few days before the actual onset of depression the person's energy may be very high, at the extreme stage of denial. The manic may perform very well socially—so agitated, in fact, as to be abnormal. Eye movements become faster. There tends to be a total loss of communication with the self, hence the desire to be with others, but accompanied by the fear that all the reaching out will prove to be superficial. [MG]

Primary depression is due in part to a general shutdown of the body-mind's energy system, and is usually misdiagnosed. The low energy level of depressives involves both internal and external energy. It is actually a blockage of the inner-outer exchanges of energy that normally take place in humans. The external factors comprise other people and the natural environment. [DR]

One way this happens is through a suppression of the individual's inner resources, creating a shell around the emotional body and a lack of internal communication: mental to emotional to physical. [JF]

At the emotional level the depressive oscillates between extremes, and has much difficulty in understanding mixed emotions, in taking emotions back to their causes. By the time the emotions catch up with the individual during the depression, there is a nearly complete loss of the life energy which fueled them. There is then the tendency to regather the energy by re-idealizing the same goals, rather than modifying these goals through internalization. The cyclic pattern continues. [MG]

The loss of self-respect is a characteristic symptom:

The common underlying characteristic is a turning inward into the self, leading to characteristics such as self-dislike, self-disgust and self-hate. But these are indicators of other, deeper factors within the body, which in turn are manifestations of energy residues in the unconscious from previous lifetimes in other bodies. It is an overlapping and a non-integration of the mental and physical bodies, and sometimes the spiritual and mental bodies as well. [VY]

The feelings of separation also lead to a strong sense of unworthiness. The strong drive arising out of the fear of not providing for the self, not supporting the self's worthiness, leads to an externalization in which attention is strongly focused on the environment as the source of love, notoriety, honor and acclaim—the manic phase. The psyche demands a natural counter-balancing, however, and since no internalization abilities have been built this leads to the depressive phase. [MG]

The individual's childhood environment can have a physical effect:

For many depressives the problems began with a lack of caring when they were in utero. If the child is welcomed and loved from the time of conception forward, there is less likelihood of many difficulties in the physical. [JF]

There is also extreme scattering and denial in depressive patients. The first depression often occurs when failure is encountered; they are unable to integrate that failure experience into the self....The strong level of denial produces high acidic conditions within the blood system, leading to a build-up of the blood's toxicity (white cells). Also, lymph flow tends to be stagnated. [MG]

Manifestation through the Nervous System

Whatever is happening at the emotional level manifests through the nervous system, and subsequently throughout the physical body. One intuitive described the typical situation as follows:

> The chain of cause-and-effect, while not linear, can be traced through the nervous system. The depressive episodes are usually brought on by pressures or demands upon the sympathetic nervous system—[actually] by an over-stimulation of both the sympathetic and autonomic nervous systems. This may be internal or external. It works through two major reflex points, the coccyx and the medulla oblongata, then spills over into the parasympathetic ganglion just at the base of the skull, then into the autonomic system, bringing about the condition described. The brain tends to enter an alpha rather than the normal beta state, and an almost autonomically induced state of meditation occurs....The brain waves fluctuate rapidly between the beta and alpha states. As the individual tries to function (especially socially) during these periods, the body becomes confused and disoriented which leads to a retreat from the normal sympathetic responses, hence shortness of breath, agitation of muscular tissues, stimulation of the adrenals, and even the development of ulcerous conditions. The entire survival system is kicked into function, leading to paranoia, which the individual seeks to suppress. Eventually more endorphins are produced, relieving the pressure in the nervous system, and the depression passes. [KR]

Physical changes may occur within the body's cells:

> The deeply buried residues sometimes manifest as an enlargement of the cells surrounding the posterior pituitary. [VY]

> Manic depressives tend to have a greater thickness of neurological tissues throughout the entire parasympathetic and autonomic nervous systems, and particularly in the parasympathetic ganglion. [KR]

These neurochemical changes accompany a general chemical imbalance in the body. In technical terms, there is sometimes an overproduction of morphine-like substances (endorphins). Neurotransmitters become involved. Disruption in the mechanism of calcium absorption upsets the delicate balance of hormones, particularly serotonin and the thyroidal hormones, and this results in the oscillatory recurrence of manic and depressive episodes. The entire endocrine system, especially the adrenals, is depressed, producing erratic eye movements and shallow breathing.

> The chain of events immediately leading to depression begins with an acid-alkaline imbalance in the body, in which the acidity causes deterioration of a certain prethyroidal (not parathyroidal) hormone [TRF? TSH?] and a molecule containing phosphorus [which may be the same]. It propagates like a chain reaction or disease. As a result this hormone loses its absorptive capacity. The effect is not steady, but consists of brief and minute interruptions in the hormone's normal behavior. There are periods when certain elements may be taken into the body so it can be reversed temporarily, but the seed has been sown. It reaches the thyroid gland, and eventually the adrenals. [LH]

> As a depressive episode approaches, the level of acidity in the body increases and the iron level drops, leading to detectable changes in the musculature. B-vitamin assimilation and the calcium level in the blood drop. Antigens within the blood and water retention increase. Erratic eating patterns set in, leading to difficulty with bowel movements. [MG]

> The weakness first affects certain of the brain's neurotransmitters, which are so sensitive to the drugs sometimes given that they enter a period of over-activity then shut down completely. The over-activity manifests as irritability and emotionality, erratic thought patterns, perception of higher levels of reality, and sensory over-sensitivity. [DR]

The Role of Nutrition and Environment

There was clear agreement that while a poor diet is not a primary cause of depression, it definitely contributes to the seriousness of the disorder and the timing of the manic and depressive episodes, because these physical expressions depend on the body's nutritive state. Meat and dairy products are largely responsible, and typically a deficiency of vitamins B2 and B12, calcium, phosphorus and zinc. There may be either an excess or deficiency of sodium and potassium. In addition:

> There is a particular amino acid [which one?] occurring in eggs, spinach and beans that may be present in excess. [DR]

One may expect mineral imbalances, cellular disruption, growth problems and so on, with consequent changes in blood chemistry and long-term tissues (skin, hair, etc.). The mineral imbalances typically involve lithium and copper, and, because of a tie-in to the adrenals and thyroid, also sodium, potassium, magnesium and calcium. [JF]

Clearly, improved nutrition is a potential area for treatment.

Influences from the environment can also trigger or worsen manic and depressive episodes. These include changes in one's geographical location, magnetic and electromagnetic fields, chemical and sonic pollution, and even the phases of the moon. They work through the nutrient choline and the red corpuscles:

Magnetic fields affect the body through the iron molecules (magnetite) within the red corpuscles. A static (direct-current) magnetic field such as the natural magnetic field of the earth itself has a generally positive effect, physiologically and psychologically, [for they are] important for the activities of choline as well as other body substances and function. Choline is in part the final and critical building block of one of the isolated psychochemical structures...directly connected with depression. Choline deficiency can arise from exposure to harmful alternating fields, such as are produced by power lines, microwave equipment, wiring in houses and industrial environments. This causes a degeneration of the red corpuscles. The effects on choline activity are largely cumulative, and are strongly moderated by other factors, such as the type and level of nutrients taken into the body....The body tends to adapt to moderate-strength alternating fields, but in so doing its balances are upset. Both thinking and behavior are affected. [KR]

Summary of Causative Factors and Mechanism

In summary, the expert intuitives indicate that no particular single factor or set of factors is solely responsible for mental depression. They explain primary depression as a total system imbalance in which genetic, biological, psychological, environmental and spiritual factors all interact and contribute in a complex cause-and-effect pattern. The interplay and the relative importance of many of them vary greatly from one depressive individual to another, and even over time.

Nevertheless, some of these factors are common for many depressives, and could therefore be investigated through medical research and experimentally for treatment, thus offering some hope for symptomatic relief and perhaps actual control of the disease. Important subcategories of primary depression might be identified and studied individually. All of these newly identified factors merit further study.

Detection and Measurement of Key Factors

The intuitives urge clinicians to monitor both the psychological and physiological condition of depressed patients, both initially and throughout their treatment, to the extent that such tests are available. Simple and reliable noninvasive means for measuring the state of the body's neural and chemical systems, particularly the levels of lithium and certain hormones, are not presently available and will need to be developed.

The intuitives described several methods for doing so, by using techniques such as urinalysis, polarized light on acupressure points, infrared scanning, and chemical analysis of saliva (for the acid-alkaline balance in the body). One can also monitor blood for iron level and any build-up of toxicity (white blood cells), though the samples must be taken consistently and at the right times.

Mineral analysis of hair and tissue are useful for observing the body's nutritional state. Even structural changes in brain cells can be detected:

> The enlargement of cells near the pituitary might be detected by one of your scans, similar to light or laser scan [tomography?]. In other cases there will be a small but detectable change in the voltage or flow of electromagnetic waves of the physical brain structure on the lower occipital lobe— essentially an EEG scan, but at a higher frequency and looking more for the occurrence of transient (spike-like) pulses than the steady frequencies now measured. [VY]

More detailed information will be needed before most of these measurement methods can be developed and applied.

It would also be very helpful to predict the times when depressive and manic episodes are about to occur, so that one may apply effective treatments (such as the administration of lithium) only at such times instead of continuously. We were told that a refined version of astrology, not yet developed, would be helpful for this purpose.

The Treatment of Bipolar Depression

It will surely not possible to find a single treatment for bipolar depression, just as no one expects to find a single treatment for cancer. The intuitives agree .

Recent decades have seen the development of a number of new treatment strategies for mental illness in general, mainly based heavily on drugs but also physical therapies and psychotherapy. Still, there is still a pressing need for treatments that would be more effective, safer, faster-acting, reliable and predictable in their effects. For depressives the intuitives proposed various approaches, some of them totally new.

Establishing a healthy, balanced diet is the first and easiest step toward treatment: eliminate meat and all stimulants, reduce intake of sugars and chocolate and take appropriate vitamin and mineral supplements. Such nutritional balancing sets the stage for other treatment modalities that would not otherwise be effective. This approach to treatment is certainly safe and is directly accessible to all patients and their families.

It is important to balance the diet of a depressive. The person has typically gone inward and is paying little attention to it, so the physical body is not working well. [VY]

Choline administration through nutritional supplements is recommended for the treatment of depression. [KR]

A loss of minerals, especially potassium salts, usually accompanies entry into the depressive state, so there is then a need for calcium, magnesium, manganese and zinc supplements. [MG]

There is typically a deficiency of vitamins B2 and B12, calcium, phosphorus and zinc, and an excess or deficiency of sodium and potassium. [DR]

Many times there will be difficulty with the recycling of blood riboplatelets [presumably ribonucleoprotein] in the spleen, so the iron content of the blood must be kept high to assist this organ. [MG]

In a clinical or hospital setting it may be possible to regulate hormonal levels to control the timing and intensity of episodes.

Hormones play an important role in the cyclical or periodic manifestation of manic and depressive episodes. Most important are the endocrine hormones, particularly serotonin and the thyroidal hormones. [DR]

The Proper Use of Lithium

The consensus indicated that administering lithium carbonate has positive effects but is usually prescribed in doses that are too large, for too long, and continuously rather than only when needed. Lithium also has certain negative long-term effects, which are usually overlooked:

Giving lithium is like giving a baby a bottle to help it fall asleep: its main value is short-term. Lithium should be used sparingly, and only for situations threatening to self or others. There must be allowance for…the individual to experience what he or she has caused for its own self….It creates a dependency, and prevents the small intestine, kidney and liver from functioning properly. [MG]

Lithium tends to muddy up or deaden the energy fields of the body thus slowing responses, dulling sensitivity to their environment and generally reducing their ability to deal constructively with their own condition.…Generally speaking, lithium is too gross a treatment for the body. [VY]

The degree of absorption of lithium varies, depending upon what foods are taken into the body at the same time. Root vegetables such as beets, turnips, rutabagas and carrots, grown in deep, mineral-rich soil, cooked so as to retain the juices…if eaten about 1 1/2 hour before taking the lithium, will tend to make the absorption of lithium more uniform. Some experimentation will be needed to get this right. [VY]

Lithium damage (to memory function) is almost irreversible.…There is a drug mixture containing silicon, currently used for treatment of schizophrenia and paranoia, that would be better than lithium for controlling manic depression....One can also administer serotonin-producing substances such as psychedelics but they must be used in a very particular way. [DR]

Controlling the Environment

Some of the environmental influences mentioned above, both beneficial and hazardous, are relatively easy to regulate by technological means. For example, an artificial magnetic field approximating the earth's field can be created quite easily to assist those who live or work in magnetically shielded environments. Electrical shielding, also simple to install, can help those sensitive to alternating electromagnetic fields.

The social environment can also be regulated:

As the depressive stage is being entered it can be helpful for the manic depressive to move into a stabilizing environment where he or she may help others directly, particularly at tasks where thinking is not required—e.g., serving in soup lines. [MG]

Sunlight (even artificial light, if it is full-spectrum) can be of direct benefit to depressives, especially those whose depression is not of the violent type. It is also wise for these individuals to be located in a rural environment, away from densely populated areas—though not, of course, to the point of loneliness. [JF]

Meditation and Body Work

Meditation techniques were repeatedly stressed as a helpful means of self-healing, particularly for relaxing the body, calming the mind and shifting the denial process. Assistance may be required when starting the practice. Meditation should not be attempted during an extreme phase of the manic-depressive cycle, however.

One suggested therapy for such a person is to apply himself to meditation....This can lead to an alleviation of the stresses. [KR]

The best therapy for use between depressive episodes is a combination of meditation and fasting. A juice fast lightens the body's attention on the autonomic responses of digestion and assimilation, reducing some of the physiological ill side effects associated with the depression. Such fasting is also useful in shortening a lengthy depressive episode. [KR]

Body treatments such as massage, acupuncture and physical exercise also have their place:

> For treatment, one can use baths containing selected minerals such as silicates and sulfur compounds, adjusted to the individual's needs. [DR]

> Both magnetic and chemical treatments are more effective if accompanied with massage, deep relaxation and even hypnosis to increase general circulation. [KR]

> Other stabilizing influences for depressives would be massage, hatha yoga and hypnosis, [the latter] to assist them to find their own center and for giving suggestions, but not for analysis....The lymph flow tends to be stagnated. This may be aided by acupuncture, using heat and either electrical stimulation or physical manipulation of the needles. [MG]

> For more aggressive types, physical work is recommended. [JF]

Psychotherapy

> "It is cruel to say that someone controls his illness, even insanity, even though the statement is true at the soul level....Indeed, the illness is a wise decision and a healing where there have been circumstances which the person cannot handle." [Emmanuel]

The expert intuitives indicated that psychotherapy can be very helpful in treating most manic depressive individuals, though it needs to be given a special "twist" for this particular condition. The emphasis should be on working intimately with the depressive on the psychospiritual level, rather than only the psychological, employing at the same time appropriate drugs, nutritional balancing, massage and other physical and chemical means of balancing the body-mind to support the psychotherapeutic process. Traditional psychoanalysis is *not* called for.

There is a place for conversation—"setting a pattern of trust"—but the talking is not the real work. There are many therapeutic modalities that can be effective, different ones for different individuals. There's no one answer at this level....This [work with depressives] is more of an art of being, an art of trusting, an art of attunement, than it is a particular tool. In particular, the therapist needs to assist patients in developing and trusting their own intuition and inner guidance. [VY]

They must learn that one may have these deep feelings without being harmed by them or harming others. [JF]

As the depressive state begins, the task of the therapist is one of not believing and not accepting the preceding frenzied activity as being useful, productive or enjoyable, not being fooled by the facade; but rather by looking deeper and speaking more honestly when regarding the situation. The therapist can also help to set firm limits as the mania starts to recede; e.g., no legal decisions, no driving, and especially no drugs. [MG]

Less traditional recommendations include the following:

It needs to be understood that many times the depressive state must be respected as a self-induced moratorium, in order that there can be a regathering of the body's energy forces. [MG]

It is always valuable for such individuals to achieve some degree of self-understanding of how they are creating their own condition, especially at the more subtle levels. This may involve recognition of some of the karmic factors, but should be done skillfully so as not to lead them to blind acceptance of karmic destiny, as if they are simply victims of cosmic forces. Finally, their experience can greatly assist other depressives, for they hold the potential to reach, to touch, to enlighten and especially to inspire others. [JF]

Other opportunities for assistance include teaching, in the most simple ways, the awareness that the total self cannot be annihilated, and that the desire to hurt others only hurts one's self. [MG]

Past-life therapy can be directly beneficial in some of these cases, for example, when dealing with karmic residues from abuse or guilt. Such therapy can result in the gradual atrophy of unnecessary neurological tissues. [KR]

Many of these susceptible children [manic depressives] are high achievers who are seen as gifted, but who cannot accept failure in any form. This stage must be distinguished from ego-building, a time when competition is useful. [MG]

Treatment modalities will be improved, partly technologically through the use of energy tools, but mainly through attitudinal work....Therapy will shift [in the future] toward allowing much greater responsibility on the part of the depressive, with the therapist working much more intimately and at deeper levels than is done at present. [VY]

Communication skills need to be taught more thoroughly ....They [the therapists] need to be encouraged in greater risk-taking. [MG]

Summary on Treatment

The intuitives provided an abundance of interesting recommendations on supportive treatment. Some of these amount to a reallocation of emphasis among known treatment methods, while others are totally new, untried approaches. The counsel was particularly strong in favor of nutritional balancing, control of environmental factors and an enhanced and improved version of psychotherapy. They emphasized again that there is no one answer for all those suffering from mental depression, so individual tailoring of the treatment regimen is essential. Careful timing is also important: a treatment helpful at one time may not be appropriate at another time.

Finally, the intuitive team encouraged the trend emerging today among therapists towards more intensive and intimate work with individual patients, and toward shifting responsibility for the healing away from the therapist and toward the patient. They stressed the importance of regarding the depressive disorder as a challenge at the psychospiritual level, one in which the depressive needs to work through his own existential crisis rather than to "undergo treatment." For this work a healthy physical body is especially important, including the avoidance of stimulants and excessive medication. The clients must be given loving support and the freedom to do for themselves what no one else and no amount of chemistry can do for them. Sometimes the depression needs to be honored as simply a time for inner work, not a condition to be "cured." In highly creative individuals it can be simply a time for greater self-understanding.

Future Research on Bipolar Depression

The inquiry as a whole generated dozens of specific and attractive topics for further investigation, as mentioned in the sections above. A few could be carried out immediately, without seeking further information, though the majority will require additional intuitive input to elicit necessary specifics before laboratory research and patient trials could be profitably and safely undertaken.

No strong consensus emerged for a single preferred future research strategy, probably because the inquiry was too poorly focused for such specifics to be given. Nevertheless, a few suggestions emerged:

> The most fruitful research direction that should be pursued is in the study of neurotransmitters, then erythrocyte membrane transport. Hormones are involved but are not in themselves such an important research approach. Genetics is secondarily relevant for research, though not for treatment. [LH]

> The most productive future research will be in the study of membranes of neurological tissues; also, the ability of the conscious mind to influence the parasympathetic and autonomic nervous systems. Understanding other physiological aspects, including hormonal imbalances and heredity, will turn out to be byproducts of these findings. [KR]

> This project can best be carried forward through publications....It will be best to work mainly on the attitudinal rather than the research aspects. When scientific validation tests are conducted, they should be done within a clinical setting. [MG]

At the psychological level, as already noted, the future approach to treatment should incorporate more intimate interaction and risk-taking than is conventionally practiced in psychotherapy today.

Validation

A thorough comparison of these findings with existing, present-day knowledge from medical science was beyond the scope of this preliminary study. Indeed, most of intuitive findings are not sufficiently specific to allow meaningful validation, because we did not explore deeply enough to discover the particular situations in which they apply.

Suffice it to say that the findings agree generally with established knowledge about mental depression on several points, such as the roles of neurotransmitters and hormones and the existence of a genetic propensity, all now widely recognized.[7]

Individual Patients vs. Broad Understanding.

The intuitive inquiry also generated information not included here about several individual patients. Once given the patient's name and location, the intuitive provided highly detailed information about the individual, offered helpful suggestions about the nature of his particular disorder and described possible therapeutic interventions. including treatments ranging from the chemical and physical to the physiological. For example, one intuitive [NT] provided exact laboratory values of plasma chemistry and hormones, whose values were later verified in the laboratory, and also described the clinical course of one patient's depression over the previous five years with such detail that the psychiatrist [PG] had to check the dates and details from his own notes. The intuitively provided information was completely correct. Another [JF] described some new diagnostic instruments.

This high precision on individual patients was in direct contrast to the vagueness of the general inquiry. When our questions arose from attempts to extend existing models and theories or were broad "why" and "how" questions rooted in the prevailing paradigm, the responses were helpful but not very specific. When they dealt with specific action to be taken in a situation or for a particular patient, they were clear, accurate, definite and to the point.

Careful study of the intuitives' responses showed that, in virtually every case in which we encountered ambiguity and disagreement, either among the intuitives or between the intuitives' statements and existing knowledge, we could trace the problem to limitations in the questioning or weaknesses in the underlying knowledge base. When we reworded the questions for a

---

subsequent session, by making them more specific, eliminating ambiguities and preconceptions, or removing their reliance on a particular model or theory, the answers improved. We realized only later that for the inquiry proper, existing knowledge about mind-body processes was too scanty for us to ask the right questions, and this deficiency prevented clear answers.

Our intention in this study may have been more "pure" when questions were asked about individual patients, out of a strong desire to help them, than when the questions pertained to a general theory of depression. The latter was sincere enough, but was driven to some extent by curiosity. It may have been limited by the lack of a clearly defined purpose more than just "understanding primary depression," as we sought the information we thought we wanted.

It is striking that some of the observations and recommendations which at the time of inquiry (around 1980) were totally unexpected, improbable or contrary to existing beliefs, have since been impressively validated. For example the measurement of melatonin in urine, at that time unknown, has since turned out to be the preferable way of monitoring melatonin excretion.[8] Intermittent use of lithium, at that time considered heretic, has since been often shown successful.[9] Nutritional prevention of recurrences by omega fatty acids is now the fastest growing new approach.[10] Low magnesium levels have been identified in mood disorders.[11] The use of visible light for the treatment of affective disorders has been positive.[12] And the intuitive insight that the children of bipolar parents are unusually gifted has been confirmed since by several authors.[13]

On the other hand, there are several areas of disagreement with established knowledge about depression. Just as in the SIDS study, medical science does not acknowledge the existence of individual consciousness before birth, nor does it give any value or relevance to the notion that an individual may come into life with essentially non-genetic predispositions and purposes ("karmic factors") which have their origin in prior existences ("past lives") of the individual. Nor does medical science attach any great value to the psychological and psychospiritual factors that are claimed here to underlie particular nutritional and hormonal imbalances, emotional and even physical symptoms and behavior. Yet, it is just these factors that the intuitives claim to be the most important factors in a proper understanding of mental depression. If medical science could acknowledge these aspects as genuine and possibly relevant, this recognition alone could well set an entirely new direct for future research and treatment.

There is already much in common between the findings presented herein and the models developed in transpersonal psychology on the strong role of the unconscious mind in creating mental and physical disorders, and especially the validity and importance of the psychospiritual dimension.[14] For instance, it encourages psychotherapists to lean more toward regarding bipolar depression as a unique opportunity for self transformation and deep healing than as a mental disease to be "cured." Blocking painful symptoms and suffering through heavy drugging is not always the most helpful treatment, even though it may help in the short term. Finding the proper balance is the challenge.

Review of the Findings

The intuitives' report on bipolar affective disorder revealed that a relatively simple set of symptoms hides a complex disorder. It has its origin in a host of causal factors. Most lie deep in the unconscious at the psycho-spiritual level, and manifest genetically, neurochemically, physiologically and psychologically. Each depressed individual has his own unique pattern of imbalances. There is no single, universal treatment for the disorder, though almost all patients could benefit from the correction of nutritional imbalances; reduced reliance on lithium, body work; and (for many) an enhanced, bold form of psychotherapy that encourages greater self-responsibility than is the typical practice. The intuitives also offered some new treatment modalities and suggestions for future physiological and psychological research.

This study yielded a broad, albeit somewhat disconnected, picture of bipolar depression, covering its causes, mechanism and treatment. It may be seen as a fragmentary beginning for a self-consistent, multi-disciplinary and broad-ranging hypothetical picture on the disorder. It embraces but goes well beyond the single-disciplinary view of depression that has so far dominated medical research and clinical practice. Still, much more needs to be understood about this complex condition before a new, revised theory is possible. If intuitive investigation can be continued, a deeper study should be able to refine and extend what has been learned so far.

This experiment on depression was perhaps the most self-educative of all the Intuitive Consensus experiments in revealing weaknesses in our approach. The subject of depression was more complex than originally expected, even more than the earthquake study presented in Chapter 7. The problem we had posed revealed our incorrect assumptions about the size and simplicity of the chosen task, hence our unrealistic expectation that the results we sought might be immediately utilized.[15]

Overall, the consensus in this experiment was generally satisfactory except in a few of the recommendations for further work and in some of the answers to very broad questions about the causes and mechanisms of depression. There were no indications that information was being withheld, though some of the replies seemed more incomplete than they might have been—not surprising in view of the naiveté of many of the questions. We left many suggested ideas unexplored, and did not follow up well on those contributions made by one intuitive and not mentioned by the others. The consensus included numerous opportunities for validation, but most of these will require further clarification before they can be carried out.

In spite of these difficulties, much valuable information emerged. In one way it was the most perceptive and challenging of the several inquiries undertaken, in that it uncovered important issues not even suspected and that could be investigated further in later inquiries and new research.

If you are yourself a patient, or are directly involved with a depressed individual as family member or caregiver, you may find some useful ideas and suggestions herein. Do be warned, though, that the information presented here consists not of facts but mainly unconfirmed hypotheses, offered to stimulate further study, The conditions for safe application of this information have not yet been worked out. You would do no harm to encourage a depressive to adopt a healthy diet, engage in moderate physical exercise or undergo massage, and cleanse his environment—all identified as safe practices that are commonly deficient in a depressive's life. For the other suggested therapies, however, careful experimentation and confirmation will be required first and this must be carried out only under the supervision of a qualified professional who can accept responsibility for the consequences.

> *"If there is sickness in the body, all the healthy organs must fight against it, not only one, but all. For one sickness can be death to them all." [Paracelsus]

• Endnotes—Chapter 9

1* This study was carried out in conjunction with Dr. Paul Grof, M.D., Royal Ottawa Hospital, Ottawa, Canada. His participation was essential and is greatly appreciated. The material presented here is abstracted from a longer report (Grof & Kautz, 1993). Thanks are also due to Nancy Thorwaldson, who helped to compile and integrate the intuitive information, as well as Nel Thompson and the other participating intuitives.

2 From "Dark Hearts" by D. H. Lawrence.

3* See, for example, Keller & Baker, 1991, Hilty et al, 1999, and Bland, 1997.

4 Akiskal et al, 2000.
5 Schou, 1995.

6* ACIM, paraphrased.

7 See, for example, Grof, 2002, Grof, 1997, Berk et al, 2001.

8 Brown et al., 1995.

9 Grof, 1983.

10 See for example: Stoll et al, 1999, Locke & Stoll, 2001.

11 Libiger, 2001.

12 Reichborn-Kjennerud & Lingjaerde, 1996, Papatheodorou & Kutcher, 1995, Leibenluft et al., 1995, Kripke et al., 1992.

13 See, for example, Duffy, 2001, DelBello & Geller, 2001.

14 See, for example, Vaughan & Walsh, 1980.

15* This point was made even more clearly in a subsequent attempt (1999) to try to determine the particular gene responsible for Bipolar Depression in an important subset of patients, namely, those who have a family history of the disease and who respond well to lithium treatment. Genes were identified, but the consensus failed completely. The reason soon emerged from laboratory studies of these patients' DNA: our assumption that there is only a single gene, which seemed reasonable at the time, was incorrect,. There are actually several. In the end it may turn out that *all* the different genes indicated by the intuitives are correct.

CHAPTER 10

LIVING FOOD[1*]
THE LIFE FORCE IN HUMAN NOURISHMENT

"Americans and Europeans are literally eating themselves to
death.…The 'good life'…has metamorphosed into a cruel joke as
Americans, overweight and plagued by the diseases of affluence,
suffer from their own excesses."
[Jeremy Rifkin]

This exploratory research study on human nourishment was undertaken for
an outside agency, which suspected that the qualities of food contributing to
human health reside not only in its known chemical nutrients, but also in subtle, possibly non-chemical aspects they called its "life force." They believed that
new information about the life force, along with information already known from other sources, would allow mankind to obtain more efficient nourishment from food so he could enjoy good health while eating only very small quantities. They reasoned that if such a dietary change could be demonstrated and applied, it would also allow more people to be fed with lesser food, thus alleviating global malnutrition and starvation. These problems are among man's most serious challenges as the population of the planet continues to increase and global weather changes inflict more droughts on inhabited areas.

The notion of "life force" is not new but has no credence in nutritional science. Freshness is recognized as important but nutritional scientists tend to see food only as a collection of chemical nutrients, necessary for survival but which must "unfortunately" be grown agriculturally instead of being produced in food factories more efficiently. The recognition of these nutrients has certainly been a huge advance for human health on this planet. Still, most people still feel there is something life giving about natural food, going beyond its chemical constituents, even when it tastes better than artificial food.

The notion of "life force" is prevalent only in certain non-Western traditions—Hindu, Buddhist and Taoist—where it is known by terms such as qi, ki or chi, prana or "vital energy."[2] The term is being used loosely in recent decades by alternative health practitioners to refer to an invisible energetic factor felt to be influential in health and healing, not specifically to food alone.

Goals and Approach

The purpose of the study was to answer two basic questions for its sponsor, namely:

(1) What is the life force in food that makes it supportive of human life?

(2) How can strong life force in food best be created, preserved and utilized by the human body?

These two questions were first expanded into fifteen specific subquestions, around which the topics covered in the following sections have been organized.

Once again, the questioning in this experiment was broad rather than deep, and this forced us to make the best use of a limited effort. We tried to identify lines of inquiry that could be explored further in the future. A second round of inquiry sessions may have resolved some ambiguities and an apparent contradiction. The consensus was already very good, however, so we and the sponsor chose not to expend the additional effort, in the hope that a full-scale, deeper inquiry might follow at a later date.

We expected the findings from this study to be useful in three ways:

- As a source of *basic information* for understanding better the true nature of human nourishment.

- As a compilation of *suggestions and ideas* of particular steps that might be taken to help find a solution to the world nourishment problem.

- As a *demonstration* of the value of a professionally executed intuitive inquiry, applied to an important global problem.

What Is the Life Force in Food?

The CAI inquiry began with a clarification of this initially vague concept of "life force" as it applies to foods: whether it really exists, what it is, how it is contained in or associated with foods, how it relates to the traditional nutrients such as vitamins, proteins, minerals, etc., and how it functions within the human body.

The three intuitives confirmed unanimously that food does indeed contain a non-physical energy, or life force, distinct from the chemical nutrients currently recognized by the nutritional and medical sciences. For example:

It has been shown through various ways of thought in the past that what you would call "prana" or "chi" or "ki" or various other ways of looking at energy that are relatively unknown in the traditional sense…are present in many different food substances and other substances that are taken into the body. [JF]

There is also that element of…life force present in the living tissues of food, more than just the chemical components—the proteins, the carbohydrates, and such. It is the same life energy that is in humans—that's the resonating factor.…When the essence of the life force is still present, the food has a higher residual value in the body. [LDM]

This life force acts directly as energy upon the cells and the chemistry.…The energy is passed on [when food is eaten].…There is a life force inherent in fresh food. [RW]

They went on to say that this life force is not a monolithic element, as we think of sunlight or water, say, but rather a multifaceted energy or category, more like vitamins, minerals and proteins (such as A, B6, E, etc.; calcium, iron, etc.;

and the 20 amino acids).. It takes different forms in different foods and food classes.

> There are many...hidden nourishments,...similar to what you call vitamins and minerals,...not merely one that you would call "life force."...Each individual plant or animal has its own life force. There are also genus life forces, peculiar to a particular plant or animal....What they all have in common, of course, is energy—"life energy." [RW]

> Each of these [food] substances carries one different aspect of the entire vibration of that plant or animal from which it is derived. In addition, each...has targets [within the body]....[Life force] is as sophisticated and complex as the complicated physical substances such as vitamins, minerals, proteins and so on. [JF]

> It is a singular energy sustaining all of existence. It just takes a variety of forms....The grain has...value by virtue of its higher life force, so long as it is prepared to retain this higher life force. [LDM]

> The life force involved with living, breathing animals and living, breathing plants is far more significant than that of grains. [RW]

Life Force and Traditional Nutrients

While the life force in food exists over and above the nutritional chemicals, it may work through them. The life force is only one of the essential nutrients in the human body.

> This life force affects the chemical makeup of the food substance...in the way in which the atoms and molecules themselves interact with each other to produce chemical compounds. You cannot separate one from the other...though you can have the chemicals without the life force in the same way that you can have a body without a soul. [RW]

> This [life energy] has its basis in fact upon the lattice structures that are naturally formed as various substances come together. These have patterns which hold the information....The forces themselves are not contained within the substance but they are simply carried by the substance. [JF]

A proper understanding of the way life force works in the body requires consideration of man's "subtle energy bodies." These are not part of Western physiology, but in Eastern traditional thought these subtle bodies, called astral, causal, etheric, etc., are the various levels of a human's energy field that can be thought of as surrounding or encasing the physical body and giving rise to it.[3] The life force in foods is claimed to interact with these subtle bodies more than with the physical body.

> The subtle bodies...are nourished by the substances [vitamins, minerals, etc.] as well....Protein substances...[affect] a change at the higher levels, the etheric and astral body levels in the individual....Certain vitamins, and most importantly all of the amino acids, tend to affect the boundaries between the subtle bodies, particularly between the physical and etheric bodies....As they [these substances] are recognized in the physical body, [they] are modulated or changed by the individual's own etheric or astral bodies. They then exert a powerful influence in how the substances make their way into the physical body. This is why the simple understanding at a chemical level is insufficient. [JF]

> These governings [by the etheric body]...are derived from the patterns present in the DNA, as well as from the conscious thought of the individual—and...from certain aspects of the unconscious. The deep aspects of the unconscious...are found in the astral body. These exert a powerful influence over the physical body, and tend to go around the influence of the etheric body. [JF]

The Roles of Water and Sunlight

The intuitives explained that the water in food is a primary carrier of the life force, though seeds and grains also serve as a vehicle in a more limited way:

> [The life force] cannot act directly upon your physical reality....It acts through the cells, and water is the key element. [RW]

> Water is seen as the primary carrier of such information....Water...will be seen to be very active, able to transfer the highest amount of living force and to vibrate most easily at 4 degrees Centigrade....This significantly increases the life-force substance available....When water is taken from

open, running streams at this temperature [and used] to feed and nourish crops...this will significantly increase the life-force substance available. [JF]

Sunlight also plays an essential part.

At the higher vibrational levels, which generally correspond to the activation of glands within the physical body of animals and man, the sun [is crucial]. In plants the sun has a different purpose, for here it is for the creation of the chlorophyll....If food is grown without exposure to sunlight, then there is the deliberate destruction of its vibrational characteristics. [JF]

If you dry [fruit] in the natural sun...you have a better product. [LDM]

The obvious correction here [to weakness in the immune system] is to bring some of the life-force energy back into the food substances. Exposure to the sun is the best way to do this. A portion of ultraviolet light in the range closest to the visible is most useful. [JF]

The Detection and Measurement of Life Force

Is it possible to measure the amount of life force in a sample of food with some kind of instruments? Not so easy, say the intuitives, though there are indirect ways to do so.

This was done in ancient times, and it is possible to create such devices again now. This is best done now by biological means. It is more difficult...by physical or chemical means, but it can be done. To do so a small quantity of the food is exposed to...high-intensity microwaves, powerful levels of stress or heat. One will then notice that molecular changes in the encroachment of micro-organisms tend to be speeded up in those foods with less life force, and is a little slower with those with more life force. [JF]

Science does not yet have the measurement capacity to distinguish the life force itself. It will come...perhaps in a combination of...scientific instrumentation and the sensitivity of individuals. [It's like] enzyme activity—this would be the closest correlation that science can now address. But an individual, developed and trained, could simply hold his hand over the food and register the life force. It's a rather simple technique....But you'll probably do it the other way first [with technology]. [LDM]

Some of the soundest intuitive advice on nutrition came from intuitive Edgar Cayce. Most of Cayce's 10,000 personal readings included dietary advice. Many of his recommendations seemed strange at the time they were given, but have since been discovered by nutritional scientists to be correct and are now part of authoritative counsel on healthy eating; for example, reduction of intake of sugars, fats and refined carbohydrates; maintenance of a proper acid-alkaline balance in the body; eating locally grown, unprocessed food; the value of particular foods such as yogurt; and the negative consequences of eating large amounts of meat.

Not yet acknowledged by science is Cayce's advice that a healthy diet should contain at least as many vegetables and fruits as all other foods combined; the serious effects of negative attitudes and emotions on digestion and health (e.g., never eat when tired or upset); and even the mind's clarity is highly dependent on a healthy food intake.

Dietary needs are now known to be highly individual despite much advertising and government propaganda. It is not enough just to consume a long list of "necessary" nutrients, for they still need to be properly absorbed, they interact with each other in complex ways, and these physiological processes depend upon enzymes and hormones that derive from one's psychological state (mostly stress).

The vibrations generally work at frequency levels that are difficult to detect with anything, except [perhaps with] what is understood as…'molecular emission spectroscopy'…in the microwave range.…[It] would be of benefit to explore for a deeper understanding of this, but to a large extent it is a secondary phenomena that is reflecting the primary interaction between the etheric and physical bodies. [JF]

It would be very difficult to measure it *per se*.…Best would be to measure the water content and the chemical content of fresh cells as compared with aging and cooked cells, and to work out the ways in which your body absorbs the various forms. You will [then] be able to find out how the life force stays. One of the discoveries would be that…certain vitamins are less important to the life force than…others. [RW]

The food's general appearance is an approximate indication:

There will generally be a direct correlation between

It is becoming clear that the primary factor in establishing and maintaining physical and mental health is the *mind*, since it determines one's appetite, what foods are actually taken into the body and how they are assimilated. When the mind is healthy in this way, the body simply compensates, even if some accepted dietary rules are broken.

The best option is to work out your dietary needs for yourself. This must be done by personal, independent experimentation, using information, good sense, sensitivity—and especially your intuition, which is enough by itself if it is strong enough. Until it is, be guided initially by four principles:

- Quantity: Eat the minimum amount of food you need for good health, considering your personal energy expenditure (exercise, physical work, etc.) and other purely biological needs.
- Quality: Include in your diet all essential nutrients, but try to avoid foods that are fatty, artificial, not fresh or contain toxic additives.
- Balance: Consume your chosen food in appropriate proportion; avoid excesses and combinations difficult to digest together.

the life-force energy and the sensory appearance of the food....The rancidity, the rottenness, the creation of mold, the various ways in which the food softens—all of these things that generally help you determine whether the food is good or not—are directly related to the life-force energy available in the food....The guide here is how the food appears under the conditions you impose upon it. This will be unique to each food substance. [JF]

Spoilage is almost synonymous with loss of life force inasmuch as it pertains to the needs of human consumption. [LDM]

We can make a rough estimate of the degree of life force contained in food just by noting the degree to which it is fresh and not decayed. [RW]

Obviously, grains, seeds and oils do not follow this simple rule so closely.

- Flexibility: Respect your felt needs, desire for enjoyment, and common sense as you select, prepare and eat (slowly!) your food at each meal.

The Uniqueness of Individual Needs

A complication is that nutritional needs vary greatly from person to person; in fact, they are unique to each individual:

> [Especially] important is the state of consciousness in which the individual habitually dwells. If he dwells in a state of agitation, paranoia, extreme anxieties or tremendous pressure, the food taken may be almost as a poison in the digestive process.... The more a person is grounded in their being...then the higher the degree of utilization of that food. [LDM]

> Food substances that impart the characteristics that the individual requires will be seen as beneficial. [JF]

> Two people essentially similar in make-up may still require different qualities of food....Food substances that might suit one body in a particular phase of development might not suit that same body in a different phase. [LDM]

It is impossible to set up a universal standard for adequate nourishment through vitamins, minerals, proteins, etc., and especially for the life-force component.

The Consumption of Particular Foods

The eating of meat is for many persons a difficult issue:

> Your body is far more willing to synthesize the life force from plants than from meats....[But] meat has certain life-force energies that can be useful....It is most concentrated in...fresh red meat. But this [meat] is not absolutely necessary for your body, and you may find substitutes for it. It also has a tendency to suppress certain vegetable life forces, most of which are found in seeds....The state of mind of a creature at death also plays a role, [for] there is a deep, intimate connection between the killer and the killed. Hand-killing...is preferable because there is a transfer of life energy there. [RW]

> The vibrations taken into the human frame for many, many generations relating to dead animals have created within individuals a certain dependence upon such substances. The protein is easily absorbed, and is

important....[People] now have choices towards less meat, lighter meats, and ultimately no meats....This makes it imperative that individuals at this time reconsider their use of meat....It has already been shown in a number of interesting experiments that the white blood cells and other characteristics in the blood are able to transmit emotions....The blood itself of the animal carries these emotions into the individual....The thought form from eating non-meat substances naturally results in a higher degree of consciousness and greater sensitivity. [JF]

And, to the point of the primary motivation for this study:

A vegetarian lifestyle could easily support a population several times greater than is already present on the earth, while meat eating would not. [JF]

Milk products present another problem.

Milk that has been refined by being homogenized and pasteurized may be of benefit, in that it...diminishes the risk of bacterial infections, but it does not have much life force when compared, for example, to a cultured product such as yogurt....[For cheese,] it again depends upon the processing. Some of it...is kind of a natural factor, but some...is highly industrialized. (Does most processing tend to diminish the life force present in milk?) To a large extent. [LDM]

The intuitives mentioned certain foods as being particularly healthy:

Food substances derived from growing seeds, early in [their] life, will have large amounts of chlorophyll and will in general be very beneficial. This includes sprouts....Substances will be extremely beneficial at this time that grow in large amounts of water and can take minerals from the ocean, as in the sea vegetables....Ginseng, which can be heated...and still impart a powerful signature aspect of the life force remaining within the plant...is generally beneficial for many individuals....There is a nourishing of life-force energy that strengthens the individual deeply. [JF]

Sprouting is one of the ways to extend the life force tremendously in all foods that can be sprouted. [LDM]

The use of very freshly grown sprouts in a salad is beneficial beyond simply the chemicals involved. [RW]

The Growth and Harvesting of Foods

The amount and quality of life force depends upon the manner in which the food is grown.

> Just as your own life force and the way you feel is very dependent upon your own chemical intake, so too for plants and animals. Even though they have the same chemical nutritional value, the diet of freshness as opposed to chemicals in plants, and the diet of food as opposed to hormones in animals, work in a similar manner....The love, the manner in which the plant or animal is grown, [is] another point....The animal that is named performs better than the one which is not. [RW]

> The individuals that find the foods and work with them should be appropriately uplifting, helpful and supportive....If an individual involved in the process [of growing] is continually projecting powerful, negative, hatred-filled thought forms at the alfalfa sprouts, they will impart relatively little life-force energy to most individuals [who consume them]. [JF]

Unfortunately, environmental problems are affecting the amount and quality of life force available today in growing food. One intuitive spoke forcefully on this issue:

> Air pollution [and acid rain] are important factors because the substances that land on plants affect the absorption of sunlight energies....All that is needed is a more frequent washing down of the plants...with uncontaminated water. [JF]

> There is a great difficulty on the earth...in the soils themselves, due partly to humanity's continued use of chemical fertilizers,...and partly to the pulling out of trace minerals....It is important to bring more of these basic trace minerals into the substances that the plants pull their nutrients from, be it water or soil. This is well documented in [the book] *Secrets of the Soil*.[4] [JF]

Much of water currently utilized for the development of crops is contaminated....When you say 'fresh water,' it is very difficult to understand this now. Fluoridation, for instance, is all-pervasive in your own time period; fluoride substances can now be found in the highest mountain snows....[To] deal with...these substances...cannot always be done by chemical means, or by [trying to] understand them simply at the physical level. [JF]

Contaminated water can sometimes be cleansed by a certain vortex action—an interesting possibility for further research.

Even water that is somewhat contaminated with various ground pesticides, substances of bio-unavailable nature (such as large molecules of iron, copper or other heavy-metal based substances) can be moved in a vortex action, powerfully and quickly. This will cause a dissociation of these substances...in such a fashion that they...are easily released deep into the soil and thus unavailable to the plant's own roots....It is likely that devices that make use of this vortex principle will be understood more importantly in the future. [JF]

The quality of available sunlight is currently worsening, placing crops further at risk.

Sunlight energy is likely to undergo a significant change on the earth over the next three-year period. This has to do with the reduction in the ozone layer, of course. It will increase the amount of ultra-violet [light] available to the plants....[It] will very likely impact crop production significantly and affect the various methods of cultivation. It may even be necessary to shield such plants with such as a filtering mechanism—a plastic, a tent or some such thing—in the immediate future. If the tent material can be derived from cross-linked polyethylene, which filters [out] primarily only the damaging ultra-violet, but still permits some of the [near]-ultra-violet...(a little closer to the visible spectrum), then there will be additional benefit in terms of the life force available to the plants. [JF]

Food substances contaminated with herbicides and pesticides are yet another matter:

If it is contaminated it may be something that can be removed. Some of the pesticides, herbicides can simply be washed away [or] be alleviated through cooking. Once it is ingested there is tremendous difficulty in removing it. [LDM]

Dealing with food that became contaminated before being prepared for consumption can be a problem, but there is a simple solution, already indicated above, for screening out food that is not healthy for the body.

The self already knows that this food works and that food does not. [So] train individuals to sense the quality of the food, so that something such as a pollutant will register. The human body is the finest sensing instrument there is. This [method] cuts through all the technicalities. [LDM]

Generally speaking, hybridized plants possess a weaker life force, even though the hybrids may be more robust in other respects.

Certain plants that have held their own species identification over long periods of time, avoiding hybridization, cross-breeding and so on, tend to have a greater concentration of life force. For after all, the vibrational attribute is then unadulterated by outside vibrations, and is in many cases strengthened by the cultivation of these plants by individuals who wish to see that the plant species remains true and pure. An excellent example of this is ginseng, which can be heated, pass through critical temperature, and still impart a powerful signature aspect of the life force still remaining within the plant, though not so much as the life force of the sun. [JF]

Sometimes hybridization works in reverse, by taking a food very rich in nutrients, though small in bulk, and making it bulky but losing some of the nutrients. [LDM]

A hand-picked vegetable receives an energy boost at the time of death....The manner in which [such foods] are picked out of their natural habitat plays a role in how they respond chemically. Methods of harvesting grains are not important in terms of the life force, simply because the grains themselves change to such a degree by the time they are ready to be eaten, but the methods [of harvesting] play a role in other [foods]....A hand-picked plant or one dug-up by an animal responds better than one that is machine-picked—the life force remains stronger. [RW]

Food Processing, Preparation and Preservation

Current methods of food processing are the greatest destroyers of life force.

> By the time the wheat or rice is processed, the energy has become more diffuse. A cereal in which the wheat is less processed would prove more useful. What is left [after processing] is pure chemistry!...By the time you are eating a piece of bread, the difference between [processed] organically and non-organically grown wheat is so minuscule that it does not matter. [RW]

For the most part the heating of food, which may take place during processing or when the food is prepared for eating, diminishes the life force. (For some foods there is not much choice, of course.)

> If the food substance is heated, the molecular bonds shift slightly. Extreme heating [results in] an erasure of the various vibrations within the food. [JF]

> [This life force] is generally deprived...when it is cooked—not always, but in large measure. Many of your grains, when prepared in a simple manner...even cooked rice...still contain a fair amount of life force....Most items that have been placed in the oven have been diminished of any life force...but it is not a hard and fast rule. [LDM]

> The energy is passed on somewhat more strongly in uncooked rather than cooked food. [The best way to cook is] that which takes the least amount of time—excluding the microwave. Pan frying is preferable to steaming.[5*] [RW]

> [The life force] is diminished [when it is cooked, but] meat would not be palatable for most people without cooking. (Is this also true for fish?) Fish, too. [LDM]

Generally speaking, the effects of freezing are not so severe:

> Freezing just slows down the life force....Refrigeration does not kill the apple, but it diminishes the life force somewhat. [LDM]

> Freezing tends to extend, albeit artificially, the longevity of the life force. The chemistry is altered by the freezing, so some of the benefits are lost,

but...the life force is kept stronger [because it] remains within the original water molecules, and these molecules are preserved long after the freezing....Freezing raw [food] is more beneficial than freezing [it] cooked. [RW]

Drying foods generally removes most of the life force, for the same reason, but some methods of drying are better than others. (Again, grains are an exception.)

If drying is done below the critical temperature then a large portion of the vibration still remains within the food. There is not as much water available, of course, so it is not as easily transferred to the person. [JF]

Drying is rather weak for preserving the life force. [RW]

Drying may leave the life force present. If you take dried peas, for example, they can be planted and they will grow; obviously, then, the life force is still present. If [fruit] is dried without artificial additives, it still sustains some degree of life force. But if you add your sulfur dioxide, your smoke, it kills the bacteria (if this is a problem) or the bugs of the insect variety, but it does not then sustain much life force because what is left is not very healthy in the human body. If you dry [fruit] in the natural sun or in a natural heating environment, without chemistry added, you have a better product. [LDM]

The deleterious effects of heat in the processing and preparation of food has already been noted. But what about microwave cooking?

Microwaves tend to remove the life force very quickly. It is not the temperature, it is the radiation, which distorts the entire chemical make up. [However,] the microwave preserves more life force than eating out of a can. [RW]

Bombarding [foods] with microwaves, while it creates a more stable shelf life, also removes a large portion of the vibrations....These extreme conditions are to be avoided....There is a deprivation of various life-force energies...by bombarding the food powerfully with radiation, microwaves. The actual levels of microwaves...from most microwave ovens is far greater than should be permitted. This causes significant cellular changes and other difficulties within the person....If the critical temperature is not exceeded, then most of the life force will then still be available within that food. [JF]

Some foods…[are] benefited more by microwave cooking than by ordinary cooking, but not much. It's more the radiation [that is destructive]. [LDM]

The majority of food substances lose most of their life force when they are physically processed through grinding, compressing and extracting:

If you grind it [rice] and make it into a flour, then you pretty much diminish any life force present. If you take the juice of the cane plant, for example, you have a relatively healthy juice, but if you extract it to the point where you end up with a crystalline substance known as common table sugar, you have no life force left at all—you have truly a drug. If you use a cold press on the olive, and do not cook or heat it, the life force still resides in the oil to some extent, but when the same oil is heated [in order] to extract a higher percentage, it drives out the life force. It has incidentally changed the way the oil affects the [blood] vessels, because of the cholesterol process in the body. [LDM]

Again, it is the primary effects of extremes, particularly extremes of temperature, that are to be avoided. Obviously, if one has too much pressure and creates molecular change, such as entirely new substances, then there will generally be deleterious effects. But under such conditions there will also be significant heat, so again you need to avoid excessive temperature. [JF]

When you take out one part in that way, you completely shift the life force. The difference between one sort of [processed] oil and another is dependent upon the chemical makeup of the oil, not the life force. [RW]

If one simply removes the encroaching substances—primarily those microorganisms that cause rancidity, color change and rottenness—as in vacuum packing in an inert atmosphere (such as nitrogen or argon), this simply excludes the ability of such bacteria to encroach upon and increase the biological rotting or changing of the food. Such preservation techniques still maintain the life force. [JF]

Deterioration of Life Force with Time

Life force tends to weaken in foods with the passage of time, but there are exceptions:

> The life force 'dwindles.' The importance of the various elements that make up the life of wheat become less important as time goes on....[But] the life force involved with living, breathing animals and plants is far more significant than that of grains....Storage techniques which tend to maintain the true freshness of the plant tend to keep the life force stronger....At this point in your technology it is almost impossible to artificially enhance or lengthen life force....Life force tends to be preserved in the same way that life is preserved. [RW]

> (Is this life force lost in foods after they are harvested?) It depends upon the food. Some foods sustain the life force for quite some time...potatoes,...and those kinds of vegetables that are growing so that they survive the cycle of seasons, so as to regenerate the seeds later in the season....The life-force energy is sustained in [some] foods that essentially don't spoil....Many of your grains, when prepared in a simple manner, still contain a fair amount of life force. [LDM]

Recommended Diets

What kind of diet, then, can be recommended for optimal health? The answer is not surprising.

> It will depend to a large extent upon the particular individual. However, by and large, substances that are grown in the sun, have strong natural characteristics, bring minerals and various vitamins easily into these plants, are grown in soils or water conditions that naturally have available all of the various substances the plant might require—all of these things are powerful and impactful. [JF]

> In your society...more salads and fresh fruits; in the cold time of year some soups; perhaps a bit of fish upon occasion. Avoid a lot of heavily prepared foods. Living fruits would be at the highest level of vibratory energy. The banana is no longer alive; it is dead. [LDM]

For some individuals who are involved in a raw-food diet, or one that consists primarily of such foods as these vegetables, sea vegetables and sprouts that we mentioned...only a small quantity of such substances as cooked food or meat may be necessary at various times in their own evolution....This is why the macrobiotic diet, which is so focused upon cooked foods, can be so beneficial, particularly to individuals in a weakened state. [JF]

It is important for the balanced life-energy meal to contain the leaf, the root, and to a lesser but necessary degree, the seed. The flower is not important....At a meal you [need to] have a piece of fruit or an orange, or a fresh salad, along with whatever cooked foods are served. [RW]

[Consume] those [food substances] grown from sun and water in the most basic ways, and not cooked; [also] sprouts and sea vegetables...and vegetables grown with all-organic and other compounds available to the plant, again not cooked. [JF]

Exercise is stressed for everyone on a high-life-force diet.

Those foods with greater life force...suggest that the person find exercise activity....So you could take a low-quality food and much exercise and still have an enhancement more powerful than with high-quality food and no exercise. [LDM]

Sprouted grains and seeds have already been mentioned as one of the best ways to bring freshness into the diet. It might not be too difficult to persuade the public to rely more upon sprouting.

Rather than saying, 'You can be healthier by eating less,' you can simply say, 'Take the amount of food you have, sprout it and you'll have more.' [Also] whatever has the higher life force generally tastes the best—the taste buds will very quickly [tell the consumer] which is best. [LDM]

One should be somewhat cautious about food mixtures.

Mixing vegetable life forces...is far more satisfactory than mixing animal life forces. A stew with three or four different types of meats or fish, or a meal with chicken and shrimp—these clash to a certain degree. [But for] aged and cooked materials it [the clash] is minimal compared to the other effects. [RW]

The Effects of Various Diets

Fortunately, for those long accustomed to a low-life-force diet, there is a way out.

In your general Western orientation you will find that far too much substance, and too little vitality, is placed in the body. Coupling that with the lack of nutrition through exercise, the net result is a lot of bulkiness about your bodies, a lot of sluggishness in the energy cycles. [LDM]

The current Western dietary practice has tended to focus…upon cooked foods, animal products and so on….After [dietary habits] have reached a certain point, generally a dependence upon the physical substance remains…to the exclusion of other foods that might provide more beneficial life-force patterns….An individual is able [then] by force of thought, by particular meditative practice or other means, to lessen this dependence upon the physical substance….Proper nourishment involves consciousness. [JF]

[Those with a high-life force diet] would feel better and their emotional tone would be better. Their creative thought capacity, their ability to resolve problems…would be enhanced—all of the things that give the quality of life a higher tone. [Also], you would need far less bulk than you would otherwise. [LDM]

Assuming that all…factors even out, the use of fresher, life-force food [will result in] the individual feeling less hungry, so there would be less starvation for life force in the body. The 'salad' life force, over a long period of time, creates a change in the craving system of the body…How to ease this adjustment? Break all the habits!. [RW]

Determine the quantity of the food, the heat intake [required] to perform a given set of activities, then consume food [with] enhanced life force within [this] lesser quantity….It is not that there is more heat energy in the high-life-force food, but the body derives a higher energy [from it]. This is also obviously true in animal husbandry. [LDM]

One may ask, what would be the consequences of subsisting on a sustained diet of zero life-force foods, as would occur, for example, for explorers in Antarctica, sailors in submarines, and astronauts in space stations and on a multi-year trip to Mars?

> Over time a number of interesting effects will likely take place, relating to the shut-down of the etheric and astral bodies....A gradual diminution of life force would likely create several difficulties in the immune system in the individual....It is dependent to a large extent upon the consciousness of the individual....At the chakra center with which the individual has the most trouble in his own life, what would normally be easily transmuted by the food substance into that individual will then be gradually reduced....Under stressful conditions one's performance would degenerate, and then one would see greater and greater mistakes, certain sluggishness in mental capacities and other things. [JF]

> Over a long period of time the individual will tend to eat more—unless, of course, there were appetite suppressants thrown in—and will tend to become sluggish, both physically and in thoughts...more difficult to exercise...necessary to get more sleep...more liable to get sick...lack of life energy....This accounts for some of the sluggishness present in Eastern Europe and the Soviet Union, where there are not enough fresh vegetables to eat. [RW]

A diet rich in high-life-force foods would have the opposite effect. Indeed, there are reliable reports of exceptional individuals, yogis from the Far East and others, who subsist healthily on little or no food.[6] Few persons can handle the higher energies, however..

> [There are] those persons of an extremely high state of consciousness who have mastered the ability to absorb energy directly and have no need of food to transfer the energy into the body. The least of their concerns is how to get by without food. [LDM]

> Many individuals will be able to shift their own consciousness to a deeper awareness of food. As a result of this, their ability to nourish [themselves] at higher and higher vibrational levels will likely continue, and they will in point of fact need less and less of the physical substance. Capabilities...and potentials within the person will be strengthened....[Other] individuals...

unable to deal with the higher vibrations, and having no ability to understand them, might then go into a period of weakness,…a shutdown state…and must return for a time period to a diet…with less life-force energy. [JF]

Understand that your body would be totally overwhelmed by totally fresh foods all of the time.…Fanatics and pure fresh-food vegetarians, may find themselves aging prematurely over the course of several years. [RW]

If a diet containing high-life-force foods could be provided to these travelers to remote places it would greatly benefit the mission:

If you are able to allow the individual to have a diet rich in those things which have life force still present, then they would feel better and their emotional tone would be better. Their creative thought capacity, their ability to resolve problems—all of those factors that are critical in a situation such as the South Pole or in space—all would be enhanced. So when you consider the costs involved in scientific investigations, etc., the quality of the food would be a very cost effective way to give a higher level of assurance that the mission will be carried through in as complete a manner as possible. [LDM]

[Subsistence on high-life-force foods is possible] if the individual is able to extract the sufficient vibration from the food as is necessary for that person's own way of being. [But he must] extract life force from other means as well, such as direct absorption of sunlight and pulling energy of various forms directly from the atmosphere, [a process] not commonly recognized today.…It is generally true that one cannot so easily live on small quantities of food if the food has a minimal amount of life force.…For most individuals this would be a difficult process, primarily because of the interaction between the astral body and the physical.…It is not simply that the higher life force available in the food is directly nourishing; rather, it changes the individual's consciousness more easily…so that the extraction of energy from these other means is increased. [JF]

In other words, the benefits of a high-life-force diet lie not only in the food substances themselves but also in the change of consciousness that is necessary before such a diet can be followed.

Can high-life-force foods aid those who are starving? Yes, but the answer is qualified, for the starvation conditions need to be corrected first:

One must [first] get one's health back in shape before these higher life-force foods can be appropriate. [JF]

The tremendous tension created by the lack of food is itself the major problem....You need the basic elements...but you may have a simple high-life-force food that is basic to nutrients needed by the body....Look at the very nature of the foods being shipped [to starvation areas] and how they are prepared. [Try] to bring things to a sprouted level. [LDM]

From a broader perspective, there is an issue as to who is really starving the most, and why.

If you want to broaden the scope of nutrition there should be the nutrition of the mind and nutrition of the spirit...[as well as] nutrition of the body-physical in terms of physical activity and nutrition through food-stuffs....[Life force] has very little to do with feeding the starving multitudes. It has much to do with allowing mankind to stop starving spiritually, which is the greater starvation. Those who are in the midst of wealth and heavily endowed with all the abundance that society may give may indeed be starving. [LDM]

And also:

Persons involved in helping to solve world hunger could be solving their own spiritual hunger if they demonstrated how to subsist on very little food by raising their consciousness. [They could] stand as examples of what it means to live without food,...of what is possible. The unlimited quality of human potential would then become more apparent....So it begins to create a valuable merging of awareness [through] experiencing the human process everywhere on the planet, including the most deprived state of human hunger. [LDM]

In summary, as your consciousness expands, your particular diet becomes less important for three reasons: (1) your fears, beliefs and emotional needs become less crystallized in specific food substances and habits, so you can tolerate and subsist on a wider range of foods, even some "bad" food or very little food; (2) your appetites and food preferences automatically change to conform more closely to what your body truly needs and can handle; and (3) you become intuitively more aware of the proper quantity, quality and kinds of food required at any moment. You may then eat properly without being disturbed by emotional factors and other pressures on eating habits.

Nutrition and Consciousness

As we examine the findings reported here for what they imply for our own lives, we are confronted from the start with the fact that our nutritional preferences and "needs" are dependent upon our state of mind. Personal experiences of food vary greatly, depending upon the extent of one's self-awareness. Most of us can confirm this observation at the psychological level, for we all know that our appetites, what we interpret as "hunger," are largely a reflection of our emotions, not physical sustenance. We know that the consumption of food often plays a security role for us by helping us feel comfortable and taken care of (if not actually loved) by being fed well, just as it did when we were infants. (Note especially the craving for sweets!) Food can also serve to suppress unwelcome feelings, which show themselves soon enough if we're forced to skip a meal or two. Most persons are also familiar with the light "high" state that accompanies non-eating. (If you've ever fasted for a few days you know well what I'm speaking about..)

When we turn from our personal feelings about food to outer authorities, we find contradictions. Nutritional scientists and government authorities are urging us to consume at least 2000 calories and 40 or more grams of protein every day, even more than this for heavy workers and pregnant women.[7*] Can we believe such advice? Not all practitioners agree, and the experiences of millions of healthy people who follow much reduced diets in non-Western countries bear witness to the fact that something is seriously missing in such recommendations. (It looks as if someone is trying to sell us a lot of food!) These requirements apparently arise out of the assumption that too little is dangerous (surely correct in the extreme) and too much of these ingredients is harmless (doubtful). In recent years they are being questioned as heart attacks and other common causes of death have been traced to the over-consumption of heavy foods. Anyway this view disregards the now well established fact that personal nutritional needs are not universal but vary greatly from person to person—a point made by the expert intuitives.

Still further along the consciousness scale, many master teachers and acclaimed "enlightened" individuals say they need very little food to survive and remain healthy. This is both their philosophy and their practice. Some go so far to assert that it matters little what one eats so long as his consciousness is well developed, for he then takes from his food only what he needs and is not harmed by the rest of it, even impurities. This is a difficult claim for Western scientists and even most lay persons to accept.

The upshot of all this is that we in the Western world have acquired from our societies a set of beliefs about our personal nutritional needs, and we have accepted these beliefs without examining them for ourselves, diverted as we are by momentary pleasure and gratification through eating. The message is clear: each one of us needs to become aware of these restrictive beliefs, to question them honestly for himself (setting aside habitual pleasures for the moment) and to discard those not fit ting his personal world. Be prepared for some surprising discoveries!

The final step is to bring his intuition to bear, in order to learn what are his personal nutritional requirements. His inner mind knows. His pleasure, health and well being can only improve.

Recommendations for Further Work

What action can be taken to support interest and activity in live food? Primarily, and perhaps obviously, this may be done through education of the public; support of organizations, companies and farms that use organic, natural methods that preserve life force, as opposed to chemical methods for enhancing their products; new studies on how to preserve life force; and interaction with the traditional medical and health communities to help them understand and accept the principles espoused here. One could also publicize the case histories of individuals who have attained a state of improved strength and health as the result of eating particular foods.

Finally, there is formal research:

> [Success] depends upon acceptance that the life force can be…technically validated as a quality [of foods]. Create scales…one for grains and another

for vegetables....Identify food substances already being utilized in which the life force could be enhanced, so these foods...could be utilized more efficiently. [Conduct] experiments to show that [properly] combined diets [can] enhance the quality of the protein that the body may assimilate....Conduct [research on] the qualities of the life force, interfacing the intuitive element with the development of science to make known this life force. Make measurements that can qualify this [life-force] concept as true, then go back to teach people how to utilize [it]....[Determine] how to meet the needs of those in today's world who are starving physically of malnutrition....This kind of research has real application, down through all levels of society and through all strata of your culture. It is not uniquely adapted just to solving the problem of physical malnutrition, [but] is something that keys into all the elements of human potential and its awakening. [LDM]

In addition to these suggestions, other specific research topics were mentioned within the intuitive sessions. Clearly, they need to be made more specific and filled out before being carried forward into formal programs.

- Conduct experiments with animals to show that they subsist better on less food if fed more high-life-force foods, such as a mixture of sprouted grains.
- Study the "vibrational characteristics" of persons who grow foods, and especially how these affect their interaction with the foods.
- Study groups of people willing to follow certain diets limited in some areas and reinforced in others (e.g., by high-life-force foods), to reveal how general body health is affected by diet..
- Let a [cooked] food substance be ingested by an individual, and shortly thereafter.... measure the white blood-cell count in his blood...From this you can determine the critical temperatures of various foods. For example, the critical temperature for carrots is about 190° F. This is a characteristic of white blood cells that is unknown at this time.
- Investigate the use of strong vortex action to make polluted water safe for plants.
- Monitor carefully the particular states of psychological and physiological ill health in astronauts who have subsisted on low-life-force diets for several months.

- To measure indirectly the amount of life force in a sample of food, expose a small quantity of the food to high-intensity microwaves, then measure the rate at which micro-organisms are growing in the food.

- Investigate the use of molecular emission spectroscopy for the detection and measurement of life-force energy.

Fasting

An occasional multi-day fast can be of great benefit, for it tends to bring a new and fresh perspective on life into one's daily routine. The practice has a long religious tradition, of course, but in this traditional context it is usually regarded as an act of sacrifice, discipline or penance, not as the rewarding pleasure it can be.

One benefit of fasting is a forced confrontation with the feeling of low energy, even exhaustion, which typically arises during the first two days. The experience leads to the discovery that normal vitality arises not only from food, as we have been taught from childhood, but also from breathing and moving—and a positive attitude. When feeling weak one may regain strength merely by breathing fully and evenly with a relaxed and fearless state of mind. The apparent loss of energy was just an unreal belief that a missed meal produces weakness! And indeed, a fear of weakness produces weakness.

Fasting also reveals that what we call "hunger" is not only and not necessarily a purely physical need, but is largely "psychological." False hunger, or "appetite," usually disappears after two days of fasting. When the fast is over even a mouthful of food takes on a unique, wonderful quality. While the body certainly needs food to survive, the thrice-daily eating practice is then seen as only a comfortable, socially sanctioned habit.

Finally, fasts can show you that you can function much better when consuming much less food than habit and convention dictates. The usual large quantities are simply not necessary. The body and mind work best on rather little food, so long as it is nourishing, clean and in balanced proportion.

Awareness of these facts about true food requirements provide a valuable reference point when emotional challenges lead to excessive consumption, or the opposite extremes of an austere eating regime or fanatical preoccupation with diet. The broader perspective provided by a fasting experience tends naturally toward understanding and moderation. The experience also stimulates greater sympathy for those suffering from obesity or other eating disorders.

If you are healthy and ready for a personal exercise in physical and mental nourishment, you may like to try fasting for yourself. Begin slowly, perhaps with a three-day juice fast. Gradually taper off on solid foods during subsequent fasts in succeeding months. Keep a journal to record what you are feeling and learning.

Evaluation

A thorough comparison of these findings with established nutritional science was beyond the scope of this study, but there is clearly good agreement on many principles of good nourishment: the importance of ingesting traditional chemical nutrients for good health, the value of fresh food and a balanced diet, avoidance of pollutants and highly processed food, the need for exercise and fresh air, and so on.[8] There is lesser agreement with the recommendations of physicians, nutritional scientists and government bodies on the constituents of a proper diet. (Indeed, these various sources do not agree well with one another.)

Nutritional science does not acknowledge as important many of the intuitives' claims. It does not recognize that there is any nutritional value to the "liveliness" of food, beyond the loss of some of its chemical nutrients as it becomes less fresh, and the obvious fact that spoiled food should not be eaten. Nor does science attach any value to the psychological and "energetic" factors that the intuitives claim to underlie the growth, harvesting, preservation and preparation of food, through the attitudes of those performing these tasks. Even more, interactions between food and human consciousness—awareness, beliefs, spiritual aspects, etc.—have found no place in the scientific view of nourishment, beyond the observation that overactive emotions (such as stress) or dependency drugs or alcohol can distort one's appetite, prevent proper digestion and impair one's health. Eating disorders such as bolemia and anarexia can have even more serious effects, of course.

There is much in common between our findings and certain portions of Eastern philosophy and medicine, most notably the very existence of life-force and the important role of the mind as a factor in nourishment.[9] On the other hand, the Eastern view does not value several factors that modern science has found to be crucial to good health; for example, the essential part played by trace minerals and the associations between nutritional deficiencies and specific diseases. Certain energetic features of foods as espoused by various Eastern medical systems were not mentioned by the intuitives at all. (Indeed, there are contradictions among these systems.)

The next logical steps in utilizing this information appear to be these:

(1) Conduct further intuitive inquires so as to expand and deepen the understanding of human nourishment emerging from this inquiry, and to build up thereby a sound basis for future theory and research; and

(2) validate crucial portions of this new knowledge (as listed in the previous section), using investigative laboratory research, so as to make the findings more widely acceptable to the scientific community and hence to the world at large.

This experiment was fairly successful for a preliminary study in view of its abundance of detail, clarity, steady flow of information and good consensus. The initial motivation and hope—that the widespread consumption of live food can reduce the total amount of food needed—was supported by the intuitives, but only with the severe stipulation that the participating consumer must not be chemically undernourished and must have already developed such an elevated state of consciousness that he can subsist on a light diet of high-life-force foods. Neither of these two conditions is satisfied for the masses of impoverished individuals on our planet. Consequently, the sponsor's original hope for the study turned out to be unrealistic.

On the positive side, the expert intuitives clearly identified high-life-force foods as very important for health. A new opportunity is laid before us as to expand our collective understanding of this factor of "life force" in food substances, and especially how we may benefit, individually and as a society, by developing improved methods for growing, harvesting, storing, preparing, eating and assimilating the food we eat.

> "If you want to build up your physical body, you need to eat meat.
> But if you want to develop yourself spiritually, you must avoid
> meat. Animals are meant to eat one another, but that is not man's
> function or purpose." [Sattya Sai Baba]

• Endnotes—Chapter 10

[1]* This chapter is adapted from a report (Kautz, 1990). I am grateful to the Schweissfurth Foundation for their support of this work and for permission to reprint the material herein.

[2] See for example, Murphy, 1992, p. 257+.

[3] See for example, Mishlove, 1993, p. 139.

[4] Tompkins & Bird, 1973, Tompkins & Bird, 1989.

[5]* Additional inquiry will be needed to resolve this last point, since it appears to contradict the prior statements about the negative effects of high temperature on life-force.

[6] Murphy, 1992, pp. 502-505, Bynum, 1987.

[7]* For dietary requirements, now called RDI—Recommended Dietary Intakes, see NAS, 2000.

[8] See for example, Truswell et al, 1986, Truswell, 1983.

[9] See for example, Chopra, 1993.

CHAPTER 11

HIDDEN VOICES

THE INTUITIVE RECOVERY OF
FOREIGN LANGUAGE

"The words of the language, as they are written or spoken, do not seem to play any role in the mechanism of thought....Conventional words or other signs have to be sought for laboriously only in a secondary stage." [Albert Einstein[1]]

Since intuition appears to be capable of recovering lost history, as shown in Chapter 6, might it also be able to retrieve a spoken language not learned by the intuitive? This seems like a more difficult task since human language involves such a mass of intricate, highly organized and culturally based detail. Language may even fall outside of what superconscious memory holds; or, if it does not, it may be far beyond what can pass through the subconscious mind of the intuitive. Even if foreign language could be obtained intuitively, it may demand that the expert intuitive possess special capacities not needed for other intuitive work.

Most claims of intuitive language recall have turned out to be invalid when investigated carefully but a few well-confirmed cases do indeed exist. Identifying the particular language spoken, making certain it is genuine, and verifying that it was never before learned by the speaker can all be challenging tasks.

In this chapter we examine several instances in which persons appeared to speak foreign languages they never learned, including three genuine cases—two investigated by Dr. Ian

Stevenson and one by CAI—in which the intuitive engaged in meaningful dialogue with an investigator in the foreign tongue. A further inquiry deals with the nature of ancient language in contrast with modern languages. We consider then the relevance of language to spoken human communication and daily life, and how man might evolve language to be a more effective vehicle for interpersonal and societal communication.

Intuitively Received Foreign Language

Many persons are able to produce a sequence of sounds that imitate an unfamiliar foreign language but is only gibberish. On the other hand, if someone utters such speech that is a real spoken language, one he never learned, we would take greater notice. The term for speaking a genuine unlearned language is *xenoglossia*.

To establish the validity of a claim of xenoglossic speech requires first that one must verify that the alleged "language" is indeed a valid language. Second, the speech must make coherent sense and should not require extensive interpretation to be understood. Third, the samples of speech must be long enough; short samples of gibberish can easily coincide with one or more of the world's 4000 or so natural languages.

Fourth, and most difficult, one must show conclusively that the speaker never learned the language in question or was so exposed to it that he may have picked it up. This test normally requires that one examine the speaker's entire biographical background to be sure he never acquired the presumed foreign tongue, incidentally or unconsciously, from television, reading books, babysitters, self-study or exposure to foreigners. Such a thorough examination is out of the question for most persons. Consequently, few fully verified cases of xenoglossia have been found.

Before considering cases of valid xenoglossia we need to look first at a more widespread and better known form of apparently foreign speech, one lying between gibberish and xenoglossia.

Speaking in Tongues

We have already noted that discoveries and insights tend to occur when the rational mind is at rest and normal thinking stops. At such moments the contents of the inner mind may emerge on their own. This happens during sleep, but it may also occur when the mind is wholly or partially "dissociated"—that is, functionally separated from wakefulness—such as falling asleep, during meditation, awakening, reverie, or the ingestion of certain psychoactive chemicals. One example of such altered-state behavior is "speaking in tongues," also called glossolalia, in which one speaks what appears to be an unfamiliar foreign language.[2]

Glossolalic speech has been practiced in religious settings as a form of "inspired" communication since at least the time of Pentecost. The Bible says of Jesus' disciples that "they began to speak in different tongues" to the multitudes, and "every man heard them speak in his own language."[3] The latter sounds more like "hearing in tongues," but the speaking interpretation persists. The disciple Paul later encouraged tongue-speaking,

My first significant exposure to glossolalia was accidental. One afternoon in the late 1970s I was researching intuitive languages in the library of the British Society for Psychic Research in London. A loud voice from a room nearby, speaking what sounded like a foreign language, interrupted my reading. The coincidence was too great to ignore! I raced upstairs to find that the voice emerged from a tape recording of an elderly American woman, Mrs. Blanch Bobo, who had visited the Society that very morning, seeking an explanation for her ability to speak "foreign languages" spontaneously. It was not hard to track her down to a London suburb. We reconnected in Los Angeles several times over the next few years, I made many recordings of her speech., and took them to international conferences to try to locate someone who could identify any of her "languages." No success., but the effort led into a serious study of glossolalia.

Blanche's background fit her glossolalic ability well. Her parents had been traveling revivalist preachers who conducted revival meetings in barns and tents in the Midwest in the early 1900s. Growing up in this environment she became devout, determined and self-confident, possessed with a strong child-like faith. She was not one to sit still for long, and was more than willing to learn what life had to teach her. She endured decades of difficult life adventures, with one demanding trial after another. While totally uneducated (perhaps an asset!), she was just graduating from college at age 65 when I knew her.

but claimed that its value lay more in listening than in speaking to God.[4] He also said, "Tongues are a sign not for those who believe but for unbelievers."[5]

Glossolalia is practiced today in Christian Pentecostal and charismatic church congrega-

> *I came to learn that much of Blanche's strength lay in her ability to release her mind from its miseries by going inside herself, where she found nourishment, strength and peace — and incidentally the strange voices that brought us together. I found much to envy in this woman, and am grateful even today for the lessons that her example of a full and courageous life taught me.*

tions, and in a few religious services in other cultures, where it is regarded as a divine gift to an especially devout person. The speech is sometimes "interpreted" by an a second individual, also believed to be inspired, who purports to explain in common language what the tongue-speaker is presumably saying. Such utterances are almost always in the form of short lectures, not conversation. Brief, recognizable phrases from known foreign languages sometimes creep into glossolalic speech.

Is glossolalia a real language? There is no evidence that it is and fair evidence that it is not. Many books discuss glossolalia at length but do not provide answers to the basic questions about it: What does it mean? How is it produced? How does it relate to ordinary language? In what sense might it be "divinely inspired"? Some of these reports come from religious enthusiasts who try to describe subjectively the ecstatic state of tongue-speaking and what it means to them, but they do not explain for someone who has not experienced it how to do it or how it works. Other accounts are written by psychologists and sociolinguists who attempt to analyze the strange utterances. However, without personal experience with the phenomenon they are too far removed from it for their academic explanations to be satisfying. These two approaches, analytical and experiential, do not seem to be able to manifest in the same individual.

Two findings on glossolalia are firm, however. Linguistic studies of glossolalic speech samples reveal that the pattern of sound frequencies do not match those of known languages. The number of different sounds is too small, and the sounds used the most often are used too often. Second, speakers are not able to repeat afterwards what they just said. These two discoveries make it doubtful that the alleged speech is a real language.[6]

Attempts to identify particular samples of glossolalic speech as xenoglossy have yielded no convincing results. Most instances claimed to be xenoglossic were very short utterances, or there were no trustworthy witnesses, or no assurance that the speaker was indeed ignorant of the language allegedly spoken. In some cases it was discovered that the speaker had reverted to his childhood language. Some psychologists have suggested that glossolalia might be a lost, primitive form of human speech, so ancient that it no longer resembles modern languages. This idea does not fit the current understanding of how human languages evolved. Moreover, primitive people do not speak primitive languages: "Every culture which has been investigated, no matter how 'primitive' it may be in cultural terms, turns out to have a fully developed language, with a complexity comparable to those of so-called 'civilized' nations."[7]

The hypothesis has also been advanced that discarnate entities or "beings" are trying to speak through glossolalists but are too unskilled to create meaningful speech. This may be happening but we have no basis on which to confirm or deny it.

The best professional, common-sense judgment at this point is that glossolalia is a sequence of random speech sounds, and is literal nonsense. The sounds themselves are genuine and the sonic and melodic patterns of ordinary speech are preserved, but the speech lacks syntactical, semantic and organizational significance. It appears that during glossolalic speech the brain's cognitive center that organizes sequences of sounds into meaningful utterances releases hold of its normal regulation, resulting in an uncontrolled sequence of sounds, a free-form, improvised "verbal jazz" or dance of sounds. It may have meaning o the speaker or listeners, perhaps as a creative expression similar to music and dance, but it has no literal significance.

Enter the Intuitives

An Intuitive Consensus inquiry on the phenomenon of glossolalia agreed with the interpretation that the event at Pentecost was more of a hearing than a speaking of foreign languages. But the utterance of strange sounds was only part of the process:

> It was translated within themselves....It only *sounded* that different languages were spoken....The subconscious was allowed to take over, at least in the beginning....When they said, "We heard them speaking in their own

language," the more proper interpretation would be, "we heard the message in our own language." [AA]

There was such a oneness of being and spirit that all the barriers which usually block man's mind were removed for a temporary period. Because of this there was a recall in the unconscious mind of the many stages it had been through....Through this were the many, many sounds that were that day brought forth. [LH]

The intuitives also corroborated the "verbal dance" interpretation and provided an explanation of its mechanism and significance:

It is a removal of the learned patterns and...inhibitions as far as speech is concerned. It's just a letting go of themselves and forgetting for a little while. It's a tremendously freeing experience, but I don't see it as being a language. [SR]

What happens psychologically, and perhaps even neurologically, is that there is a distinct separation between what we call the personality and the more impersonal part of the self. This allows in turn for the person to act, to move, to vocalize in a very uninhibited way, because there's no monitor or censor there whatsoever....You fall into the part of yourself from which you have to give some kind of expression that has nothing to do with rationality—being logical or being reasonable, none of that. [AAA]

There are actually different forms of this phenomenon. Some are instances where one is able to speak in a totally foreign language to themselves, and yet one that could be recognized or utilized. [i.e., xenoglossia]...Second, there are those who are of their own subconscious minds projecting this through their great desire to be able to allow it to flow forth from themselves...just a conglomeration of sounds [glossolalia]. [LH]

In some cases glossolalia may be just poor channeling, as suggested:

Discarnate entities are attempting to talk through these people, those who are not developed mediums, and it is comes out as gibberish. [GB]

Glossolalia was said to have a positive purpose: to strengthen the underlying non-verbal (telepathic) aspect of speech and to awaken the speaker's outer mind to greater attunement with its inner counterpart. For example:

The purpose is for his [the speaker's] own edification, for preparing him to be a channel for the power, wisdom, understanding and knowledge from God,…from the universe. It is also to be taken as a learning process, to keep oneself attuned and to raise the vibratory state on the physical, emotional and spiritual plane of the individual. [AA]

Thus, while glossolalic speech is meaningless in an ordinary literal sense it comes closer to the deeper, non-verbal levels of human communication by giving expression to the unconscious component of ordinary speech. This is a direct mind-to-mind communication link—termed telepathy in parapsychology and the "mindspeak" of science fiction—which has been suggested as underlying all human communication. It is the aspect we sometimes observe (or experience) between mothers and their infants, between intimate couples, among very close friends and sometimes with the very old who are presumed to be senile. If we could all learn to "converse" better in this deeper language, perhaps we may be able to bypass some of the limitations of words by communicating directly at this level. To be able do so would surely facilitate intuitive reception as well.

Xenoglossia

The most renowned, albeit invalid, candidate for xenoglossia arose from a Hungarian woman who spoke hundreds of phrases in a strange language she claimed to be "Martian." Her unusual speech turned out on investigation to be a French-Hindustani mixture of her own making, created (allegedly unconsciously) from her native French and an early exposure to a Hindustani nurse-maid.[8] It is surprising that such a synthesis is possible, but whatever it may be, it is not an instance of xenoglossy. There are also documented records of young twins who invented their own private "language," one useful to themselves but not recognizable to parents or colleagues. Some maintained it into adulthood as an effective means of communicating with one another.[9] These cases also do not qualify as xenoglossic.

Bozzano studied 35 cases of reported xenoglossic speech, which he called "polyglot mediumship."[10] He brought attention to the phenomenon and his reports are interesting, but his cases are too poorly documented to qualify as valid examples of xenoglossy.

Several individuals approached CAI with samples of written text in an apparently foreign language, with the assertion that they had written them from an altered state of consciousness. In some cases they claimed their source to be angelic, Atlantean or extraterrestrial. The psychic literature also reports several such cases.[11] None of these samples of alleged written xenoglossia were credible. In any case, verification would be difficult or impossible to carry out, and none was attempted.

The best existing examples of xenoglossia were investigated in depth by Dr. Ian Stevenson, M.D., professor at the University of Virginia at Charlottesville and well known for his massive accumulation of solid evidence in support of reincarnation. He discovered and verified two cases of xenoglossy, one in German and the other in an obscure dialect of Swedish no longer spoken.[12] Both speakers produced their language in an altered state of consciousness. Most significant, both studies included *responsive* dialogues, not just monologues, in the foreign tongue, thereby ruling out the possibility that the foreign phrases were merely repetitions from memory.

The Rosemary Case

A third case of xenoglossia occurred in the 1930s and 1940s in Blackpool, England.[13*] The language which the trance medium "Rosemary" spoke appeared, and was claimed by her, to be ancient Egyptian from the 18th Dynasty (about 1400 BC).[14*] The phonetically transcribed record of her speech, is voluminous: nearly 5000 phrases and sentences, within much other material in English given over a 25-year period. About 10% of the language expressions were responsive, spoken in dialogue with Dr. Frederick Wood, an organist and composer, who learned a little Egyptian in the course of his task as transcriber, supporter and friend. A few of the phrases were sung by Rosemary and recorded by Wood in musical notation.

Ancient Egyptian is a very dead language. It died out in the early part of the Christian era after persisting in Egypt for at least 3000 years. The written, hieroglyphic form is now well understood, even to its grammar and vocabulary, following its successful decipherment in 1821. Unfortunately, however, written Egyptian *contains no vowels*, so it is not known how the spoken language actually sounded.[15, 16*] Genuine spoken Egyptian has not been heard for nearly 2000 years! Obviously, Rosemary could not have learned how to speak the language during childhood or later.

Wood carried out a detailed analysis of the Rosemary xenoglossy, though not according to the rigors and standards of modern linguistics and egyptology. His work nevertheless showed that Rosemary's language at least bore a very close resemblance, in both grammar and vocabulary, to classical written Egyptian. Her vocalization (pronunciation of vowels) appears to be consistent over many years and is a reasonable version of what linguistic reconstruction would predict for the colloquial form of an early Middle Eastern language. Her Egyptian speech corresponds at least moderately well to the written form, for a language spoken when few people could read and write and when written languages were formal and managed by a social elite. There is little doubt at this point that the Rosemary xenoglossy is actual Egyptian. If properly analyzed and documented it should satisfy any interested linguist that it is indeed genuine.

A long-term project was begun to conduct this formal analysis and documentation. Its goal was to make a convincing case that Rosemary's alleged Egyptian matches its written counterpart according to currently accepted egyptological criteria.[17, 18*] To this end, the entire database of 5000 phrases and sentences was entered into a computer so that its translation (actually, it's more like decryption) could be carried out as thoroughly, accurately and systematically as possible. The project is still unfinished; it awaits a professional with the requisite interest and skills to complete it—and perhaps the time must be right for scholars to accept it.

Is it possible that Rosemary created, perhaps unconsciously, an artificial vocalization system for ancient Egyptian, and then spoke it consistently for 25 years? Under the circumstances such a task cannot even be imagined. Her personality, background and social position show her to be one of the least likely candidates for such a linguistic construction, which is difficult even for linguistic specialists. Nor is there any indication that she was interested in carrying out such an task, even if she was able. Moreover, to carryout this task entirely unconsciously is almost beyond human credibility, according to even the most extravagant theories on the capabilities of the unconscious mind.[19]

The Rosemary case promises to provide the best evidence yet that intuition is capable of regenerating and conveying human language. If the results of the proposed study are positive, and if it is presented properly, there will be an extra bonus for it will provide a reasonable basis for accepting the *content* of Rosemary's Egyptian text, as well as the rest of her many channeled discourses (in English). These contain detailed descriptions of daily life and work, political activities, cultural actiuvities, spiritual beliefs and religious practices in 18th-dynasty Egypt during the reign of Amenophis III (the father of Akhnaten).[20]* This information fills in important gaps in what is presently known from the documented history of that period, and much more. The Rosemary case may also aid linguistic studies of other ancient Middle-Eastern languages.

Finally, the Rosemary Records contain a fine spiritual message, beautifully expressed. It consists largely of now familiar teachings about the meaning of human life, man's role on planet Earth and the ever-present reality of the non-physical dimension of human existence—essentially the perennial philosophy mentioned earlier. It explains how the intuitive recovery of a very old language by a modern mind is a demonstration of the persistence of individual human consciousness over millennia of time. This portion may be interesting to some of those who are seeking answers to personal existential questions, and are drawn to this case out of their professional interest in linguistics, archeology or history.

Intuitives Speak About Ancient Language

CAI's intuitives also provided information about the Egyptian language of the 18th dynasty. They attested to the genuineness of Rosemary's Egyptian speech and reported that her description of life in ancient Egypt is generally accurate, though incomplete, because (as is known) many foreigners and diverse subcultures lived in Egypt at that time. The form of Egyptian language spoken by officials and priests and the versions spoken in the streets were said to be quite different, though mutually comprehensible. While the court language was formal, indirect, third-person, poetic, musical and more-or-less stable over time, the street forms were just the opposite: informal, direct, in first- and second-person, guttural, monotonic and continually changing. Rosemary's speech was said to be intermediate between the two, and was the form in colloquial use among family and friends in the court and upper society. Dr. Wood did not understand these differences between the formal court, colloquial court and street languages, they said, and his attempted translations were therefore sometimes in error.

The Egyptian language of this period (in all versions) was said to be notably different from well-studied modern languages. It was more symbolic, esoteric and rich in multiple meanings. At its best it reflected more directly the thought of the speaker than do our languages today. It was more honest—excessively polite in style but much more direct and to the point—in contrast to present day speech (at least in the West) in which the complexity of the language is used to hide the speaker's feelings, even when he does not intend to do so. Ancient Egyptian was also sparse, rich in long silences and slowly paced, so the receiver had to listen carefully and intuit the meaning of what was spoken to him. To help resolve multiple meanings its speakers used body language extensively—not just hand gestures but a rich counterpoint of movements of face and body. The original Egyptian language that Rosemary allegedly spoke enjoyed all of these ancillary qualities, though Dr. Wood left no written mention of her manifesting them in trance.

Memory too was a well-developed art in ancient Egypt. Despite the widespread illiteracy at the time,

> [Ancient] man had an extremely well-trained, sharp mind. There was sharp, clear thinking and knowing. He communicated without a lot of words....[For] the pictures that we see as hieroglyphs or whatever...and think they're very primitive, this one picture means many things and represents a whole story in itself. If I focus on this picture I know what is being said. [LH]

In addition, speech was used as an instrument, intended to achieve an effect. People believed without any doubt that spoken language had great power to heal or to hurt: to transmit love and concern, or else to manipulate other persons. They tended to speak much more cautiously and respectfully than we do today. Language bonded their friendships and family relationships, but they also felt vulnerable to the words of priests and others in authority. This belief allowed both blessings and curses to be effective as they were intended.

> The priests...knew the sounds that could bring certain things about. This might sound magical but...it was more like knowledge that was learned. [LH]

> Personal names were felt to reflect the intimate qualities of the person. They were private and not revealed indiscriminately, for they could be used maliciously by others to take away energy. So people had multiple names. Their "true" names were written on monuments only after death to make permanent the memory of them. [DF]

They also regarded speech as a form of intimate, creative expression, like a dance would be. Not everyone understood the subtle, deeper meanings in the language.

> In the Egyptian language were words that described interior rather than exterior events…There were signs and symbols, not now perceived, that clearly differentiated for them these differences….The language represented the strong, dual nature of private and mass existence…and one affected the other….Certain symbols and letters stood for certain words, and for the priests they stood for something else entirely…. Only those in the know could [understand] the inner language…The keys and interpretations, carefully hidden by the priests, were in a series of twelve followed by a certain character that meant a precise quarter-second pause. When this appeared three times it meant the signal for the inner language. [JR]

The sonorous, musical quality of the language was no accident:

> Intonation came through the priesthood first,…long before 3000 BC. It had been brought down to express beauty, artistic quality, sorrow and joy, and especially to put a cloak of protection around one. [AA]

The written language was another matter entirely:

> The writing was formal and controlled, with a smaller vocabulary than the spoken language….The written language was limited. Not all things could be translated in that sense….There are wider differences between the spoken and written languages of 1400 BCE than between any modern languages. [AA]

Future Studies of Ancient Languages

Could one deliberately seek to retrieve particular ancient languages by intuitive means? Yes, we are told, but there are severe limitations not arising in other intuitive inquiries. The intuitive recovery of early language appears to be subject to the same natural conditions as the remembrance of past lives. One's motive for retrieving the ancient language must first be clear and proper. A high purpose must be served, one related to the state of consciousness of the individual, before he will be able to handle the information suitably. In this way, they say, the "beings" or "energies" who can assist with the transmission of the language will be attracted to participate. Namely:

It would be extremely difficult to find that perfect channel who could submit to this and allow these languages to come forth, and also interpret at the same time....Your purpose must be one of pure education and enlightenment. It must be of a nature which will call forth only those souls or beings who can project the positive words and natures. Note that in the past there were those [beings] of the lower natures, and this is not that which you wish to call forth. [LH]

In addition, the intuitive must possess some degree of linguistic skill before the ancient language can come through. None of CAI's intuitives were able to communicate in foreign tongues, or at least they did not feel they could do so and I did not press them.

The difficulties of translating and understanding ancient speech and writing lie deeper than mere linguistic skills and techniques:

Many of the spoken and written languages that have come down are opaque to you because you do not have the kind of free subjective knowledge upon which they are based....The present interpretation of reality, and the language you use to express it, impedes your interpretation of those past languages, even when you are able to read the symbols, for you read only the most exterior surface of them.... In its own way the English language was far freer back in your past, before the beginning of what you think of as the industrial age....There are [now] more words, but less meaning to any particular word, and so there are fewer bridges between one word and another....Children, learning to speak, are in a much better position than an adult is...for they are still free of a large amount of structure [JR]

There were not the fine variations of words that there are at the present time, yet the vibration that went with the word was as important as the thought that was behind it. Words were of lesser density, and there was a truer sound and more inflection given with each word. There were sounds that were important, and these sounds when combined [often] had more meaning than the word itself....The picayune qualities of man have forced him to putting more emphasis into the degree of the word rather than the depth or the meaning of the word. In so doing he has learned to twist the meanings and feelings in such a way that they have lost their importance. Even the animals of his day will recognize the feeling that is behind the word....The importance is that which is projected from his being. [LH]

Even if the world's greatest scholar in the Egyptian language could somehow be transported back to ancient Egypt, he would have difficulty communicating with Egyptians. This would occur because the infrastructures of his learned Egyptian, modeled on modern Western language, would not match those of his communicants.

These accounts remind us of the great loss of subjective content which accompanied the development of civilization as we know it today. It is difficult to imagine what human communication was like in these earlier times. Anthropologists' reports about the apparently difficult languages of isolated, primitive cultures that have survived into modern times tell a similar story. Even experienced Western speakers of modern Asian languages such as Japanese and Chinese speak of an undefinable communicative quality that is not readily accessible to them.

Scholars who study how language and culture influence one another say that it's all very complicated; indeed, so is the whole subject of language as a mental phenomenon. Notable advances have been made over recent decades, stimulated mainly by the drive to make computers "understand" human language, but even so it still looks as if the problem of learning how the mind generates and comprehends language is a very difficult one. This universal, commonplace and almost effortless human activity we call "language," which we all learn so naturally and practice every day of our lives, is still one of life's greatest mysteries. The understanding of it that we seek is not likely to be achieved for at least several decades—even with technological and intuitive help.

The Future of Human Language

We also asked how human language will evolve over succeeding generations. The intuitives were not very encouraging on this point:

> [Future language will be] more and more intricate in its finer definitions, and yet less and less important as true feelings are being discovered and dealt with....The words will continue, for man does enjoy expressing himself, but he will also be able to perceive beyond those words which are given. Try as he will to improve his language and words and finer meanings and definitions, he will not be able to explain or describe those things that are of great depth, for they require an impulse or a sensing rather than an expressing. [LH]

More effective language will not be arrived at until the inner freedom of the self is allowed its own way. That will automatically change the artificial language barriers that you have chosen as fences and walls about your own experience. [JR]

Presently, the world is not ready to return to a language such as the [ancient] Hebrew, Arabic languages and even some of the court languages in Babylon which resemble the Egyptian. These types of languages speak to the soul, and in the spiritual sense the language of the growth of the soul….But it would be helpful if it would. [AA]

Will mankind ever be able to speak a universal language?

This is an admirable ambition. However, it will take several centuries before this can be accomplished. [LH]

Why Learn about Ancient Languages?

Ancient languages are of primary and direct concern to only a few scholars. Others cannot claim that such knowledge is immediately practical, nor is it directly relevant to everyday life or to the interests of most of the population. Still, such studies are relevant indirectly, for they provide a doorway to the discovery of fundamental principles about the nature of human communication and the human mind. I have alluded to this doorway several times in the foregoing sections. But what are these fundamental linguistic principles of human communication? How are they important to us as individuals? How might we apply them in our personal lives, even indirectly?

First and most obviously, these principles deal with one of the limits of intuition itself—that is, how far one may go in acquiring knowledge through intuition. The cases of genuine xenoglossia presented above provide a significant example: they reveal that intuition is capable of recovering information as complex and detailed as spoken human language. They support the acclaimed principle that *human experiences are never lost*, once they have occurred, but are somehow "recorded" for later recall as memories. (We can rightly say that time itself can be transcended through intuitive retrieval.) Therefore, to the extent that past experience is relevant to daily life, we are being reminded that there is little if any limit on what can be brought forth to bear in the present.

Some parapsychologists have cited these cases of genuine xenoglossia as evidence in favor of reincarnation, but this argument is not valid. As shown in Chapter 6, for an individual to receive information about the past does not in itself mean that he lived at that past time. While intuition can provide access to past languages and can yield information about them, it does not automatically invoke the notion of past lives. This doesn't mean that reincarnation is wrong, but only that the xenoglossic examples do not prove it to be right. On the other hand, if intuition is accepted as a valid human faculty, then the great volume of intuitively received information on past lives greatly reinforces the notion of reincarnation. It also supports the related concept of karma, the principle of enduring accountability for one's behavior over successive lifetimes.

Linguists Consider Channeling

The speech of channels through whom an "entity" or some other alternate personality claims to speak is often strangely accented and noticeably distinct from the channel's normal speech. It might be possible to learn something about the normal language-producing portion of the mind and brain, which is not very well understood, by studying channeled speech.

At CAI's suggestion a volunteer team called itself the "Babel Inverted Group" addressed this question.[21*] It consisted of two psycholinguists, two psychologists, a channel [NS] and a few others. The team analyzed several samples of trance speech from accomplished channels. No single consistent pattern was shared by all the samples, but the team was able to derive a few interesting observations from frequently occurring features:

• The cultural heritage claimed by the channeled entity typically skewed the channel's ordinary speech, but only inconsistently and imperfectly in comparison with immigrants from these cultures. This observation applied across the board to accent, intonation, voice quality, rhythm, prosody, choice of vocabulary, word order and sentence formulation. It suggested that the language style is being *affected*, as a mimic or actor would do.

• Many channels display no accent or speech peculiarities at all. This suggests further that the speech peculiarities often observed are not natural. In any case the accents and styles do not appear to have anything to do with the content of the intuitive communication.[22*]

- The usual accents in channeled speech are English and British Indian. This performance might be explained by its prestige value in U.S. culture. Most Americans today would not expect a Spanish accent, say, to convey authority.
- The names adopted by entities—Ecton, Ma Fu, Joshua, Indira, Zartu, for example—are typically imbued with the charm of far-away places and times, implying wisdom and lending a patina of authority to their messages. Unknown are names like "Harry," "Fran" or "Bob."
- The pronouns "we" and "us" instead of "I" and "me", etc., are common, suggesting, as is often claimed by the entity, that "it" is a collective of entities rather than a single one. Again, this plural form adds authority to the speech. Think of the English Queen saying, "We are not amused."
- The speech style is usually thoughtful and clearly enunciated, uses middle-class vocabulary and phrasing and a touch of sophistication. The language was sometimes obscure but was not intellectual, neither did it embody street slang. These are the same characteristics of speech as used by public figures such as politicians, businessmen and clergy who strive to be popularly understood.

These observations suggest that the energies or entities that communicate through channels do not have personalities, names and voices of their own, and they seem to create these features as they communicate through the channel's mind. If this is indeed true, then it would be natural for them to fashion personalities, names and speech styles as comfortable, reassuring and conducive of respect as they can. Surely this is what any of us would do if we wanted to communicate an important message, but had no suitable body, personality or language of our own and had to work through a willing intermediary.

A deeper study, using these observations as a starting point, could be very interesting. A finer analysis of channeled speech styles may reveal how the speech production portion of the channel's mind is being interacted with or influenced by the entity. Also, the speech patterns of different channels who claim to be working with the same entity (this sometimes happens) might be compared, to help distinguish the stylistic features of the channel from those coming from the entity. Finally, some entities might be willing to experiment with other voices and personalities than those chosen so we could learn how they are interacting with the channel's mind.

Second, the intuitive information presented above on the nature of language partially confirms the suspicion of many modern psychologists that human languages, especially Western languages, are a very limited vehicle for exploring and explaining the significant activities of the inner mind, especially the unconscious mind.[23] Even the important questions to be posed for study cannot necessarily be well formulated in ordinary language. This lack implies that the successful researcher must rely less heavily upon the language-based methods of science and psychology, and has to dig deeply into his own unconscious for a direct experience of the languages he wishes to study. This point was also made by the intuitive team. One intuitive had this to say about the matter:

> Your languages…are structured according to your conscious beliefs. The words that you use are purposely structured to follow your conscious interpretation of reality at that level. They follow all of your prejudices. Behind words you find images, but…the images are already structured.…Your language defines, in society's terms, the bounds with which you can explain your experience. It structures your experience from the outside. [JR]

While our communications with one another are limited by the languages we speak, our internal dialogues are much less constrained. As noted earlier, when we formulate questions in our inner minds and try to listen for answers, we are more free to bypass human language. Words may be helpful when first learning how to conduct these internal inquiries, though our best teachers tell us that we may learn how to bypass language and communicate with the superconscious solely in terms of impressions, feelings and the kind of instantaneous comprehension that occurs in dream experiences, for example. Indeed, this is just how intuition works!

Third, and closely related, human language may be used by anyone as a gateway for comprehending his true nature, through the "inner language of the mind." This step, once taken, then opens the door to understanding the entire reality of which we are an integral part, the entire human psyche:

> All words lead to One, and all words come from One. Only by the study of it [language] can it be as one who studies the earth or its rocks or its people and their personalities. Each of these things is an expression of the All.…The study of language is one way of truly understanding man.…This is a fruitful search and yet it is also an endless one. [LH]

In other words, human language is one of man's privileged means for learning about himself, first by communicating interpersonally, through the sharing of individual experience, and then intrapersonally, the inner dialogue to "know thyself"—first with words and then without them.

Direct mind-to-mind communication, or "telepathy," is part of this experience. It is a phenomenon most of us feel we touch from time to time but are still not so sure about. Parapsychologists have proven convincingly that telepathy takes place occasionally between certain people. One intuitive had this to say about the subject:

> The structured languages that you know are used by Western society to impede telepathic communication, not to give rise to it. Your words are used to point to the differences rather than similarities in experience, to categorize and unify it....When you are not [so] connected to the physical organism, you do not think in the same way....The language of telepathy does not fit in, therefore, with the structured languages that you know....Great changes must occur when you try to transmit telepathical messages on a conscious basis, using your structured languages. The material is squeezed into words that are not large enough to contain them. [JR]

Fourth, the intuitive message about human language offers a reachable ideal or standard for ordinary interpersonal communication. This goal is one toward which we might well strive to attain, first and most essentially as individuals and then as a society. Here we find the highest purpose of language as a vehicle of communication; namely,

> ...to be able to communicate more perfectly those things which stand within him as beliefs and emotions, so that he can describe to others the pathway that he has taken in such minute detail that they will be able to see the signposts and follow the path of their own. [LH]

Cultural anthropologists tell us that even today some non-Western cultures practice an intimate form of dialogue in which they communicate with each other much more effectively than we do in our civilized societies. Just visualize such a scene (as described by two of the intuitives, though not verbatim here) in which two ancient Egyptian friends are conversing with one another.

> Each listens very carefully and intuitively to the other, and can perceive the intended feeling and meaning behind every expression. Their speech

is melodious, as if they are speaking pieces of music, and is well articulated, intimate and trusting. It is accompanied by modest body language. Their slow dialogue includes long pauses for reflection and careful choosing of words and phrases. The voice is used here as an instrument of compassion and healing, and is directed toward the other with genuine affection, like a caress or loving touch.

Our Western cultural conditioning does not prepare us for such depth in our conversations, so few Westerners among us know how to speak and listen in this intimate way. This example of speech communication invites us to overcome our conditioning, thereby enriching ourselves and one another accordingly. Much personal power resides in the practice of such intuitive and compassionate speech and listening.

One finding from the intuitives' information on language is that modern man suffers from a serious imbalance between his "inter-" and "intra-" communication habits. That is, in becoming very proficient at functional, outer communication he has largely forgotten how to listen to himself. In his efforts to connect, cooperate and communicate with others, and especially when he seeks personal acknowledgment and reassurance from others, he relies too much upon his outer language and too little on his much richer, non-verbal inner dialogue. He has much to gain, therefore, by bringing his inner and outer modes into greater alignment, closer to the mode used in past times before the modern scientific-industrial age began. Man must learn again to listen acutely and intuitively to his inner voice, and to trust what he hears.

Summary

Three aspects of intuitive language were examined in this study: first, glossolalia and xenoglossia as forms of novel speech, apparently foreign and intuitive; second, ancient spoken language, particularly Egyptian; and third, what may be called the "inner language of the mind."

The cases of xenoglossia presented here show that under suitable conditions information as highly detailed and complex as a particular human language can be recovered intuitively. The exact conditions under which xenoglossy is possible are not fully known but they appear to be related to the motivations and backgrounds of both inquirer and intuitive. Most reported cases of alleged intuitive reception of foreign language, notably glossolalia, are *not* provable instances of intuitive recovery, though they may possess other intuitive features and some inspirational value for their speakers.

The team of expert intuitives provided insight on relations between spoken language, both ancient and modern, and the abstract, largely unstructured inner language of the mind. As presently practiced, man's inner and outer languages are only weakly linked. This limitation hinders not only his interpersonal communications but also his search for individual identity and deeper understanding, thus his place in the greater reality in which he lives. The intuitive message stressed the value of sensitizing oneself to this deficiency and taking steps to remedy it.

This intuitive exploration of ancient language was undertaken without any expectation that the new information could be verified evidentially. There exist no records with which to corroborate this kind of intuitive information, since scholars have no significant non-intuitive means for finding out what ancient speech actually sounded like and how it was actually employed. Many written records exist, of course, but they tend to be stylized, formal and unreliable by modern standards. Comparative studies reveal a little about ancient speech sounds, but linguists are forced to read between the lines (so to speak) and can only speculate on how ancient people actually used their languages.

This intuitive experiment has the same qualities of consensus, clarity and consistency exhibited in the best of other inquiries reported in this book. No blocking was encountered. The intuitive account does not contradict what little is known with certainty from scholarly sources. Some of the information sought was obviously difficult to convey in words—the very language deficiency being explored.

Despite limitations on verifiability, the intuitive information presented here may prove helpful to scholars seeking new perspectives and ideas on very early language. Like the other intuitive inquiries, this one was also more suggestive and exploratory rather than thorough. Further intuitive work should be able to enlarge greatly the present-day understanding of early human speech. A larger, more focused intuitive study of spoken language could surely generate a much improved body of knowledge on the role of human language in shaping inner mental processes, by taking advantage of the opportunities presented by ancient languages lying outside the present cultural context.

Other important and still unresolved linguistic issues are also ready to be explored intuitively, especially the origins of human language, how it evolved from these origins and how it interacted with other mental functions during its development. Also interesting would be the features of specific spoken languages from cultures and time periods other than 18th-dynasty Egypt, particularly those whose written versions are available and deciphered. This would include, for example, early Sanskrit and Chinese from around 1200 BCE, and Mesoamerican Indian languages during the period of the Spanish conquest. If an expert intuitive can be found who is capable of xenoglossia it may even be possible to hear one of these languages spoken again.

Other topics include learning (1) how people employed language *internally* in the past, and perhaps in isolated cultures today; (2) how one may utilize language skills to enhance intuition development; (3) how best to communicate with spoken from non-ordinary states of consciousness; and (4) the "syntax" of the inner language of the superconscious mind.

> "We have a difficult language problem these days because large
> areas of language have been laid waste by the media, by repetition of
> clichés—things that used to be meaningful but that mean
> absolutely nothing now." [Andrei Codrescu[24]]

• Endnotes—Chapter 11
[1] Hadamard, 1949, p. 142.
[2] Samarin, 1972, Malony & Lovekin, 1985.
[3] The Bible, Acts 2:4-6.
[4] The Bible, I Cor. 14:1-25, 39.
[5] The Bible, I Cor. 14:22
[6] Crystal, 1997, p. 15; Pattison, 1968, Mills, 1986.
[7] Crystal, 1997, p. 5
[8] Flournoy, 1963.
[9] Crystal, 1997, p. 249.
[10] Bozzano, 1932.
[11] Bozzano, 1932, pp. 45ff, pp. 161ff.
[12] Stevenson, 1974, Stevenson, 1976, Stevenson, 1984.
[13] Wood, 1935, Wood, 1955, Hulme & Wood, 1937.
[14*] The real name of this school teacher was Ivy Beaumont; she called herself "Rosemary" to protect her privacy at a time when trance mediums were more controversial than they are today.
[15] Gardiner, 1957.

16[*] More accurately, there are three phonetic hieroglyphs that are interpreted uncertainly as a, i and w, and the vowels of a few words have been deduced from Egyptian names that appeared in foreign correspondence of the time. Some vowels have been guessed from Coptic, a vocalized Egyptian language written in a script derived from Greek. However, the vowels for the great majority of Egyptian words cannot even be reasonably guessed. For information on vocalization, see: Czermak, 1931, Albright, 1934.

17 Kautz, 1982.

18[*] Thanks are due to a number of individuals for their interest in and support of the project reported here. I am indebted to Mr. Raymond Donovan (deceased), custodian and executor for the estate of Dr. Wood, (died in 1963), who provided access to the Rosemary Records for copying of the language portions; Mae Swayback, who entered the entire xenoglossic record into a computer; Dr. Ian Stevenson, for valuable counsel; Mr. William Roll, then of the Psychic Research Foundation, for his encouragement and support; and especially Mr. and Mrs. Charles Hooks, Tomball, Texas, for their generous financial support of the first part of the research project.

19 Murphy, 1992.

20[*] See also the discussion on Akhnaten in Chapter 6.

21[*] Group members were Dan Hawkmoon Alford, Matthew Bronson and Thomas Condon, with contributions from Arthur Hastings, Jean Millay, Nancy Sharpnack, Dio Neff, Ray West and William Kautz. This section is adapted from a published report: Bronson, 1988.

22[*] I recall a double session with channel Kevin Ryerson, in which the first part, a personal reading for a Japanese client, was accented even more heavily than the Irish brogue usually used by Ryerson in trance. The research reading that immediately followed carried no accent at all.

23 Crystal, 1997, pp. 14-15, 413.

24 Codrescu, 1997.

CHAPTER 12

HIV AND AIDS
ACCOMMODATING TO EARLY DEATH

"Your immune system is your interface with the environment. If it
is healthy and doing its job right, you can interact with germs and
not get infections, with allergens and not have allergic reactions,
and with carcinogens and not get cancer. A healthy immune system
is the cornerstone of good general health." [Andrew Weil]

The AIDS epidemic was a global shock and is still a very serious global problem.[1*] In Western countries the first public reaction arose from the obvious fear of catching this mysterious, presumed fatal disease and dying a slow and painful death. Many persons also had a hidden dread of homosexuality, initially associated exclusively with AIDS. For the most part these initial reactions soon gave way to an active and compassionate public response. Following confusion about how to deal with the disease in the face of so many unknowns, scientists, health workers, social support organizations, local and federal governments and the public at large answered the challenge with sympathetic, multilevel programs for combating the crisis. As of today (2001) AIDS is still not "cured," though the huge effort expended has been effective at tempering it somewhat, at least in the Western world, in the hope that a medical solution will eventually be found.

History of the AIDS Epidemic

The biological cause of AIDS is now known to be the "human immuno-deficiency virus" (HIV), which attacks and destroys the body's immune system for fighting off disease.[2*] Without treatment the infection is normally fatal within 2 to 5 years. The virus is passed between persons only through contact involving body fluids (blood, sexual secretions, breast milk, etc.); therefore, to block transmission of AIDS it is enough to avoid such contact— alas, more easily said than done. Almost everyone who is aware of the disease at all now knows how to prevent it. Transmission of the virus occurs today primarily through unsafe sex practices, and secondarily through shared use of needles by hard-drug users. Infection is highest among blacks and Hispanics (47% of all cases diagnosed in the U.S. in 1997). Simple tests are available to determine if one is infected. Once contracted, HIV infection has no "cure," but a few drugs now exist that slow down the progress of the infection as it evolves toward AIDS, and in most cases to eventual death.[3]

The statistics on AIDS are staggering. First recognized in 1983, the infection had spread by mid-1997 to 612,000 cases in the U.S. alone, of whom 380,000 had died.[4*] About 30 million people had become infected worldwide by December 1997, 12 million of whom had died. By 1999 infection in the U.S. had stabilized at about 40,000 new cases each year, but the worldwide figure was still increasing rapidly. In Africa alone 17 million were dead and 25 million more were infected as of 2000.[5]

Few catastrophes in history, even plagues, wars and natural events, have taken such a great toll in premature death as has AIDS.

The Medical View of HIV and AIDS

Despite the dramatic advances made by medical science since AIDS first arose, knowledge about the mechanism of HIV infection is still too incomplete. Research continues to try to understand how the disease progresses through the body and destroys the body's natural immunity. This research is also looking for a vaccine against the virus, a drug to destroy it directly or at least a way to stimulate the body to generate a suitable defense against it.[6]

The virus seems to be elusive and "slippery." There is a great variation in the rate of progress of the disease among HIV-infected persons and in how they respond to treatment: some succumb very rapidly despite intensive treatment, while others do not contract AIDS even after a decade without treatment. Only about one-third of the newborn infants of infected mothers are infected. Persons weakened by starvation, other viral diseases or excessive use of alcohol or hard drugs are at greatest risk statistically, but there are many exceptions. Other high-risk groups are hemophiliacs, those who have had sexual diseases previously and (until 1985) recipients of donated blood.

Enter the Intuitives

Our goal in this intuitive study was to try to understand better what is going on within the human body as the virus attacks the immune system and weakens it to the point where AIDS symptoms begin to develop. This inquiry was fragmentary and was not intended to be deep and exhaustive. Unlike the previous studies we did not review the literature in advance to establish the outer boundary of existing knowledge about HIV and to identify major problem areas. Specific AIDS symptoms were not pursued since these seemed to follow predictably from the destruction of the body's immune system. Alternative treatment therapies, especially oriental medicine, were emphasized, since the study team already had a special interest in this approach.[7*] (CAI and San Francisco State University were organizing at the time an international conference on "HIV, AIDS and Chinese Medicine," which took place in San Francisco in April 1993.)

We made no advance plans to cooperate with a medical research effort that could have corroborated and utilized the intuitive information. A more carefully planned intuitive investigation of AIDS might have been very fruitful, by generating information to be verified through one of the many on-going research programs. In retrospect, such a collaboration might have accelerated AIDS research significantly.

Three expert intuitives participated, each providing a one- to two-hour session. While all three intuitives had a layman's knowledge of HIV/AIDS, none was well informed about the physiological details concerning the disease and its treatment. None was HIV positive.

It turned out some of the intuitively received information was already known at the time of the inquiry, though we were not aware of it. There is little point in reporting here those portions of the intuitives' information that is now well established medical knowledge. A few portions of the findings were not only new but have since been confirmed. What remains from the study is a collection of explanations, ideas and suggestions, many of which could still be worked on. Some will probably have been explored before this book reaches its readers.

The following paragraphs focus on contributions that appear to be novel and not yet investigated, judging from a scan of the latest published theories and discoveries on HIV and AIDS. A few have already been suggested though not explored by AIDS researchers. The status of the others is unknown .

In summary, the intuitives indicated the following:

- HIV is an essential contributing factor to AIDS, though it cannot be said to be the root cause of the disease; the true cause lies in the susceptibility of the infected body.
- The virus attacks the human body only when the body's immune system has already been depressed by a "co-factor": prior poor health, over-consumption of alcohol, use of hard drugs, medical treatment with antibiotics, or in a few cases an inherited weakness.
- HIV is not a single, fixed virus but has various forms that evolve one into another, sometimes rapidly, after it enters the body.
- The virus is most dangerous when not allowed to evolve by itself—for example, when hindered by anti-AIDS drugs and under certain other conditions.
- The virus behaves quite differently in different people, so standardized antiviral treatments will always be limited in their effectiveness.
- Eastern medicine offers the most effective treatment regimen before AIDS symptoms emerge, after which point Western treatment is preferred.
- Psychosomatic and psychospiritual factors strongly determine how the HIV virus takes hold and spreads within the body.
- What can be called a medical "cure" will indeed be found, but only after many years of medical research. Even then, it will be only partially effective since it will not deal with the psychospiritual factors that govern most persons' susceptibility to HIV infection.

These points are explained more fully in the following sections.

The Origin of HIV

The origin of the virus is not known for certain by medical science, but the prevalent suspicion that it began in Africa was confirmed by the intuitives.

> The HIV virus, once contained in organisms in Africa, was transposed from that environment to the human organism. In its rapid transference from many variable forms, it became volatile and deadly. It adapted to an immuno-repressant form in order to survive the quick transference from one immune system to the next, and in order to be able to replicate over a [short] incubation period of time, resulting in the development of so-called full-blown AIDS. For this it required the presence of other parasitic or secondary infections, which are normally held in check by a healthy immune system. [KR]

> It [HIV] is not something new to mankind even though it has only appeared in the last few years. [LH]

The Fundamental Cause of AIDS

The point is made by the intuitives that, while the HIV virus is necessary for AIDS to develop, it is not sufficient by itself. It is more accurate to say that the cause of AIDS lies not in the virus but in the body in which the virus takes hold:

> You will find that all disease levels within the body physical are a dysfunction within the physical framework itself, and not so much as from invading organisms.... When the body physical is in a proper state of health, there is no invasion of disease forces. There is merely the passing through the body, as a physical host, of various life forms that connect man, as a biological being, with the elements of life itself—as a contributor rather than a taker. [KR]

> HIV alone does not cause AIDS....If the body has not been "invaded" by certain passive viruses, or seemingly passive viruses such as CMV—and [for] those who have systems that are strong...then they will not be infected by HIV when they come in contact with it. The body will fight it off. This is as true for the common cold and the flu as it is for HIV. In the case of HIV, however, the body must be far more weakened than in the case of the flu, say, [before the virus can take hold]....HIV is unusual in that it

can work with numerous co-factors. The body must be ready to receive the HIV. It can conceivably infect the body if the body is starved, or if the resistance is low due to alcohol or drug consumption. [RW]

All persons have it [the virus] throughout their life but in a variety of forms connected to that which you recognize as HIV. However,…something causes it to come forward at a particular time, when the activities of the cells cause it to be converted unto something less desirable. [LH]

These "activities" consist of a debilitating influence, a "co-factor," that demands the attention of the body's immune system. There are various possibilities:

Indeed, the autoimmune component to the HIV process is only part of the story. Actually, it's that the body cannot fight off two viruses at once. HIV is not a strong virus,…but no matter how weak the HIV is, it gets a small foothold. That is all it needs, perhaps in one lymph gland, hidden away, and then it sits until such a time as the body is…fighting off the co-factors. You could say that there is a certain amount of confusion in the body as to how to fight it off.…(What are the most common co-factors?) CMV, Herpes, Hepatitis. Hepatitis B & C are the longest lasting. [RW]

Other key factors exist, however. [Because of] the broad use of antibiotics…their immune systems have been repressed, presenting a more volatile host to the viruses present in the body. [KR]

There is a genetic predisposition in certain family traits that will cause this to come forward.…[Also,] when the system becomes dramatically acidic, you will find that this weakens the cells and allows the HIV to become more active in the system.…There are also those who have an actual change of chemical balance in their system which allows it to come forward. The result is the same. One is not more important than the other, but just in a different direction. [LH]

When infection does not occur, most of the time the HIV is…eliminated within minutes, for it [the virus] cannot fight off the body and it dies. There are then no antibodies because they are not necessary, for the white blood cells handle it within minutes. It is the white blood cells that do the "killing." This may be an approach to look at for finding your "cure.".…There are also cases where the body will naturally accept the HIV virus—that is, it has a propensity, usually genetic but it could be acquired—and a co-factor is not necessary simply because the body is weak. These [same] individuals would tend to have cancer at a fairly early age, for there is a direct relationship between a propensity toward AIDS and a propensity toward cancer. [RW]

Recent medical discoveries confirm that the highest rates of infection have been among habitual hard drug users and those previously infected with other sexually transmitted diseases. The use of antibiotics is so widespread in Western countries that it is virtually impossible to associate it statistically with a susceptibility to HIV infection. Detection of a genetic predisposition to any infection is difficult but may become easier for AIDS now that the mapping of the human genome has been completed.

As in many diseases, the mind also plays an important role in an individual's susceptibility to HIV infection. Specifically:

For instance, certain personality types or character types would be open to lower immune factors.... Mostly this factor influences persons who, much like the virus itself, have ceased to evolve. For the very fact of the virus' remarkable ability to adapt is a quality or character that many individuals have found lacking in their lives....When the virus becomes known to be present, then rapid evolution of the individual [is stimulated]. [KR]

The mind can also bring about this disease. The mind is very important here, for...a fear of the viral infection causes it to come forward....This is prevalent in many people. This fear is unseen and yet is a very real force in the world. The immune system is very sensitive to thoughts or feelings or ideas in the mind....For a child who receives these viral indications, it is not fear on their part but that of the parents around them that engulfs them. [LH]

According to one model, *all* diseases are psychoimmune, though perhaps psychospiritual would be a more definitive term. For disease is a predisposition of stress in the organism, through blocked or conditional memory, or perhaps negative thought or memory. This lowers the immune system to the point where so-called invaders may interfere with the internal harmonies of the body's own physiological function.... All states of disease are eventually linked to one's own mental well-being. {KR]

Progression of the Disease

Medical scientists have discovered that the virus takes on various forms or "strains." This property makes it difficult for both the body and external agents to fight it. The intuitives confirm that the virus evolves through several similar stages, sometimes quite rapidly, but they say this growth process is systematic and predictable:

> The virus is highly volatile. It does not mutate, it evolves. To mutate implies a random change, but this is a specific adaption or survival response. Therefore, it is predictable and expectable....The evolutionary cycle of the virus is fixed, whether treating someone who merely tests positive for HIV or somebody who has more advanced AIDS. [KR]

The T-cells are pawns in this process, incidentally destroyed in the course of the virus' activity, and their sacrifice weakens the immune system. The virus tends to concentrate in the lymph glands, thymus, spleen and a few other organs:

> It's a renegade virus. It is looking for strength-building things, not necessarily to eat or gobble. It is trying to find...other things or viruses of its own kind and grow stronger with them....It's not looking for T-cells, but if they stumble in the way, then they get depleted. The virus is not attacking the T-cells directly. [LH]

> In the tissues the key factors for the virus are to be found not only in the so-called T-cells in the bloodstream, but also in the lymph system, where the virus finds concentration even more than in the blood stream; also in the spleen and in the tissues associated with the various parts of the thymus gland system....Repressions also occur in the pituitary and the thyroid...Once the lymphatics are repressed in these activities, then the virus can penetrate into the neural tissues, eventually bringing about dysfunction in their activities in the same manner....The...thymus is the centralmost coordinator of the stimulation and the harmonizer of all the elements of the immune system itself....Both the coccyx and the medulla oblongata are secondary carriers, and of especial importance as transformers or builders of neurological energy....The medulla oblongata acts as a stimulus and storer of energy for the functions of the thyroid, and specifically for the functions of the parasympathetic ganglion. The coccyx acts as a specific storer of energy for the activities of the adrenals. [KR]

The extreme rapidity of the virus' evolution was not known at the time of this study but emerged from medical studies a few years later.

Diagnosis and Monitoring

The progress of HIV infection is usually measured by the count of T-cells in the blood, but this criterion has not proven to be completely satisfactory for revealing how close is the individual to the onset of AIDS symptoms. The intuitives say that the use of T-cell count is appropriate, but there is no universal threshold; the normal, uninfected value of the count varies considerably from one individual to the next:

> (Is there a better measure of health than T-cell count?) Monitor the viral activity in HIV patients through the pulse. Also, in any model for assessing progress against the virus, you must establish the initial baseline of the T-cells for an individual. Essentially, there will always be a lowering of the T-cells as the disease progresses. [KR]

> Clinical tests do not necessarily indicate whether a program of treatment is being effective. But T-cell count is the most accurate indicator of the state of health of the immune system at the current time [1992]. [LH]

> (When we test somebody for HIV, are we indeed testing the presence of HIV in the body, or whether or not it has taken hold, or a secondary reaction through one of the co-factors?) By and large you are testing whether HIV has taken hold. You are detecting it directly. [RW]

Treatment

The intuitives' suggestion for treatment is not to try to kill the virus by external means. This is not feasible, they say; rather, strengthen the body's immune system so the body can deal with the virus in its own way:

> (What are the best steps that can be taken to protect the individual?) Strengthening the immune system would be of utmost importance, those things which can be given or taken to increase the total body wellness....Mineral and vitamin intake could greatly reduce the possibilities of these [symptoms] coming forward. [LH]

The key element in restimulating balances with the immune system would be to seek to restimulate the functions of the thymus. The thymus is the central stimulus of the immune system....[Reduce] stress on the body, and ingest foods that are balanced in both their heating and cooling properties to the physical body. [KR]

The appropriate approach is closer to Eastern medicine, which is more personalized:

Acupuncture and Western allopathic medicine are two different ways of looking at the body, two different grids placed on the body, and both have their advantages and uses....For early intervention in HIV, Eastern medicine works better. Toward the other end of it, when the HIV is in full bloom, as it were, Western medicine is far more effective than Eastern. For the Eastern is subtle, and there is nothing subtle about the damaging effects of certain diseases.... Both have proven to be effective, and there is no reason to pick up one and discard the other. [RW]

The most superior model is to restore oriental medicine to its original course, so as to evolve the individual spiritually. Utilize a broad range of substances through cuisine, through lifestyle and through a keen awareness of personal and spiritual character. [KR]

Western treatments are limited in their effectiveness against HIV:

The allopathic model does not work particularly well with the healthy HIV patient. AZT is not a good idea for early intervention. Individuals who choose not to get tested in order to avoid the whole problem may oddly enough be making the right decision..... If you give a powerful drug early on, you are strengthening the virus's hand by weakening the body, on the one hand, and making the virus more able to combat that drug, on the other. So as the body weakens, that drug will no longer be effective....As the body changes, different treatments are required. This is something that your Western medicine doesn't seem to understand. If there is a large amount of the HIV [present], and the body were to be given a sufficient amount of AZT, eventually the body will have problems simply because it is dealing with a constant series of poisons. In the long term it would be the drugs that kill the individual, not the HIV. [RW]

However, Western drugs can help later during infection if they are applied properly:

[If you use drugs] first of one kind and then another, then another, and then perhaps back to the first, it is possible to string out the onset of AIDS virtually indefinitely. This is preferred to going on AZT for three years, or ddI for three years, for that doesn't work. [RW]

The proper time periods for using each drug in sequence will also vary with the individual.

Drugs such as AZT, ddI and other similar ones may repress the virus's progress in the blood system and they slow the virus's transmission to other elements of the thymus gland system. However, they do not penetrate much into the lymphatics, where the virus is highly concentrated and continues its aggravation....AZT can be effective in the body, adding as much as 3 to 8 years to the life span, and especially with detoxification through such actions as increasing the body's temperature through

Still fresh in my memory is an afternoon program I attended in early 1993 at Davies Medical Center in San Francisco. Ten so-called "survivors" of HIV infection, all of them still free of AIDS symptoms five to ten years after testing positive for the virus, told their stories. At that time the available drug treatments were largely untested and uncertain, both in their effectiveness and their side-effects. There was little hope that one infected with HIV could escape its ultimate consequences.

With only one questionable exception, all ten had reacted strongly to the first news of their infection. They went through stages of anger, defiance and finally determination not to accept their death sentence. They spoke about how the news had forced them to examine their attitudes about life and how they had sought and found a clearer sense of purpose than they had previously. They chose work more meaningful to them, either with the AIDS community itself or in another area of social service. For some this meant dropping out of lucrative but dull jobs. Others abandoned a careless lifestyle, including alcohol, drugs or other destructive habits. They told how they had learned to manage their leisure time differently, how their friends changed, and how they paid more attention to their physical and mental health.

What I remember best, though, is the positive, joyful energy every one of them displayed, like someone who has a full current of life running through him and radiates it outward toward others. It reminded me of active young children. It was clear that they were all trying to make the best use of their remaining years, still uncertain in number.

sweats or through other debilities that throw off toxic byproducts. [KR]

(Is there another chemical that would be much better than AZT, one that would

> *Surely this is a lesson from which we can all bene- fit. Is it really so important whether you have three or thirty years of life remaining? The choice of what you do today is fundamentally the same: how can you best fulfill yourself, your purpose in this life, in the way you choose to live each day?*

actually destroy the virus?) It will come about, but it is necessary to go through other phases first, for there is a great deal of learning which needs to take place…It is a natural substance from Africa, but native to our country, a root of some kind [shaped] like an icicle, you know. It has already been discovered, but it hasn't been related to this particular use yet. It is known in Chinese Medicine but used only occasionally. [LH]

A cure is available at the present time, even though it has not been utilized. [RW]

Eastern medicine offers the greatest hope in the long-range battle with HIV. It calls for a whole-body, whole-person approach and (again) a customization of the treatment regimen for each individual:

The isolated medical components of acupuncture and oriental herbs [will] come to be known and will correlate with key personality types, as has always been in the models of oriental medicine. Namely, all the forces of nature conspire or breathe together to force the spiritual evolution of the individual.…Observation of the physiologically altered personality, what might be called the psycho-pharmacopoeia of the personality, will in the future continue to validate already intact models of spirituality, and also oriental medicine itself. [KR]

In your acupuncture treatments seek a balance, perhaps once a week with herbs or twice a week with or without herbs. It is best if the patient is calm and relaxed, and could even fall asleep. The use of heat lamps can be effective as well. Moxibustion could prove effective as well, as it is natural, but there are certain points on the lower part of the body, related to the kidney and spleen organs, which are more effective [than others]. Some individuals use electricity, but that sounds better than it is. More natural approaches are preferred. [RW]

Both herbal approaches and acupuncture are needed in the Chinese approach. The key here is to stimulate those states that allow the body's metabolism to be stimulated by the herbs as a whole. Otherwise the herbs should not be given. When there are drugs, they should be given so that they stimulate throughout the whole body. Without the acupuncture they will not penetrate into the lymphatic systems. [KR]

One intuitive offered a detailed, four-stage, combined treatment regimen for combating HIV infection. It should be used only *before* AIDS symptoms set in.

A combination of various herbs would also be a key factor here. Methods using several antiviral substances, combined with key herbal substances, could allow for a three- to four-level assault on the virus in the body physical. This would cause the body to trigger the rapid evolution of the virus in such a way that it forces it through four stages of adaption, so as to trigger a non-immune-repressing form of the virus. Eventually, with the recovery of the T-cells, the virus then could be removed from the system. [KR]

Specifically:

The known antiviral properties of vitamin C, zinc, echinacea, shabourelle, hibiscus, garlic, cayenne, and in non-toxic dosages the so-called controversial Compound Q could be introduced in the following manner. First, non-toxic elements such as high concentrations of Vitamin C would constitute the first phase: 5-10 grams per day for 12-30 days. Second, the sudden introduction of the antiviral properties of zinc and echinacea would trigger the first two phases of mutation. Ten days of zinc and echinacea and 3-8 days of kyolic garlic in high concentrations would trigger the third phase of mutation. Finally, the non-toxic levels of Compound Q, given carefully for between 60 days to 6 months until there is no measurable amount of virus in the system, would trigger...the final phase. It will also bind to the virus, triggering a counter-T-cell stimulation in which the virus is recognized as a foreign substance. In particular, this will also penetrate into the lymphatics. Sweats of 20 minutes twice daily, preferably at ten o'clock in the morning and two o'clock in the afternoon, will raise the body's temperature 2 to 3 degrees, acting as a further catalyst on the assault on the virus, especially during the application of Compound Q. Repeat the whole cycle as necessary over six months, longer if the T-cell concentration drops, and up to 36 months if it drops to below 100....The state of progression will then eventually trigger the retrovirus's evolution to a benign and identifiable state, allowing an increase in the T-cell count. Once the virus is removed, then use the immune enhancer for immune restoration, all in this order. Administer in the cycles mentioned earlier, to match the pattern of viral evolution. The dosage of Compound Q should be non-toxic....A minute introduction of Compound Q can be correlated to the pulse rate and will be non-toxic. When combining the sugar with the so-called sweats, it should be introduced not in its concentrated, medicinally active state, but rather in its herbal state. [KR]

(Use of acupuncture in the four-cycle program of treatment?): All the cycles are present including its progressions through the meridians. Balance the overall body by placement of the needles in the principal elemental points, and by monitoring the pulse. In the first phase you should place emphasis upon the meridian points that are prevalently associated with balancing the so-called qi [chi] energies of the liver and spleen. In the second phase balance the bladder, and in the final phase monitor and balance carefully the activities of the so-called Triple Warmer. [KR]

Once the virus begins to break up by itself, one may look forward to an increase in the T-cell count by as much as 50 %. Even after the virus is out of the system, the immune system will return [slowly] to its original low baseline T-cell level because the body needs to reeducate itself after such a long exposure to immune repression. So use immune boosting herbs, principally Korean Ginseng and also the substance known as Dong Quai. [KR]

The oriental herbs may still have some value after AIDS symptoms have started:

Treat with Chinese herbs. For the acute state of AIDS use the anti-inflammatories to stabilize the condition. Then use combinations of the antivirals, perhaps in the cycles described before, then through the states of progression. Then introduce the sugar imitating substances, and perhaps Compound Q. Use the pulse [to indicate the change] from yin progression towards the yang. At the heightened moment of yang, introduce the final sugarbase-imitating elements in the cycles described before. [KR]

Psychological Aspects

> "People take on bodies partly because they can then confront physi-
> cally what they have not yet confronted on emotional and psychic
> levels. Any denial is ultimately expressed physically. An ill body is
> your faithful friend, not your enemy. Heed its guidance!"
> [Emmanuel]

Traditional medicine typically tolerates but disregards mental exercises such as
meditation and visualization as being helpful for treatment. However, many
HIV-infected persons have testified to the effectiveness of these daily practices
in their battle against the infection. The intuitives concur: such practices are
very beneficial:

> The major process of psychoimmunity in these days is the capacity of the
> mental forces to increase the stimulation, through a process of focused
> visioning, or visualization, to increase the neurological activities in various
> key internal organs....Meditation, centering on the thymus, would serve to
> increase the functions of both the neurological electrical flows reaching the
> thymus and other forces in same. [KR]

> The thought processes are also very important. It would be well to learn to
> do meditation, and [also] visualization of the suppressing of these little
> "fish" to diminish them to the minnow size again, and to "puff up" the T-
> cells so they are a good match for the invader. This is a difficult step to take
> but it can be done, and with the increase of the T-cells they will become
> stronger to protect themselves against the invasion. [LH]

> [Engage in] conscious meditation for 20 or preferably 30 minutes, twice
> daily. These are physiologically enforced states of meditation, not fatigue.
> Enter into such altered states so as to disrupt the factors of life style and
> allow the body to fully enter into a state of consciousness that overrides
> conscious superstitions, over-intellectual and other mental stimuli, and the
> lack of the natural rhythms of nature. [KR]

Research Possibilities

Future HIV/AIDS research would do well to explore the Eastern medical
approach, including the several specific herbal and drug treatments suggested

in the intuitives' accounts quoted above. One intuitive proposed a few additional substances:

> (Any new therapies for AIDS treatment?) More effectively managed models include the substance known as Compound Q, along with some promising research in the so-called sugar- imitating substances taken into the physical body; vegetarian sources of protein, such as that found in the complete protein molecule aramat; high concentrations of zinc, which interferes with a specific zinc ion base in the protein cover of the virus; also oxygenation of the blood system through hydrogen peroxide infusion; and treatment through hydrogen peroxide filters. [KR]

> Also, [conduct] research into the body's own natural immuno-repressants when there are key factors present or at certain times. These latter substances are produced...and can explain some mysteries in childbirth, namely, why some women who have a history of easy birth even though exposed to HIV quite often, experience no transference of HIV through the blood supply to the developing fetal tissues. However, for women having a history of miscarriages, HIV is transferred when they finally conceive. This is because the body is low in these immuno-repressing factors. [KR]

> [Consider also] a substance called alpha-theta-protein, produced both in men and women. The active agents here are in Dong Quai [an herbal medicine], licorice root, fruit such as guava, mango—all of these produce a yin-like state. [They participate in] the development of the fetal tissues through the nutritional and herbal benefits of the host mother in the first three months of fetal development. They are all applicable as a curative model with the condition known as AIDS, and apply to both men and women. Alpha-theta-protein is stimulated within the immune system and the integration system, and is at its highest point within the first trimester. Also, it is contained...in the products of the afterbirth. Societies that dry these and make them into a talisman or powdered medicine will be found to be low in retroviral disease and dysfunction. [KR]

Social Significance of HIV and AIDS

Taking a more perspective view of the entire AIDS phenomenon, we may ask: Is there an important lesson that individuals and society may learn from it?

First, it is necessary to acknowledge the societal factors that contribute to the disease.

The phenomenon known as AIDS is not so much a medical disease but a social disease. A characteristic predisposition of the suppressed immune system...comes from isolating minorities—so-called homosexual—or of the darker skins, or any form that is considered a minority. Whenever the collective rejects an aspect of itself, it eventually threatens the sum total of its whole....All disease spreads when you separate yourself, one from the other, be it the disease called poverty, the disease called war, or the disease called bigotry....What are you learning from this? Hopefully, that none of you is separate from another. [KR]

AIDS is in a sense a balancing agent, created out of society's disregard for what the heart truly feels, and the move toward more of just sensation in the body....The society you live in is quick to find anger, quick to find pain in others as something to shun, quick to find moral judgment over activities not in the keeping of the norm. Bypass that sense of judgment or condemnation, and just see what *is*. [LDM]

The virus stimulates growth so remarkably in those exposed to it that in the community it speeds the evolution of society—for instance, the civil benefits of those in the homosexual community. Without that catalyst the change would not have occurred. [KR]

At the level of the infected individual there are other lessons.

If someone is sick with workaholism, something will take place....It may be an ulcer, a breakdown in the system, the flu bug or something minor, but somehow there will be a point where the body says "Halt! Take a look. See what's being created." That which you call AIDS is a bigger "Halt!" It is a bigger sign upon the path of life, to show what is being created. [LDM]

Those with AIDS need to seek out their reason for being, and know that even though this disease is taking their life, it is not this life that is particularly important, but rather that of the soul, which is on-going. For through this they learn to have more empathy and understanding for those of other generations....Know that this has not been a happenstance but has been planned very well. There is a great deal of love and caring that goes into this particular situation and those who are seeking for cures and help are also those who have promised to give their time. This is not an unplanned event. [LH]

When deep love exists you will not find a need for wide expression of sexual interchange with many, many people. This is not a judgment of those who enjoy finding love with many people in a sexual sense....The inner desire is to feel the unity of existence, so the drive of sexuality is strong. The drive of love is stronger. When rightly understood, the sexual license of the time in which you live will begin to subside and there will be a better balance. [LDM]

Two non-CAI intuitive sources convey a similar message:

Illness exists first in the non-physical realm of spiritual need, emotional confusion or mental aberration. It is never primarily physical. It vibrates to stress and is an outward manifestation of inner turmoil....Illness is a teaching, a message from the soul. When the lessons are learned the illness becomes a thing of no moment. [Emmanuel]

(And what about AIDS?) All illness is created first in the mind....Nothing occurs in your life—nothing—which is not first a thought. Thoughts are like magnets, drawing effects to you. The thought may not always be obvious, thus clearly causative, as in "I'm going to contract a terrible disease." The thought may be, and usually is, far more subtle than that....Worry, hate, fear, together with their offshoots...all attack the body at the cellular level. [Neale Donald Walsch[8]]

And

A cure [for AIDS] is coming swiftly. So the time is short for you to learn the manifested teaching that AIDS offers. The moment there is a cure for AIDS, if fear has not been reckoned with, you open the way for another fearful something. [Emmanuel]

It must not be forgotten that there is more to the handling of AIDS than drugs and related treatment regimens. Already it has been discovered that the use of anti-HIV drugs to repress the virus tends to increase risky sexual behavior. Also, methamphetamines tend to make users (mainly in the gay community) very sexual. AIDS has become less of a public issue than when it first appeared. The general opinion is that it's "not as bad as it was," when in fact it is still very bad. These factors have actually increased the rate of new HIV cases in San Francisco over the last few years, for nearly one-third of the city's gay males are now HIV-positive. On the other hand, the needle exchange program worked well, for the infection rate decreased by 50% among intravenous drug users. There is no cure or vaccine on the horizon, and no reliable way to manage the infection, once contracted.[9]

What is it that makes AIDS such a great tragedy? The reason certainly does not lie not in the death itself, since we all experience death eventually. It does not even lie in the suffering associated with dying, which is already common and accepted among the elderly. It lies in the assumed *prematurity* of the death and its seeming unfairness: "Why now?" "Why me?" and "This is not supposed to happen to a healthy person." Because most of us do not understand the purpose of human life and the place of death in life, we cannot easily accept death before old age (if then), in a world we want to believe is compassionate and fair. Herein lies an important message from AIDS, SIDS and other kinds of premature death: to help us understand what the life experience is for, how each of us as an individual fits into it and what it means to enter it and take leave of it. When this is understood there is nothing unfair about death—at any age.

> "In our way, we conform as best we can to the rest of nature. The obituary pages tell us of the news that we are dying away, while the birth announcements in finer print, off at the side of the page, inform us of our replacements, but we get no grasp of the enormity of scale....The vast mortality, involving something over 50 million of us each year, takes place in relative secrecy....We speak of our own dead in low voices; struck down, we say, as though visible death can only occur for cause, by disease or violence, avoidably. We send off for flowers, grieve, make ceremonies, scatter bones, unaware of the rest of the 3 [sic] billion on the same schedule....It is hard to see how we can continue to keep the secret, with such multitudes doing the dying. We will have to give up the notion that death is catastrophe, or detestable, or avoidable, or even strange." [Lewis Thomas[10]]

The AIDS epidemic is reminding us that life is inherently worthy and potentially joyful. It is really impossible to accept it in any other way. The AIDS experience can only be serving a higher purpose, of which we humans have been largely and stubbornly choosing to remain unaware. To deprive another person of the opportunity to live freely and make his own choices is certainly wrong by any set of values. Beyond this, death itself cannot be a tragedy unless we make it so. The issue is not whether we will die, or even how or where or when, but rather the quality of the life we choose to lead in the (unknown) time left to us—whether we fully comprehend our purpose or not.

When this simple fact can be appreciated, death need no longer be feared, but can be welcomed in its own time. The presumed tragedy becomes a gift.

Evaluation of the Study

The three research sessions conducted on HIV and AIDS generated much interesting information and many suggestions for further work. However, consistent with the original intention, the study was too incomplete and fragmentary for us to pull it together into a descriptive model of how HIV is working, or even a single strong hypothesis that could be tested. Like several of the previous inquiries, we would need more sessions to fill out a complete description of how HIV infection takes root and spreads through the body, the role of the mind in HIV infection and how the infection process might be retarded or stopped through treatment, so that AIDS might be brought under control.

If our intention had been to usefully apply new intuitive information to supplement on-going research we should have conducted this inquiry a decade earlier, when AIDS was still a mystery and there was an eager openness to new approaches. We arrived late on the scene. By the early 1990s a committed international research direction had already been set in place, and it was not likely to be diverted into a different direction on the basis of even the best intuitive information.

Nevertheless, some of the intuitives' suggestions could be applied today without further inquiry. The main one is the use of Eastern medicine for the treatment of HIV infection (rather than AIDS itself). This ancient approach, already well developed long before HIV emerged, is being increasingly applied to HIV patients in the U.S. today, albeit not as the common or official method of treatment. The intuitives suggested a number of specific Chinese herbs that could be utilized. To be most effective, however, Eastern medicine demands an quite different view of the human body than the one accepted in the West, and it requires exceptionally subtle individual diagnoses. Both of these differences are unfamiliar and alien to Western allopathic medicine. The Eastern approach is being studied more carefully in the U.S. these days, though it seems unlikely that it will be accepted and widely applied in the West even over the next few decades.

While we made no systematic attempt in this study to verify the intuitive information against well established medical knowledge, I am not presently aware of any part of it that is known to be in error. As noted, a few points were corroborated by medical research reported since the study was carried out (early 1993). There was no obvious blocking of information. The consensus was good as far as it went, though there remain many pieces of information from only one intuitive and not checked with the others.

> "Death is not a failure....You have not failed when you become ill.
> When the body takes upon itself an affliction such as AIDS, the
> human personality becomes an enemy far more destructive than
> any virus...[because] you close your hearts and take terror by the
> hand....All those emotions, even without the virus, will render you
> helpless." [Emmanuel]

• Endnotes—Chapter 12

1* AIDS: Acquired Immune Deficiency Syndrome; HIV: Human Immunodeficiency Virus.

2* For a general background on the AIDS crisis and the medical understanding of the disease (as of 1999), see for example: "How HIV Causes AIDS," Office of Communications, NIAID (National Institute of Allergy and Infectious Diseases), National Institutes of Health, Bethesda, MD (June 1998).

3 Source: U.S. Center for Disease Control.

4* Studies of stored blood revealed that the virus first entered the U.S. in the late 1970s.

5 Eastman, 2001, pp. 44ff.

6 Hopkins, 1998.

7* Grateful thanks are due for the participation of Prof. George Araki, then Director, Holistic Healing Institute, San Francisco State University, and Michael Young, then Director of the San Francisco AIDS Enhancement Project and now at the Circle Health Center, Boulder, CO.

8 Walsch, 1996, pp. 187-88.

9 Eastman, 2001.

10 Thomas, 1978, pp. 98-99.

CHAPTER 13

FURTHER APPLICATIONS
INTUITIVE CONSENSUS AT WORK

"Scientific inquiry consists of three parts: first, the finding of a problem, then an inquiry into the problem, and finally, if the search is successful, the solving of the problem....All three parts of a scientific inquiry are set in motion by two mental powers. They receive their guidance from integrative powers, while they are propelled, and also supplied with suitable material, by thrusts of the imagination. The integrative powers are largely spontaneous; to mark this, we may give them the name of "intuition." [Michael Polanyi]

This chapter presents the results of applying Intuitive Consensus to three additional topics:

*   the decontamination of nuclear waste material
*   lunar effects upon water
*   elementary-school education in the United States.

These experiments illustrate further the range of information one may seek through topical intuitive studies, beyond those several already described. They also raise a few additional issues that may be encountered in the future when intuitive inquiries are carried out and applied. Finally, we mention some other topics using Intuitive Consensus that were explored only briefly.

Decontamination of Nuclear Waste

"Nuclear technology is inherently unsafe. Mankind must sooner or later recognize this fact and find a substitute source of energy."
[Kevin Ryerson]

In the mid-1980s CAI began an Intuitive Consensus inquiry to discover a feasible means for removing dangerous radioactivity from nuclear waste material. We reasoned that such a technological process would be a great boon, since radioactive wastes were (and still are) accumulating rapidly from nuclear manufacturing and research, spent nuclear reactor fuel and decommissioned nuclear bombs. According to physical science it is absolutely impossible to remove radioactivity from substances by chemical or any other means. Radioactivity decays naturally so one may simply wait for it to diminish, but this may take hundreds of years or longer. It is still difficult and expensive to store radioactive material without risking leaks into the environment.

We were encouraged in this exploration because the expert intuitives consulted indicated initially that a nuclear detoxification technology could indeed be developed. The first descriptions were interesting, but somewhat vague. They explained that the process involves first compacting the radioactive material, then inserting it in ionized or "charged" salt water in an electromagnetic field, and finally supercooling the mixture to near absolute zero (–273 degrees Centigrade) and passing through it certain high-intensity, high-frequency electric currents. For example:

The radioactive material should be put in a tank of ionized salt water....An electromagnetic process is needed to charge the water ahead of time, so that its molecules become more unstable....It would be a somewhat altered current, a "magnified" direct current....The residue which settles out will be the most radioactive....There is a project team, perhaps in Kentucky or Tennessee, which is working on this. [RW]

The nuclear waste should be compacted, then the temperature lowered as close as possible to absolute zero. Then apply a high voltage, specifically an alternating current, through the waste material....This will reduce the radioactive half-life...by stabilizing the basic atomic structure, so to say....It involves the fine line between electromagnetics and radiations....It sounds alchemical, but it does work. [KR]

However, further details about the process were not forthcoming. The flow of information slowed down and stopped.

Under further questioning two of the intuitives explained that the detailed knowledge needed to develop the decontamination technology presented a potential danger because it could lead to new weapons. We could obtain additional information but the crucial portion needed to achieve our stated purpose was simply not available. They explained further that if this technology became available too soon, it would encourage the proliferation of nuclear devices, both power plants and weapons, just when international efforts to limit and control their spread were becoming effective. They stressed that there is still a danger of nuclear weapons spreading to certain belligerent countries, and this was no time to remove the pressure imposed by the lack of a means for getting rid of nuclear material.

Here's how they described the situation:

> Neutralizing the entire waste will have to wait until a ray sort of device is discovered. Such a process will require certain changes in the concept of what radioactivity is, and how atoms and molecules move in order to engender radioactivity....This "new physics" has other ramifications—faster-than-light speed, for example....At the present time, a force that would stabilize atomic material would give whoever discovered it an awesome power. Such a ray or force could indeed trigger a holocaust on your planet, because it would be far more dangerous than being merely able to neutralize some nuclear waste....Your race is not yet ready to learn how to neutralize atomic power at this juncture. [RW]

> If the process were developed—which indeed it can—it would create a political consensus that there is no longer any danger from nuclear waste....There would be a great gung ho on building nuclear reactors, thus increasing the odds of a nuclear hazard....Whereas if the information is not developed, you're stuck with growing nuclear wastes with no way to rid yourselves of them. [KR]

This was not the first time we had experienced a slow-down in the flow of intuitive information, but this time it was a firm blockage.

Other reasons for not pursuing the intended development were also cited:

(Is this a practical process for large quantities of waste material?) Not in the immediate future. It needs to be considered, but it will take a great deal of time and money. [LH]

The supercooling process discussed earlier involves certain dangers, because it requires tremendous amounts of energy, and it may not be cost-effective....There are, of course, other processes, indeed two of them, but they also have limitations. [RW]

The balance that is needed to create it [the decontamination process] will require two groups, one working on the new scientific techniques, and the other looking at the social effects of radioactivity....The two groups must find some way to collaborate with each other....This sociological research has not been carried out, and is needed for balance. This is what will permit the experiments to be successful. [JF]

The intuitives indicated that nuclear technology is inherently unsafe, even apart from its use in weapons. (Recall the accident at Chernobyl in 1986. One intuitive [JF] indicated that eventually 50,000 people would die prematurely from radiation poisoning as a direct consequence of this catastrophe—a much greater number than that projected by Western scientists.) Mankind must eventually accept this fact and find a substitute, safer source of energy. They say that when the nuclear danger has passed, and only then, a process for nuclear decontamination can be safely discovered and developed. It will prove useful for cleansing the earth of residual, man-made radioactive material.

The intuitives' statements about the detoxification process do indeed sound like alchemy, for if true they contradict current scientific understanding about matter and energy. According to present-day physics, nuclear reactions are essential if radioactivity is to be changed, and these are possible only at high temperatures and high energies.

This observation raised a new issue for the intuitive inquiry process, which had not yet experienced such a firm contradiction with well established knowledge. Prior inquiries had revealed contradictions only at the uncertain edges of domains explored by science. An addition, this was the first time that requested information was explicitly refused.

Several years after this intuitive inquiry two U.S. physicists announced a surprising finding in what they called "cold fusion."[1] They claimed to have demonstrated experimentally that a low-temperature, low-energy nuclear reaction had been achieved. The claim was clearly heretical, and most of the scientific establishment disbelieved it. Public research funding provided support for further experiments to confirm or disprove the initial discoveries. While some of these efforts led to negative or at least ambiguous results in the U.S. and abroad, others were positive. Apparently not all the conditions necessary for duplicating the experiments successfully are yet known. Research has continued, most of it outside the framework of public funding.[2*3 4]

The recent findings lend some support to the intuitives' claim that a practical nuclear decontamination technology is possible and will someday be found.

Lunar Effects upon Water

"It has been suggested by some scientists that the primeval tidal
rhythms that nurtured our genetic ancestors in some distant epoch
have left, even now, a faint imprint on our body's biorhythms."
[Coleman Barks[5]]

According to traditional astrology the moon is associated with various human characteristics. In particular, it is supposed to exert an influence upon fluids in the human body, as well as in animals, plants and trees.[6] This connection may have arisen merely because tides are themselves fluid, but it is now well accepted in astrological lore apart from any liquid effects. Could there be some truth to this old notion?

Physics, chemistry and physiology do not acknowledge any such influence, but they do not say it does not exist. The only lunar effects upon fluids that science recognizes are the tides, and these are very well understood.[7] From a scientific standpoint it is difficult to imagine how the moon could influence humans in any other way. Variations in the reflected light, heat and gravitational force of the moon, as detectable on the surface of the earth, are minuscule in comparison with similar influences from other sources having much greater energies and larger fluctuations.

Many life processes are known to be associated with the daily cycle of day and night, the seasons and the earth's annual cycle. The sun exhibits very irregular variations (and one regular 11-year cycle) in its radiation, and the resulting solar wind affects the earth's magnetosphere and its shielding properties against cosmic rays.[8] This wind is intersected by the moon in its monthly revolution around the earth. However, by the time these fluctuations reach the surface of the earth they are much too weak to have any measurable effect inside the human body—again, as far as is known on physical grounds.

On the other hand, a number of animals (such as oysters and rats) behave in synchronism with the lunar synodic cycle of 29.5 days, even when separated from their natural habitat and shielded from moonlight and direct tidal effects.[9] It is not known how they do this. There are many reports from farmers who claim that the moon influences the rate of growth of their crops;[10] from police records that crimes are more frequent at the time of the full moon; from sociologists that women in some societies menstruate in synchronism with the moon;[11] and from hospitals that deaths, mental breakdowns and other crises are more common with the full moon.[12] In all categories except the last two, careful studies have shown little or no significant effects, but menstruation and some mental disorders are definitely correlated with lunar phase.[13] Some kind of man-moon association has to be broadly acknowledged. Still, specific effects have yet to be pinned down, and no credible mechanisms have been put forward to explain *how* these lunar effects might be arising.

An intuitive inquiry was undertaken to try to determine if this old notion has any truth in it, and if so to try to understand how the process works and what are its specific effects. We recognized that the alleged influence might be physical—that is, it may fall within the scope of presently understood physics and chemistry in a way not yet recognized—or it might involve new energies or effects not yet known to science.

The intuitive team was unanimous in affirming that there is a change in the properties of water under the influence of the moon, even apart from the human body:

> The moon influences the physical-chemical properties of water such that there is a hydration effect. That is, the water tends not to diffuse or leak out of systems during the phase from new to full. From full to new the water

becomes more volatile and diffuses out of systems, and…the dipole effects weaken. [MA]

Water polarizes under the influence of the moon. It is something like a crystalline process.…The moon neither breaks down nor strengthens the crystalline structure…but [it] discharges or neutralizes the water. The neutralization has something to do with its ions. It is a balancing process.…The effect is highest at the new moon, and is scattered on the full moon. [BR]

The moon's influences upon water to assimilate certain chemical substances, by increasing and decreasing its conductivity—this becomes the explanation of its influences on the mood structure of life forms.…It balances the activities of the sun.…[To detect this change] measure the electrical conductivity directly. [KR]

The moon acts upon electrolytes in the water. [LH].

When the moon is full the water becomes polarized. Many of the ions within the water itself have a higher energy. This energy is of low frequency—20 to 50 cycles [??]—and can be picked up if the receivers are very sensitive. Look not so much for the change per se as the cumulative effects of the change. [AA]

My interest in the mysterious properties of water led me to visit a water chemist, a scientist about whom I had heard some rather strange stories. His particular job was to create (for an environmental agency) a bottle of the purest water possible, using a variety of electrical and chemical processes to remove the last few molecules of impurities. He was slow to talk about his private experiments with water but finally told me one of them.

He reported that he once aimed intense sound waves at a tall, open-topped, thick glass jar containing some of his super-pure water. As he adjusted the frequency and intensity of the sound, the water suddenly exploded with such a tremendous blast that it blew a hole through the roof. Fortunately for him (or he would not be telling his story) the heavy jar did not break. But the experience so frightened him that he stopped experimenting with the unknown effects of sound upon water.

I was much intrigued by this result, and might have repeated the experiment (safely) if I hadn't been so busy with other tasks. There is nothing at all in physical science or chemistry to explain such an effect.

One intuitive explained that the effect occurs through a transmutation of solar energy at specific frequencies:

> The key frequency is the most prominent one in the solar spectrum, the hydrogen peak at 1200 Ångstrom. Increases in energy at this wavelength cause corresponding reactions in terrestrial hydrogen, which influences the ionic state of organic compounds. Changes in the "reactivity" of hydrogen in both water and organic chemicals influence their behavior, and are responsible for the biological variations which have been noted. [MA]

The process is still not completely clear because the concepts of "polarization," "hydration" and "neutralization," while traditionally well understood, are not usually applied to water alone. They may have a special meaning in this case.

The intuitives all agreed, there is a measurable effect of "lunar-activated" water on living systems, ranging from cells, plants and animals to the human body and mind:

> Seeds germinated in the waxing phase of the lunar month weigh more than those during the waning phase. [MA]

> The sea horse is especially sensitive to charged water, as the moon comes into the water. [AA]

> Measure the rate of growth and the mobility of a colony of paramecia while monitoring the gravitational field with a sensitive gravimeter. [KR]

> Plants are able to draw up more fluid from the source, from the earth. [SF]

> When there is the right amount of liquid in the [human] body, the moon has no effect,...but if the body is off balance the moon causes nervousness, aggressiveness or sluggishness. [LH]

The intuitives also explained (in another study) that the moon influences the female fertility cycle, which is often shifted from its natural rhythm by a civilized life-style.[14*] They said too that the moon affects infants through its position in the sky at both conception and birth, but traditional astrological ideas about this effect are greatly in error.

Clearly, these intuitive explanations go beyond present scientific understanding. A comparison with scientific knowledge could be undertaken on this matter, but an understanding beyond that reported above was not attempted. A few of the statements made by the intuitives seem questionable or incomplete, such as the 50Hz polarization frequency of water and why the 1200-Ångstrom solar radiation should have anything to do with the moon. On the whole, though, the intuitives' explanation is consistent and plausible if taken on its own merits. While physical science has not found any evidence of a lunar effect on water, other than tides, it has not demonstrated that none exists.

These alleged chemical, physical, biological and psychological effects of the moon suggest several interesting experiments one could carry out to try to detect particular forms of lunar influence upon the fluids of the earth. For example, it would not be difficult to measure the electrical conductivity, ionization level and reactivity of samples of water over the course of a few lunar months, and see if they vary as predicted; and similarly for the behavior of paramecia and sea horses, and the strength of 1200Å radiation. Alternatively, one could make careful measurements of a direct physical or psychological influence on humans instead of upon water.

When a qualified and interested researcher is ready to carry out these experiments, he would do well to work with one or more expert intuitives to obtain additional information, better hypotheses and especially a clearer understanding of the physico-chemical process involved in the lunar influence, not merely the effects explored in this study.

Elementary-School Education

> "The activities that are most characteristic of real-life learning are among the least represented in the majority of school programs. As often as not, the child's own personal reality has to remain outside the classroom until the final school bell." [Thomas Armstrong[15]]

The typical image of a school classroom is all too familiar: a crowd of bored children at their desks, lined up in front of a teacher who is reciting facts and figures at the blackboard. A recent study of 1000 U.S. schools, based on 27,000 interviews with students, teachers and parents, painted a depressing picture of present-day education: "A sterile wasteland, with little room for joy, humor, sharing of ideas or innovative activities," and so on.[16]

Yet there exist dozens of innovative schools in the U.S. in which just the opposite conditions prevail.[17] In these schools the children are given the opportunity to explore, create and discover the boundless resources of their own minds. Learning for them becomes a nourishing and fulfilling activity that richly affects their entire lives. They love school. These are outstanding and exemplary results, now well tested and reported, but for some reason the educational system as a whole has not picked them up. One can only ask: Why not?

In 1984 CAI began an inquiry into the causes and possible remedy of this crisis in education, focusing primarily on elementary-school education in the United States. We worked with a team of educators to create a list of basic questions, and inquiry sessions were conducted with seven intuitives—four in 1984-85 and three more in 1989. The findings were compiled and integrated. The questioning focused on underlying causes and the direction in which practical solutions might be found, rather than on particular theories, methodologies and specific techniques—though a few examples of these specifics arose unsolicited. Our inquiry included psycho-spiritual perspectives when these seemed relevant or arose on their own.[18*]

The educational perspective given by the intuitive team agrees well with what is today called holistic or integrative education. Several published books and many magazine articles describe this perspective well,[19] and I will not attempt to re-explain it here. The accompanying box summarizes its main principles, as presented by the intuitive team.

To readers already involved in educational reform these findings will surely come as no surprise. However, most U.S. educators do not agree with an holistic approach to education. It is not that they are united *en masse* in favor of a common alternative. Rather, they are divided on both the reasons for the obvious educational problem and how best to solve it. Their lack of consensus reveals itself in the many differing positions and policies espoused by educational colleges, professional associations and local and governmental bodies. They are split along lines ranging from conservative to liberal, religious to secular, parent-driven to teacher-driven, local to centralized management and others. The dissentions appear to run deep. There is presently very little of a common cultural, moral or even spiritual basis on which to build a unified policy or plan of action for U.S. education. It is little wonder, then, that no nationwide agreement or policy exists on how to deal with the long-standing, continuing and gradually worsening educational situation, in spite of the efforts of many well intended and hard-working individuals who are trying to contribute to its solution. All that has resulted is a very conservative approach that satisfies no one and is barely effectual.

The hope for the future lies in the exceptional schools mentioned above. According to the intuitives a public outcry will emerge early in the 21st century as a result of (1) the continually deteriorating present-day system, (2) increasing pressure to educate new kinds of children beginning to appear in the classrooms, (3) the gradual acceptance of alternative methods in public classrooms, and (4) the deeper, more "spiritual" outlook on life in general, now slowly arising in U.S. society. These four factors together will fuel a renaissance in U.S. public education, but not without widespread confusion and dissention until the change actually takes place.

These exceptional schools have already validated convincingly most of the information obtained in this intuitive consensus study. They have shown that the holistic approach really works with children. These exceptions, functioning under the general heading "alternative education," are keeping alive the necessary ingredients of future change, slowly refining them until the time when they can be picked up for use by the public school system.

One could undertake to corroborate the remaining findings of this study through additional experiments, but the question remains of who is listening for such verified results. We have already seen that ample evidence already exists in support of a holistic approach to education but it is not being heeded. For example, an experiment could be conducted to verify the recommendation that during the first seven years of a child's life the curriculum (and home training) should be limited to aesthetic, artistic and intuitive development, to the exclusion of intellectual development. Alternative schools have already taken a step in this direction. While they have not gone so far, their reported findings have not been appreciated. Perhaps some new and stronger kind of documentation would be more effective. Indeed, some of the reports on alternative education practices would be more acceptable if a simple, conclusive means could be found for measuring the effectiveness of changes in educational methods. (Written examinations definitely do *not* work.)

An Intuitive Look at U.S. Education

The major points made by the intuitive team may be summarized as follows:

- The U.S. must recognize education as its Number One priority, popularly and administratively. The changes required in the educational system are deep and transformative, not just a patching of the ailing, existing system.

- The world is changing rapidly. New kinds of children are showing up in classrooms. The abilities and skills they will need for the future are different from the familiar ones of the past.

- The potential of the human mind is much greater than is currently acknowledged. Children are beginning to show us what they are capable of when not limited by adult expectations and structures.

- For the first seven years of a child's life, cognitive and intellectual skill development, including the three R's, should take second place to aesthetic, artistic and intuitive development.

- Each child's uniqueness should be recognized and respected in the classroom, by allowing for his own mode and rate of learning, his particular gifts, his immediate interests and the emotional framework within which he learns. The classroom is not the place for mass conformance and competition.

- The traditional model of a classroom as the place where the teacher is the authoritative source of knowledge, and is responsible for transferring this knowledge into the mind of the child, is not valid. The classroom should be a place of creativity, self-discovery, freedom of inquiry and independent choice. There must be open social interchange; the child, not the teacher, should be the central focus.

- Teaching and learning are not opposites but are interdependent. Children can often teach other effectively and their own learning is aided thereby; teachers who are not also learning are a liability.

- *Inner knowing, or intuition, must be at center stage*, pervading all other modes of learning. The development of intuition and related inner-mind skills will eventually be an accepted classroom approach.

- The inner world of the child, and all it implies, must be acknowledged, respected and nurtured. Future teachers will need to enter this inner world of their children. They must develop the sensitivities, attitudes and skills for "learning from within." The days of teaching subject matter only, and judging the success of education in these terms, are passing.

- Computers and related communication technology is having a profound effect upon classroom procedures, by transferring much of the learning from the teacher into the child's hands. It will allow future teachers to focus supporting the children's individual explorations.

- Subliminal and high-speed learning will find its place for factual and linear material, acquisition of foreign languages and a few other specific learning areas.

- Care of the physical body, particularly through proper nutrition, will soon be shown to affect learning significantly, and schools will then introduce appropriate changes. Non-competitive games and practices like yoga are preferred to competitive sports.

- Future schools will find significant help from older professionals in the community who volunteer their time and experience.

- Parents need to become more directly involved with their children's learning and with the learning process itself, instead of merely sending them off each day to be baby-sat. Open discussion of family issues, even painful ones, needs to take place in the classroom.

- Private schools will continue to be the testing ground for new approaches, which will then find their way into the more cumbersome public system. These schools will be on the rise for many years yet.

- In the face of diminishing public support through tax money, public schools will be maintained in the future with partial financial support from businesses. The commercial interest will force a temporary shift in emphasis from true education toward the practical training that businesses feel they need.

I spoke with several traditional educators about the notions set forth here. Most considered them somewhat idealistic and impractical; that is, they could not imagine their own school system adopting them. Those who agreed with them acknowledged that they were not willing to "buck the system" to put them into practice in their own domains (despite the obvious fact that some of their professional colleagues had already done so successfully). This latter position, if broadly true, suggests that the individuals to whom we are entrusting our children are lacking in either the imagination or the courage to follow their convictions. Apparently the nucleus of active reformers will need to grow to a critical mass before the educational system begins to transform itself. The intuitives confirmed that when the change starts, it will take place quickly.

This study functioned satisfactorily in that it was well motivated, our initial expectations were realistic, the consensus was excellent and the flow of information was fluid and clear. The findings are reasonable and correct as far as can be determined. They agree well with an independently proven educational approach (holistic education), albeit a minority force for change at present, and they go beyond it on a few points. They contradict traditional education more at the level of principles, priorities and practices than on basic goals, ethics or values.

Very little of the intuitive information provided in this study was totally new, even at the time when it was obtained (1984-89). Its value could be said to lay more in support of its liberal position on contemporary issues and priorities in education. Summaries were presented at education conferences. Many alternative educators already understood the nature and value of intuition in education, and they recognized in our findings a valuable clarity and a sign of coming changes. They may find some encouragement thereby as they prepare for the difficult times ahead predicted for U.S. education. However, since these findings are based upon intuitive sources, already suspect in traditional educational circles, they are not likely to persuade most educators to change their perspective. Largely for this reason, no final report of this study was published.

Other Consensus Studies

Six other intuitive consensus studies conducted by CAI have been excluded from this book for various reasons: they were small and very incomplete; they provided very little new information; or they were undertaken without adequate preparation and produced information too incomplete to be useful.

- Astrology: A Critique of Traditional Astrology, and Changes Needed to Make It Correct
- Levitation: Physical Changes in Objects Undergoing Mental Levitation

- Solar Activity: The Effects of Sun Spots and Solar Radiation on Human Beings
- Pyramids: Construction Methods Employed for the Largest Eqyptian Pyramids
- Architecture: The Psychological Effects of Various Room and Building Shapes
- Crystals: The Validity and Effects of Crystal "Energy" on the Human Mind and Body

Most of these opened up areas much too large to explore within the effort available at the time, so we terminated them when this was discovered. In two we were so ill prepared that we would not have been able to understand the answers even if they had been given in considerable detail. Most arose mainly from curiosity.

Three additional studies were completed, and reports were submitted to their sponsors or published as books:

- Peace Options in the Middle East.[20]
- The Future of Japan.[21]
- The Future of the United States.[22]

These two "Future" studies contained exciting revelations when they first appeared, but after the predicted events occurred were of little interest and value. Actually, they were offered not so much as mere prediction but as *prophecy*—that is, as timely educational efforts to improve understanding of the principles underlying social change, by pointing out how social consequences follow from certain collective choices. Most were not offered as predictive phenomena to be proved or disproved; while largely correct as predictions, their correctness was not the point.[23*] Still, these prophecies could not avoid being regarded solely in terms of the predictions contained within them, and as such, they were not easily distinguishable from the numerous predictions by forecasters, futurists, amateur psychics, astrologers and latter-day religious prophets, so they seemed weak. They were unimpressive when examined ten years later, since the predicted events had already occurred and seemed obvious by that time.

This experience indicated the futility of conducting additional "Future" studies for public purposes, whether as predictions or as prophecies.

CAI also completed another large study:

- Fertility, Pregnancy and Childbirth.[24]*

Its findings covered many topics in gynecology and reproduction physiology for which medical science has not yet found explanations, as well as counsel to mothers on many common issues for which typical medical advice is incomplete or inconsistent. It also included, descriptions of what it feels like to come into life and adapt to the physical world, from the perspective of an infant being born. Some of the results of this investigation contradict established medical understanding and are therefore controversial. The completion and publication of this study appeared to be inappropriate at the time, and still seem somewhat premature.

Conclusions

The three experiments presented in this chapter were all partially successful, though for differing reasons they were not useful in their intended applications. They brought to attention four new issues.

First, the nuclear decontamination study experienced a blockage on the information desired, with the explanation that its application would have serious and harmful consequences if pursued. We had not encountered such a total blockage before. Second, this same study generated information that directly contradicts current physical theory—the well-accepted "fact" that elemental transmutation requires high temperatures and very high energies. Prior confrontations with science had only supplemented, not contradicted firmly established basic knowledge. Third, the inquiry on the effects of the moon upon fluids lent partial support to a claim from astrology, a controversial area that lacks support from better established domains of knowledge. Other systems of traditional wisdom may also contain truths that could be profitably explored through intuitive inquiry. Fourth, we learned—or were at least reminded, for perhaps we already knew—that certain topics of intuitive inquiry are limited less by a lack of information than by a lack of public agreement on how to apply information already available.

The next two chapters draw conclusions and speculate on implications of all thirteen of the experiments on the practical application of intuition presented in Parts II and III.

> *"The essence of action based on linear thinking is that it tends to force into comfortably straight lines something that by nature may want to run a less rationally predictable course. The irony is that when a larger picture of reality is taken into account, a visionary approach which allows for the *associative nature of things*—the tendency of events to associate with one another in unpredictable ways—may yield a more direct, effective means of accomplishing the most important goals....Linear reality is a subcategory of associative reality." [Christopher Childs[25]]

• Endnotes—Chapter 13

[1] Fleischmann et al., 1989.

[2]* In 1999 the U.S. Department of Energy funded the University of Illinois to set up a research facility for the study of low-energy nuclear reactions. Japanese work received a large increase in funding in 1995.

[3] See, for example, two review articles: Bockris et al, 1996, Storms, 1996.

[4] Shoulders, 1996. Shoulders most recent work shows that micro-energetic particles generated by field emission are capable of triggering nuclear transmutations, and are very likely responsible for the positive results in at least some of the cold-fusion experiments [personal communication].

[5] Barks & Green, 1997, p. 41.

[6] For a survey see Dean, 1977, pp. 60-66.

[7] Darwin, 1962.

[8] Smith & Sonett, 1976, pp. 154-171, Dean, 1977, pp. 494-496.

[9] Brown, 1954, Brown, 1959.

[10] See, for example, Kolisko, 1936, Burr, 1972, Zurcher, 1968.

[11] Law, 1980, Cutler, 1994.

[12] Thakur & Sharma, 1984, Raison et al., 1999, Hicks-Caskey & Potter, 1991, Radin & Rebman, 1994, Lieber, 1977, Lieber & Sherin, 1972, Lieber, 1978, Tasso & Miller, 1976, Campbell & Beets, 1978, Cooke & Coles, 1978.

[13] Radin, 1997, pp. 178-79.

[14]* See the last bulleted entry at the end of this chapter.

[15] Armstrong, 1988.

[16] Goodlad, 1984.

[17] See, for example, Leviton, 1995, and ref. 20 below.

[18*] This work stimulated CAI and the study team, with the support of several holistic educators, to organize a national conference on "The Role of Intuition in Education." It took place in San Francisco on August 15-18, 1991.

[19] See, for example, Anon3, 1991, Miller, 1999, Armstrong, 1988.

[20] Kautz, 1988.

[21] Kautz, 1984.

[22] Kautz & Branon, 1989.

[23*] In a later book I will have much more to say about prediction and prophecy, especially how intuitive predictions are enabled and are limited within the context of their application.

[24*] This extensive intuitive study dealt with approximately fifty key issues surrounding human conception, pregnancy and childbirth. The majority of the intuitive findings agreed well with modern-day alternative birthing theories and practices, but there were significant additions where medical knowledge has left gaps, and several serious contradictions with medical understanding. The intuitives made a number of novel suggestions about how better to accommodate to the child's needs during pregnancy, before birth and just after birth, and also described various non-physical aspects of the birth process.

[25] Christopher Childs, in "Deep Seeing: Guiding Activism Through Grace" in Noetic Sciences Review, No. 44, pp. 18ff (1997).

PART IV

INTEGRATION

CHAPTER 14

APPLIED INTUITION IN PERSPECTIVE
CONCLUSIONS FROM THE EXPERIMENTS

"The Western mind is so dominated by the rational, intellectual, scientific approach to life that it often fails to come to terms with the intuitive 'events' that just happen, quite irrationally, as a result of the spontaneous exposure of some facet of the unconscious mind....The Western mind tends to shut out intuitive prompts because it falls under the domination of that tyrant, the intellect: it becomes stagnant and inwardly insensitive. In the extreme, some persons become neurotic as a result of a personal incapacity to cope with intuitive, irrational events arising from the unconscious."
[Richard Wilhelm[1]]

This chapter reviews the collection of experimental data and draw some conclusions from them. It also attempts to generalize the findings to a broader class of topics, requirements and conditions than those actually encountered in the experiments.

We have seen in Parts II and III that *almost* any skilled intuitive may access intuitive information, on demand, on *almost* any topic, to *almost* any desired depth of detail, with *almost* unlimited accuracy, for *almost* any positive purpose. These "almosts" may turn out on further study to be unnecessary qualifications, but they must be retained for the time being until they can be established more firmly.

We examine first the experimental results and identify the key factors governing effective applications of intuition. We start with comparisons among the procedures and outcomes of the experiments and reviewing the difficulties and limitations encountered. Six important factors emerge from this analysis. This then leads to a refinement of the four conditions roughed out in Chapter 1, those that an inquiry must satisfy if it is to be successful. Finally, a few important residual issues not covered in this book merit brief attention.

Comparisons and Difficulties

In view of the varying outcomes of the experiments it will be helpful first to compare how the findings were affected by differences in subject matter, type of application, the approach taken, opportunities for corroboration, involvement of other persons and other varying factors. All have already been noted in passing, and we summarize them now:

- *Inquiries undertaken for direct personal or public benefit were more satisfactory* than those conducted to access information having only abstract, potential or long-range value. The former flowed more easily, were more tolerant to poor questioning and were usually clearer and to the point. Inquiries conducted to support individual growth were the most satisfactory of all. This observation appears to be saying that the best results occur when the step from motivation to application is humanitarian and direct.

- *Inquiries for which we had arranged the application of the results beforehand worked better* than those conducted without specific plans for applying the new knowledge.

- *Inquiries for which the consequences of applying the new information were studied in advance were usually more satisfactory.* (Sometimes the consequences could not be anticipated well at all.)

- *Inquiries that arose out of and assumed a firm base of well-established knowledge were more effective* than those that rested upon speculative, controversial or uncertain knowledge or on popular beliefs.

- *Inquires conducted with carefully prepared questions gave better results* than those carried out without such preparation, or those using poorly formulated questions. It was impossible to tell whether this improvement occurred because the questions were clearer, or because the inquirer was in a more receptive state after his preparatory effort.

- *Intuitive Consensus was not normally necessary to assure accuracy.* Accuracy depended al-most entirely on other factors, as mentioned above. The multiple sessions usually generated additional perspectives and ideas. Consensus was occasionally helpful in convincing members of the application team that the intuitive information could be taken seriously. Also, some participating intuitives claimed they were more comfortable working as part of a team than independently.

- *Occasional reliance upon intuitives who were less than "expert" was unsatisfactory.* Their deficiencies usually emerged fairly quickly during the test sessions, but in a few cases were detected only later when a demanding topic arose.

- *There were no significant differences in the information provided by expert intuitives who were already familiar with the language and concepts peculiar to the topic under inquiry, and those who were not.* The former sometimes used new terms with which they were not consciously familiar, and those not in trance often remarked that they did not understand what they were saying. Those already familiar with a topic (two were engineers, for example) might deliver more fluid descriptions, but they were just as often hesitant and occasionally even erroneous, as if they were influenced by incorrect preconceptions. These variations were minor and never a serious impediment.

- *The "mode" of intuitive reception was not significant to the accuracy, depth or flow of the information.* Expert intuitives who were channels performed no better and no worse than those who functioned fully or partially consciously.

To learn is to make mistakes, and this exploration in applied intuition was no exception. Even more than the comparisons, the errors made reveal much about how the intuitive process actually functions in practice and how to conduct intuitive inquiries properly. The most prominent difficulties encountered were these:

- *The topic chosen was too large or complex to be covered properly in only a few inquiry sessions.* We mistakenly presumed a simplicity that was not there, so the expectation that the responses to our questions would be equally simple was wrong. This problem did not arise when the subject area was narrowly limited and specific. To be sure, we did not expect definitive results in a number of exploratory studies, and a few smaller ones were entered out of curiosity, without any preparation at all.

- *The information being sought turned out to be inapplicable*, even though it was exactly what we had asked for and appeared to be correct. This obstacle arose because the persons we believed would welcome the information turned out to be uninterested, for any of various reasons: they found it incredible; they were already committed to another approach; they were doubtful about its accuracy; or they wanted it to be extensively corroborated before they would apply it. In retrospect, we should have anticipated these difficulties. We did not look well enough ahead to the intended application, and especially to the requirements of the persons who were to carry it out.

- Similarly, *we made unjustified assumptions regarding the usefulness of the information,* independent of what others may have wanted or expected. We presumed that whatever information we obtained would be beneficial and relevant to the envisioned problem area. For example, we felt it would always be helpful to recover lost objects and people, and improved technical understanding and explanations would always we beneficial. These assumptions turned out be incorrect. This deficiency seemed to arise most often in clients' personal inquiries rather than in research studies.

- *The information given challenged traditional accepted knowledge,* even though it appeared to be valid and worthy of examination. The most prominent examples were contradictions with current medical models of disease and healing; with commonly held beliefs about the absence of human consciousness before birth and after death; and with classical interpretations of history. We could trace these contradictions to doubtful assumptions underlying either the scientific paradigm, scientific methodology or long-established cultural and religious beliefs—all areas that are already controversial. This does not mean that the intuitive information was wrong, of course. Nevertheless, potential users sometimes rejected the intuitive findings because one or more portions conflicted with fixed notions they held dear. Thus, application was not possible.

- *The specific information we wanted was simply not available.* Blockage occurred because (we were told) it would have been harmful if provided, either to the individuals seeking and applying it, or to society at large if it we revealed it publicly. This barrier arose most conspicuously when the desired information, if given and used, would have allowed the development of a socially dangerous new technology, even though the positive results we sought would have emerged as well. Again, we did not consider well enough the ultimate consequences of the application. In personal sessions information was sometimes withheld because the client (or another involved person such as a spouse) appeared to be not capable of using it harmlessly.

• The simplifications and assumptions inherent in ordinary conversation complicated intuitive descriptions. For example, the intuitives sometimes made simple statements that did not include the particular conditions under which they were valid; or, the "cause" given for a situation

I should probably explain the particular role of my own intuition in this work, lest you suspect that I somehow distorted the findings through an improper use of my own intuitive abilities, whatever they might be.

I acknowledge that I utilized my intuition as fully as I was able when selecting the expert intuitives to be employed, picking the topics to be pursued and formulating the questions to be asked; also when generating ideas and offering suggestions for further work. While I have continually tried to improve my own intuition during the several years of this study (this is another story), I make no claim here about how great or how little this personal contribution might have been.

On the other hand, I did not intend and do not believe I relied on my own intuition (1) when creating the overall methodology to be followed; (2) selecting which data to pay attention to, (3) checking these data for self-consistency and corroboration and (4) drawing conclusions from them. These steps are neither intuitive nor subjective activities. They require full rigor if they are to be correct and credible. Nor did I try to compete with expert intuitives by becoming one of them, even if this would have been possible.

I feel I may rightly claim that the conclusions presented here arise from an objective observation of the intuitive process at work, and a deductive product of such data gathered by intuitive means.

ation was only one contributing factor and not fundamental. In such cases the information given was therefore incomplete. This shortcoming, not always immediately obvious, could lead later to confusion or contra-diction. Again, this language difficulty usually occurred when the questions asked were vague or otherwise ambiguous. The missing conditions sometimes emerged later, spontaneously or when asked for.

These difficulties occurred primarily in research sessions and less frequently in counseling and consulting sessions, as already noted. Most had arisen in intuitive inquiries conducted by other experimenters in the past.[2]

Note that these problems arose as much from the *application* of intuition as from the intuitive process itself. Just as when studying other human capacities, our task at CAI was to learn how to cooperate with intuition in whatever form we encountered it, not to try to shape our understanding and use of it to fit our expectations and preferences.

We found that *intuitive information was almost always available when we wanted it, could properly ask for it and could safely employ it for a worthwhile purpose.* The comparisons and difficulties reinforce and refine the four general principles or conditions for successful intuitive inquiries, suggested in Chapter 1 (and discussed in more detail below); namely, these inquiries must be (1) harmless, (2) positively motivated, (3) conducted with carefully prepared questions and (4) carried out with expert intuitives.

Limitations

The major qualities of intuitive information cited in Chapter 1 can now be understood better than when the series of experiments began.

The exploration covered a wide range of subject matter, from deeply personal to broad societal, from the distant past to the emerging future, from theoretical to practical, from philosophical and spiritual to highly detailed scientific/technical, even lost human language. It revealed that there are *very few limits* on the kinds of information one may access intuitively. This finding opens the question: are there any limits at all?

A few limits follow immediately from the condition of harmlessness. Topics such as the development of lethal weaponry, new means for burglary and paranormal technologies for mental intrusion are very likely excluded. Other inquiries are surely disallowed because they lead to a mixture of positive and negative consequences, whether apparent or hidden from view at the time. We may also suspect that valid and relevant information, especially personal information, is not always available because the recipient is not able to utilize it, as often noted.

There are certainly communication limits. For certain kinds of information the explanatory detail needed to convey it requires specialized definitions, language and background. This is especially the case in sciences such as mathematics, chemistry, biology and medicine. Even outside of science certain kinds of information are sensitive to subtle distinctions and must be exceptionally precise to be useful. Philosophy, religion, law and some other fields are subject to similar problems because they deal with knowledge expressible only in terms of erudite concepts, narrowly defined terminologies or highly specialized systems of thought. Inquiries in these areas may experience difficulties that only a specially qualified intuitive can handle. (Recall the Egyptian language example in Chapter 11.) Finally, we may be sure that there are domains of knowledge so far outside of human experience and understanding they cannot be communicated through words at all, beyond what the even most expert intuitive could receive and convey.

Of course, an expert intuitive may still be able to obtain this kind of knowledge for his personal use if he can access it directly without the necessity of human language. The deepest esoteric knowledge, the spiritual wisdom attained by the most devout seekers and those who are genuinely enlightened is said to be completely ineffable and therefore available only in this directly experienced manner.

The intuitive counseling sessions showed that very profound personal knowledge is generally accessible to intuitive inquiry for individual self-understanding. There are strong indications that such information is accessible by anyone, who has developed his own intuition well, so long as it is constructive and helpful and he is open to hearing and applying it. There appear to be few (if any) limitations on the content of such personal information, except what the individual himself might be blocking out.

In summary, we have shown that while the kinds of information obtainable through intuition are limited, these limits are not highly restrictive in practice. They lie well beyond the limits that govern other known means of generating new knowledge. Moreover, according to the collective experience gained here, they appear to arise mainly, if not totally, from the inquirer and his cultural mind set, rather than from the superconscious source itself. That is, they lie in the biases, beliefs, preconceptions and other incorrect interpretations and assumptions about reality, held both individually and collectively. Some are intricately tied into the constrictions of human language. Many of them have an emotional or egoic origin. Much future experimentation will be required to understand the roots of these limitations and define them more precisely.

Accuracy

> "Rational knowledge and rational activities certainly constitute the major part of scientific research, but that is not all there is to it. The rational part of research would, in fact, be useless if it were not complemented by the intuition that gives scientists new insights and makes them creative. These insights tend to come suddenly, and characteristically, not when sitting on a desk working out the equations, but when relaxing in the bath, during a walk inthe woods, onthe beach, etc. During these periods of relaxation after concentrated intellectual activity, the intuitive mind seems to take over and can produce the sudden clarifying insights which give so much joy and delight to scientific research." [Fritjov Capra[3]]

Accuracy is not always the most important component of intuitive information but it is the most common in demand by users, and is the main issue in corroboration. Moreover, the other valuable attributes of intuitive information depend on its accuracy to a greater or lesser extent: if information is not reasonably accurate, it is not of much use.

The track record for the accuracy of information provided by the expert intuitives was excellent on all matters for which the accuracy was actually checked. *All attempts made to corroborate information that was specific and clear, and that could be compared with known and reliable non-intuitive knowledge, were successful.* There were no known errors.

However, rather little of the information could be checked so thoroughly. Much of the non-specific intuitive information was too vague or incomplete to allow full verification for applicational use or for acceptance by society at large. The most common problem encountered was that the only prior knowledge available for corroboration was not itself trustworthy. Still more could have been checked but it would have been too expensive or time consuming to do so. Much other information was probably correct but could be checked only partially, so the result was uncertain and full accuracy could not be certified. This included a few cases in which the intuitive information seemed incredible and very important but no way could be found to verify it. There were also a few examples where seemingly unlikely information turned out later to be correct. Contradictions with established knowledge, scientific and public were frequent, though all of these fell in subject areas that not fully explored and were already controversial.

At this point, then, the case is strong, but not firmly demonstrated, in favor of the accuracy of intuitive information when it has been properly gathered. For the moment, "proper" means the four conditions set out in Chapter 1 as necessary for successful intuitive retrieval. This observation adds support to the conjecture that errors in intuitive inquiries always come from the intuitive during subconscious translation, not from the superconscious source. If this conjecture could be somehow proven to be true it would be immensely valuable, for it would indicate exactly where one should apply effort to improve further the accuracy of intuitive inquiries. Until proven, however, the theoretical distinction between the expert intuitive and the superconscious source as the seat of errors is not very relevant. Users want reliable information, free of mistakes, and are not concerned where the mistakes come from, and how.

Information obtained intuitively cannot be assumed to be inherently correct but it must always be checked further. This being the case, one may rightly ask, what good is it? The answer is the same for new information from *any* source, for it must always be corroborated by independent means. *Until new information is properly corroborated it cannot contribute to new knowledge.* How it is corroborated depends on how one chooses to regard it and intends to apply it. Like all sources of information, intuition should be seen as a resource for hypotheses, ideas, perspectives and apparent facts that *may* turn out to be true when checked. If one is willing to experiment with uncertain and invalidated information, he may find it to be immediately useful, in which case the application is its own corroboration. In contrast, if he accepts new intuitive information from others out of the stubborn or naive belief that it is inherently correct and reliable just because it is intuitive, he may be wrong, and he invites subsequent disappointment. The difficulty arises less from incorrectness than from uncertainty—that is, not because the information is wrong (which is quite possible) but because he is not sure that it is right.

Intuition is useful not only for factual information, if carried out properly, but also for more profound knowledge not easily communicated in words, even though it may contain incorrect or contradictory details. The problem arises largely because factual information is only a carrier or vehicle of deeper knowledge, even wisdom, and is secondary to it. We can expect that whoever or whatever is transmitting such information intuitively is less concerned with detailed accuracy than with the main message, just as you and I do when passionately relating an important matter to someone we care about. Indeed, the whole notion of "accuracy" is based on a massive structure of human knowledge that does not fit nicely into how knowledge is organized in the superconscious.

Accuracy is important, of course, though qualities such as relevance, completeness, novelty and sincerity are sometimes even more important. For example, the information may be sought only for inspiration, encouragement, perspective or a reminder of something already known but forgotten. It may be a simple serendipitous insight, when a complex issue bursts into clarity, a solution to a problem is seen or a crucial decision becomes obvious. In such a situation trivial errors can usually be tolerated. This was demonstrated especially in the counseling experiment, where the main usefulness of the information given lay less in its substantive and factual nature than in its insightful and personal inspirational quality. This experience also revealed yet another important factor besides factual accuracy that makes intuitive counseling so effective, namely, the communication of compassion and deep concern.

Development and Learnability

> "The regular practice of meditation is the single most powerful
> means of increasing intuition." [Frances Vaughan[4]]

These experiments were not designed to determine how intuition should be developed by one who desires to do so, but valuable information on this matter emerged incidentally in the course of the work with the expert intuitives. (CAI's intuition development classes also contributed here.) The experience gained reinforces all three points made in Chapter 1 regarding the nature of intuition development: (1) the development requires more *unlearning* than learning, mainly to circumvent previously acquired mental habits, beliefs and emotional conditioning; (2) the student must rely largely on his *feelings* to enhance sensitivity to his inner mind; and (3) the conscious mind, as the *director* of the unconscious, is in primary control of the removal of barriers and unfolding of intuition.

It has been said that intuitive skill can be learned but not taught. This claim may be valid in one strict sense of teaching—as a pedagogical means for cloning knowledge from one mind to another—but it is not true in the common sense of learning, that in which most skills are taught and learned. True teaching not only provides new information but also stimulates the learner to experiment and practice for himself. It instills positive motivation and self-esteem, and induces an essential trust between teacher and learner. Intuitive skill can certainly be taught in this larger sense of "assisted self-learning."

A competent teacher and an exposure to other learners and practitioners may aid the effort, but testimonies from competent intuitives show that *one may develop his intuitive ability completely on his own.* The learning process does not appear to depend significantly, if at all, upon personality type, profession, education, gender, other interests, intelligence, family and social environment, or childhood background. All of these factors differed widely among CAI's expert intuitives. Their testimonies about what they did to develop their intuitive skill also varied considerably in both kind and degree. These reports may be suggestive as to how one should proceed, but *no single, favored approach to learning intuitive skill emerges from their collective experience.* Learners naturally differ in the number and kind of specific obstacles they must overcome. In other respects no evidence emerged from this study that intuitive capacity is an individually inherited "gift," or is acquired during childhood, though this possibility cannot be ruled out.

Learning to use one's intuition is little different from learning a language or how to drive a car. The only known prerequisites are those that facilitate *all* learning: the belief (or knowledge) that it is possible, sufficient self-confidence and the will to actually do it. All indications are that no one who is capable of living a normal life is so heavily handicapped that he is barred from learning to enhance his natural intuitive ability. (Indeed, what are commonly considered handicaps are often assets!)

Some persons have developed their intuition to a high degree, though they do not try to communicate the intuitive information they receive directly to others. While they do not qualify as expert intuitives, who must be able to respond to questions, some of them practice their developed ability successfully and inconspicuously in particular lines of intuitive work where question asking is not necessarily required: medical diagnosis, investment management, criminal investigation, societal forecasting, and many others. Further, I have known a few powerful intuitives who utilize their ability only for their own self-understanding, without any external applications at all.

Universality

The claim that intuition is a truly universal human capacity derives from four observations. First, it is known that a human being cannot function without a direct-knowing channel, since his other means of knowledge acquisition are insufficient for normal life. This follows because the capabilities of man's reasoning faculties are well understood, as are the limitations of his senses and memory. The intellect and the data it works with can go only just so far in generating new knowledge. Man needs intuition to survive.

Second, universality is supported by the large number and wide variety of practicing intuitives, those who have deliberately chosen to develop their intuition and have successfully done so. This number includes those on the CAI staff, whom I came to know well, as well as many others who have demonstrated their abilities publicly. These intuitives are very varied in their personalities and come from a wide variety of backgrounds. They can therefore be said to be a cross-section of the public.

Third, recent experiments in parapsychology revealed that almost all those who were Remote Viewing subjects, many drawn from the general public and even several skeptical individuals, were able to perform acceptably. In Targ and Puthoff's words, "We have not found a single person who could not do remote viewing to satisfaction....The indications are that this is a widespread human talent."[5]

Finally, the universality of intuition is also supported from philosophic sources. The esoteric teachings of the world's major religions, especially those from the Far East and Middle East, include these same claims of the universality of "inherent knowledge" or "direct knowing" in one form or another. This ancient tradition says that all knowledge is accessible to whomever sincerely seeks it, and there are no fundamental limits on what a human being may come to know.

For these reasons, if intuition is not a completely universal capacity, it is very nearly so.

Mechanisms

This book has focused on intuition primarily as a kind of practical behavior, something one *does* and *uses,* and only secondarily as a notion or theory to be tested, a mental process whose internal workings are to be studied, understood and explained. The mechanisms of intuitive functioning have been limited here to a simple working model and speculations on how intuition appears to function within the human mind as commonly understood. Nevertheless, the strong historical evidence for intuition, along with the results of the several experiments, have brought this working model a step closer to validity as a valid model of the mind, one in which intuition is included along with other known faculties.

Specifically, these new findings (1) add credibility to the existence of a super-conscious, or collective unconscious, mind (whatever one chooses to call it), including a huge and profound knowledge reservoir, and they delineate some of its important properties. (2) They clarify the role of the subconscious mind as a translator, shaper and filter of superconscious information when it occasionally finds its way to consciousness. (3) They highlight the intuitive reception process as the primary means by which this higher-level knowledge reaches the conscious mind. Finally, (4) they confirm some of the subconscious obstacles that hinder the intuitive process: an overactive rationality, unreal beliefs, early negative conditioning and hidden fears, to name the most common.

Theoretical questions about the internal mechanism of intuition are numerous and they run deep. They will surely occupy scholars, especially philosophers, psychologists and neurophysiologists, for many years to come.

Remote Viewing

"To me, the value of remote viewing lies not in so-called practical applications....[It] rests with the experience itself." [F. Holmes Atwater[6]]

Remote Viewing (RV) was introduced in Chapter 1 as an extensively researched alternative to the type of intuitive inquiry explored in the CAI experiments. It consisted of a long series of carefully executed exploratory experiments in conducted at the Cognitive Sciences Laboratory of SRI International and the Defense Intelligence Agency of the U.S. government from 1972 to 1995.[7] A full comparison of CAI's approach to intuitive inquiry with RV is not called for here. Some of the results from RV are not yet publicly accessible, and present knowledge of it is derived entirely from others' written reports (not from my direct experience with it). Nevertheless, a few important observations are possible at this preliminary point.

Practical studies of RV showed it to be a valid and significant form of intuitive practice. Many of the experimental results were truly impressive as evidence of intuitive functioning. The publication of these findings within the scientific community, and according to accepted scientific standards, was undoubtedly an important accomplishment. also, the experimenters showed that almost anyone can receive valid target information, testifying once again to the universality of intuitive ability, as noted above.

The main purpose of the RV project was to generate evidence that it "worked," not so much to provide information for direct application but rather as a future possibility, including the assessment of potential Soviet RV capability. The project was generally successful in this purpose, though it never achieved full reliability, for there were ambiguities and failures among the very impressive successes, even when the goals were clear and specific and the intuitives or viewers were well qualified. The most experienced of the viewers reported difficulties and limitations. CAI's expert intuitives also encountered these kinds of shortcomings, but only occasionally. They may have arisen with RV because of its evidence-oriented research approach, driven by the desire for information about a remote target of no importance except for the experiment itself. Also, the laboratory protocol may have worked better if the RV subjects were simply asked for the desired information directly, on the assumption that is readily available, without any preconceptions about how it should be received.

The limitations may also have arisen because the intended application (as governed by the sponsor of the research) was military intelligence, a questionable motivation at best. I don't believe one can reasonably expect the superconscious to take sides in a high-level political game by revealing an opponent's secrets while still guarding one's own; to do so would not be impartially beneficial to all parties involved. If we could assume that the collection of intelligence information is a harmless and humane activity, for a worthwhile purpose, then the four conditions could be said to be satisfied. However, in the presence of the extensive secrecy in which intelligence information is collected, the consequences of its application and the deception in which those involved occasionally engage, there remain serious questions about whether the first two conditions are met. We do not know what actually occurred during the experiments, what may have been omitted in the reporting, and (for some of the reports) whether the published findings are indeed correct. Indeed, harmlessness and positive motivation were never mentioned by the RV researchers as factors that might influence accuracy and reliability.

Comparison with CAI's findings shows that unrestricted and harm-free intuitive inquiry can access information much more accurately and reliably than was shown in the RV experiments as reported. Unrestricted intuitive inquiry is capable of providing much deeper and more complex information than was demonstrated in the RV studies.

Conditions for Successful Inquiries

"The history of science makes clear that the greatest advancements in man's understanding of the universe are made by intuitive leaps at the frontiers of knowledge, not by intellectual walks along well-traveled paths."
[Andrew Weil[8]]

We may now summarize the main procedural lessons learned from the experiments as a set of four conditions to be satisfied, or guidelines to be followed, when carrying out an intuitive inquiry and applying the resulting information. These conditions are refinements of the tentative versions described in Chapter 1, which were based on early CAI experience as well as others' previous findings on the practical use of intuition. We summarize them first, then discuss each more fully.

First, the intuitive inquiry and all of its consequences must be *harmless* to all persons who could possibly be affected by it. This includes those generating the questions, the inquirers, the intuitives, the individuals who are to apply the information, other individuals who may be unknowingly involved, and in some cases the general public as well. To this end, the inquiry must take into account the entire context in which it is conducted: preparing the questions; receiving the responses; interpreting and evaluating them; obtaining corroboration as needed; and the actual application of the information. This condition must hold *even when the consequences of the application cannot be clearly foreseen.* Just as in scientific and other discoveries, this principle establishes prime responsibility for the consequences, though in the intuitive case the desired information may not even be forthcoming if harm could arise from it.

Second, and closely related but distinct, the inquiry must be *well motivated*, meaning it should be driven by a positive, humane purpose, well intentioned by those participating in it—not just to the inquirer himself but also the entire project team—the expert intuitive(s), those generating the questions and those utilizing the answers for the application at hand. It applies even if the eventual consequences are seen or would turn out to be harmless. For self-inquiries this condition requires that the individual's intention is sincere and he is open to accepting and heeding the information sought.

Third, the inquirer must *prepare carefully* all questions to be asked of the expert intuitive or himself. They should be clear and unambiguous, as simple and specific as possible, and free of bias and questionable assumptions. They should be solidly based, probing outward from certain knowledge. They do not necessarily need to be formulated in words and written down, but if not they should be implicit in the inquirer's purpose and intention.

Finally, the inquiry effort should utilize only *expert* intuitives, oneself or others, for bringing through the desired information.

One might argue that the first two conditions are required for *any* serious inquiry, not just an intuitive one, and this may be so. Their necessity follows here from the particular characteristic of the intuitive process: its benign nature, whose essential quality is independent of personality, language, conditioning and emotion, except that any of these can interfere with intuitive reception. Intuition is responsive only to intention.

As far as can be determined these four conditions are natural and implicit rather than the result of CAI's particular approach, the particular individuals who were involved or the particular topics selected for study.

In retrospect, all four seem perfectly reasonable for intuitive inquiry, perhaps even obvious in retrospect. I might well have anticipated them at the outset of the exploration but did not do so, at least not fully. Intuitive inquiry seemed at the time to transcend so well the accepted limits on the breadth of knowledge available that I assumed we could bypass the rules that ordinarily apply when seeking answers to questions. The situation turned out to be just the opposite: firm ground rules for questioning and application are essential when conducting intuitive inquiries.

Several publications over recent decades (mentioned earlier) contain reports in which other experimenters with intuition sought technical or similar factual information. Almost all of these attempts yielded information that was not credible, not useful or both; it was either vague, erroneous, too abstract, not responsive to the questions asked, impossible to verify, simply inapplicable or a combination of these shortcomings. *In every one of these unsuccessful cases of which I am aware, at least one of the above four conditions was not satisfied.*

Let us look more closely now at these four conditions, clarify them somewhat and see more specifically what they demand in practice. We may also ask, are they strictly necessary, or could one or more be relaxed in certain situations?

Harmlessness

The harmlessness condition agrees well with CAI's experience but it cannot be stated with full certainty and assurance because (1) harmful effects are not always apparent or foreseeable and (2) the notion of what constitutes "harm" is itself not precise.

While considerable protection seems to be built into the intuitive process, we do not yet understand its mechanism and its limits well enough to be able to be fully and automatically assured of harmless application. It may turn out that exceptions exist that allow dangerous information to leak through or intuitive mischief to be carried out under certain conditions. The few instances in which blocking of information was conspicuous during our study may have been only sporadic, peculiar to the particular situation at hand and not representative—or they have been only the tip of a huge iceberg. There could have been situations in which we unknowingly received dangerous information that fortunately never reached those who would have misused it. It may even turn out that there are certain kinds of knowledge that are simply not present in the superconscious, at least not in a recognizable form—a kind of cosmic ignorance—though this is difficult to imagine.

Popular legends, fictional literature and movies contain many examples of supposed transgressions by malicious mystics, evil witches, black magicians, resentful gods and others. However, I know of no solid evidence that these presumed effects actually occurred as described, or if they did that they were enabled by intuition.

Harm, as ordinarily thought of, can arise anywhere along the chain of consequences that follow the receipt of a piece of intuitive information. Some of these consequences may be clearly beneficial, while others may be very much the opposite. To verify for certain that all effects of an inquiry are going to be harmless, the entire chain has to be considered. Such thoroughness is rarely possible.

The notion of "harm" is ambiguous not only from the standpoint of limited foreknowledge but also because it is subjective, a matter of personal belief, conscience and experience. What one person regards as unquestionable benefit may well be seen from another's point of view as harmful. Conversely, even a selfish or malicious intention may turn out to have great benefit from another's perspective. Most persons would probably accept a broad criterion such as "the greatest good for all concerned," but few would agree on what this means. For some persons, doing to one's neighbor what he would like to be done to himself can include some very bizarre, antisocial and harmful acts.

New knowledge is not always a good thing, of course. In the modern world we place great value on education, learning through experience and the reduction of ignorance whenever possible, yet we all know persons who are so busy accumulating knowledge that they neglect to apply what they have learned, to relate to others or to live normal lives. The issue is most apparent for applications, where the most commonly valued action can occasionally have drastic negative effects. Transporting medical knowledge to a third-world culture can greatly reduce infant mortality, saving many lives, but the resultant increase in population can increase mortality even more when the society is then not able to feed itself properly. Similarly, administering drugs to heal someone from a disease can deprive his immune system of the ability to defend itself against a later, more serious disease. It may also deprive him of an important inner experience arising out of his pain. The decisions in such situations can be challenging indeed, especially when the consequences cannot readily be seen in advance. Who can say with confident authority what is harmful and what is not?

Like other human attributes that carry power, knowledge has its proper place in life, but it must be balanced against other attributes toward a humane purpose. In practice the conscientious inquirer can only design his inquiry to balance the anticipated benefits, as he sees them, against the harm or risk of harm that may result, to the best of his awareness and ability at the time. He should certainly include in his inquiry questions about possible consequences, and then remain alert and humble for unexpected effects and any new information that may arise as the application proceeds.

From another perspective it is remarkable that blockage occurred at all: that a natural mental process should be regulated by an apparently external condition of beneficence. Thoughts, feelings, imagination, reasoning and emotions are all seen as unconstrained mental activities, free of any inherent regulation and quite capable of being misused. At least, no such regulation is apparent. I cannot think of any other human mental faculty, except perhaps "morality" and "conscience," that is automatically regulated to prevent resultant harm to others, even (or especially) when the individual is not aware of the consequences. Could it be that there is something deep in the human mind, perhaps a beneficial "intelligence" in the superconscious, that serves to govern the intuitive process on behalf of the greater good? Even when intuition functions in support of the inquirer's purpose, is it looking ahead to consequences he cannot see? It seems so.

Motivation

> "We have here '…a whole new way of thinking and feeling, a flexible and open way of perceiving reality that is not based on certainty or security.'"
>
> [Pema Chödrön[9]]

Similar considerations hold for the requirement of a "positive motivation." Regardless of the harmless or harmful consequences of the inquiry effort, it must somehow benefit the inquirer, inquirers and application team members. It must make a positive contribution to their well-being, understanding and growth (in the broadest sense). When intuitives proclaim information without good purpose, it is useless even if it is accurate and amazing. This condition goes beyond requiring only that the team members ought not to be harmed by the effort; it demands further that they be positively benefited by it. To this end, their individual and collective intention must be cooperative, harmonious, open and supportive of one another. This requirement includes all participating parties, even entities or "beings" that may be involved through one or more of the participating channels, for these "beings" sometimes have private agenda of their own they wish to fulfill, just as do the others participants.

The history of intuitive inquiry is replete with examples of questioning that was pointless except to entertain or generate evidence for something already known and obvious. While the CAI experiments never had an obviously malicious motive, some of the larger inquiries suffered from a lack of clear understanding between the inquirers and those whom we expected to carry through on the application, so the collective intention was not cooperative. In a few cases a "being" sought to shift the goal of the effort to a more fundamental level, and those of us looking for more practical answers were frustrated that we could not obtain more direct responses to our questions. (Of course, the "being" may have been the wiser, but there was still a lack of harmony.) Some of the smaller CAI-initiated inquiries arose more out of curiosity than from a recognizable beneficial purpose. While no blocking was apparent, the lack of clear intention showed itself in perfunctory responses to our questions and too little useful information.

During intuitive counseling we discovered afterwards that two of CAI's clients had deceived us about their intention, which was different than what they had stated and was not obviously positive. Seeking evidence for their parapsychological experiments may have been a legitimate motivation (apart from the deception), depending on their ultimate purpose, but it was not consonant with our stated purpose. CAI turned down other requests to participate in such experiments, on the grounds that their potential benefit was not sufficiently constructive, even though the result itself might been of some small help to those conducting the experiments or the participants. A few clients asked for private information about other persons, and the intuitives refused them.

This condition suffers from a few of the same uncertainties as the first. It also raises the same question: is it an inherent, fixed principle, or are there exceptions?

The two conditions of harmlessness and positive motivation as stated here derive from empirical experience, not from theory or speculation. They appear to come from the emotionless, non-judgmental and will-free character of the superconscious mind. It is not understood how and why they should exist at all, but until they can be better defined they must be respected for the purpose of intuitive inquiry. Both need to be explored further in subsequent studies of applied intuition.

The Inquiry Process

"'There is no use in just telling you and satisfying your curiosity,'
said the sage. 'Better that you *know* it than simply be *informed*'."
[Swami Amar Jyoti[10]]

In every one of the experiments an unmistakable correlation emerged between the quality of the questions asked and the quality of the responses.

The sad history of poorly conducted intuitive explorations by others prompted us from the start to design the research effort around well focused requests for new information, rather than open-ended and largely goalless experiments of the "let's see what will happen" type. Indeed, the manner in which questions were formulated and posed during intuitive inquiries for specific information played a surprisingly critical role in the quality and depth of the intuitives' responses.

We observed very soon that the superconscious mind (our name for the source even at that time) requires a specific, unambiguous and unassuming form of discourse if it is to respond with clear and accurate answers. For example, when asking about a certain past or future event that is designated by a common name, it may be necessary to circumscribe the event more precisely in place, time, person or other features, since the name may also apply to similar situations or individuals that could easily be confused with the one the inquirer has in mind. When asking about the properties of something, or how something works or where to find it, it is well to ask first if it really exists, and if so, is there more than one of them? Stating the purpose of a proposed activity or project may not be necessary, but stating the purpose behind a specific request can be helpful just to make the question clear. Finally, as noted earlier, it is easy to overlook one's biases and expectations about the situation under inquiry. Firming up the questions can help reveal these unspoken assumptions.

I can only speculate why such a meticulous mode of questioning is so necessary for specific intuitive inquiries when it is not required in ordinary human discourse. Nor is it so stringent a requirement in personal intuitive inquiries (see below). The suggestions offered at the end of Chapter 1 still appear to be the most likely explanations; namely:

- The huge size of superconscious memory demands very specific direction for inquiries.
- The superconscious has no specific intention of its own, so the inquirer must provide it.
- The superconscious is responds only to the inquirer's deeper intentions, not irrelevant details that are not consistent with them, and especially not those that are not harmful or that the inquirer is not yet ready to accept and use.
- The context or infrastructure of superconscious knowledge is too broad for interpreting what the inquirer does not specifically ask for.

Indeed, these possible explanations are just how we might describe our responses to a small child's probing, poorly stated questions, when he cannot understand answers that are direct and to the point in adult terms.

Judging from CAI's experience the superconscious mind responds somewhat like a very intelligent but unemotional and undirected knowledge mirror. It functions abstractly and without a program of its own. (This does not mean that it is devoid of human values and concerns.) It reflects back to the inquirer the same vagueness, ambiguities and imprecision that exist in his questions, as if it did not "know" any better, and refuses to guess. Thus, questions in conventional language need to be translated into the "language" of the superconscious, which is more clear, precise and reliable, even though it is not fundamentally literal and word-based.

The subconscious mind of the intuitive assists in this translation, but it cannot translate what is not present in the questions, and it is similarly limited in translating answers back to the inquirer. Other subjective mental capacities such as imagination, dreaming and believing, all strongly related to intuition, also influence the translation-interpretation process through the subconscious. Some of this influence may benefit the translation but experience suggests that most of it does not. A clear mind works best.

In intuitive counseling, and to a lesser extent in intuitive consulting and searches for lost objects and people, the situation is improved. While there is still a noticeable correlation between the quality of the questions and the quality of the responses, the formulation of the questions was found to be less critical. Expert intuitives often provided appropriate counsel despite the poor quality of the client's questions. It was common for the intuitives to answer written questions even before they were posed, and often without their being asked at all. They seemed to be answering "the question behind the question," as if they already knew what the inquirer most wanted or needed to hear, even if he did not say so. Their responses were typically simplified and carefully phrased, apparently in response to what the recipient was able to accept and use. To be sure, inquirers were sometimes oversensitive to the very issues they raised in their questions.

Clearly, some kind of enabling factor was present in personal counseling that was not present in the search for factual information ordinarily regarded as "objective." Why was this so? I think we should rightly expect that direct human benefit and personal growth should have a higher priority and purpose, a more positive motivation, than attempts to enlarge ever more complex systems of knowledge. This explanation will surely seem obvious to many. I would agree, but was surprised that it should turn out to be so important. I feel now that the real reason for the difference is not so simple.

Dialoging with the superconscious appears to much like conversation with a devoted and trusted friend. You know he has your well being at heart, and he will not lie to you, but there is always the possibility of misunderstanding and you must allow for this in the exchange. If he a very wise capable friend, you may safely assume that any errors are your own mistaken interpretation rather than his mistransmission. So it goes when obtaining personal counsel from the superconscious through an expert intuitive.

When the inquirer practices intuition for his own benefit and is sufficiently expert, we know he may obtain new knowledge directly, without words and explanations. Appropriate intention is still needed, but he may bypass much or all of the tedious process of communicating verbally. That is, it is not always necessary for him to formulate his needs as specific questions and hear the answers through verbal statements. Herein lies an important difference— surely a very significant difference—between intuitive information accessed personally and that obtained through another intuitive, provided both are expert.

In order to formulate questions well in future intuitive inquiries, we will first have to understand better how knowledge is organized within the superconscious mind. We will need to know how the elements of knowledge in the superconscious are identified and recalled during inquiry, and then conveyed to the subconscious mind for translation. In other words, we must understand better the "language" the superconscious uses as it interacts with the subconscious mind, and how this language relates to ordinary language. Studies of the human unconscious over the last fifty years have extended understanding considerably, but answers to these unresolved issues are not yet known.

Expert Intuitives

Little need be said about expert intuitives beyond that offered in Chapter 2. Only some of their characteristics can now be seen more clearly in the light of the experiments.

It has been demonstrated that CAI's expert intuitives were able to access the superconscious source for satisfactory answers to almost all questions put to them, to communicate these answers back to the inquirer, and to do so with compassionate concern when this was called for. Expertness is obviously not essential for accessing intuitive information sporadically, for anyone can do it and we all do so. However, expert competence is essential if a breadth of intuitive information with high quality (accuracy, clarity, relevance, etc.) is to be obtained consistently and on demand.

It would be wrong, however, to claim that all expert intuitives performed equally. Besides the differences pointed out earlier, their ways of answering questions were often very different from one another, even when the answers were essentially the same. Their responses varied in depth of detail, vocabulary, style and point of perspective. None of these differences were so pronounced that they stood in the way of clear answers. There was never an outright breach of accuracy on clear matters about which one could speak of accuracy at all. There was no indication that errors occurred when the conditions for successful inquiries were satisfied. Other desirable qualities besides accuracy—precision, completeness and relevance, in particular—were sometimes affected but not significantly so. Only the future will tell whether these minor shortcomings would become limiting in other kinds of inquiries and with other expert intuitives.

Regarding Intuitive Consensus, one may ask: could the intuitives' common responses to the same question sometimes be simultaneously wrong? Could a team of intuitives all subconsciously distort a piece of superconscious information in exactly the same way, perhaps out of a culturally shared and mistaken preconception? No signs of such a conspiracy were ever observed, even for a wide range of subject matter, among several intuitives and over a time period of many years. This is not a proof that it did or could not happen, since validation was not attempted on all consensual information but it is difficult to imagine a superconscious mechanism that would provide verifiable and correct consensual information through several expert intuitives on most occasions, while at the same time generating identical but incorrect information on other occasions. These observations suggest strongly that faulty consensus does not occur at all.

There is, of course, a looseness in the definition of "expert." It arises from a vagueness in the criterion of "high quality" of information used when candidate intuitives were tested. Indeed, a few failures slipped through the testing protocol, though not from a lack of intuitive competence but because it was not possible to work with them for other reasons. Since expertness is defined in terms of the quality of the information provided, which was thoroughly and adequately verified in the experiments, there need be no doubt that the intuitives who contributed were other than expert.

The four conditions, when suitably defined, and according to present understanding, appear to be both necessary and sufficient for successful intuitive inquiry. That is, all four conditions are required and no others seem to be needed. Once again, these conditions, when properly interpreted, can be said to apply to *any* search for knowledge, not just an intuitive one. Only future research and accumulated practical experience will reveal if this claim is strictly true without further qualification.

Depth of Intuitive Perception

"We may have some idea that a place of ultimate understanding exists—but heaven is not necessarily somewhere else. It is within

the nature of our minds....We just accept each situation as it comes,
and follow our inner guidance, our intuition, our own hearts."
[Tarthang Tulku[11]]

From time to time expert intuitives were able to tap unusually high (or deep) levels of knowledge. Most of these profound responses occurred in life readings, when there was an obviously strong personal need, though it also happened occasionally when seeking specialized technical information. Of course, from others' testimonies it is always difficult to tell for certain just how deeply their personal readings affected them. I can report from my own personal readings that the information given to me was sometimes very profound, well beyond what I would ever expect from the most wise friend or counselor. I have come to expect such responses from the superconscious. It is my task to be open, eager to learn and actively humble in the face of a source (perhaps my deepest self) that is much better informed and very much wiser than my conscious self. When a client satisfies these conditions, I believe he will receive profound guidance.

Again, we are all aware of the multiple levels at which parents give answers to their children's questions. They want to respond truthfully, not being misleading in their responses, but they must step down their answers to conform to the child's limited ability to understand what he is told—and to do so compassionately, without condescension.

Is there a level of deep perception and "expertness" beyond that observed in the CAI experiments? Reports on the accomplishments of certain Eastern teachers and masters indicate that there certainly is. These individuals typically resist documentation of their abilities, they customarily decline examination and they avoid impressing others with a display of their skills. Still, a few trustworthy reports show that they have on occasion provided exceptional information on topics they could never have been exposed to—clear evidence for a strong intuitive ability.[12*] Western observers close to them say they are able to see deeply into the lives of others totally unknown to them, and are unusual in their compassion toward other persons. Some of these masters claim themselves that they have access to whatever knowledge they want, all because they can be safely entrusted to handle it without misuse, either accidentally or deliberately. Perhaps it is this perfect harmless quality that enables them to be so intuitively all-knowing.

This experience and these reports suggest again that while the upper limit of intuitive knowing is not known, it is much higher than that observed in past applications of intuition, and also n the majority of the CAI experiments. It seems likely that we can look forward in the future to another, stronger wave of intuitive performance and application, and a new breed of super-expert intuitives.

Residual Issues

The treatment of intuition in this book has omitted a number of issues important to the explanation of its functioning and application. At CAI we studied each of these to the point of achieving a preliminary understanding, though the findings on these issues are too incomplete to be included here as conclusions. They will surely emerge on their own in future research on intuition, and as the understanding of intuition and its practice become more widely accepted. Suffice it to acknowledge briefly just four of them.

First, future applications of intuition within the public domain will raise serious *ethical questions*. The informed public must realize at some point that competent intuitives can apparently probe into the activities, and even the thoughts and intentions of others. For example, organizations that maintain their sense of security by maintaining secrets (justified or not) will naturally feel threatened by this realization, especially when they recognize that they are not even aware of whether, when and by whom their secrets might be intuitively probed. They will feel (rightly) that they have no power to prevent the intrusion. Competitive enterprises such as businesses, governments and the military will be forced into other options: to employ intuitives of their own; to expand their means of detecting security violations, using more sophisticated protection systems; or to give up the secrecy of their confidential activities. Smaller institutions will be similarly vulnerable.

At the individual level such intuitive probing could have an even greater impact, probably arising more from the fear and suspicion of personal violation than from the intrusion itself—just as for existing threats that their secrets will be revealed (like blackmail). The public may demand that criminal legislation and investigative bodies protect them against intuitive invasions of their personal and institutional privacy, but such measures will be difficult if not impossible to carry out. Conventional means of detection, investigation and proof are hopelessly inadequate.

On the other hand, it may turn out that such offenses cannot actually occur, at least to the extent just envisioned, because of the self-protective feature of intuitive inquiry. If true, this fact will lessen the offenses, though the public need only *believe* they can occur for the social issue to arise. These and other examples will require the solution of some challenging ethical puzzles. Some of them could make present-day social issues such as euthanasia and abortion seem like child's play.

Then there is the issue of who is responsible when a channeling intuitive provides counsel that turns out to be wrong—or is at least ambiguous and misinterpreted. Is it the channel, the inquirer or perhaps the "being" who is accountable?

Second, the topic of *prediction and prophecy* is a complex one and asks for clarification. The intuitive experiments show that prediction of the future is sometimes possible, beyond what can reasonably be expected, forecast or guessed by non-intuitive means. Some predictions seem to contradict the scientific notion of causality, as well as the commonly held principle of freedom of personal choice: "If my future is predictable do I really have any choice about it?" It is not yet clear just when such predictions are incorrect, where the notion of causality might be wrong, and what is really meant by "free choice." Also, many people assume that since intuition has been able to make correct predictions a few future events, well beyond the chance of reasoning or guessing, then they should be able to make any other statements about the future—certainly not so.

Predictions are implicit in *prophecy*, which is a kind of wise counsel, often intuitive, in which information about the future is given as a warning in order to avoid certain consequences: "Turn from your slovenly ways or your city will be destroyed!" warns Jehovah in the Old Testament of the Bible. But even famous prophets were sometimes terribly wrong. Prophecy has the power to effect changes, both societal and individual, when the listener has enough fear of the predicted outcome, confidence in the prophet or guilt over his hidden activities or intentions. Apart from their effects, intuitive predictions appear to vary greatly in their depth of perception, as if they come from different levels that seem to have different credibility. This raises the question of how one may reach the deepest level through an expert intuitive, oneself or another, with due regard to the receiver's ability to be aided by the new information about the future.

The basic question here concerns the extent to which intuition allows an inquirer to step across time into the future when seeking new information. We still need to learn which kinds of future events are predictable and which are not; how to access the most profound predictive information; and the particular conditions (perhaps beyond the basic four) that must be satisfied if accurate and constructive intuitive predictions are to be obtained. A few answers are available, but present understanding is incomplete.

Third, following the above discussion on *blockage of intuitive information*, there remains the issue of how the conditions of harmlessness and positive motivation are actually operating. To what extent does the superconscious regulate the intuitive channel to assure that only "safe" information can come through it? What is the fundamental principle or natural law that governs how this regulation is taking place? Does the regulation exist solely to protect against the release of potentially dangerous information (as in the nuclear example in Chapter 13), or are there other criteria at work as well? May this regulation be overridden in certain circumstances, either by a master intuitive who can assure responsible use, or by a malicious intuitive, say, who wants to misuse the information? Has a shield of protection been operating throughout mankind's evolution to protect against accidental, socially harmful discoveries? We may wonder if certain areas of inquiry are being regulated even today. CAI's work with intuitives suggests only beginning thoughts on these issues, and no satisfactory answers.

Fourth, we need to understand *how the intuitive process is working inside the human mind*, to a much greater extent than was explained in Chapter 1 and extended in this chapter. The impressive historic literature on inherent and innate knowledge, remarkable discoveries and useful insights provides ample evidence for the existence of intuition as a human capacity but it says very little about *how* it is functioning, at least in terms familiar to psychologists and others who make it their business to understand the workings of the human mind, especially at its unconscious levels.

Part of this deeper understanding of the intuitive process emerged from CAI's study. It largely confirmed and refined the model of the mind presented in Chapter 1. It also provided a partial explanation of the limits of intuitive inquiry—how far one may go in obtaining new information. This work also shed light on how intuition is related to cognitive activities such as reasoning, concept formation, imagination, language, perception and pattern recognition, as well as its place within established disciplines such as psychology, religion, philosophy, parapsychology and medicine. These topics must await further study, another day, and perhaps another book for their explanation.

One step we may take immediately is to try to generalize the experimental experience reported here by envisioning future applications that now appear to be possible.

> "Knowledge comes from within, not from without. As a man
> thinks, so are his surroundings. The eyes of curiosity see only what
> is not so, and it is not only a man's lips that ask questions. The eyes
> and the taste and the touch are all inquisitive, seeking to learn from
> without what shall deny the truth within. He who sees the dawn
> must wait for it; and even so, if he is blind, it will be darkness to
> him." [Talbot Mundy[13]]

• Endnotes—Chapter 14

[1] Wilhelm, 1967, Intro.

[2] See, for example: Schwartz, 1978, Schwartz, 1983, Goodman, 1977, Cayce & Cayce, 1971.

[3] Capra, 1975, p. 31.

[4] Vaughan, 1979.

[5] Targ & Puthoff, 1977, p. 4.

[6] Atwater, 2001, p. 134.

[7] Puthoff & Targ, 1976, Targ & Puthoff, 1977, Puthoff, 1996, Targ, R., 1996, McGoneagle, 1993, Morehouse, 1996, Atwater, 2001.

[8] Weil, 1973, p. 150.

[9] Chödrön, 1991.

[10] Jyoti, 1988, p. 13.

[11] Tulku, 1977, p. 85.

[12*] The list of credible reports is long, but the following are representative: Brunton, 1984, Sandweiss, 1975, Yogananda, 1985; see also the extensive survey by Michael Murphy in Murphy, 1992.

[13] Mundy, 1924.

CHAPTER 15

IMPLICATIONS
THE FUTURE OF APPLIED INTUITION

"There are more things in heaven and earth, Horatio, than are dreamt of in your philosophy." [Shakespeare[1]]

We are now in a position to make some observations about which areas and fields of knowledge can best take advantage of intuition as a powerful knowledge resource, and perhaps for other purposes as well. In this final chapter we examine the future implications of applied intuition as it is allowed to play a stronger role in human activities—for society as a whole, its various institutions, working teams, and especially individuals. We will ask: What will be the impact of the practice of intuition when it gains more widespread acceptance and is more extensively used?

The Potential of Intuition

"Let the mind be enlarged, according to its capacity, to the grandeur of the mysteries, and not the mysteries contracted to the narrowness of the mind." [Sir Francis Bacon]

The discovery of any powerful and readily accessible means for generating new knowledge is certain to have widespread effects in many areas and at multiple levels of human affairs. The widespread practice of intuition will change the way in which society works and in which individuals live their lives, for we all spend much of our time and energy acquiring information, both factual and personal, and evolving it into understanding, knowledge and ultimately wisdom. Intuition stands today as the most powerful new means available for expanding human knowledge.

Knowledge is not the only ingredient of right living and a healthy planet, of course, but it is a primary and essential one. Since ancient times ignorance has stood as a major barrier to mankind's continuing evolution and well-being. Examples of the terrible consequences of ignorance are still around today for all to see. Other ingredients of right living—action, will, courage, commitment, compassion and service, for example—are equally essential, though all are stimulated and supported by the pursuit, achievement and application of relevant knowledge and understanding. Mankind's gradual progress over the millennia of history is solid testimony to the great value of continually increasing knowledge, as it is held individually by society's creators, sages and leaders, and then collectively by the general populace as "common knowledge." There is no law, man-made or cosmic, that forces us humans to remain ignorant of whatever we want to know and are able to handle responsibly. Life is saying: all knowledge is accessible, and all persons may possess it.

Intuition has already played a major part in this long trail of human development. Acknowledged or not, it has always supplied crucial information where and when it was needed, thence the rich knowledge that gradually evolved from it. It has provided mankind the vehicle for tuning into and accessing basic human principles from his superconscious source. It is here that we find the roots of the wisdom required to utilize effectively our other human qualities. As each of us learns to tap this vast knowledge resource, and to do so well, he opens his personal doorway to become a fulfilled human being—self-realized, self-actualized and self-responsible—and then to share his enhanced capabilities and skills with others.

The recent proliferation of technologies for replicating and exchanging information presages a "new age" of commonly shared knowledge among all the world's people. As our communication and computer systems improve in their coverage, capacity and ease of use, we can rightly say we are entering a historical era of "free and abundant information." Soon no one will be able to claim that he is denied access to the information he wants and needs to live his life as fully as he desires. Education especially will be a major recipient of this advance, since it rests so strongly upon self-empowerment of young minds through the acquisition of knowledge and the rich experiences it induces. Many societal problems will disappear as acceptable solutions emerge in areas now governed by the rampant ignorance that induces a self-centered perspective, possessiveness, isolation, resentment, foolish choices, antagonism and fear. These negative human qualities lead in turn to controversy, poorly motivated behavior and much suffering.

Changes in social values over the last few decades, as reported in recent studies, testify that this new realization is well on its way. We see a weakening public confidence in hierarchical institutions (government, business, religion, science, military, etc.) for dealing with society's greatest needs. We also see an increasing confidence in inner authority. There is now less reliance on material wealth as the preferred means of security, and more interest in a lifestyle governed by non-materialistic values and "voluntary simplicity." Notice, too, the lesser involvement with traditional religion, but a growing interest in first-hand spirituality. And don't forget the increasing and broader roles for women; a greater desire to engage in meaningful work as opposed to a routine job; and greater tolerance for ethnic, sexual and political differences (social diversity).[1] The recent popularity of books, classes and activities for gaining deeper understanding and inducing personal development shows that there is a new openness and expanding interest in the possibilities of "inner knowing" for personal purposes.

The experiences with intuition gained through the exploration reported in this book fit in well to help nudge open this gate to the future. They provide assurance that intuition is a useful human capacity, one having potential for direct practical application to benefit both individuals and society at large.

Applications of Intuition in Future Society

"There is within us a power that could lift the world out of its ignorance and misery if we only knew how to use it, if we would seek and find."

We have seen that intuition is most useful when it can serve as a source of fresh ideas, new perspectives, specific information or guidance/inspiration. By these means it can aid tasks such as the solution of problems, the making of decisions, the generation of understanding and the enhancement of creativity generally. Its broad capability makes it directly applicable to almost all human activities—individual and collective—but mainly those that depend strongly upon the *acquisition of knowledge and understanding* for their successful accomplishment. It will be valuable at this point to look at the particular knowledge based areas where intuition will have the most impact.

Science certainly stands at the top of this list, at least in the Western world. This is not because scientific knowledge is most important to mankind's development but because it has become so widely respected for its breadth, reliability, credibility and apparent relevance in a largely materialistic society. It constitutes the most extensive and self-consistent repository of consensual knowledge mankind has ever known. Indeed, the very purpose of science is to generate new knowledge and understanding, and it offers a powerful methodology for doing so. The boundary between what is known and what is not known is clearer in science than in any other knowledge domain. Science also provides a powerful means for validating information derived from other, non-scientific ways of obtaining new knowledge. We can expect that the various disciplines of science and its derived fields, despite their limitations in representing and explaining reality, will yield the most evident, impressive and impactful applications of intuition in the foreseeable future.

The "hard" and natural sciences, including mathematics, physics, chemistry, biology, astronomy, etc., provide abundant examples of unsolved problems, unresolved issues and recognized but unexplored topics of study, all amenable to intuitive investigation. Intuitive inquiry could aid physics, for example, by creating theories for explaining confusing experimental data and by generating ideas for new experiments. It might even be possible to untangle the seemingly complex relationships among the known fundamental particles, explain the confusing enigmas of quantum theory, resolve classical paradoxes and help to evolve the currently sought "theory of everything" that would unify gravity, nuclear and electromagnetic forces. Chemistry, biology and genetics are equally replete with important fundamental problems.

Intuition can contribute insights and the "gestalt" required for advances in even its most abstract disciplines such as mathematics, computer science and the more systematic aspects of philosophy. These areas are well known for their profundity and intellectual precision. They are best explored through the investigator's own intuition, rather than through expert intuitives, thereby bypassing language limitations.

Intuition can also help to resolve common meta-issues of science, those which are not readily decidable within science itself. For example:

- choosing which particular topics to investigate, out of various possibilities,
- identifying candidate approaches to pursue,
- anticipating the consequences when scientific discoveries are applied,
- zeroing in on ethical issues that may arise from application, and
- learning what else besides new knowledge is needed for successful application.

This last three items are a reminder that the introduction of intuition into scientific studies may often soften the hard, rational stance that science normally follows. It will force scientists to take into account relevant non-scientific issues that are easy to disregard. As noted earlier, an intuitive approach may also reveal new applications of existing scientific knowledge and create new viewpoints for interpreting past observations.

These capabilities of intuitive inquiry also extend to applied science: engineering, technology and many of the practical arts. Here the problems are determined by what is likely to be useful rather than the desire for knowledge and understanding (though the line between the two is not at all sharp). The challenges are therefore more pragmatic. These areas are especially needful of detailed information (facts) and must often take into account complex human requirements. The CAI experiments show that such details and complexities are available intuitively. At the same time practical results tend to be more easily verified direct applied than in the hard sciences. While these fields usually demand less inspiration and new perspectives (except for inventions) than scientific research, they require greater attention to the consequences, since applied work tends to arise out of expediency, contemporary pressures and short-term demands.

The implications of applied intuition can easily be imagined in the creation of future communication and information systems, energy sources and distribution, medicine (including its many subfields), agriculture and food technology, architecture, defense, transportation (including space flight) and the protection of natural resources. Advances are needed in all of these fields to ameliorate and eventually solve the well recognized and interdependent global problems: environmental destruction, poverty, sickness, overpopulation, political oppression and war (and other misuses of power), as well as their less tangible origins in greed, ignorance, prejudice, dishonesty, resentment, hate and lack of compassion generally.

Given the opportunity, the widespread practice of intuitive skills can contribute significantly to the creation of global understanding and cooperation, tolerance, prosperity, hope, freedom, sharing of resources, individual health and fulfillment and a healthy planet. It can help generate the individual self-understanding that leads to personal fulfillment, a posture of caring and responsibility for other individuals and for all mankind, and the motivation of love and service that fuels all beneficial activities.

The social sciences, liberal arts and humanities also have a role to play. These applications deal mainly with non-informational factors such as visioning, will, positive values and compassion, so they are less knowledge dependent. What is needed here is not so much factual information as a comprehension of the deeper and often complex issues that underlie and govern the more applied problem domains.

Philosophy, psychology and religion contain countless opportunities for worthwhile intuitive inquiry, primarily in the pursuit of new ideas and perspectives and the gradual winning of the deeper understanding. These areas impact education, public preferences, governance, law, public policies, commerce and political activities. Admittedly, some of the problematic topics in these fields are erudite, specialized and highly academic, so it is difficult to ask suitable questions and to corroborate the responses. At the same time, many of their aspects are just the opposite: they are fundamental to a common understanding and appreciation of how man may live on Earth peacefully, naturally and abundantly, as cells in the single body of humanity, with due respect for his creative origin and his role as a part of the Great Cosmic Design, however it might be seen. History, literature, anthropology, law, political science, education, linguistics and economic theory, along with their applied facets, all have a part in this endeavor. They benefit from the knowledge, perspectives and inspiration intuition provides.

Finally, we have the creative arts. These are not based on informational knowledge at all but are highly dependent on inspiration. The artist's own intuition enhances the inner (non-material) component of his creativity by revealing to him important hidden aspects of his own nature, and therefore human nature in general. This kind of inner perception has been demonstrated many times over by the world's most respected painters, musicians, writers, dancers and poets. These creators are also supported by others who provide new means and materials for manifesting and communicating their works. Apart from enhancing the artists' individual creativity, therefore, intuition can assist in developing new technologies for artistic expression, production and distribution—for example, new materials and media, computer and communication systems, mass replication devices and broadcast services.

Some Examples

We may appreciate the future implications of applied intuition better if we look at specific tasks to which intuitive information could be applied to assist in solving on-going and future knowledge-based problems. The number of possibilities is huge. The samples that follow are representative only, obviously not exhaustive and not necessarily the most important. They include efforts both large and small, theoretical and practical, specialized and of broader interest, and for use by either an individual or by society at large. They are grouped into fields, but many overlap two or more disciplines. A few (not distinguished) are best carried out through one's own intuitive practice rather than through expert intuitives.

- Economy, commerce and business: Work out the optimal distribution of national and global resources. Within a given company, determine the preferred markets, products and services, packaging, advertising, sales efforts and production methods. Screen present and new employees for suitability for the jobs to be filled. Explore new opportunities for research, expansion and diversification. Determine how better to serve the needs of employees. Predict the future market for a particular product or service.

- Environment: Find a practical way to remove heavy metals from ocean fish (and other toxic chemicals from water, soil, the atmosphere, factory smoke, auto exhaust, refuse, etc.). Anticipate future climate changes that will threaten agricultural areas of the globe. Determine an active means for replenishing the earth's ozone layer. Find a practical and safe way to locate and destroy buried land mines. Develop inexpensive biodegradable containers for food and other consumer products.

- Physics: Design an experiment that will detect gravity waves. Determine the nature of the "ether" and its properties. Discover the properties of zero-point energy and how to tap it as an energy source or means of communication. (See the accompanying text for more samples in physics.)

- Energy: Find a source of energy that is renewable, transportable, inexpensive, environmentally safe and not adaptable to lethal weaponry. Determine how better to contain a meltdown or other disaster in a nuclear reactor. Locate economical and environmentally safe resources of petroleum, (and minerals and other raw materials). Develop compact, rechargeable, efficient and environmentally safe batteries. Find a more efficient material for converting light into electricity (solar cells).

- Transportation: Check for dangers in an upcoming space flight. Design a practical, efficient and non-polluting engine for automobiles. Find new fibers and other materials that are strong and durable but flexible.

- Medicine and health: Understand the specific role of the mind in the spontaneous healing of cancer. Find a means for removing HIV from an infected body. Determine the key factors that cause aging and how to reverse them. Understand what one's own body needs to cure an illness and to maintain good health. Find a cure for cystic fibrosis (and countless other diseases).

- Agriculture, nutrition: Derive a new strain of wheat that can thrive at high altitudes. Anticipate the next famine in Africa. Discover a way to control a common crop infestation without upsetting the ecological balance. Work out a safe and effective way to destroy cocaine plants en masse. Learn how to grow, harvest and store food crops so as to preserve the freshness or "life force." Determine one's optimal personal diet, including the identification of foods to be avoided.

- Criminal investigation and justice: Identify particular offenders and where to find them. Locate missing evidence. Develop non-lethal "weapons" for apprehending criminals. Provide fair judgment in the court, in cases where evidence is insufficient or contradictory. Generate insights for resolving complex ethical issues that arise in creating and enforcing laws.

- Linguistics: Regenerate the Proto-Indo-European language. Assist in the interpretation of historic texts in ancient languages. Determine the relationship between language, thought and behavior. Determine how language evolves in the infant mind. Assist in making computer translation systems more accurate. Find a teaching method for very rapid language learning.

- Archeology, history: Locate lost documents that will reveal the history of the Etruscans. Locate a worthwhile exploration site for learning about pre-dynastic Egypt. (e.g., Imhotep's grave). Track down material evidence of man's migration from Asia to Alaska. Verify legends of an ancient civilization in the Gobi Desert, and where to find specific evidence of it. Assist archeological teams in determining where to dig and what will be found there.

- Religion: Provide insightful re-interpretations of classic religious writings. Work out how to strengthen the spiritual nucleus of Christianity (and other religions) so as to better support the universal individual search for meaning and understanding. Enrichen one's own religious experience through intuitive practice. Find out what happened to Jesus during the unreported years of his life (ages 12 to 30).

- Psychiatry, psychology, psychophysiology: Understand the function of dreaming within the human mind, and especially its daily necessity as an integration and healing process. Determine what allows and triggers spontaneous remission and self-healing of mental disorders. Discover how human memory (storage and recall) functions within the brain-mind system. Find a effective and safe drug for moderating the effects of schizophrenia. Determine a treatment regimen to cure a particular individual suffering from bipolar depression.

- Education: Develop a method to teach intuition development to young children.

- Consciousness Studies, Parapsychology:[2*] Find the "seat of consciousness" within the human body-mind system. Discover the "inner language" of the subconscious mind. Determine where non-physical energies (prana, qi, chakras, etc.) interface most closely with the physical body or brain. Determine the conditions necessary for physical objects to be teleported. Discover the mental process involved in channeling, how it works and its limitations.

Implications for the Individual

"By favour of the gods, I have, since my childhood, been attended by a semi-divine being whose voice from time to time dissuades me from some undertaking, but never directs me what I am to do. This

> prophetic voice has been heard by me throughout my life....Up to
> now the voice has never been wrong." [Socrates[3]]

We have already seen in Chapters 2, 3, 5 and 13 four examples of areas in which
intuition may directly benefit an individual. This "use" of intuition involves
the acquisition of both specific information to meet his particular needs, and
personal counsel to help him deal with broader matters: career and relationship challenges, emotional problems, expansion of sensitivity, improving self-
esteem, accelerating personal development and especially confronting
existential life issues. Since most of these problem areas are already well recognized in psychology, religion or philosophy, individual applications of intuition may build upon these fields as a basis for further and deeper inquiry.

Many personal benefits ensue directly from the *societal changes* predicted
above. That is, a wider public appreciation of intuition can be expected to
stimulate individual interest and confidence generally. It will encourage many
persons to undertake intuition development, understand their own intuition
better and eventually incorporate its practice into their relationships, employment and daily life. Those whose professional work brings them in contact
with the specific fields of application listed above will probably be the first to
be inspired to explore what intuition can do for them. The young will be especially stimulated as intuitive practice enters education.

At a more personal level, *intuitive counseling* will be able to play a significant
role in all aspects of the personal growth process. A qualified intuitive counselor can induce a significant acceleration, so long as the individual client
approaches the interaction with openness and a willingness to learn and grow.
This kind of counseling assists by bringing forth the key, missing information
needed for self-understanding, and doing it with sufficient sensitivity, depth
and compassion to render it acceptable and therefore useful. It is safe to say
that *anyone* can benefit from intuitive counseling as soon as he is ready for his
next stage of growth. Also, the best intuitive counsel carries with it a spiritual
quality ordinarily lacking in ordinary psychotherapy and psychiatry.

Many positive benefits follow from deliberately undertaking a program of
intuition development. They are coming to public attention ever more forcefully nowadays as the value of intuition is becoming better appreciated. Little
has been said in this book about personal intuition development. Information
is readily available in many publications and training programs. (See the
Appendix for a listing of some of these resources.) I can do no more here than

to cite the most salient benefits that can be expected to ensue, omitting explanations of how they actually come about.

First, a well developed intuition is an especially valuable asset as one works through the universal difficulties of *human relationships*: parent-child, couples, supervisor-employee, within families, cooperating teams, etc. For most persons this relationship area constitutes their main arena of personal development. Regular intuitive practice allows the participant in a relationship to understand better how his own role contributes to whatever issue is up for consideration and resolution at the moment. He can then understand more clearly the position of the other party. Obviously, more is involved than intuitive knowing, but a strongly functioning intuition can provide the key increment of missing knowledge needed to break through the emotional barrier.

Second, and closely related, any serious effort toward enhancing one's intuition automatically reveals the *emotionally based barriers* that are blocking its manifestation. These barriers are the same ones that block all aspects of living a full, satisfying life. Intuition alone is not enough to eradicate them, for the barriers weaken the very perception, understanding and acceptance needed to resolve them. Nor is an intellectual approach to removing them going to work. Most essential is a certain inner release process, involving a different part of the mind: a partnership of will and awareness, or intention and attention. Intuition plays a strong supportive role in this release, especially during the calmer moments after emotionally dominated periods. These are times when the pain of active involvement with the problematic issue can still be remembered, so there is a stronger than usual motivation for self-examination, confrontation with the barrier and correction of the problematic condition. This is just the time to seek for answers and inspiration from a different source. An actively working intuition, whatever might be its stage of development, provides access to that source. Conversely, each step of melting out these emotional barriers improves one's intuition.

Third, apart from the issues and problems of relationships and emotional growth, intuition has a major role to play in the act of *maintaining continual self-awareness* during one's daily life. We can all become more effective at our activities, and more satisfied with their consequences, if we remain conscious and attentive of what we are doing and thinking as we go about our daily tasks. This attitude is responsive but not reactive. Thoughts and actions are then performed deliberately, with full heart and mind, and with a sense of the purpose for which they are being done. Perfection is not necessary, for gradual effort generates gradual improvements. A working intuition aids this process, and again, such a highly aware state of mind aids intuitive proficiency.

A direct consequence of this kind of personal intuitive effort has practical applications and implications in helping to resolve life's typical problems, for example, which job to take and which career to follow, whether and whom to marry, whom to trust, how to deal with difficult family members (adolescents, elderly, parents-in-law, etc.), neighbors and coworkers, health issues, money issues, personal challenges (one's own anger, jealousy, resentfulness, greed, fear, etc.). These include real-life issues such as the scenarios of movies and fiction are made: love triangles, the mother whose son is on drugs, the pregnant teenager, choices between evils, the abusive husband, the unfaithful wife, the children of divorce, standing up to malicious authority, lying to save someone's life, etc. Certain life-death issues such as abortion, euthanasia and life prolongation, for which no simple solutions exist at a social level, can also be resolved personally through reliance on one's own intuition.

Beyond Knowledge

*"Intuition is a comprehensive grip of the principle of universality, and when it is functioning there is, momentarily at least, a complete loss of the sense of separateness." [Alice Bailey[4]]

Most of this book has focused on the use of intuition to obtain *information* that can be applied toward the build-up of understanding, knowledge and eventually wisdom. Such an acquisition is certainly a legitimate and worthy undertaking, even though it is only a stage and a means, not the end of the seeker's path. In fact, it is easy for some persons to become caught up in the pursuit of knowledge as a temporary fascination, an apparent but illusory shortcut or a diversion. Some may use it as a means of wielding influence over others through the power that knowledge carries—while forgetting that knowledge alone can never provide true satisfaction and fulfillment.

Actually, *the most significant aspects of intuition have little to do with the accumulation of knowledge.* In the preceding chapters we touched on this facet without pausing to explore it. We should examine it briefly now as an acknowledgment of intuition's greater value besides just making us smarter.

The first of these realms of "beyond knowledge" is the role intuition plays in releasing and expanding one's deepest capacities, intuitive as well as others, in the cause of what is variously called inner growth, spiritual development and sometimes "soul growth." This particular "application" of intuition was mentioned earlier in the discussion of intuitive counseling (Chapter 3), in the previous section and elsewhere as a concomitant of intuition development. The target of personal growth is the deep aspect of the Self (suitably defined), rather than the more visible personality and one's behavior and the thoughts that are associated with them. The purpose of personal growth is the enlargement and refinement of this deeper Self. It takes place through an awareness and acceptance of its natural and fundamental place in one's total existence. This Self is not an abstract, functional and obscure component of the mind, as (for example) reasoning, imagination and conscience tend to be. Instead, it is the very essence and prime part of your being. You do not "possess" a deeper Self. It *is* yourself, and more truly *you* than what your thinking mind thinks you are, even though your on-going awareness of this Self may be fuzzy, fleeting and limited.

To embrace this Self is to "wake up" to your true nature. For most persons this awakening occurs very gradually, throughout a lifetime, largely outside of awareness. That is, it takes place almost entirely within the unconscious mind, and there is little or no deliberate effort, with only occasional flashes of insight and a great deal of resistance to it. This need not be so. One may awaken from this dream at any time by stimulating and feeding it with conscious attention and intention. The working process for this awakening is *self-inquiry*. The goal is *self-understanding*. The final result is variously called *self-realization*, self-actualization or enlightenment.

Those most qualified to teach us about these matters agree that the path of inner growth is the only path there is, the only game in town. Steps along the path may be postponed, denied or neglected, but it is in the nature of human life that they are unavoidable. Most persons opt for this slow, painful course before finally accepting an opportunity to step out of it. As the years go by, and as one continues to reject the changes in consciousness being urged upon him, the pains of procrastination and inattention gradually mount, arising naturally out of his unawareness, insensitivity and ignorance. If no life changes are undertaken intentionally, then the resulting suffering increases, and eventually becomes overwhelming through disorientation, confusion, physical disabilities and depression. Life seems to be a series of random, meaningless events, with the individual a helpless victim of what appear to be external influences and circumstances.

The key invitation life offers each one of us is *to acknowledge and become fully aware of being on this path of growth, and to accept life as a sequence of corrective lessons for enabling and encouraging this growth.* We are asked to proactively and cooperatively participate in the experiences that the process offers us, with the confidence that, whatever they are, they are exactly the right "lessons" we need for our next step. We have "chosen" them at some deep level of our being as an expression of our personal pattern of deficiencies and incompletenesses. The choice to accept or reject this grand invitation is a fundamental, critical and existential one. It is profound because so much depends on this single decision.

When the path is accepted, the effects come forward naturally and gracefully. They automatically generate a strong sense of purpose, which translate into specific objectives and goals for successive stages of development. Awareness of this purpose provides the main mind-tool for making wise choices, large and small, since a basis for decision is now at hand. It also facilitates the solution of problems, also large and small. Since learning has become the order of the day, it accelerates through experience, an acceptance of one's errors (past and present) without guilt or remorse, and a similar toleration of the errors of others without blame or resentment. Each event and situation is seen as a self-selected opportunity for growth, not a misfortune to be undergone as a result of bad luck or "fate." Your sense of duty emerges from within, not without, so every externally begrudged "I must" becomes a consciously chosen and joyful "I want."

As self-understanding improves in these ways, the fantastic design behind your entire life experience also becomes clearer. "Understand yourself and you understand everything else," say our wisest teachers. This realization covers the common mysteries of suffering (your own and others', local and global); the rhyme and reason behind your birth, illnesses and death; why the world (natural and societal) is the way it is; the surprising "chance" meetings with certain other persons. Continual growth and change, not stability and security, become the order of the day. The dynamism and "nowness" of daily life makes it much easier to let go of past associations, worn-out beliefs and habits, and even relationships when they are no longer relevant to what is happening in the present. This letting-go also applies to the host of fear-based emotions that have taken root in imagined, unreal futures, and that are so limiting.

With these releases you may then see your entire life in clearer perspective, appreciate the progress you have made so far, and even begin to glimpse portions of your future. You can also live with a strong feeling of bonding with all of life, growing ever closer to your creative origin.

The Intuition Gateway

> "The greatest insight, thought and art concerning the human condition and its divine aspirations are rooted in the phenomenon of inner vision."
> [José and Miriam Arguelles[5]]

Intuition has such a central place in this development because it is the human mind's communicative faculty that links the outer self with the inner self, the conscious mind with the unconscious, the known with the not-yet-known. An active intuition permits between these largely disparate parts of the mind. Once your intuition is developed it allows the crucial internal dialog to take place between your conscious mind and the rich knowledge in your superconscious, which is so wisely assisting your growth. This deeper essence is what enables awareness and acceptance in the first place, followed by the emergence of crucial information, then knowledge, then understanding—all of which enable the consequences just cited.

Intuition is your open gateway to the mysteries of the Universe, your personal means of eventual liberation from the limiting bonds of ignorance, attachment, suffering and limited compassion. This wonderful capacity, which you already possess naturally and which enables so many of the abilities and skills you may develop from it, is by far your best ally as you enact your role in the great drama of life.

Intuition therefore works at its best when it is allowed to operate at this intimate level of personal enhancement, rather than serving only as a source of factual information. It also works better when you are able to rely upon your own intuition rather than upon that of an expert intuitive—that is, when you can become your own expert. This is mainly because you are then free to pose deep questions and receive new ideas and answers without having to rely so heavily on the descriptive languages of ordinary interpersonal communication. Of course, before you reach this point you may take valuable counsel from expert intuitives, for they can be important aids in your intuition development and are always ready to help.

Finally, acceptance of the spiritual path and recognition of the broad purpose of your life also leads toward valuable character traits and personal qualities that follow naturally from the inner rewards sketched above. These include self-confidence, integrity and personal power; moral strength; insight, true intelligence, keen judgment and wisdom; acceptance, patience and gratitude; fearlessness; trust and the ability to forgive; self-responsibility; tolerance, openness and broad-mindedness; total responsibility for your life; and indeed, the capacity to love and be loved, that root quality that interacts with and enables all the others.

This list of personal qualities that emerge from the serious personal development of intuition surely sounds like the promises of an over-zealous revival preacher or a campaigning politician. In this case, though, the rewards are real and the offer is genuine. They are well-proven and guaranteed by the experiences of many others who have followed the intuitive path toward self-discovery.

The Ultimate Intuitive Experience

"This [intuition] is absolute knowledge founded on the identity of
the mind with the object known." [Plotinus]

We have only scratched the surface here on what intuition offers to an individual as he moves through this waking-up into a much larger domain, this deeper experience of his existence. Past the level of self-development described above, there is a further stage of intuitive experience consisting of a profound perception and experience of both human nature and the natural world, even the entire universe and what has been called "ultimate reality." It is difficult to describe and understand this inward path well through explanation alone, but is too important to neglect, so we must try.

I am speaking now of a kind of individual intuitive experience that lies well beyond ordinary knowledge and even beyond wisdom as commonly thought of. It is a grand extension of ordinary perception in that whatever is perceived (and there appears to be no limit at all) is not objectified as being "out there," amenable to observation and description, but is sensed as if it is inside the seeker himself and is part of his own being. This is the kind of intuitive inquiry in which *the conscious mind accesses the superconscious directly*, bypassing the subconscious almost entirely. Such acquisition is subjective and intimate, outside the limitations normally imposed by sense modalities, preexisting concepts, verbal structures and knowledge frameworks.

What is this deep intuitive place like? Sorry, there are no maps. Even the most lucid descriptions fall pitifully short of clarity, simply because ordinary objective language is too feeble a vehicle to hold them. While some (perhaps many) expert intuitives and enlightened masters have been there, they cannot tell us much about their adventure of exploration. We can speak here only of a few of its features, as reported by them and by various other explorers of the mind who trained themselves to perform

Life talks to me in my sleep, and also during meditation and in the state just following meditation. It tells me what I need to know about myself, often anticipating conscious awareness of what is missing, or assisting a conscious formulation of what I would like to know. It's way ahead of my thinking mind, both in the scope of what is important in my life and in a depth of understanding appropriate to my particular issues and questions. I can't imagine living without this kind of ready assistance.

Where is it coming from? I don't know. But I know I am not the only one who hears these kinds of signals, so I assume that we all share this same source and this same capacity, at least in some overlapping way. Some say this inspiration comes from their "guide." That's OK, though I find no need to personalize it, except perhaps through the wisdom and compassion exhibited by our best examples of humanness. Others call it "God." I have no argument with this interpretation either, while noting that my God is only rarely the same as others' Gods. Still others attempt to explain it in psychological, philosophical, scientific or mystical terms. These efforts seem worthy enough, although I find them unsatisfying as are almost all attempts at descriptions and explanations of my own experience

I can only say, this inner source feels like a very deep part of me, not something I am observing and have the right to talk about. My capabilities to commune with seem primitive and paltry, miles away from true enlightenment, whatever that is. I know I have hardly begun to tap what is there for me.

The most important thing, though, is that it is there, it is always accessible, and the illumination, protection, wisdom and love it provides is exactly relevant to my needs.

such unusual access.[3] (Actually, a few found themselves there inadvertently.)

First, this "place" is said to be the center where everything in the universe is accessible to the exploring mind. It is as if all space collapses into a single point. Time too shrinks into a single moment, so that every event is equally and immediately present. What is experienced, therefore, depends only on where the inquiring mind places its attention. Without a focus there is only chaos, confusion and perhaps overwhelm (as may happen in a dream), but with appropriate intention, applied consciously or unconsciously, then whatever is desired is immediately at hand—and not just as information or knowledge but as *direct experience* (again, as in a vivid dream).

Second, even with strong intention this exploration may be challenging because what the explorer experiences is so much shaped by the beliefs, incompletenesses, insensitivities and insecurities he brings with him. Whichever of these shortcomings have not already been worked through and resolved attract a dose of material appropriate to their resolution. The spaceless, timeless center at which these experiences occur may be protective and compassionate, as is usually described, but it does not allow a full experience when the mind of the inquirer is not prepared to undergo it. Cleaning out these shortcomings is therefore an important and essential part of the preparation for such exploration. Such cleansing is exactly what one does in intuition development, and in fact it is what the entire life process is about, as sketched above.

Third, the reports of these explorers show that they were able to experience, first of all, the natural world far beyond the limited ranges and sensitivities of the senses. They speak of "hearing" music with a richness exceeding the normal range of tones and qualities, as well as inner visions the human eye could never see. Sometimes the various sensual impressions merge together (synesthesia). They say they have immersed themselves in the whirling of electrons in atoms, and can "watch" in a single glimpse entire solar systems in their galaxies. They experience directly the nucleotides within the spirals of the DNA helix, the 100-billion-cell nerve network in the brain, and the tight social network of six billion humans on planet Earth, all in a single comprehension. Space and time are expanded or compressed to fit the experience, so each of these events is seen as a single unity, all at once, not as separate parts. No wonder they cannot explain in detail what they experience!

The experience is even more profound when it is focused on a chosen human being. Body, mind and soul are perceived fully and compassionately, with sudden and complete understanding, including the manifold psychospiritual aspects. When there is an intention to heal, the necessary background information and relevant counsel emerge spontaneously, just as occurs in intuitive counseling but much more so.

Not every explorer reports all of these kinds of experiences, of course, but the overlap is sufficient to provide substantial agreement and validate the perceptions as a common experience, not just individual fantasy (which would be amazing enough).

The fact that a handful of explorers have accomplished these feats of experiential perception show that they are humanly possible. Since most of them were attained deliberately, with committed effort, it is very likely that other persons can attained them too. The record suggests that they are be accessible to everyone as an expanded version of the kind of intuitive inquiry reported in the preceding chapters. The possibilities for growing new knowledge and achieving very deep understanding through this deeper level are truly staggering!

There remain many important questions. For example, what enhancement of intuition development is necessary if one wishes to explore through such deep inquiry? Are the four conditions stated (harmlessness, etc.) still sufficient, or do they need to be refined and extended for this new level? What are the limitations of this form of inquiry? How can the explorer's discoveries be effectively communicated to others? (This last challenge may turn out to the greatest obstacle.)

Still further, we may ask what is happening to the explorer himself as he probes these profound mysteries? If the experiments reported in this book are any guide at all, they are saying that he enters into a space of self-knowing that is so greatly expanded that he transcends his own prior limits of self-knowledge. This is the state described as *self-realization, nirvana, or enlightenment* in the esoteric traditions of ancient cultures throughout the world, and well preserved even today. While this state lies well beyond full description, they agree that it involves a shift of identity from the ordinary ego self (that which is transcended) to the realization of and identification with a higher or deeper Self, which may rightly be thought of as the Absolute, or "All That Is," or God. The new sense of Self, they say, is experienced as a unity with everything that exists, where we are truly "All One." It also reveals the purpose, process and perfection of this unified existence, this greatly expanded notion of "life." It also explains the fairness behind human suffering, among other classic mysteries that are revealed.

To achieve this realized state is said to be the destination of the universal path we are all called upon to follow, whether we realize it or not. It shows itself as the universal longing to return Home, at any price, but this will be allowed only when we are fully ready. It is the only effort required of man, and there is truly nothing else worth doing. This is not a moral prescription for a virtuous life or a dogmatic declaration of externally imposed duty, but a self-created destiny. Indeed, each one of us, at the deepest core of his being, chose at one time to undertake this long journey, and even participated in creating the Grand Rules of Life by which the game was to be played. We have almost forgotten this now, but we can begin to remember it again—with the help of our intuition.

> "The great world is inside. This [outer] world, which looks so huge and magnificent, is the microcosm. The macrocosm is our inner life. It just reverses science."
> [Coleman Barks[6]]

• Endnotes—Chapter 15

[1] Shakespeare, 1906, pp. 870-907.

[2*] Such studies might well include the role that intuition plays in scientific, psychological and even parapsychological experiments. For example, is double-blindedness assured when both experimenters and subjects can anticipate an outcome intuitively? Are scientific experiments that employ prediction as proof compromised, when intuitives can foresee the outcome? Does a researcher's unrecognized intuitive ability compromise the way his experiments turn out?

[3] Xenophon, 1907.

[4] Bailey, Alice,...10-2/5

[5] Arguelles, 1972.

[6] Barks, 1997.

BIBLIOGRAPHY

Note: The sources of some of the quotations included in the text are cited only by author, without page number: ACIM (Anon6), Rumi (Barks, 1995, Barks & Green, 1997), Emmanuel (Rodegast & Stanton, 1985, 1991)), Seth (Roberts, 1970, 1972, 1988), Sanaya Roman (Roman, 1986, 1987) and Tao Te Ching (Lao Tse, 1972).]

* Abrahamsen, Aron, *On Wings of Spirit* (Virginia Beach: ARE Press, 1993).
* Adamo, R, C., & F. Enns, "Study of Atmospheric Electrical Processes and of their Association with Earthquakes," Final Report, Project 8063, SRI International, 1981; for US Geological Survey.
* Agor, Weston H., "The Logic of Intuition: How Executives make Important Decisions," Organizational Dynamics, (Winter 1986).
* Agor, Weston, *Intuition in Organizations* (Newbury, Park, CA: Sage Publishing, 1989).
* Akiskal et al, "Re-evaluating the prevalence of and diagnostic composition within the broad clinical spectrum of bipolar disorders" (Review), Journal of Affective Disorders. Vol. 59 Suppl., No.1, pp.S5-S30 (Sep. 2000).
* Albright, W. F., *The Vocalization of Egyptian Syllabic Orthography* (New Haven: American Oriental Society, 1934).
* Aldred, Cyril, *Akhenaten, King of Egypt* (Thames and Hudson 1988).
* Aldred, Cyril, *Akhnaten and Nefertiti* (Viking, 1973).
* Anon1, "Radio 'Signals Before Quakes?" Science News, vol. 121, p. 200 (1980).
* Anon2, *The Urantia Book* (Chicago: The Urantia Foundation, 1955, 1981).
* Anon3, *New Directions in Education: Selections from Holistic Education Review* (Brandon, VT: Holistic Education Press, 1991).
* Anon4, The Irish Times, 28 Nov. 1991 and 22 February 1993.
* Anon5, "Tangshan: Portrait of a Catastrophe," Science News, Vol. 111, p. 388 (1976).
* Anon6, *A Course in Miracles* (three volumes in one), (Tiburon, CA: Foundation for Inner Peace, 1982).
* Arguelles, José and Miriam, *Mandala* (Berkeley: Shambala, 1972).
* Armstrong, Thomas, *In Their Own Way* (Tarcher, 1988).

* Assagiolli, Robert, *Psychosynthesis* (Hobbs Dohrman, 1965).
* Atwater, F. Holmes, *Captain of My Ship, Master of My Soul* (Hampton Roads, 2001).
* Bailey, Alice A. *From Bethlehem to Calvary* (Lucis Publishing Co., 1937).
* Bailey, Alice, *From Intellect to Intuition* (Lucis Publishing Co., 1932).
* Bakirov, A. G., "The Geological Possibilites of the Biophysical Method" in The American Dowser (August 1974,) pp. 110-112.
* Barakat, N., L. Dolphin et al., "Electromagnetic Sounder Experiments at the Pyramids of Giza," Final Report, NSF Grant No. GF-38767, (Menlo Park, CA: Stanford Research Institute, 1975).
* Barks, Coleman, *The Essential Rumi* (Castle Books, 1997).
* Barks, Coleman, and Michael Green, *The Illuminated Rumi* (Broadway Books, 1997).
* Beckwith, J. B., "The Sudden Infant Death Syndrome," Current Problems in Pediatrics, Vol. 3, p. 3-36 (1973).
* Bennett, E. A., *What Jung Really Said* (New York: Schocken Books, 1967).
* Berger, Arthur S., & Joyce Berger, *Encyclopedia of parapsychology and psychical research*, (New York: Paragon House, 1991).
* Berk, M., et al., "Emerging options in the treatment of bipolar disorders," Drugs, Vol. 61, No. 10, pp.1407-1414 (2001).
* Bernstein, Morey, *The Search for Bridey Murphy* (Doubleday, 1956).
* Bird, Christopher, *The Divining Hand* (Dutton & Co., 1979).
* Bird, J. M., *Plate Tectonics, Selected Papers from the Journal of Geophysical Research* (Washington, DC: The American Geophysical Union, 1972).
* Blackburn, Gabrielle, *The Science and Art of the Pendulum: A Complete Course in Radeisthesia* (Ojai, CA: Idylwild Books, 1983).
* Bland, R, "Epidemiology of Affective Disorders: A Review", Canadian Journal of Psychiatry, Vol. 42, No. 4, pp. 367-77 (May 1997).
* Bockris, J. O'M, G. H. Lin and R. T. Bush, "The Rediscovery of Cold Nuclear Reactions," Fusion Facts, Vol. 7, No. 11, pp. 1-5 (May 1996).
* Bolt, B.A., *Nuclear Explosions and Earthquakes: The Parted Veil* (San Francisco: Freeman & Co., 1976).
* Bolt, Bruce A., *Earthquakes: A Primer* (W.H. Freeman, 1978, 1993).
* Bond, F. B., *The Gate of Remembrance: The Story of the Psychological Experiment which Resulted in the Discovery of the Edgar Chapel at Glastonbury*, 2nd Ed'n (Blackwells, 1918).
* Bozzano, E., *Polyglot Mediumship (Xenoglossy)* (Rider, 1932); translated from the Italian edition.
* Breasted, J. H., *A History of Egypt* (Scribners & Sons, 1933).
* Bronowski, J., *The Ascent of Man* (Little-Brown & Co. 1973).

* Bronson, Matthew, "The Voice of the 'Other'—Linguists Consider Channeling," New Eyes (CAI), Vol. 4, pp. 3-6 (Fall 1988).

* Brooke, Hazel, et al, "Case Control of a Study of Sudden Infant Death Syndrome in Scotland, 1992-95," British Medical Journal, Vol. 314, p.1516ff (May 24, 1997).

* Broomfield, John, *Other Ways of Knowing* (Inner Traditions, 1997).

* Brown, David F., "Consciousness in Business," New Realities, Vol. 1, No. 3, p. 17 (1977).

* Brown, F.S., "Persistent Activity Rhythms in the Oyster," Amer. Jl. Of Physiology, Vol. 178, pp. 510-514 (1954).

* Brown, F.S., "Living Clocks," Science, Vol. 130, pp. 1534-1544 (1959).

* Brown, G.M., M. Steiner, and P. Grof. "Neuroendocrinology of Affective Disorder," in Anonymous, pp. 461-474 (1995).

* Brunton, Paul, *A Search in Secret India* (York Beach, ME: Red Wheel, 1984).

* Bucke, .R., *Cosmic Consciousness* (Dutton, 1969; original 1901).

* Budge, E. A. Wallis, *The Gods of the Egyptians* (Methuen, 1904; Dover, 1969).

* Burr, H.S., *Blueprint for Immortality* (London: Neville Spearman, 1972).

* Buskirk, R. E., D. Frohlich & G. V. Latham, "Unusual Animal Behavior Before Earthquakes: A Review of Possible Sensory Mechanisms," Rev. Geophys. and Space Physics, Vol. 19, No. 2, pp. 247-270 (1981).

* Bynum, C. & R. Bell, *Holy Feast and Holy Fast* (Univ. of Calif. Press, 1987).

* Calais, Eric, & Bernard Minster, "GPS Detection of Ionospheric Perturbations Following the January 17, 1994 Northridge Earthquake," Geophys. Res. Ltrs., Vol. 22, No. 9, pp. 1045-48 (May 1, 1995).

* Caldwell, Taylor, *I, Judas* (Atheneum, 1977).

* Campbell, D.E., and J.L. Beets, "Lunacy and the Moon," Psychological Bulletin, Vol. 85, pp. 1123-1129 (1978).

* Capra, Fritjof, *The Tao of Physics* (Berkeley: Shabala, 1975).

* Carroll, Lewis, *Alice in Wonderland* (Henry Altemus Co.,1905; Grosset & Dunlap, 1946).

* Carter, Howard, and A. C. Mace, *The Tomb of Tutankhamen* (3 vols.) (Cassell,1930-33).

* Cayce, E.E. & H.L. Cayce, *The Outer Limits of Edgar Cayce's Power* (Harper & Row, 1971).

* Cayce, Edgar, *On Atlantis* (Warner Books, 1999).

* Cayce, Evans Edgar, *Edgar Cayce On Atlantis* (Paperback Library, 1968).

* Chacon, M. A., and J. T. Tildon, "Elevated Values of Tri-iodothyrodine in Victims of Sudden Infant Death Syndrome," Journal of Pediatrics, Vol. 99, No. 5, pp. 758-760 (1981).

* Chamberlain, David B., *Babies Remember Birth and Other Extraordinary Scientific Discoveries About the Mind and Personality of Your Newborn* (Ballantine Books, 1988).
* Childs, Christopher, "Deep Seeing: Guiding Activism Through Grace," in Noetic Sciences Review, Vol. 44, pp. 18ff (1997).
* Chödrön, Pema, *The Wisdom of No Escape* (Shambala, 1991).
* Chödrön, Pema, & bell hooks, "Beyond Right or Wrong: A Conversation between Pema Chödrön and bell hooks," The Sun, No. 258, pp. 11-14 (June 1997); originally in Shambala Sun.
* Chopra, Deepak, *Ageless Body, Timeless Mind* (Harmony Books, 1993).
* Codrescu, Andrei, "Disappearance of the Outside," What Is Enlightenment, No. 12, p. 61 (Fall/Winter 1997).
* Coe, Michael, *Breaking lthe Maya Code* (Thames and Hudson, 1992).
* Cone, Polly, *Wonderful Things: The Discovery of Tutankhamun's Tomb*, NY Metropolitan Museum of Art (Acorn Books, 1976).
* Cook, James, "Closing the Psychic Gap," Forbes, Vol. 133, No. 12, pp. 90-95 (1984).
* Cooke, D.J., & E.M. Coles, "The Concept of Lunacy: A Review," Psychological Reports, Vol. 42, pp.. 891-897 (1978).
* Crystal, David., *The Cambridge Encyclopedia of Language,* 2nd Ed'n (Cambridge Univ. Press, 1997).
* Cummins, Geraldine, *The Childhood of Jesus* (London: Psychic Press, 1937
* Cummins, Geraldine, *The Manhood of Jesus*, Parts I & II (London: Psychic Press, 1949).
* Cutler, W.B., "Lunar and Menstrual Phase Locking," Cas. Lek. Cesk., Vol. 133, No. 4, pp. 103-110 (Feb. 1994).
* Czermak, W., *Die Laute der Aegyptischen Sprache* (Wien: Arbeitsgemeinschaft der Aegyptologen und Afrikanisten in Wien, 1931).
* Darwin, C. H., *The Tides* (W. H. Freeman & Co., 1962).
* Davies, K., & D. M. Baker, "Ionospheric Effects Observed Around the Time of the Alaskan Earthquake of March 28, 1964," Jl. of Geophys. Research, vol. 70, No. 9, pp. 2251-53 (1965).
* Davison, C., "Luminous Phenomena of Earthquakes," Discovery, Vol. 18, pp. 278-279 (1937).
* Dean, E. Douglas & John Mihalasky, Psychic, Vol. 6, No. 1, pp. 21-25 (1974).
* Dean, Geoffrey, *Recent Advances in Natal Astrology: A Critical Review, 1900-1976* (Rockport, MA: Para Research, 1977).
* Deikman, A., "Intuition," in Palmer, Helen, Ed., *Inner Knowing: Consciousness Creativity, Insight and Intuition* (Tarcher/Putnam, 1998).

* DelBello, M.P., &, B. Geller, "Review of studies of child and adolescent offspring of bipolar parents," <u>Bipolar Disorders,</u> Vol. 3, No. 6, pp. 325-334 (Dec. 2001).
* Derr, J. S., "Earthquake Lights: A Review of Observations and Present Theories," <u>Bull. Seis. Soc. Amer.</u>, Vol. 63, No. 6, pp. 2177-2187 (1973).
* Dogen Zenji, "Shobogenzo," in Kennet, J., *Selling Water by the River* (Vintage Books, 1972).
* Dolphin, L., et al., "Applications of Modern Sensing Techniques to Egyptology," Final Report, NSF Grant No. INT76-00414, (Menlo Park, CA: Stanford Research Institute, 1978).
* Dolphin. L., "Geophysical Studies around the Sphinx," private report (1978); see www.ldolphin.org.
* Dormion, P. & J.P. Goidin, *Khéops: Nouvelle enquette*, and *Les nouveaux mystéres de la Grande Pyramide* (Paris, 1987).
* Dowling, Levi H., *The Aquarian Gospel* (DeVorss & Co., 1972; orig. 1907).
* Drury, Allen *A God Against The Gods* (Doubleday, 1976).
* Duffy, A., et al., "Measures of attention and hyperactivity symptoms in a high-risk sample of children of bipolar parents," <u>Journal of Affective Disorders</u>, Vol. 67, Nos. 1-3, pp.159-165 (Dec. 2001).
* Durrell, Lawrence, *The Alexandria Quartet: Clea*(Penguin, 1960).
* Earthquake Research Group, Academia Sinica, "Some Characteristics of Animal Behavior Prior to Earthquakes," <u>Proceedings, International Symposium on Earthquake Prediction, 1979</u> (Paris: UNESCO, 1980).
* Eastman, Dale, "Dr. Coates on Risky Sex," <u>San Francico Magazine</u>, Feb. 2001.
* Emerson, J. Norman, "Intuitive Archeology: A Psychic Approach" in <u>New Horizons</u>, Vol. 1, No.. 3, p. 18 (1974a).
* Emerson, J. Norman, "Intuitive Archeology: The Argillite Carving" and "Intuitive Archeology: A Developing Approach," Department of Anthropology, University of Toronto, 1974b.
* Emerson, J. Norman, "Psychic Archeology," in <u>Psychic</u>, pp.23-25 (Sep./Oct. 1975).
* Erman, A., *Life in Ancient Egypt* (Dover, 1971).
* Esmael.,F., ed., *Proceedings of the First Interntional Symposium on the Application of Modern Technology to Archeological Explorations of the Giza Necropolis* (Cairo, 1988).
* Evernden, J. F., Ed., *Abnormal Animal Behavior Prior to Earthquakes,* Conference Proceedings (Menlo Park, CA: US Geological Survey, 1976).
* Eysenck, H.J., & D.K.B. Nias, *Astrology: Science of Superstition* (Penguin, 1984).

* Feuerstein, Georg, "Consciousness, Spirituality and Noetic Science," in <u>Intuition</u>, No. 4, pp. 20-25+(1994).
* Feuerstein, Georg, "Intuition in the Boardroom: An Interview with Charles Nunn," <u>Science of Mind</u> pp. 34-42+(August 1993).
* Feild, Reshad *Steps to Freedom : Discourses on the Alchemy of the Heart* (Watsonville, CA, U.S.A. Threshold Books 1983).
* Fleischmann, M., S. Pons & M. Hawkins, "Electrochemically Induced Nuclear Fusion of Deuterium," <u>Jl. of Electroanal. Chem.</u>, Vol. 261, pp. 301-308 (1989); erratum, Vol. 263, p. 187.
* Flournoy, Theodore, *From India to the Planet Mars: A Case Study of Somnabulism with Glossolalia* (University Books, 1963); translated from the French original (1900).
* Foucart, G., "Imhotep," <u>Revue de l'Histoire des Religions</u>, Vol. 48, p. 362 (1903).
* Franquemont, Sharon, *You Already Know What To Do* (Tarcher, 1999).
* Fraser-Smith, Anthony C., et al., "Low-frequency magnetic field measurements near the epicenter of the M 7.1 Loma Prieta Earthquake," <u>Geophysical Research Letters</u>,Vol. 17, pp. 1465-68 (1990).
* Friedlander, S., and E. Shaw, "Psychogenic Factors in Sudden Infant Death Syndrome: Some Dynamic Speculations," <u>Clinical Social Work Jl.</u>, Vol. 3, pp. 237-278 (Winter 1975).
* Friedman, Milton, "Intuitives in Washington," <u>Intuition</u>, No. 7, pp. 21-27 (1995).
* Gadamer, Hans-Georg, *Philosophical Hermeneutics*, trans. by David Linge (Univ. California Press, 1976).
* Gardiner, A. H., *Egypt of the Phaoros: An Introduction* (Oxford, 1962).
* Gardiner, A. H., *Egyptian Grammar* (Oxford Univ. Press, 1957).
* Gauquelin, M., reported in Dean, 1977).
* Gauthier, H., "Un nouveau monument de dieu Imhotep," <u>Bulletin de l'Institute Francais d'Archeologie</u>, Vol. 14 (1918).
* Geller, R., "Earthquake Prediction: A Critical Review," <u>Geophys. J. Int.</u>, Vol.131 (1997), pp. 425-450.
* Geller, Uri, & G. L. Playfair, *The Geller Effect* (Henry Holt, 1986).
* Ghiselin, B., *The Creative Process* (New American Library, 1952); originally, *La Raisonment Mathematique* (Paris: Ernest Flammarion, 1908).
* Gibran, Kahlil, *The Prophet* (Knopf, 1951).
* Giles, F. J., *Ikhnaton: Legend and History* (Farleigh Dickinson University Press, 1972).

* Glass, Philip, & Robert T. Jones, *Music by Philip Glass* (Harper & Row, 1987), and Glass, Philip, *Akhnaten: An Opera In Three Acts, Libretto* (Pennsylvania: Dunvagen Music, 1984).
* Gold, Thomas, The Deep Earth Gas, lectures given at Univ. of Sydney, Australia (1979).
* Goldberg, Philip, *The Intuitive Edge: Understanding Intuition and Applying It in Everyday Life* (Tarcher, 1983).
* Goodlad, John I., *A Place Called School: Prospects for the Future* (McGraw Hill, 1984).
* Goodman, Jeffrey, *Psychic Archeology* (G. P. Putnam, 1977).
* Govinda, Lama, *Foundations of Tibetan Mysticism* (Samuel Weiser, 1969).
* Grant, Joan, *Far Memory* (Avon Books, 1969).
* Grof, Christina, & Stanislav Grof, *The Stormy Search for Self* (Tarcher, 1990).
* Grof, P., "Mood disorders—new definitions, treatment directions, and understanding," Canadian Journal of Psychiatry, Vol. 47, No. 2, pp. 123-124 (Mar. 2002).
* Grof, P., "Affective disorders: discovery and recovery," Canadian Journal of Psychiatry, Vol. 42, No. 5, pp. 461-462 (Jun. 1997).
* Grof, P. and W. H. Kautz, "The Nature and Treatment of Mental Depression: An Intuitive Consensus Study" (San Franacisco: The Gaia Institute, 1993).
* Grof, P., "Lithium update: selected issues," in F. Ayd, ed.,*Affective disorders reassessed*, (Baltimore: Ayd Medical Publications, 1983).
* Grof, Stanislav, *Beyond the Brain: Birth, Death and Transcendence in Psychotherapy* (Albany: State University of New York Press, 1985).
* Hadamard, J., *The Psychology of Invention in the Mathematical Field* (Princeton Univ. Press, 1949).
* Haich, Elisabeth, *Initiation* (Palo Alto: Seed Center, 1974).
* Harman, W.W., & H. Rheingold, *Higher Creativity: Liberating the Unconscious for Breakthrough Insights* (Putnam, 1984).
* Harvey, Charles & Suzi, *Principles of Astrology : The Only Introduction You'll Ever Need* (London: Thorson's, 1999).
* Havel, Vaclav, "The End of the Modern Era," New York Times, 1 March 1992; from a talk delivered at the World Economic Forum, Davos, Switzerland, 2 February 1992.
* Heaton, T. H., "Tidal Triggering of Earthquakes," Geophysical Jl. of the Royal Astron. Society, Vol. 43, pp. 307-326 (1975).
* Hicks-Caskey, W. E. & D. R. Potter, "Effect of the Full Moon on a Sample of Developmentally Delayed, Institutionalized Women," Perceptual Motor Skills, Vol. 72, No. 3, Pt. 2, pp. 1375-80 (June 1991).

* Hilty, D.M., K. T. Brady & R.E. Hales, "A Review of Bipolar Disorder Among Adults, <u>Psychiatric Serv.</u>, Vol. 50, No. 2, pp.201-13 (1999).
* Hopkins, "Q&A: AIDS Vaccine Being Tested," <u>IntelliHealth Health News</u> (Baltimore: John Hopkins University, 2 March 1998).
* Hulme, A. J., & F. H. Wood, *Ancient Egypt Speaks* (London: Psychic Book Club, 1937).
* Hurry, J. B., *Imhotep, the Vizier and Physician of King Zoser and Afterwards the Egyptian God of Medicine*, 2nd Ed'n (Oxford Univ. Press, 1928, 1978).
* Huxley, Aldous, *The Perennial Philosophy*. (Harper & Bros., 1945).
* James, William, *The Varieties of Religious Experience* (Amer. Library, 1958).
* Jennings, Paul C., Ed., Committee on Scholarly Communication with the People's Republic of China, Report No. 8, *Earthquake Engineering and Hazards Reduction in China*, (Washington, DC: Nat. Acad. Sciences, 1980).
* Jones, David, *Visions of Time: Experiments in Psychic Archeology* (Theosophical Publishing House, 1979).
* Jung, C.G., *Memories, Dreams and Reflections* (Vintage, 1965).
* Jung, C.G., *C.G.Jung's Letters*, Vol. 2, Bollingen Series 95 (Princeton University Press, 1973).
* Jung, C. G., *The Archetypes and the Collective Unconsciouss*, Collected Works, Vol. 9.1, Bollingen Sesries XX (Princeton Univ. Press, 1959).
* Jung, C. G., *Psychological Types* (Pantheon Books, 1964; Princeton Univ. Press, 1990).
* Jyoti, Swami Amar, *Spirit of Himalaya* (Ward, CO: Truth Conscioiusness, 1988)
* Katagiri Roshi, in Goldberg, Natalie, *Long Quiet Highway* (Bantam, 1993).
* Kautz, Willliam H., "The Rosemary Case of Alleged Egyptian Xenoglossy," <u>Theta</u>, Vol. 10, No. 2, pp. 26-30 (1982).
* Kautz, William H., "Earthquake Triggering: A Psychic Exploration," <u>Psi Research</u>, Vol. 1, No. 3, pp. 117-125 (Sept. 1982) and Vol. 1, No. 4, pp. 101-116 (Dec. 1982).
* Kautz, William H., "Liveliness in Food: Key to Human Nourishment," Center for Applied Intuition, for the Schweissfürth Foundation, Munich, Germany (Feb. 1990).
* Kautz, William H., "Peace Options in the Middle East," Center for Applied Intuition, for the Sadat Peace Foundation, New York (1988).
* Kautz, William H., "Sudden Infant Death Syndrome," <u>Applied Psi Newsletter</u>, Vol. 1, No. 4, pp. 4-6 (1984).

* Kautz, William H., "The Intuitive Historian: Reconstruction of the Life of Imhotep," <u>Phoenix: New Directions in the Study of Man</u>, Vol. IV, Nos. 1 & 2, pp. 61+(1980).
* Kautz, William H., and Melanie Branon, *Channeling: The Intuitive Connection* (Harper and Row, 1987).
* Kautz, William H., "The Future of Japan," Center for Applied Intuition, for Comet Research Institute, Chiba, Japan (1984).
* Kautz, William H., & Melanie Branon, *Intuiting the Future* (HarperSanFrancisco, 1989).
* Keller, M.B. & L. A. Baker, "Bipolar Disorder: Epidemiology, Course, Diagnosis, and Treatment," <u>Bulletin of the Menninger Clinic</u>, 55(2): 172-81 (Spring 1991).
* Kenawell, W. W., *The Quest at Glastonbury: A Biographical Study of Frederick Bligh Bond* (Helix-Garrett, 1965).
* Kerr, R. A., "Quake Prediction by Animals Gaining Respect," <u>Science</u>, Vol. 208, pp. 695-696 (1980).
* Kim, V.P., & V.V. Hegai, "On possible changes in the mid-latitude upper ionosphere before strong earthquakes," <u>Journal of Earthquake Prediction Research (Japan)</u>, Vol. 6, (1997).
* King,C-Y., "Radon Emission on San Andreas Fault," <u>Nature</u>, Vol. 271, pp. 516-519 (1978).
* Klaus, Marshall H., & John H. Kendall, *Maternal-Infant Bonding* (C. V. Mosby Co., 1975).
* Klaus, Marshall H., *Bonding: Building the Foundation of Secure Attachment and Independence* (Perseus, 1996).
* Klimo, Jon, *Channeling: Investigations on Receiving Information from Paranormal Sources* (Tarcher, 1987).
* Knopoff, L., "The Triggering of Large Earthquakes by Earth Tides," <u>Trans. Amer. Geophys. Union</u>, Vol. 50, No. 5, p. 399 ff (1969).
* Koestler, Arthur, *The Act of Creation* (Dell, 1964).
* Kolisko, Lili, *The Moon and Plant Growth* (London: Anthroposophical Foundation, 1936).
* Kondo, G., "The Variation of the Atmospheric Electric Field at the Time of an Earthquake," <u>Memoirs Kaioka Magnet. Observatory</u>, Vol. 13, pp. 11-23 (1968).
* Kornfield, Jack, <u>A Path with Heart</u> (Bantam Books, 1993).
* Kraus, J. F., and N. O. Borbani, "Post-neonatal Sudden Unexplained Death in California: A Cohort Study," <u>Amer. Jl. of Epidemiology</u>, Vol. 95, No. 6, pp. 497-510 (1972).

* Kraus, J.F., S. Greenland & M. Bulterys, "Risk factors for sudden infant death syndrome in the US," Collaborative Perinatal Project., Intern. Jl. Epidemiology,Vol. 18, pp. 113-120 (1989).
* Kripke, D.F., et al., "Controlled trial of bright light for nonseasonal major depressive disorders," Biological Psychiatry, Vol. 31, No. 2, pp. 119-34 (Jan.15, 1992).
* Krishnamurti, J., in Chandmal, Asit, One Thousand Moons (Abrams, 1985).
* Krishnamurti, J., The Awakening of Intelligence (London: Victor Gollancz, 1973.).
* Kubler-Ross, Elizabeth, On Death and Dying (Macmillan, 1969).
* Lao Tse, Tao Te Ching; Feng, Gia-Fu & Jane English, transl'rs (Vintage, 1972).
* Law, S.P., "The Regulation of Menstrual Cycle and its Relationship to the Moon," Amer. Jour. of Obstetrics and Gynocology, Ser.. 1, Vol. 137, No. 7, pp. 834-839 (1980).
* Lee, W.H.K., et al., "A summary of the literature on unusual animal behavior before earthquakes," U.S. Geological Survey, Open File Report, 1976.
* Lee, W.H.K., & S Wang, "Abstracts of articles on Chinese earthquakes and related studies," U.S. Geological Survey, Open File Report 76-460, 1976.
* Leibenluft E., et al., "Light therapy in patients with rapid cycling bipolar disorder: preliminary results," Psychopharmacology Bulletin, Vol. 31, No. 4, pp. 705-710 (1995).
* Leonard, R.S., & R.A. Barnes, "Observation of Ionospheric Disturbances Following the Alaskan Earthquake," Jl. of Geophys. Res., Vol. 70, No. 5, pp. 1250-53 (1965).
* Levine, Stephen, Who Dies: An Investigation of Conscious Living and Dying (Anchor/Doubleday, 1982).
* Leviton, Richard, "Why Do These Kids Love School?" Intuition, No. 6. pp. 14-22+(1995).
* Libiger, E., Personal communication to Paul Grof, 2001.
* Licauco, Jaime T., ESP, Meditation and the Business Executive, paper presented at the conference "Steps Beyond," sponsored by the Young Presidents Organization, Cebu City, The Philippines, 26-29 October 1991.
* Lieber, A.L., "Human Aggression and the Lunar Synodic Cycle," Compr. Psychiatry, Vol. 18., No. 4, pp. 369-274 (Jul-Aug. 1977).
* Lieber, A.L., & C.R. Sherin, "Homicides and the Lunar Cycle," American Jl. of Psychiatry, Vol. 129, pp. 69-74 (1972).
* Lieber, A.L., The Lunar Effect: Biological Tides and Human Emotions (Doubleday, 1978).

* Locke, C.A., & A.L. Stoll, "Omega-3 fatty acids in major depression," <u>World Review of Nutr. Diet.</u>, Vol. 89, pp.173-85 (2001).
* Lott, D. F., B. L. Hart & M. W. Howell, "Retrospective Studies of Unusual Animal Behavior as an Earthquake Predictor," <u>Geophys. Res., Letters</u>, Vol. 8, No. 12, pp. 1203-1206 (1981).
* Malony, H. & A. Lovekin, *Glossolalia: Behavioral Science Perspectives on Speaking in Tongues* (Oxford Univ. Press, 1985).
* Masters, Edgar Lee, *Spoon River Anthology* (Signet, 1992).
* Mauk, F. L., & J. Kienle, "Microearthquakes at St. Augustine Volcano, Alaska, Triggering by Earth Tides," <u>Science</u>, Vol. 182, pp. 386-389 (1973).
* May, R., E. Angel & H. Ellenberger, Eds., *Existence* (Basic Books, 1958).
* McGoneagle, Joseph, *Mind Trek: Expl;oring Consciousness, Time and Space Through Remote Viewing* (Hampton Roads, 1993).
* McMoneagle, Joseph, *Remote Viewing Secrets: A Handbook* (Hampton Roads, 2000).
* Mihalasky, J., Extrasensory Perception in Management," <u>Advanced Management Journal</u> (July 1976).
* Miller, Ron, *Caring for New Life: Essays on Holistic Education* (Brandon, VT: Holistic Education Press, 1999).
* Mills, W.E., ed., *Speaking in Tongues: A Guide to Reseach in Glossolalia* (William B. Eerdmans Pub'rs, 1986).
* Mintzberg, Henry, *The Rise and Fall of Strategic Planning* (New York: Free Press, 1994).
* Mishlove, Jeffrey, *The Roots of Consciousness* (Random House, 1975; Marlowe & Co., 1993).
* Morehouse, T, *Psychic Warrior: Inside the CIA's Stargate Program* (Saint Martin's Press, 1996).
* Moszkowski, A, *Conversations with Einstein*, (Horizon Press, 1970).
* Moulton, D. G., "Odorant Outgassing Preceding Earthquakes and Olfactory-Guided Behavior in Animals," <u>Abnormal Animal Behavior Prior to Earthquakes, Proceedings of Conference XI</u>, USGS Open-file Report 80-453 (Menlo Park, CA: US Geological Survey, 1980).
* Mundy, Talbot, *Om, The Secret of Arbor Valley* (Carroll & Graf, 1924).
* Murphy, Michael, *The Future of the Body* (Tarcher/Putnam, 1992).
* Myss, Caroline, *Anatomy of the Spirit: The Seven Stages of Power and Healing* (Random House, 1997).
* Naeye, R. L., "Brain-stem and Adrenal Abnormalities in the Sudden Infant Death Syndrome," <u>Amer. Jl. of Clinical Pathology</u>, Vol. 66, pp. 526+(1976).
* Naisbitt, John, *Megatrends* (Warner Books, 1982).

* NAS (Natural Academy of Sciences), Recommended Dietary Allowances—RDA, (1988); see http://www.nal.usda.gov/fnic/dga/rda.pdf]; and Dietary Guidelines Advisory Committee, Report of the Dietary Guidelines Advisory Committee on the Dietary Guidelines for Americans, 2000, US Department of Agriculture (2000).
* Nitsan, U., "Electromagnetic Emission Accompanying the Fracture of Quartz-Bearing Rocks," Geophys. Res. Letters, vol. 4, No. 8, pp. 333-336 (1977).
* Odent, Michel, Entering the World : The De-Medicalization of Childbirth, (London: Marion Boyars, 1989).
* Oike, K., "Precursory Phenomena and Prediction of Recent Large Earthquakes in China," Chinese Geophysics, Vol. 1, p. 179-199 (1978).
* Oliver, Frederick, Phylos the Tibetan: A Dweller on Two Planets (Harper & Row, 1817; Rudolf Steiner Publications, 1974).
* Orlowsky, J. P., R. H. Nodar & D. Lonsdale, "Abnormal Brainstem Auditory Evoked Potentials in Infants with Threatened Sudden Infant Death Syndrome," Cleveland Clinic Quarterly, Vol. 46, No. 3, pp. 77-81 (1979).
* Ornstein, Robert, The Psychology of Consciousness (W. H. Freeman & Co., 1972).
* Osbon, Diana, The Joseph Campbell Companion (Harper Perennial, 1991).
* Otis, L. S., and W. H. Kautz, Biological Premonitors of Earthquakes: A Validation Study, Final Report (Menlo Park, CA: SRI International, 1981); for US Geological Survey.
* Panigrahy, A, et al.,"Decreased kainate receptor binding in the arcuate nucleus of the sudden infant death syndrome, "Jl. Neuropathology & Exper. Neurology, Vol. 56, No.11, pp. 1253-61 (Nov. 1997).
* Papatheodorou, G, & S. Kutcher, "The effect of adjunctive light therapy on ameliorating breakthrough depressive symptoms in adolescent-onset bipolar disorder," Journal of Psychiatry & Neuroscience, Vol. 20, No. 3, pp. 226-232 (May 1995).
* Parikh, Jagdish, Intuition: The New Frontier of Management (Oxford: Blackwell's, 1994).
* Park, S.K. et al., "Electromagnetic Precursers to Earthquakes in the ULF Band: A Review of Observations and Mechanisms," Reviews of Geophysics, Vol. 32, No. 2, pp. 117-132 (May 1993).
* Parrot, M., & M.J.S. Johnston (Eds.), "Seismoelectromagnetic Effects" Phys. Earth Planet. Inter., Vol. 57, pp. 1-177 (1989).
* Pattison, E.M., "Behavioral Science Reserch on the Nature of Glossolalia, Jl. of Amer. Scinetific Affilliations, Vol. 20, No. 3, pp. 74+(September 1968).
* Peirce, Penney, The Intuitive Way (Beyond Words, 1999).

* Peterson, D. R., and N. Chinn, "Sudden Infant Death Trends in Six Metropolitan Communities, 1965-1974," Pediatrics, Vol. 60, pp. 75-79 (1977).
* Pinker, Steven, *The Language Instinct: How the Mind Creates Language* (HarperPerennial, 1995).
* Planck, Max, *Scientific Autobiography, and Other Papers* (London: Williams and Norgate, 1950).
* Plato, *GreatDialogues of Plato*, W.H.D. Rouse, transl'r (New American Library, 1956).
* Plotinus, quoted in Klimo, 1987,p. 308.
* Poincare, Henri, "Mathematical Creation," in Ghiselin, B., *The Creative Process* (New American Library, 1952); originally, *La Raisonment Mathematique* (Paris: Ernest Flammarion, 1908), pp. 33-42.
* Pondy, Louis R., 'The Union of Rationality and Intuition in Management Action," in S. Srivasta, ed., *The Executive Mind* (San Francisco: Jossey-Bass, 1984).
* Popper, Karl, *The Logic of Scientific Discovery* (Springer, 1934, and Basic Books, 1959).
* Prophet, Elizabeth Clare, *The Lost Years of Jesus* (Summit University Press, 1984).
* Purcell, Jack, "Lazaris on Intuition," audio cassette tape (Fairfax, CA: Concept Synergy, 1984).
* Puthoff, H. E., and R. Targ, "A Perceptual Channel for Information Transfer over Kilometer Distances: Historical Perspective and Recent Research," Proc. IEEE, Vol. 64, (1976), p. 329+.
* Puthoff, H.E., "CIA-Initiated Remote Viewing at Stanford Research Institute," (Austin, TX: Institute for Advanced Studies at Austin, 1996).
* Radin, D.I., and J. M. Rebman,"Lunar Correlates of Normal, Abnormal and Anomalous Behavior," Subtle Energies, Vol. 5, No. 3, pp. 209-238 (1994).
* Radin, Dean, *The Conscious Universe* (HarperSanFrancisco, 1997).
* Raison, C. L. et al., "The Moon and Madness Reconsidered", Journal of Affective Disorders, Vol. 53, No. 1, pp. 99-106 (April 1999).
* Ram Dass, *Still Here: Embracing Aging, Changing and Dying* (Riverhead Books, 2000).
* Ray, Michael & Rochelle Myers, *Creativity in Business* (Doubleday, 1986).
* Redford, D. B., *Akhenaten, The Heretic King* (Princeton Univ. Press, 1984).
* Reichborn-Kjennerud, T, & O. Lingjaerde, "Response to light therapy in seasonal affective disorders: personality disorders and temperament as predictors of outcome," Journal of Affective Disorders, Vol. 25/41, No. 2, pp. 101-10 (Nov. 1996).
* Remen, Rachel Naomi, *Kitchen Table Wisdom* (Riverhead Boloks, 1996).

* Renault, Mary, *The Persian Boy* (Bantam Books, 1973)
* Richardson, W. & J., & Lenora Huett, *The Spiritual Value of Gemstones* (DeVorss & Co., 1987).
* Rikitake, T., "Earthquake Prediction," Developments in Solid Earth Geophysics, Vol. 9, pp. 1-357 (1976).
* Roberts, Jane, *Seth Speaks : The Eternal Validity of the Soul* (Prentice Hall. 1972).
* Roberts, Jane, *The Nature of Personal Reality* (Prentice Hall, 1974; Bantam Books, 1988).
* Roberts, Jane, *The Seth Material* (Prentice Hall, 1970).
* Roberts, Jane, *The Unknown Reality, Vol. 1* (Prentice Hall, 1977).
* Roberts, Jane, *The Way Toward health : A Seth Book*(San Rafael,CA: Amber-Allen, 1997).
* Roberts, Kenneth, *Henry Gross and His Divining Rod* (Doubleday, 1951).
* Rodegast, Pat, & Judith Stanton, *Emmanuel's Book* (Bantam, 1985).
* Rodegast, Pat, & J. Stanton, *Emmanuel's Book II* (Bantam, 1991).
* Roman, Sanaya, *Opening to Channel* (Tiburon, CA: H.J. Kramer, 1987).
* Roman, Sanaya, *Personal Power Through Awareness* (Tiburon, CA: H.J. Kramer, 1986).
* Rossi, Ernest, and David Cheek, *Mind-Body Therapy* (Norton & Co., l988).
* Rowan, Roy, *The Intuitive Manager* (Little Brown & Co., 1986).
* Ryerson, Kevin & Stephanie Harolde, *Spirit Communication: The Soul's Path* (Bantam, 1989).
* Samarin, W. J., *Tongues of Men and Angels* (Macmillan, 1972).
* Sandweiss, S.H., *Sai Baba: The Holy Man and the Psychiatrist* (Prashanthi Nilayam, India: Sri Sathya Sai Books and Publication Trust, 1975).
* Santos, C., Prediction of the 1972 Managua, Nicaragua, Earthquake from Groundwater Changes, translated from Spanish by E. L. Krinitzsky, Translation No. 73-7 (Vicksburg, MS: US Army Corps of Engineers, 1973).
* Sat Prem, *Sri Aurobindo: An Adventure in Consciousness* (New York: India Lib. Soc., 1904).
* Schou, Mogens, "Prophylactic lithium treatment of unipolar and bipolar manic depressive illness," Psychopathology, Vol. 28, pp. 81-85 (1995).
* Schroeder, L., & S. Ostrander, *Executive ESP* (Prentice Hall, 1974).
* Schultz, Barbara, "Intuition in Business", in Intuition, No. 7, pp. 14-21 (1995).
* Schwartz, S., & Rand de Mattei, "The Discovery of an American Brig: Fieldwork Involving Applied Archeological Remote Viewing," in Henkel,

Linda A., & Rick E. Berger (Eds.), *Research in Parapsychology 1988* (Scarecrow Press, 1989).

* Schwartz, Stephen A., & H. E. Edgerton, *A Preliminary Survey of Eastern Harbour, Alexandria, Egypt, Combining both Technical and Extended Remote Sensing Exploration* (Los Angeles: The Mobius Group, 1980).

* Schwartz, Stephen A., *The Alexandria Project* (Dell, 1983).

* Schwartz, Stephen, A., *The Secret Vaults of Time* (Grosset and Dunlap, 1978).

* Schwarz, B. E., *A Psychiatrist Looks at ESP* (New American Library, 1965).

* Seed, John, et al., *Thinking Like a Mountain: Toward a Council of All Beings* (Philadelphia: New Society Publishers, 1988); p. 70-71; reconstruction by Ted Perry of a 1854 speech by Chief Sealth (Seattle).

* Sethe, K., "Imhotep, der Askepios der Aegypter," <u>Untersuchungen zur Geschichte und Altertumskunde Aegyptens</u>, Vol. 2, No. 4 (1902).

* Shakespeare, William, "Hamlet," in Craig, W. J., Ed., *The Complete Works of William Shakespeare* (Oxford Univ. Press, 1906).

* Shanks, Bradford, "Mirror" (early poem).

* Sharadze, Z.S., et al., "Disturbances in the Ionosphere and the Geomagnetic Field Associated with the Spitak Earthquake," <u>Izvestiya, Earth Physics</u>, Vol. 27, No. 11, pp. 989+(1989).

* Shlein, S., "Earthquake-Tide Correlation," <u>Geophysical Jl. of the Royal Astron. Society</u>, Vol. 28, pp. 27-34 (1972).

* Shoulders, K. &. S., "Observations on the Role of Charge Clusters in Nuclear Cluster Reactions," <u>Jl. of New Energy</u>, Vol 1, No 3 (Fall 1996); see the authors' references for relevant patents.

* Silverberg, R., *Akhnaten: The Rebel Pharaoh* (Chilton, 1964).

* Simpson, J. F., "Earth Tides as Triggering Mechanisms for Earthquakes," <u>Earth and Planetary Science Letters</u>, Vol. 2, No. 5, pp. 473-478 (1938).

* Smith, E.J., & C.P. Sonett, "Extraterrestrial Magnetic Fields: Achievements and Opportunities," <u>IEEE Transactions on Geoscience Electronics</u>, Vol. GE-14 (1976).

* Smith, Huston, *Beyond the Post-Modern Mind* (Wheaton, IL,: Theosophical Publishing House, 1989).

* Sögyal Rinpoche, *The Tibetan Book of Living and Dying* (Harper-Collins, 1992).

* Stearn, Jess, *Edgar Cayce, The Sleeping Prophet* (Bantam/Doubleday, 1967).

* Stevenson, Ian, "A Preliminary Report of a New Case of Responsive Xenoglossy: The Case of Gretchen,' <u>J. of the Amer. Soc. for Psychical Research</u>, Vol. 70, pp. 65-77 (1976).

* Stevenson, Ian, *Unlearned Language: New Studies in Xenoglossy* (Univ. Of Virginiia Press, 1984).

* Stevenson, Ian, *Xenoglossy: A Review and Report of a Case* (Univ. of Va. Pres, 1974).
* Stoll, A.L., et al., "Omega-3 fatty acids and bipolar disorder: a review," Prostaglandins Leukot. Essential Fatty Acids, Vol. 60, No. 5-6, pp. 329-337 (May-Jun. 1999);
* Storms, Edmund, "Review of the 'Cold Fusion' Effect," Journal of Scientific Exploration, Vol. 10, No. 2, p. 185 (1996).
* Sullivan, Dierdre, "Portrait of a Prophet," in Omni, pp. 42-50+(April 1992).
* Suzuki, D. T., *On Indian Mahayana Buddhism,* E. Conze, Ed. (Harper and Row, 1968).
* Targ, R., "Remote Viewing at Stanford Research Institute in the 1970s: A Memoir," Journal of Scientific Exploration, Vol. 10, No. 1, p. 77+(1996).
* Targ, R., & H. E. Puthoff, *Mind Reach: Scientists Look at Psychic Ability* (Delacorte Press, 1977).
* Task Force on Infant Sleep Position and Sudden Infant Death Syndrome, "Changing Concepts of Sudden Infant Death Syndrome: Implications for Infant Sleeping Environment and Sleep Position (RE9946)", Pediatrics, Vol. 105, No.3 (2000).
* Tasso, J., & D. Miller, "The Effect of the Full Moon on Human Behavior," Journal of Psychology, Vol. 93, pp. 81-82 (1976).
* Teng, T-L., "Some Recent Studies of Groundwater Radon Content as an Earthquake Precursor," Jl. of Geophys. Research, vol. 85, No. B6, pp. 3089-3099 (1980).
* Thakur, C. P. & D. Sharma, "Full Moon and Crime," Brit. Medical Journal (Clin. Res.), Vol. 289, pp. 1789-91 (Dec. 22, 1984).
* Thomas, Lewis, *The Lives of a Cell: Notes of a Biology Watcher* (Viking, 1974; Penguin, 1978).
* Tompkins, Peter & Christopher Bird, *Secrets of the Soil* (Harper & Row, 1989).
* Tompkins, Peter, & Christopher Bird, *The Secret Life of Plants* (Penguin, 1973).
* Tributsch, H., "Do Aerosol Anamolies Precede Earthquakes?" Nature, Vol. 276, p. 606-608 (1978).
* Trungpa, Chognyam, *Shambala: The Secret Path of the Warrior* (Shambala, 1984).
* Truswell, A.S., et al., *ABCof Nutrition* (Amer. C. Phys., 1986).
* Truswell, A.S., *Recommended Dietary Intakes Around the World,* Nutrition Abstracts and Reviews, Vol.. 53, No. 11, pp. 940-1015 (Nov. 1983).
* Tulku, Tarthang, *Gesture of Balance* (Emeryville, CA: Dharma Publishing Co., 1977)

* Ulumov, V. I., et al., "Light and Electrical Effects Connected with Earthquakes," <u>The Tashkent Earthquake of 26 April 1966</u>, Pt. 1, Chap. 5 (Tashkent: F. Akad. Nauk Uzbek SSSR, 1971); (in Russian).
* Valdes-DaPena, M. A., "Sudden Infant Death Syndrome: A Review of the Medical Literature, 1974-1979," <u>Pediatrics</u>, Vol. 66, No. 4, pp. 597-614 (1980).
* Vaughan, Frances, & Roger Walsh, *Beyond Ego: Transpersonal Dimensions in Psychology* (Tarcher, 1980).
* Vaughan, Frances, "The Role of Perception in Psychotherapy," presented at the conference "Opening the Intuitive Gate: Intuition in Psychotherapy," San Franciosco, CA, Center for Applied Intuition and John F. Kennedy University, 1989.
* Vaughan, Frances, *Awakening Intuition* (Anchor/Doubleday, 1979).
* Vaughan, Frances, *The Inward Arc: Healing and Wholeness in Psychotherapy and Spirituallity* (Shambala, 1986).
* Verny, Thomas R., *The Secret Life of the Unborn Child* (Delta, 1994).
* Wakita, H., et al., Hydrogen Releaase: New Indicator of Fault Activity," <u>Science</u>, Vol. 210, pp. 188-190 (1980).
* Walsch, Neal Donald, *Conversations with God* (Putnam, 1996).
* Walsh, Roger, & Frances Vaughan, Eds., *Gifts from a Counse in Miracles* (Putnam, 1995).
* Walsh, Roger, & Frances Vaughan, *Paths Beyond Ego: The Transpersonal Vision* (Tarcher/Putnam, 1993).
* Walsh, Roger, *Essential Spirituality: The Seven Central Practices to Awaken Heart and Mind* (Wiley, 1999).
* Waltari, Mika, *The Egyptian* (Putnam 1949).
* Weber, Robert J., *Investive Minds: Creativity in Technology* (Oxford Univ. Press, 1992).
* Weil, Andrew, *The Natural Mind* (Houghton Mifflin, 1973).
* Wheeler, John A., "Law Without Law," in Wheeler, John A. & Huburt Zurek, *Quantum Theory and Measurement* (Princeton Univ. Press, 1983).
* Whyte, L. L., *The Unconscious Before Freud* (Anchor Books,1962).
* Wickes, Frances, *The Inner World of Childhood*, (New American Library, 1966 revised ed'n).
* Wilber, Ken, *The Spectrum of Consciousness* (Wheaton, IL: Theosophical Pub'g House, 1977).
* Wilhelm, Richard, "The I Ching" (London: Routledge & Kegan Paul, 1950); translated into English by Carl F. Baynes (New York: Bollingen Fdn., 1967).
* Wood, F. H., *After Thirty Centuries* (London: Rider, 1935).

* Wood, F. H., *This Egyptian Miracle* (London: Watkins, 1955).
* Wood, M. D., & N. E. King, "Relation between Earthquakes, Weather and Soil Tilt," Science, Vol. 197, pp. 154-156 (1977).
* Xenophon, *Anabasis, or Expedition of Cyrus, and the Memorabilia of Socrates* (London: Bell, 1907)
* Yeats, *A Vision* (London: Macmillan, 1937)
* Yogananda, Paramahansa, *Autobiography of a Yogi* (Los Angeles: Self-Realization Fellowship, 1985).
* Yoshimura, S. "Nondestructive Pyramid Investigation 2", Studies in Egyptian Culture, No. 8 (Tokyo, 1988).
* Yoshimura, S., et al., "Nondestructive Pyramid Investigation by Electromagnetic Wave Method," Studies in Egyptian Culture, No. 6 (Tokyo, 1987).
* Zehnder, Egon, Wall Street Journal, Dec. 28, 1987.
* Zelenova, T.I. & A.D. Legen'ka, "Ionospheric Effects Related to the Moneron Earthquake of September 5(6), 1971," Izvestiya, Earth Physics,Vol. 25, No. 10, pp. 848-852 (1989).
* Zhu, F-M., & Y-z. Zhong, "Macro-anomalies and their Significance in the Prediction of Large Earthquakes," in Earthquake Reseearch Group, 1980.
* Zurcher, E., et al, "Tree Stem Diameters Fluctuate with the Tide," Nature, Vol. 392 (No. 6678), pp. 665-66 (16 April 1998).

APPENDIX

RESOURCES

NETWORKING

The Intuition Network

Computer conferencing, publications, seminars, events, media activities and local groups. Jeffrey Mishlove, Director.

369-B Third Street #161, San Rafael, CA 94901; 415-256-1137, fax 415-456-2532.
Internet: http://www.intuition.org
e-mail: intuition.network@intuition.org .

EXPERT INTUITIVES

CAI has worked with all of the following intuitive counselors, certifies them as expert intuitives and recommends them for the types of readings indicated. The other CAI expert intuitives mentioned in the text and under Acknowledgements are no longer available for readings, for one reason or another.

Many competant intuitive counselors are not listed here, of course, but you are on your own to find one who is suitable for meeting your needs. When checking out intuitive counselors please keep in mind that the type of service they offer varies greatly, not only in the quality of their work but also in their mode of working and the kind of information they give. As you make inquires state clearly your needs and requirements, and ask what they can provide and what they require of you. During your session with them come prepared to ask focused, specific and relevant questions. (See the sections near the end of Chapter 2 for further suggestions on the selection and utilization expert intuitives.)

* Diane M. Conti

Diana has worked as an expert intuitive for more than twenty-five years, in addition to a long a successful career as executive of community-based not-for-profit programs. Diana applies her intuitive expertise to management and business as well as to individual readings. Her guidance synthesizes the practical, emotional and spiritual aspects of life situations to illuminate and nurture the heart and soul of the individual or organization.

Readings in-person or by telephone.
309 Via Recodo, Mill Valley, CA 94941; 415-388-9739, fax 415-380-9807.
e-mail: conticonsulting@yahoo.com

* Jon C. Fox

Jon has been channeling Hilarion since 1983, when his interest in energy devices led him to channeling as a source of new knowledge and principles. Among Hilarion's works channeled through Jon are *Starlight Elixers and Cosmic Vibrational Healing* and *Flower Essences* (Revised Edition). Jon has been building energy devices channeled by Hilarion, principally in New Physics and in areas of healing. He gives personal and research readings in California, as well as group channelings.

Readings by telephone, in-person and remote.
P.O. Box 2209, Nevada City, CA 95959; 916-478-1002, fax 916-265-0720.
Internet: http://www.hilarion .com
e-mail: fox@hilarion.com

* Sharon Franquemont

Sharon Franquemont has been an author, speaker, coach, and educator about intuition and continues to be a leading authority in the field with 33 years of experience. Her published works include *You Already Know What To Do* (PenguinPutnam, 1999), *Intuition: Seven Steps to a More Fulfilling Life* (at her web site and Amazon.com), and *Intuition: Your Electric Sel"* (6 Tape set, at her web site or from Sounds True). A 60-minute Intuitive Consulting session with Sharon focuses on identifying the main theme of this period of your life and how that theme impacts your relationships, professional life, visions of your future, well-being, and spiritual evolution.

Readings by telephone or in-person.
7960 Crest Ave, Oakland, CA 94610; 510-777-3443, fax 510-777-3445.
Internet: http://www.intuitionworks.com
e-mail: sfranque@aol.com

* Mary Gillis

I have given readings for twenty years, and they, of course, have evolved along with me. I provide readings tapered to the individual, and not a pre-set format. The content evolves according the individual's needs....I endeavor to offer a truly healing perspective so tht the recipient can focus their intent and come to much greater self-understanding. Perhaps it could be said that greater self-understanding leads to greater self-responsibility and to greater possibilities for transcending the self. I enjoy the inner intuitive states, the intimacy of sharing this with others, and touching the same in them.

Readings by mail or in person.
4415 Hamlet Court, Rohnert Park, CA 94928; 707-584-2303.

* Richard Lavin

Richard, a full-trance channel since 1981, is available for private, practical "life path" counseling sessions and channel traiining. He channels a "non-physical personality" named Ecton, whose counseling is spiritual/psychological/philosophical and is based upon concepts of unconditional love, absolute personal responsibillity and unlimited creativity. Richard resides in Honolulu, Hawaii and often works in Japan.

Readings in person and by telephone.
P.O. Box 10111, Honolulu, HI 96816; 808-734-5034; e-mail: rlavin@compuserve.com.
e-mail: www.richardlavin.com

* Penney Pierce

Penney Peirce is a gifted intuitive and visionary, as well as a popular lecturer, counselor, and trainer specializing in intuition development, "skillful perception," and dreamwork. She is the author of *Dreams for Dummies* (Wiley&Sons, 2000), *The Present Moment: A Daybook of Clarity and Intuition* (McGraw Hill,

2000) and *The Intuitive Way: A Guide to Living from Inner Wisdom* (Beyond Words Publishing, 1997). She is available for 90-minute life readings and intuitive mentoring.

Readings in-person or by telephone.
Pierce Communications, 12 Grande Vista, Novato, CA 94947; 415-898-8925 (also fax).
Internet: http://www.intuitnow.com
e-mail: penneirce@aol.com.

* Kevin Ryerson

Kevin Ryerson is an award winning consultant, expert intuitive and trance channel in the tradition of Edgar Cayce and Jane Roberts. For over 30 years he has offered consultations and retreats. Kevin authored *Spirit Communication: The Soul?s Path*. Shirley MacLaine?s best selling books *Out on a Limb, Dancing in the Light* and *It?s All in The Playing* highlighted Kevin?s intuitive abilities. Kevin is well known and respected for his balanced and integrated world view and experiences that inspire and change people?s lives.

Readings by phone and in-person.
P.O. Box 151080, San Rafael, CA 94915 ; 415-356-9887, fax 415-267-6939.
Phone 415-356-9887
Fax 415-267-6939
Internet: http://www.kevinryerson.com
e-mail: kevinryerson@earthlink.net

* Richard Wolinsky

Richard Wolinsky is a trance channel in the style of Jane Roberts, whose Seth classes he attended for two years. He has a graduate degree in philosophy and an extended background in psychology, hypnosis, metaphysics and mysticism. For the past two decades he has worked as a magazine editor, free-lance writer and radio interviewer....Richard is uniquely qualified to deal with many philosophical principles involved in the so-called New-Age message. The personality he channels, Martenard, is both loving and challenging in the ways he helps clarify individuals' own understanding of their life purposes, current difficulties, spiritual explorations, relationships and psychic gestalt.

He enables individuals to confront their own problems in their own way with love and understanding.

Readings in-person, by telephone and remote.
P.O. Box 1173, El Cerritto, CA; 510-525-5344, fax 520-525-5344.
e-mail: richwol@well.com

INTUITION DEVELOPMENT

The Internet is today the best resource for finding intuition development seminars, workshops, classes and intuition coaching, both for individuals and for business and government organizations. The many capable training sourcesthat now exist may be accessed easily through www.google.com or another search engine. CAI can recommend the following specific trainers and training programs for above-average or better quality of training. Most have written books or prepared audio or video tapes describing their particular approach. Books may be obtained through www.amazon.com, www.abebooks.com or other similar purchasing sites. Tapes are available through www.soundstrue.com, www.newdimensions.org, www.bigsurtapes.com, www.thinkingaloud.com, for example.

* **Marcia Emery:** 1502 Tenth St., Berkeley, CA 94710; phone 510-526-5510; fax 510-526-9555; www.powerhunch.com; e-mail: PowerHunch@aol.com.

* **Sharon Franquemont:** 7960 Crest Ave, Oakland, CA 94610; phone 510-777-3443, fax 510-777-3445; www.intuitionworks.com; e-mail: sfranque@aol.com

* **Penney Peirce:** Pierce Communications, 12 Grande Vista, Novato, CA 94947; phone & fax 415-898-8925; www.intuitnow.com; e-mail: info@intuitnow.com.

* **Nancy Rosanoff:** 109 Sunnyside Ave., Pleasantville, NY 10570; phone 914-769-7226, fax 914-769-4473; www.intuitionatwork.com, www.rosanoff.com; e-mail: nancy@rosanoff.com.

* **Barbara Schultz:** 22 Forbes Avenue, San Rafael, CA 94901; phone 415-456-6441, fax 415-456-1044; fax 415-456-1044; e-mail: BLSIntuit@aol.com .

* **Helen Palmer Workshops,** 1442A Walnut Street #75, Berkeley, CA 94709; phone 866-366-8973; www.authenticenneagram.com; e-mail: eptpoffice@aol.com

MAGAZINES

I am aware of no current magazines devoted exclusively to intuition (except the last entry below, which is no longer published) but the following exemplary list includes those that honor intuition and discuss it occasionally. The websites often contain sample articles and in some cases the entire magazines. Newstand and and even professional magazines come and go continually, so the following list must be regarded as temporary.

Common Boundary, 5272 River Road #650, Bethesda, MD 20816; 301-652-9495; www.commonboundary.org.

Journal of Consciousness Studies, Imprint Academic, PO Box 1, Thorverton EX5 5YX UK;+44 1392 841600, fax:+44 1392 841478; PO Box 7147, Charlottesville, VA 22906; 800-444-2419, 804-220-3300, fax: 804-220-3301; www.imprint.co.uk/jcs.html

Kindred Spirit, Foxhole, Dartington, Totnes, Devon TQ9 6EB, England;+44-1803-866686, fax–866591; www.kindredspirit.co.uk.

New Age Journal, 42 Pleasant St., Watertown, MA 02172; phone 617-926-0200; e-mail editor@newage.com .

New Perspectives: A Journal of Conscious living, P.O. Box 3208, Hemet, CA 92546; 909-925-6117.

Noetics Review, Institute of Noetic Sciences, 101 San Antonio Road, Petaluma, CA 94952; 707.775.3500, fax: 707.781.7420; www.noetic.org.

The Quest/Journal of the Theosophical Society in America, P.O. Box 270, Wheaton, IL 60189; 630-668-1571, ext. 318, fax 630-665-8791; www.theosophical.org

Revision: A Journal of Consciousness and Transformation, Heldref Publications, 1319-18th St., N.W., Washington, D.C. 20036; 800-365-9753; www.heldref.org.

Shambala Sun, 1345 Spruce St., Boulder CO 80302; 902-422-8404, fax 902-423-2701; www.shambalasun.com.

Tricycle: The Buddhist Review, Dept. TRI, Box 3000, Denville, NJ 07834; 800-783-4903. 800-873-9871,+44 208 553 5020; www.kable.com/pub/trym/subservices.asp, tricycle.com.

What is Enlightenment?, Moksha Press, P.O. Box 2360, Lenox, MA 01240; 413-637-6000, fax: 413.637.6015; www.wie.org.

* The following are no longer published, though back issues are available in some cases:

Gnosis, The Lumen Foundation, P.O. Box 14217, San Francisco, CA 94114; 415-974-0600, fax 415-974-0366, e-mail: gnosis@well.com.

Personal Transformation (formerly Lotus), Lotus Customer Service, 4032 S. Lamar Blvd., #500-137, Austin, TX 78704; 800-775-6887; www.personaltransformation.com]

Intuition: A Magazine for the Higher Potential of the Mind, San Francisco, CA; www.intuitionmagazine.com.

BOOKS

The following suggested reading varies from basic, uncomplicated treatments of intuition to attempts at scholarly explanations in psychological or parapsychological terms; also from early classical presentations to the latest knowledge. Some contain how-to instructions for intuition development, and a few cover the psychospiritual aspects that the interested inquirer is inevitably drawn into. All are drawn from the preceding Bibliography, where additional resources may be found for deeper or more specialized study. All may be obtained through local bookstores or ordered directly from www.amazon.com, www.abebooks.com or another similar Internet source.

* Anon, *A Course in Miracles*, (Tiburon, CA: Foundation for Inner Peace, 1982) [three volumes in one].
* Broomfield, John, *Other Ways of Knowing* (Inner Traditions, 1997).
* Chödrön, Pema, *The Wisdom of No Escape* (Shambala, 1991).
* Palmer, Helen, Ed., *Inner Knowing: Consciousness Creativity, Insight and Intuition* (Tarcher/Putnam, 1998).

* Franquemont, Sharon, *You Already Know What To Do* (Tarcher, 1999).
* Goldberg, Philip, *The Intuitive Edge: Understanding Intuition and Applying It in Everyday Life* (Tarcher, 1983).
* Harman, WillisW., & H. Rheingold, *Higher Creativity: Liberating the Unconscious for Breakthrough Insights* (Putnam, 1984).
* Klimo, Jon, *Channeling: Investigations on Receiving Information from Paranormal Sources* (Tarcher, 1987).
* Mishlove, Jeffrey, *The Roots of Consciousness* (Random House, 1975; Marlowe & Co., 1993).
* Peirce, Penney, *The Intuitive Way* (Beyond Words, 1999).
* Radin, Dean, *The Conscious Universe* (HarperSanFrancisco, 1997).
* Roberts, Jane, *Seth Speaks : The Eternal Validity of the Soul* (Prentice Hall. 1972).
* Rodegast, Pat, & Judith Stanton, *Emmanuel's Book* (Bantam, 1985).
* Roman, Sanaya, *Personal Power Through Awareness* (Tiburon, CA: H.J. Kramer, 1986).
* Ryerson, Kevin & Stephanie Harolde, *Spirit Communication: The Soul's Path* (Bantam, 1989).
* Targ, Russell, & Harold E. Puthoff, *Mind Reach: Scientists Look at Psychic Ability* (Delacorte Press, 1977).
* Vaughan, Frances, & Roger Walsh, *Beyond Ego: Transpersonal Dimensions in Psychology* (Tarcher, 1980).
* Vaughan, Frances, *Awakening Intuition* (Anchor/Doubleday, 1979).
* Walsch, Neal Donald, *Conversations with God* (Putnam, 1996).
* Walsh, Roger, & Frances Vaughan, Eds., *Gifts from a Counse in Miracles* (Putnam, 1995).
* Wilber, Ken, *The Spectrum of Consciousness* (Wheaton, IL: Theosophical Pub'g House, 1977).
* Yogananda, Paramahansa, *Autobiography of a Yogi* (Los Angeles: Self-Realization Fellowship, 1985).

0-595-27584-?